THE AFGHANS

Also by Åsne Seierstad

With Their Backs to the World

The Bookseller of Kabul

A Hundred and One Days

The Angel of Grozny

One of Us

Two Sisters

THE AFGHANS

THREE LIVES THROUGH
WAR, LOVE AND REVOLT

ÅSNE SEIERSTAD

TRANSLATED BY SEÁN KINSELLA

virago

VIRAGO

First published in Norway in 2022 by J.M. Stenersens Forlag
First published in Great Britain in 2024 by Virago Press

1 3 5 7 9 10 8 6 4 2

Copyright © Åsne Seierstad, 2022, 2024
Translation Copyright © Seán Kinsella, 2024

The moral right of the author has been asserted.

Map by Barking Dog Art, based on an original drawn by Audun Skjervøy.

All rights reserved.
No part of this publication may be reproduced, stored in a
retrieval system, or transmitted, in any form or by any means, without
the prior permission in writing of the publisher, nor be otherwise circulated
in any form of binding or cover other than that in which it is published
and without a similar condition including this condition being
imposed on the subsequent purchaser.

A CIP catalogue record for this book
is available from the British Library.

Hardback ISBN 978-1-4087-1793-6
Trade Paperback ISBN 978-1-4087-1794-3

Typeset in Perpetua by M Rules
Printed and bound in Great Britain by
Clays Ltd, Elcograf S.p.A.

Papers used by Virago are from well-managed forests
and other responsible sources.

Virago Press
An imprint of
Little, Brown Book Group
Carmelite House
50 Victoria Embankment
London EC4Y 0DZ

An Hachette UK Company
www.hachette.co.uk

www.virago.co.uk

*This translation has been published with
the financial support of NORLA.*

Contents

| Author's Note | xi |

Part One

Will	3
Unrest	11
The Desert of Death	17
A Bright White Light	24
The Base	28
Play	33
To Read Oneself	42
Attempts	53
On the Wing	62

Part Two

We Who Love Death	71
Home	80
The Making of a Warrior	91
Fire in the Tent	101
Fathers and Sons	107
ABC	117
First She Fell for His Voice	129

Winning Some Hearts	146
The Surge	151
Best	171
Minister of Martyrs	178
Trapped	189
The Great Game	208
My Heart Will Go On	222

Part Three

Collapse	231
The Victor	248
Lost	255
Exile	266
Time for Tenderness	274
Do You Want to Meet the Taliban?	283
Rector Redbeard	295
Visiting the Dead	305
Eclipse	318
Four Dresses and a Mobile Phone	333
The Runaway	346
The Boys Are Coming!	356
Out of the Shadows	370
The Women and the Caliph	374
Running Up That Hill	385
A New Life	401
The Basis of the Book	417

Author's Note

This is a documentary account. It is based on testimonies which I have tried to present as directly as possible. My ambition is to always stay in the perspective of the person that tells their story.

The reader who would like to know more about my methods before starting the book may go directly to the chapter 'The Basis of the Book' at the end.

Part One

Will

The fever rose.

Was she losing her?

The little girl's cheeks were crimson. Her forehead was moist, her eyes glassy.

The shaman placed amulets and herbs on the child's chest. He had written verses on tiny scraps of paper that Bibi Sitara was to put in water. She shouldn't try to make out what was written on them before drinking the water, or they wouldn't work. That instruction was unnecessary. Bibi Sitara couldn't read.

The pregnancy had been tough. The shaman had come to see her back then too. She had wanted to know if the child was healthy and would live. He had urged patience. Everything would go well if she drank the sacred water.

He told her she was carrying a girl, who would be the pride of her mother, and that they should name her Jamila, 'the beautiful one'.

He had been right. The child was born healthy, and she was truly lovely, with deep, grey-brown eyes, pale skin and a heart-shaped face. Until her fever interrupted their playing, she had been her sisters' doll. She was dressed up, carried around, rocked and fussed over. They swaddled her in strips of sheet and wrapped her up in embroidered ribbons so that she could barely move.

Now they peeked warily in.

Bibi Sitara felt her baby was slipping away. She sent for another holy man, this time a local mullah. He sat next to the sick child reading Quranic verse until nightfall. Like the shaman, he received generous payment.

After the mullah's visit the mother remained with her daughter. There was something else the shaman had said when she was pregnant. That the girl would be something special. Bibi Sitara had thrust the thought aside because she had no desire for a remarkable child. On the contrary, she just wanted an ordinary daughter.

After a week the baby's fever broke. Bibi Sitara thanked God. Everything was as *He* commanded. Alhamdulillah. God be praised.

In time they forgot the girl had been sick.

Her sisters resumed playing with her. Jamila was given dresses, necklaces, piercings in her ears. Perhaps because she was so well looked after and seldom wanted for anything, no one worried about why she never got to her feet. She continued sitting propped up by cushions, or she pulled herself across the floor with her arms and wriggled like a snake.

One day, as her mother was changing the girl, it struck her that one leg was thinner than the other. It'll probably even out, she thought. Some time later she noticed that the leg appeared to be slightly shorter.

She lifted the leg and when she let go it fell limply.

Again, she called the shaman. More prayers, amulets and pieces of paper. But to no avail. One leg wasn't keeping up with the other.

The mother remained convinced that Allah had a plan.

Unbeknownst to them, a virus had affected the girl's nervous system. It had attacked the brain stem and damaged the spine. The infection had first weakened the leg, then paralysed it. The illness had a name – poliomyelitis.

Jamila was born in 1976. Polio had been eradicated in most of Europe, but in Afghanistan it remained rampant. The virus thrived in poor areas, spreading through dirty water, through faeces and droplet infection.

There is no cure for polio, only a vaccine, but Jamila's parents had never been offered one. Nor had they ever been to a doctor. They preferred a *malang*, who cured with lines of verse and the laying on of hands. Traditions passed down from shaman to shaman were not viewed as contrary to the teachings of the Quran; a malang had been endowed with the abilities to heal by Allah.

Jamila's father and his brothers shared several houses around a large yard. Jamila went from age two, to three, to four to five, without getting up. She crawled at speed behind the other children. But when they ran out into the street, she remained behind on the sun-warmed window ledge. The wide trousers worn beneath her dress, which concealed her crooked leg, were thin and frayed at the knees. Her knee joints had become her feet.

'You should let a doctor examine her,' one of the aunts told her mother. Perhaps there was a cure. 'She'll become a burden to you. The way she is now, she'll never marry.'

No one cared that Jamila could hear what was said. It was assumed that a physical handicap also affected the thoughts and mind.

'No one wants a *langak*,' the aunts sighed. A cripple, yes, that was what she was, sitting there on a cushion with her legs in a heap. It must be a punishment for something the family did, the parents thought, penance for the sins of the forefathers. Nothing happened in life by chance, everything had recurring power, even if the suffering was visited generations after the misdeed was committed. Thus was God's judgement righteous, albeit arbitrary.

Then there was black magic. Someone wanting to harm the family might have looked at her with the evil eye. Only the shaman could remedy that type of devilry.

No doctor would ever touch his daughter, Jamila's father decided. Apart from the humming of prayers and water from the holy well in Mecca, her leg received no treatment.

When Jamila was four, her eldest brother had a daughter. One day, she noticed how the toddler stretched her arms towards the edge of the table, pulled herself up – and stood. Later, surreptitiously,

Jamila tried doing the same. She gripped the table, tensed the muscles in her arms, held on tightly and tried pulling herself up.

One day, when she was leaning against the table, her hands on the smooth surface, it happened: she stood.

She practised persistently. The muscles in her healthy leg increased in strength. Her balance improved. Eventually she could let go of the table.

The next time her niece came to visit, Jamila observed how, after raising herself up, she held on to the edge of table and moved along it.

When Jamila was alone, she copied the movements. Suddenly her mother was standing in the doorway. Jamila stumbled and fell to the floor.

'You don't need to!' Bibi Sitara shouted, startled by the ungainly movements. 'I can fetch things for you.'

Jamila grew up in a family where girls were not supposed to desire anything. The more passive the better. Life, their mother impressed upon them, was to be lived with open hands. Never grasp for anything. In that way her daughters would get what others let slip through their fingers.

Now that Jamila had seen the world at eye-level, she refused to crawl. She hopped on her good leg or limped along. When her niece got a walker, Jamila begged to have one too. Finally, her mother asked a carpenter to knock one together. It was made of wood, with legs running down to some small wheels and a handgrip. For indoor use only. The world outside was off limits.

Each morning, when the boys put on their school uniforms, grabbed their bags and hurried out, their sisters stayed at home. Reading could disturb and disrupt, give them thoughts they shouldn't have; learning could cause trouble. Their value on the marriage market would fall. That was the primary focus. Their value. Their market value.

A traditional arranged marriage was a transaction. In the pot lay the girl's qualities: her age, appearance, skills. Family, clan, earthly possessions. Honour, reputation, status. All this amounted to a price that parents could negotiate with the family of a suitor.

Ibrahim was ambitious on behalf of his children; his concern was how they could be parlayed into alliances, like families had done through the centuries.

Until marriable age, therefore, it was important to maximise the value of his daughters. There were certain factors you couldn't do anything about, such as clan or family status. Other qualities could be polished. Being unseen consolidated their purity. No men would *see* Jamila's sisters. No man would *hear* their voices. No one would *know* their names. Should a woman's name get around, she was already sullied. Jamila's father drove home these vital lessons to his children. When he had guests, his daughters sat silently in a different part of the house.

Ibrahim was born into clan rule in Ghazni, a city on a mountain plateau in the south-east of the country. Raised in poverty, he had begun life tanning hides on the dirt floor at home. Before reaching his teens, he had opened a vending spot outside the family's little mud house, offering what people would always need: coffins.

He was a true self-made Afghan. Like coffins, clothing too would always be in demand, and from dresses and shawls he expanded into food, then on to bicycles, motorcycles, cars and trucks. Finally, he went into the lucrative business simply termed *import-export*. Out with watermelons, pomegranates and grapes, in with ventilation systems, blow dryers, concrete and cement. He bought large plots of land where he pictured erecting shopping centres. The boy who had never learned to read and write properly, managed to make the most of the good times after the Second World War as Afghanistan got its first bank and its first power plant.

Jamila's parents moved from Ghazni to Kabul, where Ibrahim believed the future lay. He hired two Indian secretaries to keep track of money and contracts. The king – Zahir Shah – who had ruled since 1933 was a master in exploiting his country's position between the world's two superpowers, both of which helped build and arm the country. A road was started at one end by the Soviet Union and completed by the Americans at the other. The Soviets constructed a modern airbase at Bagram, while the US built dams and bridges. Under a mountain pass in the Hindu Kush, Soviet engineers blasted enough rock to create the highest tunnel in the world, connecting the north and south of the country.

The king had lofty ideas. He brought in American engineers to transform the rocky desert in Helmand into an oasis. The plan was to build a model city of leafy avenues, swimming pools, cinemas, tennis courts and schools, all powered by generators from the enormous dams that were to be built. It began well. In Little America, as the place was known, farmers cultivated cotton and wheat. But the soil was shallow. Irrigation led to salt accumulation and the destruction of crops. Without proper maintenance the soil deteriorated, and investments were lost. Gradually the farmers went over to growing opium poppies instead, while the desert gobbled up the oasis.

Jamila admired her father from a distance. She knew she was a disappointment, one that the influential businessman could neither adorn himself with nor be proud of. That was just how it was. She craved his acknowledgement but seldom saw him. One of her favourite things to do was sit behind the wheel of one of the cars parked in the courtyard. A Mercedes, a Rolls-Royce, a blue Ford. She would sit there daydreaming, pretending to drive until her brothers came home from school. Then she had to vacate the driver's seat.

Sometimes Jamila would take a peek in her brothers' schoolbags while they were out. Pulling out the books, she would first look at the pictures, then at the beautiful flowing patterns – the Persian alphabet.

The books were always snapped shut before she was discovered. She knew the plan.

For her sisters – get married.

For her brothers – work in their father's businesses.

For her – stay with her parents for as long as they lived.

As her father's income grew, he had taken on servants, housemaids and a gardener.

What use was *she*?

She had practised walking without crutches for a long time. She would move one leg forward, pull the other one behind her, and stabilise her body before lifting the first leg again. She took one step, then another. Forcing herself to make her limp as inconspicuous as possible. One step, two steps, three steps, ten!

Her legs were just about able to carry the weight of her body.

She was walking.

She could walk!

Now that she was standing on her own legs, and walking on them no less, she couldn't wait any longer. She knew what she wanted. She wanted to go to school like her brothers. Behind the patterns in the books lay a hidden world, she was sure of it.

Ibrahim just shook his head.

'That's not for you!'

'Let me try!' she pleaded.

'Out of the question!'

'Please!'

Her father was not accustomed to being contradicted. Her brothers didn't make any trouble, they followed the path he had set out for them. Her sisters never asked for anything.

Langak! Langak! Cripple!

In the end her father had surprised everybody. Jamila was allowed to accompany her brothers to school.

Cripple!

Out among the neighbourhood children she soon became used to their jeers.

The adults didn't care. The children lived in their own world. No one had taught them not to deride what was different. You looked down on weakness, scorned defects. Best to distance yourself from someone affected by the evil eye, God's vengeance or whatever it may be. Her brothers didn't defend her; on the contrary, they were embarrassed by her hobbling and having to walk to school with her. They asked their father to be spared. Couldn't she just stop attending? Their sister was merely a nuisance. It was mortifying. What use was schooling to her?

But her father had made a promise. Jamila would go to school until she learned to read.

Holding her head as high as she could, Jamila drew her bad leg behind her.

The books, the pens, the teachers. How she loved it! Soon she was top of the class. At the end of the year, she came home with a report card none of her brothers were even close to achieving.

'That's it,' her father smiled when the school year was over. 'Now you can read and write.'

When the next school year began, the plan was for Jamila to stay at home with her mother and help in the garden. Pickle plums. Rinse beans. Crack almonds. Jamila wanted to go back to school.

'Stop bothering me,' her father told her.

Jamila held up her index finger and looked at him imploringly.

'One more year, just one more year, one single . . .'

No one quite knew why, but Ibrahim yielded. New glowing report cards followed.

Every year the same procedure. She would hold up one finger in a gesture of supplication.

Every year she was granted *just one more year*.

Unrest

Even before Jamila was born, there was growing discontent in the country. A new progressive constitution had been enacted in the mid-1960s. Political parties were formed, freedom of the press announced, women were admitted into the government administration and burkas were banned in the civil service. Words like democracy and equality ran through Zahir Shah's speeches.

Reform began at the top. Kabul University attracted a wide range of intellectuals. Secondary schools, where children of the elite filled the classrooms before being sent to study in the West or at technical colleges in Moscow, were established.

The nightlife in the Afghan capital surged: Pakistanis came for weekend trips to drink whisky, sheiks from the Gulf to dance. Young Westerners stopped off on the hippie trail to India to smoke opium and try the local hash. The street scene, fashion magazines, even the youth rebellion drew inspiration from Paris.

At the same time only one in ten Afghans could read and write. Kabul was a bubble. The modern hairstyles, miniskirts and sleeveless blouses were quite real, and yet illusory.

The urban and the rural were two separate worlds. While jazz was playing in the capital, people outside the cities lived as their families had done for centuries, from hand to mouth. They grew nuts, apricots and carrots. On the mountainsides, sheep and goats grazed. Large parts of the country lacked clean water; people were starving and children dying of simple diseases.

By the end of the 1960s discontent had escalated. Several newspapers called for regime change. Stalinists and Trotskyists, benefiting from the king's attempts at a democracy they wanted to abolish, took to the streets. Students threw stones at the police.

Deeper rumblings spread through the countryside, supported by young intellectual Islamists in the cities. Were the goings-on in Kabul in accordance with Islam?

The mullahs didn't think so.

While the young girls of Kabul listened to the Beatles, women's daily lives elsewhere went on behind high mud walls. Indoors they were born and indoors they would die. Ideally, only twice in her life should a woman leave her home, both times clad in white: as a newlywed brought to the house of her husband, then when she was borne out, wrapped in a burial cloth.

The king himself was more Westward-looking than socialist-oriented. As the unrest spread, he sought help from across the Atlantic, but the USA had its hands full with the war in Vietnam. So the Afghan ruler sought closer ties with the Soviet Union, militarily as well as economically.

When drought struck in the early 1970s, without Zahir Shah seeming to take much notice – the throne was shaking.

On a hot July day in 1973, while the king was resting in Italy after an eye operation, his cousin took over the royal palace. Prince Daoud had been sacked as prime minister a decade earlier when Zahir had reintroduced direct royal rule. Now he had engineered a comeback.

Without a drop of blood being spilled, in a coup led by a handful of officers, he seized power from the sovereign who had ruled since he was a teenager.

Daoud abolished the monarchy and declared a republic. The Marxists who supported the coup were given several seats in the cabinet but were gradually squeezed out. At the same time, the new ruler cracked down on Islamists he feared might undermine the regime. The leaders of the Muslim Brotherhood were imprisoned or fled to Pakistan.

The royal administration had held a protective hand over Jamila's father. When the king failed to return from Italy after the coup, Ibrahim shifted allegiance to the new powers. Daoud wasn't necessarily bad news for business. Monarchy or republic, the country needed what Ibrahim sold.

The new constitution of 1977 was framed in revolutionary rhetoric, and policies included both land reforms and nationalisation, but in practice the regime continued as before: centralised, autocratic and repressive. Power lay with the army and bureaucracy.

While Ibrahim's businesses continued to grow, the outspoken press was clamped down on and dissidents were silenced.

Still occupied with their own war in South-East Asia, the USA continued to cut funding to the country. To move away from the Soviet sphere of influence, Daoud turned to non-aligned countries like India, Iran and Egypt. The chief of the Soviet Politburo, Leonid Brezhnev, raised the issue on a visit Daoud made to Moscow. The former prince is said to have replied tersely that he would cooperate with whomever he pleased and would not be dictated to by anyone.

His bold response sealed his fate. The Kremlin was pulling the strings when Afghan Marxists, led by the poet Nur Muhammad Taraki, occupied the presidential palace in April 1978. After several hours of intense fighting, Daoud and his entire family – twenty-seven in all – were executed, in the same way the Bolsheviks had disposed of the tsar's family after the revolution of 1917.

Massacres spread throughout the country. In rural districts the communists proceeded with a heavy hand. Mullahs and their congregations were imprisoned, tortured and killed.

The new government did not sit for long. In September 1979, after just over a year in power, Taraki was assassinated in the palace he himself had seized. His prime minister, Hafizullah Amin, whom Moscow had actually wanted to get rid of, took over.

It was under Amin's regime that the difficulties began for Ibrahim. The conditions for private capital worsened and it was subjected to tighter restrictions. Radical reforms were implemented, aimed at limiting how much land and property one family could own. Ibrahim, like many others, had some of his land seized. Taking power from the upper class would lead to support from the common folk, Amin believed. But the reforms were neither popular nor productive. The farmers, fearing expropriation, allowed the harvest to fail, and food shortages led to civil unrest.

Despite clear warnings from his own generals, Leonid Brezhnev decided to invade his southern neighbour. On Christmas Eve 1979 Soviet troops landed at Kabul airport.

The Kremlin's strategy was to stabilise a new regime, then withdraw the troops after a couple of weeks. They would first occupy the cities where support for the communists was strongest, then supply the Afghan army with ammunition and support, allowing it to defeat the resistance in rural areas. The plan was never for Soviet soldiers to engage in combat.

The coup itself went quickly. Like his predecessor, Amin was shot in the presidential palace, the Arg, after first being poisoned by his Russian cooks.

The superpower had taken over an independent, non-aligned country and installed new puppets. Of all the mistakes Brezhnev made, the invasion of Afghanistan was the most fatal. The elderly chief of the Politburo hadn't anticipated the Afghans' collective will to defend themselves. The Cold War was about to turn hot.

The CIA programme to arm Afghan guerrillas was codenamed Operation Cyclone. It was the costliest covert operation the intelligence agency had ever embarked upon. Initiated by President Jimmy Carter in 1980, it would outlive his presidency and be inherited by Ronald Reagan. Carter's security advisor, Zbigniew Brzezinski, who had promised 'to give the Soviet Union their own Vietnam', was passed down with it.

Expenditure accelerated under Reagan, and when Brzezinski enquired as to the limits of spending, he was told 'there are no budgets'.

By the time Jamila started asking for *one more year*, Afghanistan had become the site of an ideological contest between the world's two superpowers, but the real war had yet to reach the children of Kabul. The Soviets protected the regime in the capital; there was peace and quiet in the streets and children at play in the schoolyards. It was in the mountains and the countryside the rockets fell. That was where children were being maimed. Fathers killed. Mothers snatched away.

Not that children in Kabul didn't notice some change. The Islamic confession of faith disappeared from the morning schedule at school and boys and girls began sharing classrooms. The girls no longer wore headscarves. Those who signed up for communist children's activities gained advantages and a red pioneer scarf. Jamila did everything to avoid wearing one. That was her protest.

In class, you could no longer tell friend from foe. Some of the parents worked for the Soviet occupiers, others had parents who wanted the foreigners out.

Yet the invasion would introduce Jamila to the feeling of being part of something bigger. One February night, in the first winter the Soviet soldiers spread across the country, the people gathered behind what would come to characterise resistance: Allah.

A quiet stream of men defied the curfew, taking to the streets or going up onto the rooftops. The women went out into their backyards and looked upwards. To Jamila it sounded like they began to hum. But it was not a song; it was a prayer. They were reciting. Like a battle cry directed at the aeroplanes above their heads.

The voices could be heard all through the night. Allahu Akbar. Allahu Akbar. *Allahu Akbar.* God is great, God is greater, God is greatest!

The little, very special girl crawled up onto the window ledge and heard the many-voiced praise, sung in harmony, one voice taking over for the next.

There and then she felt that God was listening.

The Desert of Death

You get out of bed, build the fire, boil some water, perhaps warm up some of yesterday's bread and suddenly you're dead. Someone who doesn't know you has ordered an attack. Red-hot shrapnel hits your village before dawn, penetrating bodies, puncturing lungs, breaking hearts. Metal at temperatures of hundreds of degrees smashing skulls, ripping off fingers or entire arms, stopping everything – a dream, a yawn, a train of thought, a half-spoken word.

Death usually came from above. By the time you heard the plane or the hissing in the air, it was too late. The plane had slipped its payload. A bomb ripped through roofs and tent cloth and hit you at home. Families who had run inside during an attack were charred when the house ignited; entire broods of children huddled behind an outhouse turned to ash. Villages razed to the ground so the rebels could not hide there.

It took some people longer to die. If the main artery in your leg is severed, it takes two minutes. If it's your arm, you have ten minutes before bleeding to death. Missiles, bombs, bullets ended lives that had barely begun, lives carrying life, already long lives.

Multiply this by a million.

And we are still only halfway through the war.

Death also came from the ground. Landmines were laid on mountain slopes, along roads and riverbanks. Farmers lost hands and legs in the fields; children were blinded by explosives they mistook for toys. Soil that could no longer be cultivated, pasture where animals could no longer graze – yet another war crime on top of all the others.

Death was all around; you just had to get used to it.

* * *

The first time Hala looked her husband in the eyes, he was lying in the yard with two holes in his forehead.

His teeth were shattered. Limbs stiff. His chest riddled with bullets. His eyes wide open.

It felt as though the ground was rumbling beneath her. She had run out to the yard as they were carrying him in, without caring that the men around him were not part of the family. In death, God was merciful, as surely the neighbours were too. The trembling under her feet intensified. The ground was undulating, causing her to sway.

As Hala stood tipping from side to side, she looked her husband in the eyes. Not a sob, not a single tear escaped her. Finally, she could look at him without being afraid.

The blood had blackened on his skin; he was covered in gravel and sand, his tunic brown with blood. She touched his arm. During their marriage their gaze had always swept past one another. If he looked at her, she lowered her eyes; if he spoke to her, she bowed her head. Only when she was certain he wasn't looking at her did she dare look at him. And only when his head was turned in another direction. Warily, always warily.

She was ten years old when they married. Wasir was much older, thirty, maybe forty. She didn't know. Several years passed before they had children. Six in total. Four sons – Hassan, Yaqub, Raouf and Bashir – and two daughters, who no one outside the family knew the names of. Now they were fatherless. From now on they had only her.

She thought of his voice. Her husband used to recite from the Quran every morning and evening, often for hours. It was so beautiful. She had always wanted to ask him if he could teach her the words but had never dared. Now he lay there. Now it was too late.

The night before, she had his dinner ready when he came home. She had boiled rice and fried some vegetables from their small plot. It was Ramadan and from sunrise to sunset no food or drink was to pass their lips.

She had spread a sheet on the floor and placed the dish between them. He had blessed the food before the family began to eat. They clumped the rice together with their fingers or scooped it up with sauce on a piece of bread. After dinner her husband had gone to the mosque to conduct the evening prayer.

Mussahi, a village of just a few houses along a small river in unyielding farmland, had become important to the rebels due to its strategic location thirty kilometres south of Kabul's city limits. To the east lay the foothills of the mountains, to the west lay the fields, and beyond them, the main road to Kabul. Further east lay the province of Logar, known as the Gates of Jihad. Important supply lines ran through the barren province, as large quantities of weapons were smuggled in from Pakistan.

In Mussahi, *mujahideen* – fighters who had taken up the struggle against the Soviet Union – and the villagers were often one and the same. They were fathers, brothers and male cousins. The resistance was based on – and run by – tribal networks and clan leaders; they *were* the village.

The word *mujahid* derives from *jihad*, holy war. Mullah Wasir would be given lists from the mujahideen detailing what they required – food, clothing and equipment – then he would send out men to try to obtain the supplies. Hala would often cook for the fighters when they came down from the mountains to eat before they disappeared once again.

The mujahideen could not manage without the villages. They were the circulatory system in the resistance movement.

Some days previously, local fighters had carried out a successful attack on the closest Soviet position. Allah had provided help. Several of the infidels had been killed, Hala had heard.

After her husband went to the mosque, Hala nursed the baby and put the other children to bed. Their father would want tea when he came home, so she filled the pot and placed it on the fire. But he was slow in coming.

Perhaps he had decided to stay behind in the mosque. Prayer during the time of fasting gave extra credit in paradise, so maybe he wanted to stay there overnight.

She heard gunfire, then it went quiet. It hadn't come from the direction of the mosque, so she gave it no further thought. Eventually she went to bed.

Next morning, he still wasn't home. Hala wanted to pick *shaftal*, a spinach-like plant that grew on the land beyond the wall of their yard. She had prepared a dough to make *bolani* for her husband when they broke the fast at sunset. She would chop onion and shaftal and fry it gently in oil, before rolling out the dough into thin circles, spreading the green filling over one, placing another on top, sealing it and frying it golden on each side. They were to be served freshly cooked, right from the pan.

Hala went out at dawn. She didn't bother putting on her burka; it was so early, and impractical in the fields. When she spotted a group of men a little way off she hastened to turn her face away and cover it with her shawl. Still, she noticed they were staring at her. That was unheard of. Men were supposed to be careful where their gaze fell, least of all let it rest on another man's wife.

She picked a few bunches of shaftal before hurrying back home, without glancing at the men.

They knew something she didn't. Yet not being in the same family, they could not tell her.

She went into the kitchen, checked that she had enough onions and washed the green bunches to rinse them of soil. At the same time, she kept an ear out for her husband, who could be home at any minute.

But it was Wasir's brothers who came.

*

The Ox's men had taken him from the mosque.

Wasir had always been cautious in his sermons, wrapping his message in Quranic verse; there might be informers in the congregation. The traitors also had to tread carefully because the villagers might guess who they were. People who had extra cash or improved their position were suspect. They showed up now and again at Friday prayer, in simple dress like the others, worn grey, brown or dark blue tunics with wide trousers underneath. You could see it in their eyes, Wasir said, how they wanted to get away from God's house, to Kabul, to the big city, where the roads were tarmacked, where water came from taps.

Whether someone had snitched on him, no one knew. The security forces had orders to single out men in retaliation for the attack a few days earlier. They had taken the mullah and those who had stayed behind after prayer; others had been pulled from their houses. One man had refused to go and had been shot on the spot, right there by his own gate – the shots Hala had heard the night before.

Mullah Wasir and the others had been driven into the desert.

They had been lined up, shot, abandoned. Retribution was complete.

When you died a martyr, you were not to be washed. You were to meet God as you had fallen. There was no coffin, only a sheet to wrap the deceased in.

Hala stood and saw everything. The earth continued to move beneath her. It cracked. While he just lay there.

The man she had been so afraid of, so modest towards, the man who for sixteen years she had never dared ask to teach her to recite. She had loved his voice; it was deep and warm.

She had never seen him as he was now. Completely open, perfectly peaceful. She felt shy. Even in death he had that effect on her.

The Ox, as he was known, was responsible for the security services. Najibullah, who had come to power in 1986, was a tall man with a broad torso from hours of wrestling and weightlifting. While studying medicine in Kabul in the 1970s, he had joined the Afghan

Communist Party. Following the invasion in 1979, the newly qualified doctor signed up to serve the new rulers. He rose rapidly through the ranks of the security forces. His talent at breaking people down turned out to be more highly valued than his skills in caring for and healing them.

A year after the invasion, Najibullah was appointed leader of the KHAD, the secret police, built with the Soviet intelligence services as the model and brutality as the method. Tens of thousands of Islamists, holy warriors, communists from the wrong factions and random victims never emerged alive from the notorious Pul-e-Charkhi prison on the outskirts of Kabul. There, the weightlifter could bring his physique to bear. He liked to torture the prisoners personally, often to death, or he let recruits use the inmates for target practice. Prison guards slowly removed fingernails, pulled out hair and beards or chopped off body parts while demanding information on supply routes and hideouts.

Wasir's death was more merciful. A few shots, then life was over, and a new journey began.

To the gates of heaven. That was where he was now headed.

Martyrs were admitted directly to *Jannah* – paradise. They were granted the best places, near God's throne.

Life had been a struggle. Now he would be rewarded for his toil, as promised to him in the hereafter. He'd had one wife in this life, he would get seventy-two virgins in the next. Martyrs such as he would be celebrated, as he himself had preached, so he should know.

Six children were asleep in Wasir's house when the shots were fired. The youngest was three months old.

They had named him Bashir, *the one who brings tidings of joy*.

Their father was buried the same day. He left nothing behind but his clothes and his Quran. No photographs, no other possessions. All Hala had was the children. She found solace in the baby. She allowed herself to be soothed and warmed by the little body that couldn't manage without her and sucked greedily on her breasts. She didn't want to let go of the child she knew would be her last. Remarrying was out of the question. It might mean splitting up the children and she would rather die than face that prospect. She was determined that her children would not be subjected to the rootless, lonely upbringing she had experienced after losing her father as a two-year-old. Back then Hala's mother had been quickly wed to her dead husband's uncle and forced to give up her children. They became the property of her new husband's half-brother. He later gave Hala away in marriage in exchange for a second wife for himself, along with a payment of twelve thousand afghani. The young girl he took as a second wife was considered more beautiful and more accomplished, and therefore worth more, than the fatherless ten-year-old.

The house was filled with weeping women. Wasir's mother, sisters, cousins and aunts. Hala did not shed a tear. Her husband wouldn't have liked her to cry, for how could she be sad when he finally would be seated near the throne of God?

The dough she had made in the morning had finished rising. The bunches of shaftal were still lying on the counter. Someone began to chop the onions and vegetables, sprinkled some salt over them and placed them in the pan to sizzle. A neighbour helped her roll out the dough. Another placed the filling inside, put the second circle of dough on top and sealed the edges. A delicious smell pervaded the kitchen as the stuffed flatbreads were fried on the hot stone.

The children were hungry. They were given their father's portion.

Because life goes on.

A Bright White Light

Jamila's father noticed the impact on his wallet. The war was destroying roads, bridges, warehouses. Incomes across the country dropped sharply. Transport became difficult, trade came to a halt. The two Indian secretaries who had read documents for Ibrahim, processed his dictation and looked after the bills disappeared, taking a healthy chunk of his fortune with them.

The Afghan army, financed by the Kremlin, was ineffective. Purges, executions and desertion prior to the invasion had reduced the officer corps by half. During the first year of the Soviet occupation the army shrank to a quarter of its pre-invasion size. Entire units mutinied and pledged loyalty to the mujahideen.

Conscription was introduced. First the call-up. Then the recruiters at the door.

Ibrahim and Bibi Sitara worried about their sons. They had managed to keep military service at bay thus far, but an increasing number of young men were being called up. Conscription was set at age nineteen. Any attempt to evade the draft was viewed as desertion and punishable by death. The term of military service had increased to four years, and the education grants offered on completion did not tempt Jamila's brothers.

Ibrahim was in a quandary. He had to choose between his sons and the money. Letting his sons flee the country would lead to trouble with the authorities. Exceptions were only made for prominent party members and students in Eastern Bloc countries, or through bribes.

Blood outweighed banknotes. Ibrahim let his eldest son travel to Pakistan under the guise of a business trip. He gave him money to buy a house, in case the whole family needed to follow him.

Many of Ibrahim's contacts had left the country but the merchant in him wanted to stay where his businesses were. Maybe he could adjust to a war economy. He had adapted before.

Then his own people began to be arrested. First a cousin was jailed, then one uncle, then another. He counted seven relatives who had been taken by the secret police. Upon learning they were to be executed, he knew he had to act.

Several old women had been to the house on behalf of their sons, nephews and grandsons, to look at his daughters.

Like prey, Jamila scoffed. Groomed and made up. With no names. The eldest of the sisters was called the red fairy, the second eldest the green fairy, after a wedding feast they had attended in red and green dresses respectively.

One of the suitors belonged to the communist elite. He was a nephew of the regime's intelligence chief. There was no better catch.

Ibrahim used the red fairy as a bargaining chip to free his relatives. They were released when the engagement was agreed. The marriage gave Ibrahim some leeway.

Jamila was shocked by the decadence of the wedding feast. The ten-year-old stared wide-eyed at glittering dresses and plunging necklines. The women of the communist elite, without shawls, loud and bold, danced without any inhibitions. These sins would be punished, Jamila was sure of that. Just wait.

The green fairy was bargained away to a businessman with good connections to the regime. Jamila was disappointed. She knew neither of the husbands were from families her father respected. As a deeply religious man he hated the communists. The two fairies, who in childhood had played with her as their doll, had been sacrificed for a greater good.

Eventually the alliances Ibrahim had built could not protect his family any longer. He sent away his second son, followed by the third when he turned nineteen. Then the fourth also went to Pakistan. Finally, the fifth. Ibrahim feared punishment. He had seen other men fall from grace.

Time was beginning to run out. Now he, Bibi and Jamila would also have to leave.

There were roadblocks all along the road to Pakistan, so they couldn't take that route. His sons had followed the goat tracks the mujahideen used through the Khyber Pass but these mountain trails would be impossible for Jamila.

Her parents decided to send her with an uncle, on the pretext of undertaking the journey for medical treatment, then they would travel to Pakistan themselves once all the children were safe there. Her father hired a car and a driver, had an elderly uncle sit in the passenger seat and Jamila in the back. The doctor's letter was placed in the uncle's hand.

The car drove quickly out of Kabul. Soviet engineers had built a highway to Jalalabad. Low stone walls separated the twisting road from cliffs and steep slopes. After a while the car was winding its way past large stones and craters. Jamila saw the destruction she had been spared in Kabul.

Armoured vehicles passed them. On one stretch, Jamila noticed an oncoming tank signalling to them. The driver ignored this, and continued driving towards it. Soon they were alongside the tank. Jamila looked out of the rear window as they passed and saw the heavy machine gun that protruded from the turret turn slowly in their direction. The barrel was pointing straight at her. Jamila stared into the muzzle.

The last thing she remembered was the flash of light. A bright white light.

She woke freezing. She felt wet but was unable to see anything. She rubbed her eyelids. Her eyes were clogged with something sticky.

Jamila forced one eye open. She saw the windows were smashed, the remaining shards of glass shaking as the car moved at breakneck speed. There was blood everywhere. On the seat. On her. On the back of the seat in front. She uttered a few words.

The driver turned.

'Alhamdulillah, you're alive!' he exclaimed.

A pain cut through her head. She lifted a hand to her ear, where the blood was beginning to congeal.

She heard gurgling sounds coming from the passenger seat.

'*Baba!*' she shouted.

There was no answer.

The bullet from the tank's machine gun had gone through the back window, gashed Jamila's right ear, grazing her cerebral cortex, pierced the seat in front and penetrated the back of her uncle's head. Baba had been killed instantly; the sounds were coming from his body.

After the bullet hit, the driver, who was himself unharmed, had turned to look at his two slumped passengers and thought he was driving two corpses.

Jamila had her head bandaged in the next village. Her uncle's body was collected by relatives. The dead man was to be washed, prayed over, and buried the same day.

While the Soviet soldier bore the blame for one life lost, God was thanked for sparing the other.

The Base

By the time Jamila was sent across the border, over a quarter of Afghanistan's population had fled the country. Some two million had travelled west to Iran, even more into Pakistan. The war had been going on for eight years. One million Afghans would soon be dead. Millions more maimed.

Jamila and her uncle became part of the statistics. One dead. One injured.

The family settled in the rapidly expanding border town of Peshawar. The plains around the town had become one enormous refugee camp. Shacks made of mud, stone, plastic, cardboard, of whatever was to hand, were packed close together. A continual influx of new people coming into an already overpopulated country. Pakistan didn't need them. Not their labour, not their minds.

Lives were lost every week. Bombs detonated over internal disputes. People were executed in broad daylight. Rivalry between mujahideen groups as well as between the Islamists and the communist regime meant more Afghan militia leaders were killed here than on the battlefield, in assassinations carried out by the KGB, by the Ox's KHAD, by the Pakistani intelligence service or by the eternal enemy: one another.

At the same time, the illegal flow of money and weapons led to an economic upturn. The drug trade flourished. Gemstones and stolen treasure from the national museum in Kabul found new owners.

Following their flight to Pakistan, Jamila's father had become short-tempered and was given to sudden fits of rage. He had lost valuable investments and property in Kabul, and had a hard time adjusting to life in Peshawar, this rumour mill of a city which in the course of the war had become the heart and brain of the resistance.

Jamila was spared the daily sufferings and the squalid conditions of the camps. Her family had moved into a villa behind high walls, surrounded by eucalyptus and magnolia, close to the headquarters of Burhanuddin Rabbani, a sharia professor who had fled prior to the Soviet invasion, in the wake of an attempted Islamic coup. On the street outside, and throughout the entire district, his lascivious and pugnacious men swarmed. Few families allowed their girls outside.

Jamila's father shook his head. Attending school was out of the question.

Her brothers backed him up. Jamila's insistence on a life outside the house was a threat to their reputation. They were a distinguished family with a good name, and that called for a particular dignity and reserve. Ibrahim kept out of politics and war. None of the brothers joined the resistance; their time was taken up getting business connections in place. The older brothers cursed their fates and the one person in the family who refused to accept hers: Jamila.

People had sought refuge in Peshawar in several waves. First came the Islamists, who had studied sharia in Kabul in the 1970s – the first target of the Marxist purges. They possessed the power of definition in the camps and decided the direction of the resistance. On their heels followed the rural village mullahs, and finally, the people who just wanted to get away from the war.

Rabbani, the sharia professor in the next street, led the largest mujahideen group, Jamiat-e-Islami, predominately composed of Tajiks, the second largest ethnic group in Afghanistan. While Pashtuns comprised about half the population, scarcely a third were Tajiks, residing mainly in the west and north of the country. Uzbeks and Hazaras were the two next biggest peoples, each making up around a tenth of the population.

Many of Rabbani's students established their own rebel groups. In the mid-1980s there were a couple of hundred militia groups in the city. Chaos reigned. Most of the funding came from Pakistani intelligence, the Gulf and the CIA, and went to the seven largest rebel groups, known as the Peshawar Seven. Saudi Arabia contributed half a billion dollars annually, equalling the spending of the USA. Close cooperation with Pakistan's president, the authoritarian Islamist Zia ul-Haq, led to the Sunni-dominated jihadists receiving more support than the less ideological rebel groups.

Among the people who made their way to Peshawar was the Egyptian doctor Ayman al-Zawahiri, following his imprisonment for involvement in the assassination of the president, Anwar Sadat. The surgeon operated on jihadists wounded in combat and led the organisation al-Jihad. He was short of money and looking for support.

A wealthy Saudi by the name of Osama bin Laden came to his rescue. Through his father, who had restored mosques in Mecca and Medina, and died in a plane crash en route to fetch yet another teenage bride, he was in direct contact with the Saudi Arabian royal family and oil billionaires in the Gulf.

Bin Laden ran Maktab al-Khadamat – The Services Bureau – an organisation receiving crisp new dollar bills from oil sheiks in Kuwait and gold jewellery from well-off wives in Jeddah, while the Saudi crown prince donated trucks and the mosques in the Gulf sent briefcases full of cash.

The Services Bureau functioned as a hostel for Arabian fighters and as the editorial offices of the magazine *al-Jihad*. Here, in robust safes, bin Laden stored the money raised. He was the individual who brought the most money, weapons and fighters – the so-called Afghan Arabs – into the country, offering plane tickets, board and lodging as well as three hundred dollars a month per household. For no charge you were given training, indoctrination and access to his theological library.

It was the director of the CIA, William J. Casey, who convinced Congress that the mujahideen needed the very latest, light shoulder-launched missiles that could shoot down aeroplanes and helicopters.

After the CIA had supplied these Stinger missiles, and American personnel had trained the jihadists in their use, they were eventually able to cope with the overwhelming Soviet air superiority, the most important factor in turning the tide of the war in the rebels' favour.

Casey was an ardent supporter of recruiting radical Muslims from around the world to fight with the Afghan mujahideen. President Reagan called them freedom fighters. When he invited a group of mujahideen leaders to the White House in late 1987, he lauded their wisdom. In his speech to the battle-hardened guerrilla fighters, seated in the soft chairs of the Roosevelt Room, Reagan spoke of their new weapons, coordination and tactics. 'You are a nation of heroes. God bless you,' he concluded.

Fear of fighting, in addition to a promise made to his mother, meant Osama bin Laden remained on the Pakistani side of the border. It was five years into the war, during Ramadan, that he first ventured into Afghanistan, where he viewed everything – weapons, roads, trenches – as being in a sorry state. 'I asked forgiveness from God Almighty, feeling that I had sinned because I listened to those who advised me not to go,' he said. God would only forgive him if he became a martyr, he thought, terrified by how low the planes flew as they attacked, how deafening the sound of the bombs were and how blessed he had felt when the missiles that landed nearby did not explode but lay like 'black stones' around him. He felt closer to God than ever before, he told his companions.

Osama bin Laden and the ideologue behind the jihadists of the 1980s, the Palestinian Abdallah Azzam, had a concept to sell: martyrdom. It pervaded the books, pamphlets and cassettes sold at mosques and in bookshops. Azzam's magazine *al-Jihad* was grounded in the cult of death. He was the one who expounded the theory that it was every Muslim's duty – *fard al-ayn* – to wage holy war when a Muslim country was attacked. Young men were mobilised in a just war against a godless occupying power. Once the scholars had defined a conflict as fard al-ayn, you didn't need to ask your father, your mother or your imam, you could just go! A glorious death enticed the sinful, a direction triggered the listless. A poor man would get to enjoy heaven's delights, meat, fruit, even wine, and not least the fabled virgins – chaste as hidden pearls.

Together with Azzam, Osama bin Laden founded al-Qaeda, *the Base*. Shortly afterwards – in 1989 – Azzam and his two sons were killed by a car bomb on their way to Friday prayer. Whoever was behind the killing remained a mystery, the enemies too numerous.

But the Base would become known throughout the world.

Play

Bashir's earliest memory, a little trauma at the time and later something he would laugh about, was when his mother buttoned up her dress and told him, 'You're a big boy now.'

That was the end of breast milk.

Bashir was three years old. The following year he was engaged.

His cousin Yasamin had just turned one. It was Hala's doing. She had reached an agreement with Yasamin's father, her late husband's brother, that the engagement of the two children could just as well be arranged sooner rather than later.

Hala singled out wives for all her sons while they were still small. In so doing she could keep her eye on the girls and correct them from childhood on. It was about virtue. About honour. In that she was a master.

When asked if she would marry again, her reply was that she would rather *eat dirt* than find a new husband. You didn't mess with Hala. Things had changed since she was widowed. She made her own decisions, she raised the children alone, all within the framework of *Pashtunwali*, the ancestral code, which dictated the basic principles of honour and hospitality, courage and loyalty, justice and revenge.

Hala was strict with her children, and was quicker to strike than hug. She was terrified her sons would become idlers, use opium, bring shame upon her and that people would say, 'There go the four without a father.'

There were nevertheless many they could call baba. The children grew up in the backyard of Wasir's brothers, with uncles wherever they turned.

Bashir never felt he lacked a father. How could he miss something he didn't know?

When it came to Hala, there was only one man who made her shy – her dead husband. Any time his name came up she would lower her head and hide her face.

* * *

The invasion was a fiasco. For the Politburo in Moscow the loss of prestige hurt. The Soviet Union was trapped by its poor neighbour.

If only the Politburo had paid more attention to military history. Over the millennia, commanders like Cyrus the Great, Darius I and Alexander the Great had tried to conquer the Afghans and all had encountered fierce resistance. Alexander finally succeeded by a policy of divide and rule, torture and execution. But at a cost. According to legend the Macedonians lost as many men on one bloody day as in the four years it took to conquer the lands between the Mediterranean and Persia. After the conqueror's death his warriors began fighting among themselves. The mountain people struck back – as the Soviets would experience over two thousand years later – from cliffs and steep terrain.

Only in the thirteenth century did a foreign conqueror take possession of the land. Genghis Khan and his Mongol hordes had already laid waste to several civilisations between the Caspian Sea and China. His men slaughtered thousands in Kabul, Kandahar and Jalalabad. In the wake of a rebellion in Helmand men were decapitated, the women taken as slaves. Genghis Khan's successors held power for three hundred years, until the Mongols also lost out to the Afghans.

Throughout history occupying forces had never become masters of the Afghans. 'We can stand strife, stand attack, stand blood,' went the saying, 'but we will never stand a ruler.'

If only the Politburo had studied the maps more closely. The very names attested to violence. Hindu Kush – Killer of Hindus – a test of strength in summer, impassable when the snows came; crags, cliffs and mountainsides ideal for ambushes. Only to the north and south-west were there level plains; but these lay at altitude and were exposed, with names like Dasht-e-Margo, the Desert of Death.

If only the Politburo had cared about their own. The Soviet soldiers were haphazardly equipped, poorly clothed and seldom sufficiently trained in the use of heavy weaponry. Already in the first month a thousand of them had been killed. When a young man came home in a coffin, his family were disciplined. Visible grief in the workplace, over a child sacrificed for the motherland, was regarded as detrimental to the collective; the parents could be sent for psychiatric treatment.

No official statistics existed, no known registers. Young men simply did not come home. Or they returned in zinc coffins, bolted or welded shut. Parents were not to see what the war had done to their son. Or if the soldier in the coffin was their son at all. After major battles, bones, heads, random arms and other body parts were divided among the coffins so they were of suitable weight before being sealed.

Headstones were only allowed to bear the inscription of when your child was born and when he died. Only the date, never the place, never Afghanistan.

If only, if only.

In 1986, the year before Bashir's father was killed, Mikhail Gorbachev called the war a 'bleeding wound'. The superpower was changing its tune. When the new head of the Politburo launched *glasnost* and *perestroika* – openness and restructuring – peace and withdrawal were part of the equation. But how was he to do it without losing support? The puppet government in Afghanistan would surely fall, weakening Soviet strategic interests. A withdrawal could also lead to increased self-confidence and revolt in the Muslim Soviet republics in the south, and would signal an ideological defeat for communism.

The Soviets had an enormous military presence in the country, with several hundred thousand soldiers in addition to the KGB, military advisors and civilian contractors. They had a vast number of tanks and heavy armoured vehicles, but the army often got stuck in the narrow valleys, making them vulnerable. The soldiers called them *dukhi* – spirits – the fighters who suddenly turned up and attacked them, only to disappear again. The mujahideen could leave an area the Soviets had struck, leading them to believe they had won. Then the dukhi would return at night, or the next night, or the week after, when the soldiers had made camp and relaxed their guard.

The wound continued to bleed – fresh, young blood.

The costs of staying outweighed the costs of pulling out. There was no prospect of a military victory.

Gorbachev summoned the Ox – now President Najibullah – to the Kremlin. The Afghans would have to govern alone and pursue national reconciliation. Moscow promised massive support, economic and technical as well as military. In April 1988, one year after Wasir was killed, an agreement was signed in Geneva.

In February 1989 the last Soviet soldier left Afghanistan. The Politburo continued propping up the Ox until the Soviet Union dissolved into fifteen independent republics in 1991. The steady stream of roubles came to a sudden end. Najibullah was forced to resign and was immediately placed under house arrest in Kabul.

Afghanistan was also divided up, by warlords who fought, betrayed and bribed one another, then entered alliances before switching sides and fighting again. The mujahideen no longer had a common enemy to unite them. Four of the largest Islamist factions fought doggedly, with increasingly heavy weaponry, for control of Kabul. By 1992 it was civil war.

The four powerful commanders each held their own cardinal

point of the city, launching attacks on one another. People were stuck in the middle as the city was shelled to pieces. One day Bashir's house was destroyed when a missile hit the roof.

The children's play reflected reality. While in the 1980s they had captured Russians, in the 1990s they played at being Islamists of varying shades. Bashir's eldest brother, Hassan, always wanted to be from Hezb-e-Islami, the group of Gulbuddin Hekmatyar, who had relations in Mussahi. Others pretended they were the soldiers of the Lion of Panjshir, Ahmad Shah Massoud, or they wanted to be Osama bin Laden's ally, Abdul Rasul Sayyaf. The unlucky ones had to be the notoriously brutal Abdul Rashid Dostum. He was Uzbek and no such people lived in Mussahi.

The boys fired stones with catapults and gathered sticks for fighting at close quarters. As one of the youngest, Bashir was bossed around, while he yearned to be the one ordering ambushes, retreats and fresh attacks.

Outside the playgrounds, there seemed to be no end to the cycle of violence. The anarchy was absolute. Proud mujahideen did whatever they pleased. They abducted, raped and massacred; both boys and girls were exploited. The victors seized houses, ejected the occupants and gave the farmland to their own. Public property was of all and no one, people cut down telephone poles for its copper wiring, raided market stalls and sold stolen goods to scrap merchants. Many who hitherto had remained in the country now left.

When the Swedish Committee for Afghanistan built a school in Mussahi, Hala sent her sons there. First the three oldest, Hassan, Yaqub and Raouf, then the apple of her eye. She never made any attempt to hide that she favoured Bashir. He spoke clearly from an early age and always thought big; bigger than the others, she told people.

There were now two schools in the village: a *maktab*, the Swedish school with mathematics, science and Persian, and a *madrasa*, a Quran school, with prayers, recitation and Arabic. Eventually Hala took her sons out of the Swedish school. They were to attend the mosque full time so they could become mullahs like their father. Her two daughters had no need of book learning. Education was not a requisite for wives – on the contrary. The school might challenge parents' authority and you never knew what the children might pick up from others. Besides, girls' faces weren't covered in the classroom.

Hala's daughters were kept on a tight rein. From the age of nine they were no longer allowed to play outside the gate. If they went on an errand they had to go straight to where they were headed, then home. Idle time came to an end after the first years of childhood.

The boys had more freedom.

When they weren't at school or in in the mosque, they played cricket on a plain outside the village. The ball was made of hard, rolled-up material, the bat had been carved from a piece of wood.

But mostly they were warriors. During Bashir's first year at school a new group of fighters was added to the game. The grown-ups spoke about them with hope. The imam preached in admiration. The mullahs at the madrasa pointed to them as examples. They could bring peace. They were moral guardians. They were God's students. They were Allah's soldiers. They called themselves Taliban.

Talib means student in Arabic. Not any student but one at a madrasa, one seeking knowledge of Islam. With the Quran in hand this student group were going to sweep up and cleanse society. Bring peace. Disarm the population. Introduce sharia. The Talibs had spent their formative years at Quran schools. They had learned about the society the Prophet Muhammad had fought for in the seventh century – the ideal they wished to realise.

It began with a one-eyed mullah on a motorbike. He had lost his eye when a grenade splinter pierced it during a Soviet attack. His cheek and forehead were disfigured in the same explosion and, until he lost his eye, he had been known as an able marksman. While the civil war raged, he'd had a vision. The Prophet Muhammad had appeared to him and charged him with bringing peace to the country.

Mullah Omar borrowed a motorcycle and travelled around to Quran schools to enlist students. At first, few were tempted, but in time he had about fifty men. This first fifty executed a couple of local commanders, one of whom had a harem of young boys. A third commander gave them two jeeps and a truck, and their number swelled by another hundred or so men. Their first conquest was the Maiwand district outside Kandahar, where the local militia leader joined Omar. The mullah suddenly found himself with a couple of thousand fighters, several tanks, a large munitions warehouse, some helicopters and a fighter jet.

After a year, the Taliban had twenty-five thousand men under arms. They moved fast and in packs, in pick-ups with mounted machine guns, light artillery, anti-aircraft guns and rocket batteries. As the Pakistani intelligence service had grown increasingly frustrated by the chaos the mujahideen had created, they turned their support to the Taliban.

Stories about the rapid gains made by God's army were rife. They were protected by Allah, bullets couldn't kill them, they were invulnerable. Many commanders surrendered without a fight.

The movement had originated in Kandahar, in the south of the country, and fought its way north. Few believed they would take the capital but in September 1996 Jalalabad fell, and the road to Kabul lay open. Two days later the city was attacked from the south, east and north. The lightning assault forced Ahmed Shah Masoud, who controlled Kabul, to retreat towards the Panjshir Valley. He left only a small group of men to blow up weapon depots and ammunition dumps so as not to allow them to fall into Taliban hands.

The Ox was under house arrest at the UN building in Kabul. He asked headquarters in Islamabad to strengthen security. There were only three guards in the building, along with Najibullah himself, his brother, a secretary and a bodyguard.

The former intelligence chief realised too late how precarious his situation was. He had refused an offer from Masoud to accompany him northward. The Pashtun didn't want to flee with a Tajik, it wouldn't look good. He gambled on being able to negotiate with the Taliban, who belonged to the same ethnic group as him.

When the sound of shooting could be heard from the outskirts of the city, the three guards fled. Najibullah's communications grew desperate. But it was too late. A special force from the Taliban, consisting of six men, had arrived at the UN building. They located Najibullah and his brother, beat them and then drove them to the bombed-out Presidential Palace, where Najibullah had once lived. They castrated him, tied him behind a jeep and drove around the palace several times before shooting him. His brother was subjected to the same treatment. Afterwards their bodies were hung from lamp posts. Cigarettes were wedged between their fingers and banknotes stuffed in their pockets as symbols of greed and decadence.

Within twenty-four hours the Taliban had introduced the strictest Islamic social system in the world. They raised their white flag and renamed the country an emirate. The regime that would govern the capital comprised village mullahs and Islamic scholars, but also men with a background in the Peshawar Seven. None of them had any experience of governing a state, none were from Kabul, many had never set foot there before. But that was not needed as they were going to wipe the city clean of its past and steer society back to the Prophet's time, far away in the Arabian desert.

Now all the boys in Mussahi wanted to be Taliban. Bashir was nine years old and didn't just want to *play* at being one, he wanted to become one of them.

The first time he witnessed their power was when he and his mother were taking the bus to visit some relatives. A pair of Talibs had stepped up onto the footboard to take a look around. All the women were wearing burkas. Still, the students in the turbans saw something they didn't like.

'Remove that!' they ordered the driver, pointing at a photo of an Indian movie star dangling in the window. They hadn't threatened him, hadn't hit him, yet the photo was quickly taken down. Hala had squeezed Bashir's hand in triumph.

From then on he sat at the mosque reading for several hours a day. He wanted to learn the Quran off by heart. To follow the Prophet's counsel. To become as pious as the men on the bus. To become a talib.

To Read Oneself

'They're angels!'

One of Jamila's uncles had come to visit them in Peshawar. The talibs had taken control of Ghazni Province, where he lived, the previous winter, and now that they also ruled Kabul it was safe to travel along the highway. The Taliban had cracked down on the gangs, each controlling their own stretch of the road, who had threatened, robbed and beaten up any travellers who refused to hand over part of their possessions.

'God has sent them to get rid of the corrupt mujahideen,' her uncle praised. 'The Taliban are superhuman. They've come from heaven, they're angels!'

Jamila's family sat spellbound listening to his account of this new phenomenon in their home country. Now there was peace, the uncle said, and they were to be ruled under true Islam. They all agreed that the Taliban's intentions seemed to be good. Perhaps they could finally return home. A number of Ibrahim's commercial buildings in Kabul had been destroyed in the civil war. He was eager to go back. How he yearned for his city!

Jamila tried to find out more about these angels. If they wanted to rule according to true Islam, then surely that was a good thing.

In time she heard the reports about the burkas. About girls' schools being shut down. About female students being sent home. About flogging and stoning. Women no longer able to work outside the home, not being allowed to leave the house without a male guardian. They couldn't even wear shoes that made a sound!

She'd had to contend with her brothers, been so insistent with her father, and now she'd be denied the chance to make use of her hard-won education in her native country?

No, this did not sound like the work of angels.

The teenage years were a time for a girl to prepare to be married off. As this didn't apply to Jamila, she could have other dreams: high school.

Once again, she held up a finger. 'One year. Please. Just one more year!'

'You hold that finger up to me one more time and I'll cut it off!' her father threatened.

Jamila continued to plead. Ibrahim continued to threaten.

Few Afghans in Peshawar had their children in Pakistani schools. They did not have the money for uniforms nor books, so their sons were sent to school in the camps, where the teacher only needed one book – the Quran – and a piece of chalk. There was little on offer for girls. In any case, it wasn't a madrasa Jamila wanted to attend.

'Just one more year!'

Eventually her father gave in. Jamila learned passable English at home and got through the entrance exams.

The next challenge was getting to the school. It wasn't too far away, but the soldiers in the next street were constantly setting up roadblocks. They would mock her as she approached with limping steps.

'Where are you going?'

'To school.'

'What for?'

'To learn. So I can help the Afghan people,' she always replied. Few of the soldiers had attended school.

'Take a look at yourself! Go home to your mother!'

Every time the same rigmarole. Every time they let her through.

The year passed. She soaked up knowledge, read until bedtime and excelled in class. Her brothers complained that she was bringing shame on the family. Someone had seen her arguing with the soldiers. Her father had had enough. He couldn't have people talking. There would be no more school.

Her brothers' businesses had gradually picked up and they were always on the go. Ibrahim was mostly at work. Her youngest brother, the most irascible one, instructed the family's guards not to let Jamila leave the house. 'If she goes out, we'll kill you,' he threatened them. The guards promised to keep the gate shut.

The days dragged. Life was passing her by. School, homework and study were the only things that made her happy, made life worth living.

She received help from an unexpected source. From the property of her brothers: her sisters-in-law. None of them had ever learned to read and write, and now Jamila's struggle became their own. They wanted her to see and experience the world they were excluded from.

Her sisters-in-law never opposed their husbands. The plan had to be carried out in secret. They needed to use their wits to get the guards to disobey orders.

Eventually Jamila bribed the guards with money she had been given to buy jewellery.

All the women, even her mother, pretended Jamila had stopped going to school. Her sisters-in-law covered for her when the brothers asked where she was. They said she was asleep, that she wasn't feeling well, was in the kitchen or sitting in the women's room. To avoid her having to knock, they made sure to be in the back garden, next to the gate, at the time she usually came home.

Her sisters-in-law rinsed beans for her, chopped vegetables, crushed spices; chores all ostensibly carried out by Jamila. In return she helped as much as she could with her nephews and nieces, reading to them, singing and telling stories.

She feared every day of freedom might be her last. At any time she could be found out and towed back in. Even though her brothers didn't know what was going on, she had the feeling of being watched. The strictest of her brothers drove a white car. Some days every car looked like his.

The machine gun on the turret of the tank turned slowly towards her. Again and again she looked down the barrel. She felt the pain as the bullet grazed the side of her head, gashing her ear. The shock had taken root in her body. On many nights she was awoken by the white flash of light. Heard the shot. The scene was etched in her mind. The congealed blood on her uncle's throat. Her dress soaked in red. The experience was burned on her retina. The memories could not be pushed away.

Many times she'd been jolted awake, believing she was bathed in blood only to discover it was sweat. A gun had been pointed at her and fired. But just once. What about those who had survived attack after attack, like the children in the countryside, how did they sleep at night?

What she had experienced paled in comparison.

Two years of hide-and-seek passed. Her father and brothers were oblivious to what was going on. By the time her secret came to light, Jamila had managed to sit the entrance exam for Jinnah College for Women and been accepted.

'You're dishonouring us!'

Her brothers were furious.

'Do people know this? Have they seen you?'

Her sisters-in-law faced punishment. Such betrayal! It was embarrassing for the brothers not to have control over their own wives, that people had seen the family cripple go out alone without the heads of the household being aware of it. How would they recover from this loss of face?

They roared and shouted. Only Hashim, the third brother, sat quietly.

When the last fist had hit the table, Jamila's face was blotchy. Tears rolled down her cheeks. 'What am I supposed to do with my life if I don't get an education? I can't wash, can't cook, can hardly carry anything. Am I to sit at home with no purpose, is that what you all want? What kind of life is that?'

More curses and abuse flew. It was against Islam to contradict your parents. The Quran preached obedience. Women were to live hidden from the gaze of men. How could she possibly venture out of the house in this lawless city?

Hashim asked the others to calm down.

'Enough,' he said. 'You won't be punished. We'll put this behind us. But you have enough education. From now on you'll stay at home.'

It was decided she would home-school the younger children. Then she would be of use, if that was so important to her. Jamila accepted that. While her brothers were out at work she didn't just teach the younger children to read and write, but also her sisters-in-law.

There was a lot she wondered about. Like her brothers' references to what she could and could not do. 'It's in the Quran,' they always said.

Jamila wasn't too bothered what the Quran had to say about her everyday life. She wanted to learn French. That might prove important for the career she was dreaming of. She wanted to work in the UN, maybe become a diplomat or even a peace negotiator.

In scripture classes she had been the one who asked the most questions. Not that she could say she disagreed with something. To challenge Islam was *haram* — a sin. But Jamila was aware of a feeling, deep inside, that something wasn't right.

If you performed good deeds you would be rewarded in the hereafter. If you carried out jihad — with the sword, the pen, the head or the hands — men were taught they would 'find good company in paradise'.

'What sort of company?' Jamila asked a female teacher whom she really liked, and thus could challenge.

Well, a man would spend his days and nights with virgins, who were there to satisfy him in gratitude for his sacrifice.

After hearing this several times, she dared to ask, 'What about women, what do they get?'

'They'll get their husband back,' the teacher answered.

What if they weren't happy with their husband, Jamila wondered. What if the husband had mistreated them? What if death felt like peace and long-awaited freedom, and then they got the same husband back? It wasn't even practical or feasible because, after all, the men were with the virgins. What was God thinking here? No, it didn't make any sense.

'Ah, Jamila, you have so many questions, we must search, we must seek knowledge,' the teacher continued. But she was merely brushing the questions aside, Jamila felt.

Later, when ordered to stay at home, she tried to find books to garner knowledge, but all she came across were the same explanations, rendering the interpretations in the same colours.

As the home-schooling fell into a pattern, she was allowed take classes with an elder scholar a few afternoons a month. This was acceptable as the theme was Islam.

'You're such a difficult child!' he exclaimed whenever she asked about the interpretations. But she liked his lessons. They provided a way in to some of what she wished to figure out. Sometimes she tried to speak to him one-on-one, so that the others in the class didn't hear her questions. As he was an elderly man she didn't have to worry about approaching him on her own.

Finally he said, 'Learn Arabic! Read the Quran yourself! Half of the contents and most of the beauty is lost in translation.'

One had to read the original. And the original had been revealed one night in the fasting month of Ramadan, when a forty-year-old man named Muhammad had gone to a cave in the mountains above Mecca, where he liked to sit in seclusion and pray. Suddenly the archangel Gabriel appeared before him. He held up a silk cloth and commanded: 'Read!'

'I cannot read,' Muhammad stuttered.

'Read!' Gabriel insisted. Three times the angel told Muhammad to read before he had to tell him to repeat after him:

Read: In the name of your Lord Who created,
Created human from a clot
Read: And your Lord is the most generous,
Who taught by the pen,
Taught human that which he knew not.

Then the angel disappeared. Muhammad went straight home to his wife.

'What has happened to you, Muhammad?' Khadija asked. After he had told her, she went to consult a monk. She returned with a hopeful message.

'Rejoice and be of good cheer. Allah has chosen you to be his messenger.'

This was the starting point for the Quran, which night after night would be revealed by the archangel. The Quran was God's voice and God spoke Arabic. That was just how it was.

The scholar whose classes she had been given permission to attend lived far away in Lahore and only came to Peshawar occasionally. Jamila needed to find a new teacher, but that was difficult when she wasn't allowed to venture outside.

She plucked up courage. There were no more fingers left to hold up, she had to show both hands.

'Dad, just Arabic, it's only Arabic!'

He couldn't refuse to let her learn God's language. Of course he couldn't.

It turned out that a friend had just begun studying Arabic.

'You should come! The teacher is really good.'

They went to Arbab Road together, where language courses were held in a rundown building. Most of the young people there wanted to learn English and data skills, only a few had signed up for Arabic. Instruction in that language usually took place at mosques and madrasas.

They were placed in a class with six other students. The other girls were different from Jamila and her friend, who had both gone to secular schools and dreamed of university. These girls had studied at a madrasa and been subject to an Islamic school system. Jamila was impressed by their knowledge, what they could recite and what they knew about *sunnah*, *hadith*, the Prophet's way of life and his doctrines.

Arab grammar was an intricate system. Almost like mathematics. There were inflections, rules and exceptions. Every Arabic word had a meaningful root and from this root new words could be formed. It was so beautiful. Jamila loved the classes.

She was particularly interested in gender and numeral inflection. The grammar revealed that when the Quran – that is to say, God's voice, which is to say, God – said something, it was addressed to everyone. Not just to men or just to women. When it said 'Read!', it was to all. When it commanded 'Write!', it was to all. To men and women.

This was a revelation.

In the interpretations she had read, it was as though the message was only for men. But when she read the Quran in Arabic, she felt it was directed just as much to her. In not one of the important chapters was she able to see anything aimed at men in particular, or merely at women. Yes, there were different recommendations, but not concerning the most fundamental matters. On the contrary, most verses were equal and for everyone.

The punishments God imposed were also alike for men and women. If women were less able, as Jamila had been told her entire life, then why would God impose equal punishment? If women were weaker, either intellectually or physically, then shouldn't the punishments be milder? But no, they were not!

It was only due to the translations being carried out by men, due to the interpretations being written by men. As a consequence, everyone had been misguided. There were far too few female scholars, she concluded.

And she set forth these views. At home. In the classroom. Among friends. To the teacher.

She was happy with the teacher. Kakar was a handsome man with deep, slightly mournful eyes. He had a mild, pleasant and withdrawn manner, as he conjugated rows of verbs in front of the eight girls. He was open. He sought to learn. And he liked challenges.

Jamila was on the warpath.
Upon discovering anything new, she wanted to discuss it right away with Kakar, who offered his view and encouraged her to explore further. She brought her new-found knowledge to bear with her brothers.

'What you're all saying is wrong! You've misunderstood!'
'Heretic!' they retorted.
She argued with everyone.
Her brothers rebuked her. 'You're to submit to what your parents say. You're not supposed to question spiritual matters.'
'No, that's incorrect, that's not righteous. Look, here!'
Also in larger family gatherings with uncles and cousins she brought up her interpretation of the Quran. It always led to conflict.
'The Day of Judgement could come tomorrow,' she said to one of her sisters-in-law, 'and God will say to you, "I have granted you life, how have you used it?" What will you answer then?'

Jamila replied on behalf of her sister-in-law, imitating her voice:
'I washed my husband's clothes, I cleaned the kitchen, changed my children's nappies,' she mimicked. 'God won't be pleased with those answers, I can promise you that! "I gave you the universe," he'll say, "air, water, a world to live in. How did you spend your time?" When you reply, "I was a servant for my husband, for my brother-in-law, for my grandfather, I cooked nice food," then God will laugh! He'll think you hold yourself in low esteem, that you wasted what he gave you. We have a responsibility to humanity — that's what separates us from other creatures: our intellect.'

As Jamila's knowledge of Islam grew, so too did her urge to share.

On the Day of Judgement everyone will be asked five questions by God, she continued. 'You'll be asked about your life, what use you have put it to, how you have used your vigour, your talent, your knowledge, the energy and riches he gave you. And then last of all: "What have you contributed to society, what have you given to others?"'

She was an idealist and a revolutionary moralist.

'This life is a gift given to us by God,' she explained. 'We must not dishonour him by throwing it away. Youth, the best time, is here and now. Some will squander it on song and dance, on drugs or gossip. But I ask you all: how are we to make the best use of the best time of our lives?'

When Jamila was finally able to read the entire Quran in Arabic, the beauty of the text shone through to her. She felt enlightened, yes, illuminated. Some verses were so beautiful they brought tears to her eyes.

As she read more about the Prophet himself, she understood that the man who lived in the desert in the seventh century was more progressive than her own family in the late 1990s. She had been taught that a woman was the property of a man. That he needed to approve her actions, every trip she made out of the house no matter how short, whom she went with, what she wore. And if he didn't want her to work, then she didn't work. If he decided she couldn't visit her family, she didn't go. Now she realised that these rules lay in the culture, not in the religion.

She began to regard the polio and her shortened leg as a blessing. It had meant her father had let her go to school, had meant she had learned to read, had been able to study further. She loved the freedom her disability had afforded her, that her father could never sacrifice her for a good connection. She was spared both a husband and the stress of being married.

At first, she had called herself a revolutionary. Now she discovered she was also this: a feminist.

She was an Islamic feminist. The Quran was a tool for women's emancipation, she reasoned. She would use it. The stories about the Prophet's wives had huge potential for liberation, she believed. Khadija was a successful businesswoman. When they met, she was a forty-year-old widow. Muhammad was a casual labourer of twenty-five. She hired him as a driver for a caravan, eventually offering him her hand in marriage. She became his closest advisor, and he hers, and when the archangel revealed to him that he was God's messenger, she was the first to listen and to believe him. Most people in Mecca turned their back, or poked fun at him; they laughed at the idea of God speaking through such a halfwit. Khadija was the one who provided for him while he sat up in the cave receiving revelations. Through her powerful network she got people to follow him.

The Quran was revolutionary for its time, Jamila believed. Men and women were equal before Allah. God's words gave women the opportunity to be financially independent. Nothing in Islam prevented women from getting an education! That was the point she hammered home repeatedly.

Islam was misunderstood – on purpose – to suit the men who interpreted it. Or rather, who had the power to interpret it. God wanted equality but was opposed by human weakness. She was certain of that.

Her father, the strapping, strict tanner's son, had no comeback when faced with his well-read daughter. She insisted on having the last word.

Attempts

When Ibrahim was born some time in the mid-1920s, never knowing his year of birth, Afghanistan had a royal couple who were attempting to shake the country free of its past. Prince Amanullah had assumed the throne in 1919, after his father was shot during a hunting trip to Jalalabad. Being killed was the most common end for an Afghan ruler, but whoever had sneaked into the king's tent and murdered him was never caught. A brother? A cousin? The British? The Bolsheviks?

In any event, his bright son succeeded to the throne after outmanoeuvring an uncle and two older brothers. A brother could be an ally but also your fiercest challenger. Killing a relative was sometimes the quickest route to power.

While his father was still alive, Amanullah met fourteen-year-old Soraya, the daughter of a prominent intellectual family that had returned from exile. Soraya had attended the best schools in Damascus; she was well read and brimming with modern ideas. The young prince fell in love with her the first time her family had an audience at the palace – and she with him. It was a love marriage in a forest of power alliances.

Upon his ascension to power, the first thing Amanullah did was send a letter to Lenin, expressing a desire for peaceful relations. He then told the viceroy of India that Afghanistan was willing to enter trade agreements with the British but would do so as a free state. Amanullah was impulsive, impatient and ambitious. Soon he declared independence and went to war against Britain – the third war between the two countries in less than a century. A few months later Afghanistan became a sovereign state.

Amanullah enacted the country's first constitution, which in practice abandoned sharia in favour of a secular criminal code. The courts were to be independent and laws would be passed by a *loya jirga*. 'Loya' means big in Pashto and 'jirga' is a council or meeting. The arrangement had been instituted by the rulers in Kabul in the eighteenth century to legitimise their power. When important matters were to be discussed or legislation approved, an assembly of tribal chiefs and religious and military leaders was summoned. Though the king often ruled by decree, without listening to anyone.

Soraya became the first Afghan queen to make public appearances. She hunted, rode on horseback and in time participated in government meetings, regarded as a co-regent.

'I am your king, but the minister of education is my wife – your queen,' Amanullah told the loya jirga. In 1921, Soraya opened the country's first girls' school. The same year she founded a magazine for women as well as a women's organisation. She established a refuge for victims of abuse – the first crisis centre in the region.

The regents encouraged women to discard the veil, as Soraya herself had done. Inspired by Turkey's Kemal Atatürk, Amanullah announced an end to purdah – the segregation of men and women. He dissolved his father's harem, set the slave girls free and dismissed the close-cropped female guards who were dressed in men's clothes.

In 1926, on the seventh anniversary of independence, Soraya delivered her first speech.

'Do you think our nation needs only men to serve it?' she asked. 'Women should also take their part as women did in the early years of our nation and Islam.' Independence pertained to everyone. The country could only develop through education – a universal right – and women had to 'acquire as much knowledge as possible'.

It smouldered.

It glowed.

The clan leaders fanned the flames.
The mullahs stood with bellows.
Soraya calmly put more wood on the fire.

Eight years into their reign, the royal couple embarked on a grand tour of Europe and the Middle East to drum up investment and get fresh ideas. No rulers in Kabul had ever travelled further than India, but Amanullah and Soraya drew inspiration from Muslim countries such as Turkey, Iran and Egypt, where discussion of secular ideas and reforms were taking place.

They were applauded upon arrival at receptions, visits to factories and tours of power plants. Queen Soraya spoke to the students at Oxford, dazzled at the opera in Berlin. She allowed herself to be photographed without a veil, in dresses revealing bare shoulders and arms. The royal couple were stirred by what they saw in Paris, Moscow and Teheran, and fretted about how underdeveloped Afghanistan was in comparison. They needed to speed up the modernisation.

After eight months of travel, it was time to put their ideas into practice. Amanullah decided they would take the overland route home from Teheran in his newly purchased Rolls-Royce. Dejected by what they saw of their own country along the road, they made up their minds that it was no longer reforms they needed but a brand-new society.

Not long after their return, the king demanded that the thousand representatives of the loya jirga attend the next assembly in three-piece suits and black shoes, with freshly cut hair and beards. Before this broadly composed audience, he announced an even more liberal constitution than the one already enacted. He introduced a host of new rules, such as civil servants not being allowed more than one wife, a minimum age for marriage of thirteen and a prohibition on solving disputes by the exchange of women. In certain areas of the city the wearing of Western clothes became obligatory.

The smouldering of the bastions of power steadily losing their privileges caught fire. The state made greater inroads by means of taxation, conscription and radical changes to family life. When the religious leaders determined that the king's ideas were contrary to Islam, protests flared up. Opponents had had plenty of time to conspire while the royals were off travelling. Rumours were spread that King Amanullah and his queen were apostates, that they had converted to Catholicism in Europe and that the consumption of large quantities of pork and alcohol had driven them mad.

The uprising spread. For an army deserter and gang leader with the nickname Bacho-e-Saqao — *son of the water carrier* — it provided an opportunity. Like an Afghan Robin Hood, he promised food and power to the poor and fought his way to Kabul. Amanullah's attempts to negotiate support from the clans failed. In January 1929, after ten years in power, the royals fled the capital in their Rolls-Royce.

With the son of the watercarrier and his cavalry on his heels, Amanullah got his car stuck in a snowdrift on the way to Kandahar. He abdicated and narrowly escaped with his life, leaving the throne to his half-brother who ruled for three days before the water carrier's son killed him. Bacho-e-Saqao held power through terror and plundering for nine months, until he was deposed by the same elite that had elevated him. From out of this mess Nadir, one of Amanullah's generals, came to the fore, along with his brothers, and aided by the British, he seized power.

The upstart was hanged, while the royal couple were granted asylum in Italy.

Soraya's ideas had fallen on stony ground before even spreading beyond Kabul's city limits.

While all this was going on, Ibrahim was cleaning hides in Ghazni. The little boy scraped off fat, blood and sinews. He removed the hairs and cut, ripped, clipped and cleaned with salt and water. His hands became rough and sore, his back ached. Alongside him on the floor sat his parents. The family had one room where they slept, ate and tanned hides.

Siblings were born and siblings died. Only one brother survived the destitution that ravaged those outside the palaces. While

Amanullah had let intellectual life flourish in the salons of Kabul, the poor remained poor.

Ibrahim reached school age at the beginning of the 1930s. But for him the alphabet remained nothing more than some signs; there was no school in the slums of Ghazni. The city lay along a route that for millennia had been the main artery between Kabul and Kandahar, and westward to Herat and Iran, but only goods passed through; new ideas never made it this far.

Modernisation had by now been rejected, the literary salons closed and the women's organisation shut down. As was Soraya's crisis centre. Newspapers and magazines were once again subject to censorship. Burkas made a return. The new ruler restored power to the clans and the religious leaders. The revolution was over.

Ibrahim detested the work he had inherited, the fresh blood, the membrane, the rancid fat. He was disgusted by the stench of putrefaction, the sour smell of decomposing hides, and couldn't stand the bark he scoured them with, the minerals he used to toughen them, the fat he smeared on them so they softened.

He saw how his parents got up with ever increasing difficulty, hunched by sitting cross-legged all day. The boy wanted to get up from the floor. Once he was old enough, he asked his parents for permission to try his luck at something else. That was when he started selling coffins. It barely yielded a profit, but one day a local merchant stopped by. This coffin-seller had caught his eye.

'What's a fellow like yourself doing here in this little shop? I can give you canvas to sell, if you'd like.'

The merchant estimated it would take the handsome, well-built boy a month to sell the material. Ibrahim sold it all within a week. The merchant gave him dress fabric and soon that was out of stock. Colourful shawls, white veils, sky-blue burkas, everything was sold. On a trip, the boy noticed the variations in price of dried apricots, raisins and figs. He saw opportunities everywhere. His confidence increased.

One afternoon, while pulling his cart of wares, the barefoot boy lost his way in some narrow alleyways. After a while the houses got bigger, the roads wider. The people were dressed in fine tunics and wore sandals.

Suddenly he heard a shout. The next thing he knew, a stone hit him on the shoulder.

'Clear off! Get out of our area!'

He tried to turn the cart but was pelted with more stones. He squinted in the direction of the voice and saw it was just a kid.

'Get out of here, you ragamuffin!' the boy yelled again.

Ibrahim grew angry and wanted to fight back. He looked around for stones to hurl. Nobody was going to insult him like that.

The impudent kid was wearing a freshly ironed tunic with loose trousers beneath. His clothes were white, the colour of the wealthy. Ibrahim's tunic was a faded grey. He picked up a stone.

'You wouldn't dare! Don't come near me!' the boy shouted. Ibrahim threw the stone.

As it hit, something happened within him. He sensed it more than saw it.

The boy turned and ran. Ibrahim followed. The rich man's son was faster, he always knew where his next step would take him. Just as he was almost out of sight, Ibrahim saw him slip through a gate. It slammed behind him. Ibrahim looked upward. It had to be one of the most magnificent properties in the area – a *qala* – a fort with walls of dried mud. Tall trees, within what was no doubt a lush garden, towered above the gate. Ibrahim drew back but made enquiries about who lived in the big house. He was given the name of one of Ghazni's tribal chiefs.

'But unfortunately he has only daughters,' the man told him. 'No matter how many wives he takes, he produces no sons.'

Now, he was sure. The exquisitely dressed boy he had seen was no rich man's son. It was one of the daughters in the family.

She would be his.

With that Bibi Sitara's freedom was at an end.

She was a *bacha posh*, which meant 'dressed as a boy'. It wasn't uncommon for families with no sons to choose a daughter, often the youngest, to live as a boy and carry out the tasks of a son. In so doing a family could send a girl out to work, allow her to run errands, be a shepherd, or sell fruit at the market. A widow with only daughters had no one to represent the family outside the home, meaning one of them would have to imitate a boy. It was believed that transforming a daughter into a boy also increased the chances of the mother giving birth to a son. A boy would beget a boy.

A bacha posh was a half-hidden secret within the immediate family, sometimes within the neighbourhood. Some were teased but by and large they were treated according to how they were dressed — as boys.

Bibi Sitara felt strong. She made choices. As the son of the tribal chief, at every street corner she decided what direction to take and walked at her own pace. Sometimes her father took her with him to the market or bargaining. She accompanied her sisters as a chaperone if they needed to go out. They, enveloped in burkas, she, with short hair, in a boy's tunic and sandals. In trousers she was the master of her own life.

Life as a boy ended as the girl entered puberty, and it was at this stage that Bibi Sitara now found herself.

She got trapped. In female clothing, freedom had flown. She was to disappear beneath the folds of a dress, be hidden away, not seen nor heard. Filled with sadness, she slipped into her gender role. Lowered her gaze. Forced her thoughts into submission. Kept an eye out for danger rather than opportunities.

The number of suitors grew when she disappeared from the streets. The tanner's son was among them.

One morning, Ibrahim's mother stood up from the floor and the half-scraped hides. She washed herself thoroughly and dressed in the new embroidered clothes her son had bought for her. Tradition dictated that a woman of the family, preferably the matriarch, made the proposal. Ibrahim had also seen to it that any people he knew had spoken highly of him to the tribal chief and advocated on his behalf. Men negotiated with men, women with women.

The tanner's wife had to use her wits as the family could not compete on the bride price. Ibrahim's family were hard-working but had no name to speak of.

She was granted an audience at the grand house, but the girl's mother sat in silence.

The tanner's wife sang her son's praises, spoke of his talents, his business acumen and the money he had begun to make.

The girl's mother nodded politely but said nothing.

Then Ibrahim's champion drew the ultimate sword: the Quran.

'You don't approve of us,' she said to the wealthy woman and handed her the holy book – a gift one could not refuse. 'You are rich and we are poor. But you approve of this book and we all love God. As you have received my Quran we are now tied. Have mercy on us.'

It was a bold move, but it worked. The Quran linked them. Islam united them.

They had the money and the daughter; Ibrahim and his mother had the strength and the will.

Bibi Sitara hated being bargained for. She despised the thought of marrying him even more. Uncouth, dirty and wretched. But she was to have no opinion on the matter, nor did she express one. From now on she kept her thoughts to herself, forced back into the life she was born to live.

Prior to the wedding, Bibi needed to learn how to cook, wash and sew, all the things she had been spared while dressed as a boy. Choices became a vague memory. Options evaporated the moment she dressed as a woman. After the ceremony, when she left her father's house, the privileges she had been born into disappeared as well. She hated her new life, filled with work her own family had servants to carry out. Moreover, Ibrahim was strict. He had her in a burka straight away and there she stayed.

Her only distraction was a small plot in the back garden. She pondered over what to do with it. The seeds at least she could choose herself.

*

Afghanistan's most important export was what the soil yielded. The 1940s were a good decade for agriculture and the state recorded hundreds of millions of dollars in profit. After the Second World War, hides and skins – a line of business Ibrahim knew all about – provided most revenue for the treasury. Earnings on Persian lamb fur, popular in New York and Paris, were especially good. Just prior to the ewes lambing, they were slaughtered. Their stomachs were opened and the unborn lambs skinned. Their fur was used for exclusive hats, coats and muffs.

Ibrahim was in the process of building an empire.

There was just one problem.

Bibi Sitara didn't bear him any children. One year passed, two, then three, she was just as infertile. Each spring the pink flowers of the almond tree spread their soft fragrance, seeds sprouted, green shoots grew from the ground wherever she sowed. She picked lettuce, mint and spring onions. Sweet, blushing apricots fell to the ground, bulging and ripe.

She herself remained barren.

After a decade Ibrahim bargained for a second wife. He had every right. He needed heirs. He needed sons. Right before the engagement was to be announced, he visited a shaman. He wanted to know what the soothsayer saw in his future.

'You scorn your fate!' the clairvoyant warned. 'Who were you when you met your wife? And who are you today? She is your talisman! If you take a new wife you will lose everything!'

He called off the engagement.

Bibi Sitara became pregnant.

Jamila would be their eighth child.

On the Wing

The Taliban brought a peace of sorts. Hala could cultivate her plot without checking the sky for anything but rain. The farmers could transport their crop to the city without getting caught in crossfire. People met in the mosque without fear of informers. The takeover of power gave a sense of victory. They were ruled by their own.

The civil war's crime wave had come to an abrupt end. The new penalties were severe. An eye for an eye, a tooth for a tooth. A life for a life. Sometimes the Taliban punished entire gangs by cutting off the right arm and left foot of each member. The body parts were hung up on trees or posts until they rotted.

Radio Kabul, re-named Radio Sharia, announced that infidelity would be punished with death by stoning. The consumption of alcohol meant facing being whipped. Satellite dishes, TVs, video cassettes, music and all games – including chess and football – were forbidden. Even the flying of paper kites was haram. All the while the boys in Mussahi continued playing war.

For the women in the village little had changed. Hardly any of them had worked outside the home; few had ever sent their daughters to school. They had covered up since they were little girls, and as regards the new laws and rules for shoes with heels, make-up, nail varnish and tight clothing, nobody walked around the muddy paths of Mussahi like that anyway.

Hala was very pleased. She detested finery, loathed frivolity and flat plastic sandals that could easily be rinsed were her chosen footwear. She was full of praise for the Taliban, who she believed should find space for her sons in their ranks.

Hassan was going to build the country. Yaqub would make clothes. Raouf was to become a mullah. And Bashir, well, the youngest would be allowed play a little longer.

The country was, however, in deep crisis. Maternal mortality was sky high. Infant mortality was the highest in the world. Every fourth child died before the age of five. Life expectancy was a little over forty years of age.

The infrastructure was in ruins; scarcely a waterpipe lay unbroken. Millions of landmines made it hazardous to move around, let alone to clear the fields the war had laid fallow.

The educated elite had abandoned the country long ago. Many fled during the war with the Soviets, others while the civil war raged, a last wave followed after the Taliban took power. There was hardly anyone with a technical education or vocational training left. In the mines there were neither engineers, geologists, equipment or electricity. Electricians, plumbers and mechanics were gone. The only thing the country had an abundance of was explosives.

Afghans lacked self-sufficiency in everything besides opium poppies, which barely required watering. Despite the Taliban's rhetoric against foreign interference, the truth was that large portions of the population subsisted on food aid from humanitarian organisations.

Two years after the change of regime, areas in the north were struck by earthquakes. The south suffered floods. Famine occurred.

Taliban persecution and displacement of Hazaras led to widespread starvation. This ethnic group, predominately Shia Muslims, were subjected to severe oppression. In several villages Hazaras were forced from their homes, which were then taken over by Pashtuns.

Not until the Taliban's third year in power did food production increase. The talibs had one thing in common with the warlords they had replaced: they didn't care about the lives of ordinary Afghans.

*

Then an old adventurer came to visit. Osama bin Laden had returned to Afghanistan, with a new mission: global jihad.

He had gone to Sudan with his four wives and seventeen children when the civil war broke out in 1992. There he became an entrepreneur, landowner, farmer and horse breeder. But one obsession disturbed this peaceful existence. Infidel American soldiers were stationed on hallowed ground in Saudi Arabia. During his years in Sudan, bin Laden's sights had turned towards a new enemy: the USA.

From his home in Khartoum he had followed the Taliban's advance on Kabul. In May 1996 he landed in a chartered jet in Jalalabad, which was still under the control of the government forces of Rabbani. The Saudi had been invited by old mujahideen friends – Hekmatyar, Sayyaf and Haqqani – in the hope that he could help them in the fight against the Taliban. One of the mujahideen in attendance warned him, 'You are our guest, and no one can get to you. If anything happens with the Taliban, tell me. Though there is little I can do after they reach you, I will do all I can.'

When the Taliban came to power a few months later they wanted him out of the country. They wished for recognition from the international community, and to rule in peace. Their ambitions did not stretch beyond the borders of the country. Osama bin Laden was wanted by the FBI and would have to keep a low profile for the Taliban leadership to shelter him. Bin Laden sent Mullah Omar repeated invitations, but it was months before he turned up. The Taliban leader would allow the Saudi to stay on one condition: he had to promise not to plan any attacks against America while on Afghan soil.

Bin Laden avoided making any promises, merely telling the one-eyed leader – who always turned his head a little to the side when looking at someone – that jihad against America was fard al-ayn. An individual duty, not the type of jihad one could just give up.

Mullah Omar chose to close his one good eye and allowed the Saudi to stay.

*

Both the Taliban and al-Qaeda ran training camps in Afghanistan and in the tribal areas of Pakistan. Bashir had heard of such places and dreamed of going. He envisaged the brotherhood, the glorious missions.

He was twelve years old when he crept into his mother's larder and stole a sack of grain. He hauled it to the bazaar to sell. The money was enough for two bus tickets, one for him and one for his cousin.

Before their mothers noticed they were gone they had made it to the bus stop at the turn-off to the village.

Hala was beside herself with worry when Bashir didn't come home for supper. He always came on time for meals, which followed prayer times. Wherever could he be? She sent his brothers out to look. They found out their aunt's son was also missing. Someone had seen the boys board the bus that headed east. They put two and two together. Bashir had been nagging about being allowed leave for a training camp to become a holy warrior. His mother had said he was too young.

There were no phones in Mussahi, the lines weren't built, and mobiles had yet to come to the country. Searching for him would be futile. They just had to put their trust in Allah.

Hala's sister-in-law let her feelings be known. 'It must have been Bashir's idea! He talked my son into it. You've no control over him! It'll be your responsibility if anything happens to them!'

Hala couldn't argue about the first part; it probably had been Bashir's idea. As for the second, everyone had their own free will, the cousin included. With regard to the last part, Allah took on the responsibility for them now. When and how you would die was written in heaven. The broad outline of your fate was predetermined, but within that you had a duty to choose the right path.

Her own fear of what might befall Bashir had abated when, during prayer, she heard a deep voice telling her that she could safely place her son's fate in God's hands.

'They're only twelve years old, they won't manage long without us,' Hala comforted her sister-in-law. 'They'll soon be back.'

*

The only one who was not sorry about Bashir having run off was Yasamin, who was now nine years old. It was a relief he was gone.

When they were younger, they had played together like siblings. Until she discovered she was promised to him.

One day as she was hanging up the washing, a cousin had said, 'Look, there goes your husband!'

She pointed at Bashir, who had just entered the backyard.

Yasamin swiped at her. Her cousin went on teasing. 'Look at your sweetheart! Isn't he lovely?'

Yasamin went to her parents to complain.

'She's just joking,' her mother smiled. But her father told her straight, 'No, no, that's right. I've promised you to Bashir.'

Yasamin took an immediate dislike to the cousin with the unruly curls and the shrill, warbling laugh. He was gross and yucky. She fretted about how she had become shy and awkward around someone she had never bothered about. Everything became embarrassing all of a sudden. From then on, whenever Yasamin met one of her male cousins or uncles in the backyard, she turned away, pulling her shawl across her face.

'Bashir's wife! Bashir's wife!' her friends would tease as they walked to and from the mosque together. They attended the madrasa, not to be taught to read or write but to instil the teachings of Islam in them.

At home Yasamin learned the exact number of times she had to change the water to make perfect rice. She learned to boil, fry, chop, slice, rinse, bake, wash, sweep, dust and obey.

Now Bashir was gone. She hoped he'd become a martyr.

The two cousins had made it to a camp in the autonomous tribal area on the border between Afghanistan and Pakistan.

They were turned away. Facial hair was a requirement for gaining entry. But the boys were granted places at one of the Quran schools.

From the mid-1970s, Jalaluddin Haqqani, Osama bin Laden's close friend and mentor, had been building up his religious and military infrastructure in the region. In winter, when the fighting season was dormant, he schooled young men from across the Muslim world. Young extremists met for the first time. They studied, lived and trained together. The camps became mini universities for future fundamentalists.

A group of young Saudis came to the country. After a time they were sent to the USA to enter flight training. While in Afghanistan, they already knew why they were to learn how to manoeuvre large passenger planes.

They were the chosen ones.

There in the Afghan mountains they were thanked in advance by Osama bin Laden, while Mullah Omar remained unaware of the Planes Operation.

After a year of being surrounded by these men's ideas the cousins returned to Mussahi. Bashir was eager to continue his studies, but his mother, who had eventually found out where he was, wanted him home.

Late one evening Hala heard loud voices out in the yard. Outside her sons were talking excitedly.

She peeped out. A group of young men was standing by the gate.

Gradually the voices rose to cheers and thanksgiving to Allah. Cries of 'Allahu Akbar!' could be heard from several places in the village.

'What is it?' she called out.

Her sons paid her no attention.

Someone in the village had heard something on the radio.

Scattered cries of *Allahu Akbar! God is great, God is greater, God is the greatest!* could be heard.

'Am. Er. Ica,' she heard the voices say.

She went outside.

'Who is that?' she asked.

Her sons were too wound up to respond.

Am. Er. Ica. Am. Eri. Ca.

It was repeated again and again. She had never heard the strange name before. What was it? An animal, a bird, perhaps? She caught snatches of what they were saying. Something about wings. Had a huge bird flown into a building?

There were many dead, they said.

God be praised! they cried.

Eventually, her eldest son told Hala what he knew.

'America is a place, Mamma, it's a country. A very big country. On the other side of the ocean.'

Two planes had flown into two tall buildings over there.

Oh, well.

Hala went back inside. What a fuss. Worse things had happened.

Part Two

We Who Love Death

A tall, lean man stood gazing down the steep slopes of the Suleiman Mountains, in the far south-east of Afghanistan. Below lay the city of Khost, and from there a narrow road twisted its way up to the top. The man was standing at the entrance to a cave. He liked caves; they held special meaning for him. Their rock walls protected him. They enveloped him, left him at peace. Caves made him feel connected, in a way, to the Prophet Muhammad, who for years had gone up to a cave in the Hira Mountains above Mecca to meditate and pray. At last God had revealed himself to him, as he had hoped.

Osama bin Laden had travelled from his villa in Kandahar that same night. A dozen Yemeni bodyguards had packed his car full of equipment: a generator, a satellite dish, a couple of laptops, a portable TV, a tuner and some cables. They had struggled all day with the big dish, trying to locate the right satellites. Moving it from one outcrop to the next. Attaching it to the mountainside, to crags, placing it in a thicket. But they couldn't pick up a signal. The screen remained black.

A few hours after the sun had reached its zenith over the peaks of the Suleiman range, a message came over the radio. Mohamed Atta, the leader of the hijackers, had passed airport security and boarded American Airlines Flight 11.

Osama was agitated. He had travelled here to follow the operation. And now he wasn't going to get to see it!

The fifty-four-year-old kept his nerves under control by giving thanks to God and drinking sweet tea. Wrapped in a woollen shawl, flanked by his teenage sons Osman and Muhammad, he sat waiting on the thin mattress his guards had put out. Next to him was the rifle he boasted about taking from a Soviet soldier after a battle. He got to his feet now and again and looked up the sky, or watched the guards clambering about with the satellite dish. No matter which way they held it, the mountains blocked the signal.

They turned on the radio.

Only a handful of those closest to Osama knew the details of the Planes Operation. Half of al-Qaeda's inner circle in Afghanistan had in fact voted against it, which had led to conflict within the group and some of them breaking with the leader. It was too extreme and would lead to direct war with America. The Base had, however, kept the discord quiet. No details were leaked.

The attack had also been kept secret from the Taliban. Mullah Omar was not informed. Those who were aware of the plan had been ordered by bin Laden to not even dream about it, because Mullah Omar could interpret dreams.

Then – finally – news came through the ether.

One plane – two planes – three planes – four.

America was struck through the heart. Alhamdulillah. God be praised.

The world would listen to him now, would have to listen to him.

Bin Laden dispatched a messenger to fetch a young Kuwaiti preacher he had recently heard speak. He had made the preacher promise to help him no matter what he asked. Like others in his circle Abu Ghaith had heard rumours that an operation was in the offing, but had no idea of the details. Now he sat in a car snaking its way up the mountain and was suddenly a part of everything.

Night had fallen by the time he saw the slim silhouette of Osama by the mouth of the cave.

'Did you see it?' the terrorist leader exclaimed as his guest got out of the car. 'How did it look?'

The Kuwaiti nervously described the scenes from New York as he had heard them over the radio. Osama smiled.

'*We* did the Planes Operation!' he boasted.

Then he asked the preacher how he thought America would respond.

'America will not settle until it accomplishes two things: to kill you and topple the state of the Taliban,' Abu Ghaith replied.

'You're being too pessimistic,' laughed Osama bin Laden.

In total nineteen men, of whom fifteen were Saudis, had carried out the suicide attacks. Armed with box cutters, tin openers and pepper spray they had turned civilian planes into missiles. Two planes crashed into the Twin Towers of the World Trade Center on the morning of 11 September 2001. Within an hour both skyscrapers had collapsed. A third plane crashed into the Pentagon, setting one wing ablaze. The fourth team of hijackers were on their way towards Capitol Hill or the White House until the plane crashed in a field in Philadelphia.

The hijackers were all killed and took 2,977 people with them in death.

In Kandahar people poured onto the streets to celebrate. In Khost they fired shots into the air. In Kabul the Taliban wondered how they were going to get out of this predicament.

When the men in the Suleiman Mountains settled down for the night, it was still afternoon in America. President George W. Bush was on board Air Force One. There was nowhere safe for the plane of the commander-in-chief to land, so it circled in the air.

Osama had appointed the preacher to write his message to the world. It needed to be framed within the correct Islamic context. Osama had planned the camera angle, what he would wear and how the background should look. The recording had to be perfect.

Three days after the attack, Congress, with the exception of one member, voted to grant the president broad powers to use necessary force against those who had 'planned, authorised, committed or aided' the terror attacks. The one member who voted against, Democrat Barbara Lee from California, urged moderation, so as not to escalate an already tense situation. She was quickly labelled a traitor.

With the passing of the resolution, President Bush demanded the Taliban hand over Osama bin Laden and all other members of al-Qaeda.

Mullah Omar found himself in a pinch. The Saudi had played him for a fool. However, Pashtunwali forbade him from kicking out a guest. Nevertheless, the ancestral code also required reciprocity, and the guest could have showed the host respect by leaving voluntarily. The Taliban leadership council in Kandahar suggested extraditing Osama to a Muslim country, thereby avoiding sending a believer to the infidels, and letting others take on the burden of handing him over to the Americans. Washington had no interest in this; they wanted bin Laden served up directly. Consequently, he stayed where he was.

George W. Bush urged the rest of the world to get behind the USA's vengeance with the words: 'Either you are with us, or you are with the terrorists.' The president also coined the term *the global war on terror*. For the first time, NATO invoked Article 5: an attack on an ally is an attack on all members.

On the night of 7 October, bombers entered Afghan airspace. Tomahawk cruise missiles destroyed training camps, bases and weapon depots.

The terrorist leader himself spent the night with three of his wives and most of his children in a house in Kabul. His oldest wife, who had known about the Planes Operation, had implored her husband to let her leave Afghanistan before he put his plan into action. Osama demanded he keep most of the children; she was allowed to take the two youngest and the eldest, who was autistic and dependent on her. While the rockets lit up the sky, Osama bin Laden calmly recorded his video message. At last he had drawn America into war. He wasn't just America's enemy; he was public enemy number one.

*

Time and time again, luck was on his side. The CIA would find out where he was going – until he changed his plans at the last minute, went somewhere else or turned back, or they bombed buildings he had just left. On several occasions the Americans were minutes or metres away from killing him.

The logic was that the harder the Taliban were hit, the faster they would give him up. Hunting down Osama bin Laden was the highest priority.

After a week of airstrikes, the Taliban once again offered to discuss handing Osama bin Laden over to a third country. In return they demanded a stop to the bombing.

'They must have not heard – there's no negotiation,' President Bush told reporters on the White House lawn. 'They need to turn him over.'

Thus Osama got away again, while thousands of his foot soldiers would achieve the irrevocable joy he predicted: martyrdom.

'The US loves life. We love death,' was his mantra.

Bashir had turned fourteen. Life was fast-paced, exciting. No building was safe, so they could just as well go up on the rooftop and watch the aerial warfare play out. They heard the whine of the Tomahawk missiles above, the boom when they struck. They saw the sky blaze when a target in Kabul was hit. *Allahu Akbar, Allahu Akbar, God is greatest!*

The smartest boys from the madrasa in Mussahi had entered one of the Taliban's schools on the northern outskirts of Kabul. It offered board, lodging and strict discipline. War or not, the first lesson started at four in the morning, hours before breakfast. Throughout the day and evening there were classes. Those who didn't learn fast enough received a rap across the hands, a box on the ear or had their fingers squeezed.

During this period Bashir became *hafiz* – someone who has learned the Quran by heart. After memorising it in Arabic, he learned the verses in Pashto and became acquainted with the interpretations. All this in accordance with the Hanafi School, which the Taliban professed faith in.

The boys looked up to their teacher, a young mullah with whom they spent most of their waking hours. The Quran could not be questioned. The teacher used the book to underpin the message that jihad was not just a part of Islam but a way of life and explained the difference between those who went to war and those who refrained.

The faithful who sit idle, other than those who are disabled, are not equal to those who fight in the way of God with their wealth and lives, Bashir and his friends recited from the Quran's fourth chapter. God ranked those who strived above those who were inactive. *He has granted His favour of the highest reward to those who struggle in preference to those who sit at home.*

The boys in the class were born into war. Like Bashir, they had lost fathers, uncles or brothers in the fight against the communist regime, or in the civil war. From a very early age, the concept of holy war had been deeply impressed on their minds. Now they were teenagers and the Prophet was their role model, Osama bin Laden their idol. Everything was as before, except that a new superpower had replaced the old one as the enemy.

At night the teacher stood with them on the rooftop as rockets lit up the sky like fireworks. Finally it was here, the real war. Now they would get to show how brave they were.

And then they weren't old enough! The ignominy. The Taliban only accepted fighters with beards. It had to be the length of a fist clasped at the chin. Some of Bashir's peers had down on their upper lips but that wasn't enough.

They were in the middle of this glorious, all-consuming war and yet they were cut off from it. The pupils discussed how long the conflict would last, anxious about missing out. All the while they studied the Quran.

Those who disbelieve cannot expect God to forgive them and show them the way, except to Hell. There they shall be and remain, Bashir read in the fourth chapter. *And that would be easy for God*, it went on.

Kill the infidels wherever you find them, seize them, besiege them, and lie in wait for them, it said in the ninth chapter.

The boys sat cross-legged on the floor of the mosque with the Quran on a cushion in front of them, feeling life was going on elsewhere. Allah would of course set things right, but they wanted so much to help him.

Then one day the teacher had news. They were going on an outing.
To the front!
Alhamdulillah. A field trip to the war.
The closest frontline was by the village of Qarabagh, on the Shomali Plain north of Kabul. The Taliban stuck together in small, mobile groups, living among the people in the villages along the front, making it difficult for those on the lookout to give their co-ordinates to the enemy.

The summer heat persisted. There had hardly been any rainfall since spring and none at all since the outbreak of the war. The dry air turned yellow with sand dust when the bombs fell; missiles left huge craters in the landscape.

Bashir and his classmates had little hope of encountering Americans face to face. The US had only sent a limited number of special forces soldiers to coordinate attacks with the Northern Alliance, who had their base in the Panjshir Valley, north of the Shomali Plain. Their leader, the fabled Lion of Panjshir, had been killed two days prior to the 9/11 terror attacks. Ahmad Shah Massoud had been outwitted by two men from al-Qaeda, posing as journalists, with explosives hidden in their camera. Osama bin Laden had wanted the mujahideen hero out of the way before he brought the war to Afghanistan.

Now the Northern Alliance, dominated by Tajiks and backed up by Uzbeks, were operating as the Americans' ground forces. Allowing themselves to be subjugated to the cause of the infidels? A Muslim couldn't do that, Bashir thought. Traitors would end up on the losing side anyway.

Across the Atlantic, President Bush was also driven by a clear mission. God had told him, 'George, go and fight these terrorists in Afghanistan.' So he did.

Bush and Bashir could agree on one thing – there was one God. Both believed he was on their side.

The class trip to the frontline turned out to be for an indefinite period and took place without their parents' consent. None of the boys had telephones at home, so the pupils just packed their Quran and a blanket.

They discovered that war involved a lot of waiting around. You waited for the enemy, then you waited for orders. In the meantime you cleaned your weapon, cooked food, went to bed and boiled water for tea when you woke up. The boys helped prepare food, and as grapes were in season they were sent to the grape fields. Often the fruit was given to them for free when they said they came from the Taliban. The teenagers plodded along the front, meeting groups of soldiers sitting in the shade in sandals and dirty tunics, waiting for the war to come to where they were.

The airstrikes intensified week by week, with weapons the Taliban had never seen the like of. There was no way for them to respond when the enemy bombed from such a height.

Camps, mosques and ministries were hit. As were clinics and village schools, Mullah Omar's farm and several of bin Laden's hideouts.

While the two leaders dodged attacks, their foot soldiers paid a heavy toll. Arms and legs were torn off in bomb blasts, bodies cut in half or blown to pieces. The shockwaves caused bleeding from the ears and nose. Trenches became mass graves; there was hardly anyone left to bury the dead.

The Taliban had the taste of defeat on their tongue.

A few weeks after Bashir had visited the front north of Kabul, it no longer existed. The bases were bombed out, the camps pulverised. Qarabagh fell at the same time as Kabul, on the night of 13 November 2001.

Several of the soldiers they had met had managed to make it out alive, by use of an old Afghan tactic: switching sides. An Afghan fighter is not owned, only loaned, the saying went. Realising they would not prevail they negotiated a surrender. Sometimes this involved a ceasefire of a few hours that allowed them to flee, other times they joined the winning side, or simply filtered back to their villages.

It was worse for al-Qaeda. The Arabs had no place to go. Many were banished from their own countries, and should they return they would be wanted men. Afghanistan had been their sanctuary. They were prepared to fight to the last man. In some areas Taliban commanders informed their Afghan soldiers of plans to surrender while letting the Arab jihadists take up positions ahead, before shooting them in the back, to avoid them causing problems when the retreat was ordered.

By mid-November what was left of the Taliban in Kabul were corpses and grim memories. Barbers appeared on the streets equipped with scissors and razors. Beauty parlours reopened. Music could be heard everywhere. Eye-catching posters of beautiful Bollywood stars were hung up. Though, by and large, women remained dressed in burkas. A woman could never be too careful.

Osama bin Laden had disappeared into the snow-covered mountains of Tora Bora – Black Cave. He had begun fitting out the cave complex outside Jalalabad during the war with the Soviets. It was equipped with ventilation systems, mined entrances, secret exits and an electricity supply. The terrorist leader had taught his sons to memorise every stone, every stream and every trail there, because one day their lives might depend upon it.

Home

Jamila took out a pen and some paper and began to write.

Outside the window, climbing plants wound their way over the fence. Her mother's flowers teemed in intense colours. Autumn in Peshawar was hot, even now in late October. Still, when the fan was on full, Jamila's room was quite cool.

What the terrorists had done was horrible. But why should Afghans be punished for what this Saudi had carried out?

The Afghans had suffered enough. Ten years of war with the Soviets, four years of civil war, five more years with the Taliban, and now the Americans were bombing. Every morning she watched TV to see what targets had been struck. It pained her, knowing she was living in comfort in Pakistan while many at home lacked even the means to flee. The poorest remained behind.

Jamila wrote quickly, her message was simple: the US needed to stop bombing her country. She found addresses and sent her submission to the newspapers she knew of. On the TV screen she saw lifeless bodies lying scattered like dead ants. Buildings flattened. Wounded civilians.

She waited in vain for a reply from the newspapers. Of course her article was not published. She was nobody. Who cared what she thought? The war would last a long time, she feared, like the war she had experienced thus far.

But suddenly it was over.

The combination of superior air power, CIA intelligence, small pockets of special forces and local fighters had exceeded all expectations. The loss of American life was minimal.

During Ramadan, a few weeks after the Taliban's retreat from Kabul, their power base in the south, Kandahar, fell. It had taken the US less than forty days to overthrow them. Now they were just going to smoke bin Laden out of the black cave.

The terrorist's world had shrunk to a labyrinth of tunnels. Tora Bora was hit by hundreds of airstrikes each day. One bomb was so large it had to be rolled out of America's largest transport plane. The boom and vibrations could be heard and felt for miles. The rocks it hit and those hiding beneath were pulverised.

Had they got him?

While the Americans continued their hunt, the UN sought to establish peace. The international community wanted to set up a transitional government. A summit meeting in Bonn was arranged to pave a new path. As well as an array of Western diplomats, representatives from Pakistan, Iran, India, Russia and the neighbouring countries in Central Asia were invited. A few dozen Afghans – a diverse collection of warlords, old mujahideen, exiled politicians, monarchists and former communists – were also on the guest list. Seated at solid German conference tables, they were to lay the foundations for how Afghanistan would be governed.

It still being Ramadan, the Afghan delegates abstained from food and drink from sunrise until sunset. Pork was removed from the hotel menu. The wine list was only available on request.

They soon decided on a leader.

Pashtun Hamid Karzai got a call from the BBC correspondent Lyse Doucet on his satellite phone:

'Hamid, what's your reaction to being chosen as the new leader?'

'Am I the new leader?'

She told him that the news was on the BBC.

'That's nice,' Karzai replied.

What he didn't say was that he was lying wounded in a grove

in the southern province of Uruzgan, in the wake of an American air raid. He and his travelling companions had been mistaken for fleeing Taliban.

Hamid Karzai, not an obvious candidate, had suddenly become the perfect choice and the one America was insistent upon. He came from a noble branch of the Popolzai tribe, with ties to the monarchs of the Durrani dynasty since the eighteenth century. His father had been a close friend of the last king, and like his son, had supported the mujahideen in the war against the Soviet Union. When the Taliban came to power in 1996, the Karzai family had been generally sympathetic and had seen an opportunity for cooperation. But relations broke down and Hamid's father was killed by the Taliban in broad daylight. While in exile in Pakistan, Hamid engaged in attempts to undermine the movement and had contact with several Western countries as well as the CIA. After the terror attacks in the US, he returned to Afghanistan on a motorcycle, like Mullah Omar, to gather support among the tribal leaders in the south.

As well as backing Karzai, the delegates in Bonn agreed that the country needed a new constitution. This was to be drawn up by a loya jirga. Members would be chosen from the top down, as those in Bonn were.

The Bush administration convinced the delegates to pursue an American solution, a constitutional democracy with direct elections for a president. What worked in America should work in Afghanistan.

The Bonn Agreement had, however, one weakness everyone seemed to overlook.

The Taliban weren't invited.

A number of Taliban leaders had expressed the desire to surrender in order to take part in the discussions on the future of the country. No one wanted them there. The tribal leaders rejected them, the UN ignored them, and neither George W. Bush nor the Northern Alliance wanted to negotiate. The Taliban had lost. They were gone.

Like the missing trophy.

Could he still be alive?

He was.

After the Bonn Agreement was signed on 5 December 2001, after hundreds of tonnes of bombs had been dropped, Osama's voice could still be heard. As al-Qaeda used unsecure radios their communications could easily be intercepted, allowing the Americans to listen in on their crackling conversations. When a CIA operative picked up a radio from a dead jihadist, the Americans got a clear channel into the caves. Bin Laden was still in command. The fighters referred to him as the Sheik.

In mid-December, Osama bin Laden wrote his will. He instructed his wives not to remarry and apologised to his children for dedicating himself solely to jihad.

The Americans used GPS and laser range finders to pinpoint the caves, and where within them the Sheik was to be found, but no technical equipment can make up for human deception. The US had put their faith in two local warlords – a drug smuggler and a man with a brutish reputation. They offered the US a force of two thousand men, cobbled together and riddled with internal distrust. The Americans, lacking boots on the ground, paid them well to keep watch over Tora Bora.

Following a few more weeks of bombing, the drug smuggler conveyed the message that al-Qaeda wanted to surrender. All they were asking for was a twelve-hour ceasefire to allow them to climb out of the caves, come down from the mountains and hand over their arms. In an intercepted radio exchange, Osama bin Laden was heard telling his men the surrender was acceptable. The drug smuggler promised the Americans the entire leadership of al-Qaeda on a plate.

It was agreed the bombing would cease for one night to allow the fighters to emerge.

The next morning not a single fighter turned up. Instead, approximately eight hundred men had escaped into Pakistan.

Two nights later, Osama bin Laden and his Yemeni bodyguards

wandered quietly out of the cave complex. They crossed the snow-covered mountains on foot and on horseback, disappearing into the tribal area over the border into Pakistan.

While the jihadists left Afghanistan for Pakistan, many Afghans wanted to travel in the opposite direction. Homeward.

Among them was Jamila's father. He believed in Karzai, regarding him as a capable, skilful businessman. Most of Ibrahim's properties lay in ruins, but the land they stood on was still his. Rebuilding and development could now take place.

Ibrahim had only been back in Kabul once since they left, during a ceasefire in the civil war. Together with Bibi Sitara, he had driven there to check on the house. Without warning their neighbourhood, Kot-e-Sangi, was caught in the line of fire. While the fighting raged around them, they decided to flee under cover of darkness. Jamila's mother remembered stepping over bodies.

This time she refused to return until she was certain there really was peace.

The Americans are in Kabul, Ibrahim assured her. They were pro-business and would maintain law and order, he promised. In the end he left without Bibi. Then his sons followed, one by one, to help their father.

'A golden time,' Ibrahim proclaimed to old friends in Kabul. All that was needed was to clear up the rubble.

While her father fell asleep and woke up with his head full of ideas, figures and budgets, Jamila had activism on her mind. All through her studies she had been engaged in relief work.

Those with clothes to spare, give them away!

Are there shoes?

Food!

Medicine!

Her father and brothers had eventually given up and let her study at university. She had completed a master's in international politics that summer. While studying she had started her own organisation, Noor, meaning light. Education was the only way out of misery, she believed. And since very few in the camps sent their children to school, Noor visited the camps and taught them there.

But now, when her father and brothers left, a thought came to mind. Should she also return home?

To a country she barely knew but was certain she loved.

Just after New Year, she got into her uncle's car. The spectacular view through the Sarobi Pass brought tears to her eyes. It was on this stretch of road she had been shot years before. All along the route lay buildings in ruins and the rusty machinery of war.

As they neared the capital, she saw thick black smoke above the city. People were burning coal and brushwood to keep warm. The waterpipes were dry, the telephone lines silent, the lightbulbs dark.

Now everything would change.

As Jamila was returning home, foreign aid organisations were pouring into the country. Development initiatives conceived in the West needed local help. Jamila got a job with Care International. After some rapid training, she was to work as an instructor on a programme called Capacity Building for Social Workers. The others selected had, like her, spent the turbulent years in Pakistan, while those taking part in the programme had stayed in Afghanistan.

Jamila was excited. She was the youngest instructor. Full of energy, the twenty-four-year-old immediately began to speak, presenting herself and the course. She felt useful, important, and sprinkled catchy aid expressions and abbreviations throughout her presentation.

The room was restless. The participants seemed sceptical, and glared at her, almost aggressively. Some of them got up and stood by the door; a few even left. Jamila forced herself to concentrate. Her voice grew louder as she tried to speak above the rising chatter.

She went on for an hour. No one was interested. No one seemed to care.

Nevertheless, she continued to impart what she had been taught to say.

'Why is the women's group so negative?' she complained to another instructor during the break.

Her colleague shrugged.

Jamila decided to take the bull by the horns, picked up her crutches and went over to a group of women who had sat morose and sullen while she had spoken.

One of them looked her up and down.

'Here I am, much older than you, and I feel like I've wasted my life,' the woman said. 'You know more than me, you're full of vigour, you have a brighter future than me, I have none,' she complained. 'But if I'd had the opportunity, I'd be better than you.'

'I hate the mujahideen and the Taliban,' another woman said. 'They're products of Pakistan. We've suffered at their hands and here you come, well dressed and pale from Pakistan, and you're supposed to teach us how to live!'

Jamila stood in silence.

'I stayed in Afghanistan while you left! You've had higher education, we've eaten dust,' a third woman said.

Jamila was ashamed. She had seen herself as some sort of angel coming to the rescue, with lots to offer others. But she hadn't asked them about anything, had shown no interest in their experiences. She had all the solutions, wrapped neatly in Care International's eloquent language.

The women had survived war, repression, harassment, fear, and then she comes along, a young girl, and was supposed to train them.

Jamila, you're not up to this, she told herself.

The break was almost over. Group work, based on what they had done in the first session, was next. They were to do role play, with the interaction designed to lead to solutions. She had thought this would engage the participants but now everything felt wrong.

When they gathered after the break, Jamila looked calmly out over the class.

'I've come here to listen to you,' she said.

She sat in silence until the first of them began to speak. The woman uttered a few sentences, then stopped. Putting the bitter feelings into words was unfamiliar. They bore a common pain, but it ran through each of them individually, twisted and knotted in its own way. Now they were going to try to untangle it together.

Jamila also spoke. She related how Pakistanis hurled abuse at Afghan refugees in the street. How children were unable to attend local schools. How it was close to impossible for an Afghan to get a proper job. How people froze to death in the camps in winter or died of heatstroke in the summer. How the children ran about without clothes, without proper food and succumbed to easily curable diseases.

'And here I was thinking all of you were doing fine there,' one woman said.

Jamila told them how she had kept out of sight of her brothers, her father, how she had been mocked by the soldiers for her limp, how she had fought to get where she was now. Exile too tasted bitter.

Her older colleagues, who had not been met with the same resistance, were annoyed. 'You're not following the plan. You're ruining the schedule.'

'People are traumatised, they're not ready to engage with our course,' Jamila replied.

The male participants were still difficult. They challenged, scoffed and poked fun at her, making what she said sound idiotic. Or they were combative. No matter how she phrased things, they took it the wrong way. Being taught by a younger woman was humiliating.

Jamila realised that her only option was to employ her knowledge of Islam. They couldn't make fun of that. She quoted from the Quran. The verses were fresh in her mind. She cited the interpretations of different scholars, before analysing and discussing them. No one could match her in that regard. The sneers evaporated. The rebukes subsided.

She had found her sword, and her shield.

Eventually Jamila took up a position with the UN women's organisation, UNIFEM. She was tasked with identifying the needs in different areas of the country. What type of services did people want? A school? Seed grain? Would they then need more water?

Should a well be built?

The social workers she trained were supposed to go out to the villages, set up focus groups, sit down with people and ask them what they required. What had to be arranged quickly, what was an emergency, and what was needed for long-term development?

After a few months she decided to work with what she viewed as most important: education. As summer approached, she registered Noor as a development organisation in Kabul.

Noor received support from an international aid agency in setting up twenty schools. With scarcely any premises to be found, teaching would take place in people's homes. They started classes at several levels, from beginner to catch-up programmes, where girls whose schooling had ceased under the Taliban would make up for lost time, or at least catch up on some of what they had missed out on.

One day Jamila was informed that one of her pupils had killed another. The two lived next to each other, beneath tarpaulins and cardboard boxes in the grounds of the former Soviet embassy, where several hundred families had makeshift shelters. The two women had been arguing over a length of clothesline.

The younger woman had picked up a stone from the ground and beaten the older woman on the head until she collapsed.

Jamila hurried to the scene. When she arrived, the police were in the process of removing the corpse and arresting the other woman.

A crowd had gathered. They were talking excitedly, all at once, about what had happened.

'The blood was pouring from her head!'

'And from her nose!'

'And her mouth!'

They described the altercation, demonstrating the blows with their hands, pointing at the bloody rock. Several of them were laughing, imitating the action anew.

Like a rat had been killed, Jamila thought. She felt nauseous. The crowd surged. She gripped her crutches tightly, managed to remain standing. When she had regained her composure, she turned and left.

Once she returned home, she broke down.

She wasn't cut out for this. She couldn't do it. She'd have to pass the baton on to someone else.

While lying in bed, trying to recover from the experience, her thoughts turned to what war did to people. These women were traumatised, both the one who had killed for a length of clothesline and those who had laughed about it afterwards. They had seen so much death, so much suffering; they were desensitised.

She called her mother.

'Mama, I'm coming home.'

She returned to Peshawar, to her mother and sisters-in-law who had yet to follow their husbands to Kabul. She moved back into the villa, to the climbing plants and her bedroom.

She lay in bed, burnt out, but cooled by the ceiling fan.

She found an escape from the misery of Afghanistan, an escape no one could criticise her for: a PhD.

Prior to the fall of the Taliban, her plan had been to do a doctorate after her master's degree. Now she wanted to resume her studies. Sit and read in peace and quiet. She filled out the application forms for the PhD programme.

The day of the admission exam came around. Jamila was well prepared. She showed her identification when she arrived.

'Your name's not on the list,' the man at the counter said.

'There must be some mistake. I'm a student here, I've taken a master's here,' she said. 'At this faculty. I've submitted everything.'

'You're an Afghan refugee,' the man replied. 'You need to go through a different procedure to show you're suitable to continue.'

'No, I'm not a refugee. I live here. I'm registered here,' Jamila answered, standing there with her papers in her hand. She pointed out that she'd already submitted the application forms Afghans needed to fill out and had them approved.

'Yes, but that was for a master's,' the man replied.

'But . . . I . . .'

'Look, it's what the authorities require. Take a look at the rules!'

She turned to leave.

Rejected.

Insulted.

She made up her mind there and then. I'm going back to my country. Whether it's good or bad.

It's my country.

The Making of a Warrior

The old man laid out a map of Kabul.

'Let's say you want to hit the American embassy. From here in Mussahi!'

He took a compass from a small case. The instrument had two needles and a thin metal wire attached to the top.

'You centre the compass between the two points on the map. Then you pull the wire in the direction of the target. When you're sure you've found exactly the place you want to hit, and there's no difference on either of the sides, you write down the latitude and longitude. Then you have to calculate according to the map.'

Bashir listened attentively, sitting on the floor beside the old fighter. The map was between them.

Shukur lived on the outskirts of Mussahi. Bashir had walked for an hour before arriving at his gate, with the intention of mining the warrior's wisdom. The old man was renowned for his bullseyes against the Soviets.

Initially Bashir had been brusquely turned away. He understood why. Shukur might think he was a provocateur, suspect he was trying to lure him out and turn him over to the new authorities. People were being reported indiscriminately, dragged from their houses for things they had done, or not done. Giving military training to the youths of a village, outside the international force's programme, could put the honourable old man in prison for what he had left of his life.

Bashir had told him who he was, who his father was, who his brothers were. The old man had nodded but was still guarded.

'You're too young.'

'I'm almost fifteen.'

Bashir didn't want to be among the faithful who sat idle. But he needed skills that would be useful in war.

'You're my hero,' Bashir pleaded. 'You drove out the godless the last time they were here. Now our land is occupied by the infidels again and we have a duty to fight back.'

The Americans had a somewhat murky idea of who the enemy was, despite George Bush's outline of fighting *the bad guys*.

But who were *the good guys*?

Many Afghans had quickly thrown themselves over to the side of the good. The shrewd among them managed to kill more than two birds with one stone, getting rid of a bothersome neighbour they had a feud with, securing themselves the disputed land and at the same time receiving money from the Americans.

With a little luck and some agreeable witnesses, reporting *a bad guy* was enough to have the man picked up by the security forces. The squabbling of old rivals, or even older tribal feuds – everything could be solved now. War criminals, opium growers, smugglers and murderers quickly dressed in the garb of *the good guys* and received generous remuneration.

Informing for money or position went on without the foreign troops seeing through it, or caring. They were too preoccupied by the war on terror. They had set objectives and intermediate aims, which included arresting a large number of members of al-Qaeda and the Taliban.

In the struggle to meet the quota for *bad guys*, numerous rank-and-file Taliban were reported to the authorities. When the regime fell, many lower-level commanders had conceded defeat and headed home to their villages. There they resumed civilian life, pondering how they could cooperate with the new government. Some had just managed to recommend that their clan back the new president – prior to being reported as dangerous, leading members of al-Qaeda.

The good guys, including warlords, mujahideen and other old hands, as well as the Afghan security forces, were often undisciplined. During arrests they might blackmail the suspect before delivering him to the Americans. The foreigners often began the interrogations from scratch, with only the information they had been fed by informers. Without any idea of who they were sitting with, they might ask a local farmer about the whereabouts of bin Laden, or if al-Qaeda were planning new terror attacks.

Afghan tribal leaders had been almost unanimous in their opposition to armed resistance against Hamid Karzai's rule. But the brutal conduct of the new authority drove many into a rebellion. Respected men from the elder council of villages who had liaised with the Taliban, but who had never been a part of the movement, were intimidated, arrested and humiliated. While imprisoned they were hung by their arms or upside down, beaten in front of others, tortured during interrogation, denied use of a toilet and deprived of sleep. The degradation was strong motivation to seek revenge. It was impossible not to pick a side.

The Bush administration made a fatal error in blurring the distinction between the Taliban and al-Qaeda, and then tarring them with the same brush.

The two groups had partially overlapping views, but they had different goals and different cultures. Al-Qaeda was composed of Arabs and foreign fighters, and had a global objective of jihad. Its leaders wanted to strike at the US, the Saudi royal family and secular leaders in the Middle East. The Taliban, meanwhile, wanted power in Afghanistan. Their interpretation of Islam was rooted more in local traditions than in political ideology. The movement had particular support from conservative Pashtuns in the south and east of the country who wished to preserve their way of life.

To George Bush they were all *bad guys*.

The truth was that after Osama bin Laden and eight hundred of his fighters escaped from Tora Bora, there was hardly anyone from al-Qaeda left in Afghanistan. They had gone to the tribal areas in Pakistan to lick their wounds. Taliban, on the other hand, were plentiful. Many of them were definitely *bad guys*, yet they had nothing to do with the terror attacks on the US. But it was easy for the Americans' local partners to make that connection: individual mullahs became sophisticated terrorists. The Americans rarely checked carefully, sometimes not before the accused was flown across the Atlantic to the prison camp in Guantánamo Bay. It was better to round up too many than too few.

If the boy had turned him in, Shukur could be accused of supporting the rebellion against the new government. Be that as it may, Bashir had in the end been allowed access to the Mecca of knowledge. The old fighter had everything he needed: maps, a compass – and experience.

Shukur explained latitude, longitude and altitude, showed where the trails wound their way in the mountains, and where the caves to hide equipment were located. He described how maps could have different scales: one centimetre might correspond to two kilometres, or ten, or one hundred.

'Now, look here,' he said. 'Check on this list for the angle you need to set the rocket at if you want to reach a target twenty kilometres away. That's the distance from this hill to the American embassy.'

Shukur told Bashir how to build a platform from two logs. When the rocket was at exactly the right angle according to the compass, it could be fired.

'With Allah's help you'll hit the target,' he said, smiling behind his straggly white beard.

Within a couple of hours, Bashir had learned the theory behind perfect accuracy.

'These are yours,' Shukur said finally, handing him the map and the compass. 'May they stand you in good stead.'

Bashir swore he would kill many infidels with the precious gift.

THE MAKING OF A WARRIOR

'Promise me you'll be careful,' the old man said.

Bashir was overwhelmed. He smiled, thanked and praised the man.

Now he just needed to get his hands on some rockets.

Most of the old heroes were gone. The warriors Bashir and his classmates had met at the front had either been killed or fled to Pakistan. The Quran teacher was missing. Osama bin Laden remained in hiding. Mullah Omar was on the run.

Life for many, including Bashir's family, had become unsafe. They were among those who feared a knock on the door at night. 'Just like under the communists,' Hala sighed. His mother called the Americans *Russians* in the beginning – the previous foreigners who had attacked the village.

One night the knock did come.

'Where are the weapons? Where have you hidden the weapons?' The soldiers stood pointing their guns at Hala's two eldest sons. 'Show us the weapons!'

Hassan and Yaqub said they didn't know about any weapons.

'We'll kill you if you don't show us the hiding place!'

Finally the brothers were thrown in a car and driven away.

Informers in the village had fingered them as weapon smugglers. And they were. Sometimes they hid weapons in the mountains above Mussahi. Other times in a field, or in their own barn.

The soldiers returned several times. On one occasion one of them picked up a spade and let loose on the furniture.

'Just to torment us,' Hala said, cursing them as she swept up afterwards. 'Terrorise us,' she corrected herself.

Bashir swore to his mother he would avenge the insults.

Hassan and Yaqub were promised a reduced sentence if they cooperated and, under torture, eventually revealed the locations of hiding places they assumed the soldiers would find anyway. They kept quiet about the rest, which Bashir had been charged with watching over.

The weapons storage they provided was important to the

resurrection of the Taliban. The fighters were always on the move, and it was difficult to transport weapons prior to an attack without being discovered. Scattered depots were needed.

The new authorities offered good money to informers. The temptation had gone right to the heart of Bashir's kin. It was Hassan's brother-in-law who had betrayed them. He himself had helped them bury the weapons so he knew where they were. His kind would not be shown any mercy.

When the brothers were released from prison they went to Waziristan, the autonomous tribal area across the border in Pakistan that Bashir had run away to two years earlier. The border – the disputed Durand Line – was drawn up by the British and the Afghan emir in 1893 and cut through Pashtun land. The tribes who lived there wouldn't allow themselves to be ruled. Constant revolts became so costly that they were granted a degree of autonomy. Except for the main roads, the Pakistani authorities didn't patrol the area. High mountains, dense forest and baking desert made the land of the Wazirs a fortress created by nature itself. It would serve as the new heartland of the Taliban.

Bashir shared the role of the man of the house with Raouf, who was a couple of years older. The four brothers had agreed that one of them always had to be at home with their mother and sisters.

As spring approached and Raouf returned from a mission, Bashir begged his mother for permission to follow his two eldest brothers to Waziristan. How could she tolerate the country once again being occupied by infidels? He reminded her of the weapons search, how they broke down doors, smashed windows and traipsed through the house with their boots on; how the women, who never showed themselves outside, had been exposed.

Hala gave in to her favourite son. She was sure he would manage just fine. Bashir was the smartest out of all of them, after all. While the eldest boys had liked both opium and the hash that grew wild, Bashir had steered clear of all that. She gave him money for the bus and a change of clothes. He went to where the mud path met the main road, to the bus stop where he had stood a couple of years earlier, when he had stolen grain from his mother's larder for the fare.

At the border he changed buses and then, following his brothers' instructions, went into the tribal areas. The village he was heading for was called Miram Shah. To gain entry to the training camps you needed a reference; just turning up could be dangerous. The men feared infiltration.

Bashir's brothers were there to greet him. The next day he would meet the man they simply called *Khalifa*.

Jalaluddin Haqqani was born in the 1930s, in the eastern province of Paktia, and was one of the top commanders during the war against the Soviet Union, renowned for his precision and his brutality. While old mujahideen friends fought over Kabul after the war, Jalaluddin had kept to Waziristan, schooling new cadres at his own madrasa. He had been a military advisor for Osama bin Laden, while at the same time working closely with Pakistan's intelligence service.

When the Taliban took power in the 1990s he was appointed minister of borders and tribal affairs, but maintained his house, school and mosque in Miram Shah.

Following the terror attacks in the US he sought refuge there and immediately began organising fresh resistance. A week after Bush ordered the airstrikes on Afghanistan, Jalaluddin was invited to talks with the Pakistani and American authorities in Islamabad. He envisioned them offering him a role in a new government.

Was he willing to transfer his loyalty from the Taliban to the transitional authorities in Kabul, the Americans asked. What would he want in return?

Jalaluddin asked them to make him an offer.

The Americans were confident. Progress on the battlefield was fast. The trinity of the Taliban, al-Qaeda and Haqqani had as good as lost.

The offer entailed unconditional surrender. The old fighter would be brought to Guantánamo to be rapidly questioned. After telling them everything he knew about Osama bin Laden he would travel home a free man.

It wasn't an offer, it was an insult.

Jalaluddin quickly left the meeting.

He went back to Waziristan. Here he was at home and had everything he needed. While the Americans searched for al-Qaeda in Afghanistan, they were all here, with him, in Pakistan.

Jalaluddin was ready. His brothers were ready, his sons, cousins and nephews. All of them were ready.

Bashir was euphoric, on a high after the trip and excited about meeting the legend.

Jalaluddin received him on his veranda in Miram Shah. It was a warm night and they sat outside, on the concrete. There was no excess at Haqqani's place, no furniture, no carpets, no decorations. All resources went to jihad.

The older man liked to have an overview of who was in the camp. He always met the new volunteers and studied them carefully.

'What brings you here?' he asked, as he sat straight-backed and cross-legged. His beard, which was once black, had been coloured with henna, the reddish-brown dye sticking to the wispy grey hairs.

'I have come to fight the invaders,' Bashir answered.

'Well, then you've come to the right place, my son,' the caliph replied. 'But know this: you'll get no pay. There are no funds, we scarcely have any vehicles and food is low. Do you still wish to be with us?'

'I am with you until death,' the teenager answered. Boys like this, that was what they needed now.

For the next hour Jalaluddin explained in detail about life on the base. Bashir would be assigned different tasks and upon growing a beard he would be allowed fight.

Owing to his advancing age, Jalaluddin had handed over the day-to-day operations of the network to his eldest son, Sirajuddin. He had sat in silence like a rank-and-file Taliban while his father spoke. Bashir had noticed the resemblance straight away.

'Tomorrow you will meet a mujahid from Libya,' Sirajuddin said. 'He's the one who takes care of boys like you.'

That night, as Bashir lay on a thin mattress beside his brothers, he thought about how real life was finally beginning. He had arrived.

'What's this child doing here?'

The Libyan seemed surprised when presented with Bashir, who looked even younger than his years, with chubby cheeks and soft curls. His high, arched brows over big eyes gave him an innocent look.

Abu Laith al-Libi wasn't just anyone, as Bashir was aware, but a central commander in al-Qaeda. After helping drive the Soviets out of Afghanistan, he had returned to his native Libya and joined the Islamists in attempting to overthrow the dictatorship of Muammar Gaddafi, but failed and fled. He had, like so many jihadists who were *persona non grata* in their homeland, travelled via Saudi Arabia to the sanctuary Haqqani had created for men of his ilk. Now he strutted around the little village, training young boys to be fighters or suicide bombers. He was known as *Ustad-e-fedayeen*, teacher of those who sacrifice themselves.

In which group would Bashir end up?

'You're too young to be sent to war yet,' Abu Laith told Bashir when he asked when he would learn to shoot. As no states now financed them, all combat training was theoretical. The Taliban couldn't afford to waste a bullet.

The Libyan slapped him on the back and said something in Arabic.

Insha'allah al-walad sa-yakun mujahid.

Bashir memorised the sentence the next morning, and the morning after that, and the week after. Then he asked someone what it meant.

'This kid will be a great mujahid, God willing.'

Bashir smiled. A sense of complete freedom struck him. He would never live under anyone. Least of all the Americans. Here, with the new mujahideen, was the only place a man could live like a lion!

He felt life was full of meaning.

The following day they would resume training.

Some would be directed to be suicide bombers.

Others were meant to become great warriors.

Fire in the Tent

Bashir had been an errand boy in Waziristan for a few months when the caliph's son decided he was ready for a mission.

'Come after evening prayer,' he was told. On warm nights Sirajuddin and his father used to sit on the veranda of the madrasa drinking green tea and snacking on nuts. In the winter they gathered their men around the large stove indoors. Sirajuddin, who had just turned thirty, had the same broad features as his father, with deep-set eyes that nestled in the shadow of bushy brows. It lent them a strict, almost angry aspect.

Like his father, Sirajuddin was adept at using resources prudently and effectively, whether that be people or ammunition. He sent his fighters where he thought they would fit in best, where each could realise his potential, all with the old man's blessing.

The mountaintops were still white but down the sides the snow was melting into small streams. Spring ushered in the fighting season in Afghanistan. Winter was a time to withdraw, to family life, to make repairs, read the Quran and recuperate. When the earth sprouted, it was time to ready your weapons.

Bashir, still waiting for his long-desired beard to grow, had been entrusted with the key to a weapon depot. He kept it with him at all times and was the person new recruits had to seek out to be issued with equipment and ammunition. In Miram Shah there were more men than rifles.

*

Bashir's mother had also moved to the tribal areas, and his three older brothers had brought their wives. The extended family had been allocated their own house. Bashir's routine – prayer, mealtimes, study, the mosque and sleep – began to resemble his life at home. Many of the jihadists, both Afghans and Arabs, lived family lives with births and washing up in between missions. There were shortages of everything: food, clean water, fuel, clothes. But they were together, they were ready, all busy accruing rewards in the next life. The reward in heaven applied whether you cooked or killed.

Bashir was restless, and afraid. He feared something might happen before he got his chance, that the war would end without him.

In the US, George Bush was also growing impatient.

At Christmas 2001, while smoke from the explosions in Tora Bora still hung in the air, the commander of the US forces in Afghanistan, General Tommy Franks, had been summoned by the president. Despite Osama bin Laden still being free, it wasn't him Bush was occupied with in the meeting, but Saddam Hussein. The general was asked if he thought it would be too much to also take responsibility for a war in Iraq. Franks, who had just committed the blunder of not placing US Army Rangers around Tora Bora to prevent bin Laden escaping, confirmed that he could lead both operations – concurrently.

Bush announced that Saddam Hussein was in the process of producing weapons of mass destruction. He claimed the dictator had cooperated with al-Qaeda and contributed to the terror attacks against the USA. There was no evidence for any of this but Bush was eager to take out more bad guys.

'You're from Mussahi, so do you know Kabul well?' Sirajuddin Haqqani asked. He needed someone who wouldn't attract attention.

'Like the back of my hand,' Bashir lied.

Kabul Province began just past Mussahi, but he'd barely been to the capital.

'You said you'd learned how to fire rockets?' Sirajuddin continued.

'Yes,' Bashir lied again, adding, 'I also have a map of Kabul Province and a compass.'

'Good. Here's the thing . . .'

Bashir broke out in a cold sweat.

Despite his stern appearance, Bashir had never heard Sirajuddin raise his voice. When he was angry you could only sense it; he sounded just as friendly. His voice was quite high-pitched and mellifluous. Bashir could have listened to it for hours. He wondered how he spoke to an enemy.

The caliph explained what the mission consisted of. Bashir was to take another boy with him, and they were to visit a man called Abdul Rahman al-Canadi. His base was in the Muhammad Agha district of Logar, which was a good starting point for attacks on Kabul. Now he was in southern Waziristan, running a training camp, and he would give them more details there, Haqqani promised.

The jihadists often had a nationality added to their name. Al-Canadi, who was Egyptian born, had come to the training camp from Canada with his wife and child, and so was known as the Canadian. He lived a few villages away, but Bashir and Wardak, the boy picked to go along, had to take back roads and mountain trails to avoid running into the Pakistani army. A few spring snowflakes followed them along the first part of their journey. By the third night they reached the restaurant where they were to deliver a letter from Sirajuddin to the owner.

The boys were asked to go into a room behind the dining area to take part in evening prayer. Before they had finished, a man came in and told them to hurry up. Al-Canadi was waiting.

After reading the letter, he gave Bashir five hundred dollars to purchase walkie-talkies and rockets, as many as he could afford. The communications equipment was available at the Khyber bazaar, he said.

'Buy the weapons closer to Kabul,' he recommended. That was where they would be used. He told them where they could find a man he called Babai, a nickname meaning pal.

As they were leaving, al-Canadi encouraged them to invite their comrades and cousins.

'I can train them!' he offered.

Babai was hard to find. While searching, they found some time to practise firing missiles. Bashir knew many undetonated rockets were lying around outside Mussahi. In one impoverished place, rockets had been laid as roofing on outhouses, side by side like timbers, to keep the rain and snow out. One house owner emerged when the boys began removing the rockets and loading them onto a pick-up they had managed to get hold of. His protests ceased when they threatened to kill him if he made any trouble.

On another occasion they found rockets laid as a makeshift bridge over an irrigation canal.

They trained for the mission. At night they fired the old rockets from plains and fields, before quickly exiting the scene. Bashir spent time positioning the rockets at the right angle, in the direction of the hills around Kabul.

Before even locating Babai, they heard al-Canadi had been martyred, killed by Pakistani forces when he left the tribal area.

He had been shot in the face.

The five hundred dollars were burning a hole in Bashir's pocket.

The summer was drawing near. The last king of Afghanistan, Zahir Shah, was flown in from his exile in Italy to open the loya jirga, which was to appoint a president until elections were held in two years' time. The old regent had avoided conflict with the transitional leader Hamid Karzai, on learning the Americans desired a republic and not a monarchy.

The meeting had put the security services in Kabul on high alert. Almost fifteen hundred delegates were invited, of which two hundred were women. There were tribal chiefs, military leaders, imams and mullahs, some locally elected, others appointed.

Two thousand people turned up, most of them older men. The five hundred extra were former mujahideen and warlords demanding their place in the new democracy. They mingled with the delegates, intimidating and harassing those who called for their exclusion. Agents of the Afghan security service were also circulating, so the state would know what people were talking about.

After first having interfered with the electoral processes in several regions, the warlords were about to undermine the entire loya jirga. Meetings were interrupted. The UN's representative to Afghanistan regretted that voting was eroded by threats of violence, manipulation and the buying of votes. 'We are hostages of those who destroyed Afghanistan,' one delegate said. Anonymously, of course. He wanted to live.

The US ambassador, exiled Afghan Zalmay Khalilzad, kept an eye on proceedings from the sidelines. He was a regular guest at the presidential palace. Wicked tongues had it that *Zal* was the one who actually ran the country.

Prior to the loya jirga, several Taliban leaders had sought reconciliation and expressed a desire to cooperate with the transitional government. They were met with closed doors. No one with any links to the Taliban was allowed near the enormous tent where the loya jirga held its nine-day assembly.

Their only route to regaining power was to fight the regime.

When Bashir and Wardak finally found Babai, they had enough money left for four Russian rockets.

Finally Bashir was ready for *the mission*.

It was just in time.

The next night they went to some high ground west of Kabul, to the ruins of Dar-ul-Aman, a neoclassical palace built for King Amanullah in the 1920s.

The rockets were three metres long and had a range of twenty kilometres. Bashir took out the map and compass Shukur had given him. The coordinates were written down on a piece of paper. He set the angle as precisely as he could.

From the royal palace Bashir wanted to strike at those now in power. They had seized victory with the help of infidels and now wanted to write a constitution. What use was that when Afghanistan had sharia?

The boys fired the four rockets in quick succession. Then they left, without knowing where the rockets landed. It wasn't until the next day that they learned the rockets had reached their target. They had set a tent alight.

So the traitors would have to replace that at least.

CNN were informed by 'official security forces' that remnants of the Taliban were behind the rocket attack, but that it would not disrupt attempts to form a new government. The security chief of the Ministry of the Interior stressed that the rockets had landed far from the assembly tent and that several suspects had already been arrested.

By then the two friends were already on their way back to Waziristan. The new rulers should know that when the Taliban weren't invited to the table this was how they responded.

Fathers and Sons

Bashir turned sixteen. His sweet appearance had its advantages. The absence of a heavy beard and calloused hands meant he drew less attention when he was sent across the border, usually with a friend, to plant roadside bombs.

Bashir's big brother, Hassan, a car mechanic by trade, was now an explosives expert. Together with his wife, who among the women was known as the engineer, he had begun production in the kitchen.

The work required many hands and a high degree of caution. Your first mistake might be your last, Hassan impressed upon them, as he stood mixing chemicals before carefully placing the bomb in a yellow plastic container that had once held cooking oil. This kept it from exploding in transit, yet it could easily be pressed down by the weight of a tank or a car.

Bashir and his friend would go out under cover of darkness and bury the *bushka* where they knew the foreigners or government forces would drive. Sometimes the mechanism required more than the weight of a car to set it off, so that only armoured vehicles would cause it to explode. They often dug the bombs in on the side of the road, where the earth wasn't as packed down, making it harder to spot that anyone had disturbed the soil.

Haqqani's men organised the training of Bashir and the other novices. They were split into groups of ten, with two or three instructors, to learn about guerrilla tactics and how to shoot.

On the other side of the border, other young men were receiving combat drill. NATO's forces operated under a mandate of the UN security council. Their primary task was to assist the Afghan government in stabilising the country. Several countries, with the US at the forefront, oversaw the military training. The plan was for the new security forces to operate on their own within a few years, so the country would never again provide safe haven for terrorists.

In the year following the Taliban's fall from power, the movement, apart from some small and scattered attacks, almost went into hibernation. Lacking a united leadership, several groups organised themselves into different *mahaz* – fronts – from a handful of men to a few dozen who operated on their own.

Hassan learned how to make remote-controlled bombs. A mobile phone was attached to the detonator and set to vibrate should anyone ring it, setting off the bomb.

After Bashir and his friend had buried a bomb, they would hide behind bushes on the mountainside, with a clear view of the road. There they would sit, waiting for their target. They sat patiently, so far from people that no one could hear them when they sang:

> *Those who come to our country*
> *We send them back in pieces.*
> *With a yellow bushka,*
> *Filled with gunpowder.*

In March 2003, American forces rumbled across the desert in Operation Iraqi Freedom. As in Afghanistan, the regime was easily defeated. It took twenty-two days to reach Baghdad.

On 1 May, six weeks after the start of the invasion, George W. Bush, in a green pilot's uniform, was flown aboard the aircraft carrier USS *Abraham Lincoln*. In front of a large banner reading 'Mission Accomplished', he announced that major combat operations had ended and thanked the American forces for 'a job well done'.

The invasion of Iraq had required a force of 120,000 soldiers. That spring, the USA had barely ten thousand men and women under arms in Afghanistan.

The same day Bush was speaking on the aircraft carrier, defence minister Donald Rumsfeld was in Kabul to meet Hamid Karzai. They held a joint press conference at which Rumsfeld delivered a speech similar to the one Bush had just made. In his script, major combat operations were also over. Just like in Iraq, only small pockets of resistance remained.

The Haqqani Network was one such pocket. Bashir himself was barely pocket fluff.

One afternoon, a group of men were gathered at the taps outside the mosque in Miram Shah to wash their hands and feet before prayer.

The Americans were just across the border, one said. Sirajuddin had obtained rocket artillery.

The network only had the capacity to launch simple attacks into Afghanistan, enabling them to withdraw to Waziristan, where the Americans couldn't follow, as it was Pakistani territory.

Now that it was warm enough to sleep outside, Sirajuddin wanted to send a group to attack the enemy. Commander Qalam, a tall, lean, somewhat gruff man with a lined, weather-beaten face, was to lead the operation.

He was standing right next to Bashir, by the taps, saying that he needed two more men.

'I can do it!' Bashir burst out.

It was a shortcut, because only Sirajuddin Haqqani could approve who was ready for missions.

'I need grown men,' Qalam slammed.

Bashir felt the weight of the key to the weapon depot in his pocket. He had been assigned the duties of a caretaker when he was here to become a warrior! A year had passed since the attack on the loya jirga and he was yet to take part in any real fighting.

'You won't regret it,' the teenager replied.

*

Though initially rejected, Bashir got to go all the same, owing to one of the men getting wounded. With him, they were eleven. They left Miram Shah at dawn. The plan was to make camp at the border, two or three days' march away. The distance wasn't great but they couldn't use the roads, which were patrolled by the Pakistani army. The terrain they had to traverse was rugged and densely forested, and the men were carrying a heavy load: the weapons that would help them kill and win.

Exactly where the border lay, none of them knew, but on the third night they made camp at a spot Qalam picked out. Early the following morning they crossed into Afghanistan under cover of darkness and wandered around until night fell without encountering any Americans.

Every day the men kept watch on the mountainous area. The nearly-war became a new routine. Sleep, prayer, march, rest. Pray. Food. Pray. March. Pray. March. Pray. Rest. Sleep. Then morning prayer again. The group became a single ecosystem in which each of them had their place and played their part. When they ran out of food some went to a village, others found shelter in an abandoned house, where they all gathered.

But where were *the invaders*?

One night when the group were praying together before settling down to sleep, a truck screeched to a halt outside. Everyone grabbed their weapons. Then they heard one of their own call out in a low voice. A messenger sent by Sirajuddin.

'An American convoy is headed towards Gayan!' he said. 'Right now!'

Gayan was a district centre in Paktika Province. Haqqani had received a tip-off that the Americans would pass before eight the next morning.

Bashir tied his bootlaces.

The messenger knew the local area. The eleven fighters got on the pick-up, some in the front, the rest on the cargo bed.

Qalam was dressed in a sand-coloured tunic and a military jacket, with a fur vest over it. Now he ordered the men up the mountain on the Afghan side. The tall, well-built man pointed out a hilltop the

Americans would have to pass beneath on the way to Gayan. The men followed one another up the scree. On reaching the ridge they readied the rockets and sat down to wait.

A convoy of vehicles would take a long time to get through the valley. The road had collapsed, with large craters in places. A shallow river meandered along the valley floor. The enemy would have to drive through it, Qalam reckoned; the road itself was too narrow for their wide vehicles.

There!

The first Americans.

The group weren't driving, but on foot, like them. Several of them had backpacks. Even from far away Bashir could see that they were foreigners. They walked differently, the rhythm heavier, their outlines broader; they were wearing helmets, not felt hats like them. The Americans took up a position high up on the opposite side of the valley to protect their convoy.

Qalam and his men drew closer together. The Americans couldn't see them.

Suddenly they saw a third group approach on the same side of the valley as the Americans. Through his binoculars, Qalam saw it was Baitullah Mehsud, the leader of a Pakistani Taliban militia, and his group. He contacted Baitullah over the walkie-talkie and reported their location. Baitullah returned his greeting. In order to get closer and make the attack even more of a surprise for the Americans, Qalam decided they should move further up to a spur where they would have a better view. As they began to crawl, Baitullah's voice came over the walkie-talkie.

'The foreigners are above you!'

Baitullah, looking through binoculars on the far side of the valley, had seen that Bashir and his men were about to move right into view of the Americans. The warning had come just in time.

'God be praised!' they mumbled in chorus.

Qalam halted the climb and they took up a position behind some rocks.

Then Bashir saw several vehicles, perhaps a dozen, edging forward between boulders and yellow sand, down towards the muddy riverbed. During the Soviet invasion, travelling along the roads, which Soviet engineers had often constructed, had been one of the most dangerous things the Red Army could do. The mujahideen could sit tight and fire down on them with small arms and light weapons. If the guerrillas hit the first tank and the one at the rear, the Soviets were trapped. That was the reason the Americans had infantry accompanying them, who, like the mujahideen, moved along the hillside in an attempt to catch anyone planning an ambush off guard.

The line of military vehicles was about fifty metres away. Bashir and a couple of others were standing by the rocket artillery while the rest had rifles.

The armoured vehicle at the front of the convoy suddenly sped up, making a swing around a rock before continuing onward.

Qalam counted down.

'Fire!'

Bashir heard a sudden rushing sound in the air, felt the shock of the blast before the bang. Smoke rose up from the vehicle, which had stopped with a jolt. It was Abdul Manan, a friend from Mussahi, who had fired first. Then a new rocket was launched, then another and then one more.

The convoy came to a standstill.

Several of the armoured cars were put in reverse; a couple of them crashed into the vehicles behind but continued backing up. Baitullah's group now began shooting. The Americans had to repel an attack from two directions.

Contrary to what he had told Qalam, Bashir had never fired this type of rocket before. He fumbled. His fingers were stiff. He spent a long time aiming. 'Allahu Akbar!' he yelled and pulled the trigger.

Nothing happened.

He tried again. Nothing. He said a prayer. Some armoured cars pointed machine guns in their direction. Dear God . . . The boy glanced up at the American lookout post on the opposite side of the valley.

He pulled the trigger again. The rocket failed to launch. He tried to twist the rocket but that just made it fall out of the barrel. He lifted the launcher up to see if something was blocking the mechanism, pulled the trigger, and suddenly the rocket roared straight up, high over the Americans and landed undetonated on the ground far from the target.

One of the older men came scrambling down to him.

'The angle is too steep!' he shouted.

What no one had explained to Bashir was that when you were high above a target, aiming downward, you had to adjust the settings. He had five rockets and had used one; he couldn't waste the other four. If he didn't pull this off . . .

Baitullah's group continued firing at the Americans from across the valley. This was Qalam's chance to take out the enemy's men and vehicles, and quickly, before their hiding place was blown. The foreigners had more advanced weapons and reinforcements were probably on the way.

Bashir saw two soldiers heading towards a vehicle, pulling a third with them. He aimed and fired. The rocket struck the ground beside the vehicle, causing no damage. He had used up two now. First the one straight up in the air and then a miss. If he didn't score a direct hit he'd never be allowed to come along again.

He prepared to fire the third. Bullets were raining down now. A rocket hit a boulder behind them. The men around him began to run.

'Take cover!' Qalam shouted.

It was as though the commander were far away. Bashir was unaware of anything but the third rocket. All his attention was focused on it. He took careful aim – and pulled the trigger with all his strength.

'Abandon your position!' Qalam yelled as a rocket hit right next to him.

Bashir had hit the armoured car he had aimed at and loaded a fourth rocket. He fired. Smoke rose up from down by the river.

'Run!'

But Bashir had one rocket left.

'The helicopters will be here soon!' a man called out.

It was as if Bashir was in a trance. He was standing with the last rocket in his hand. Parts of the convoy were reversing. A truck was blocking the road; a few men were taking cover behind the bonnet of a vehicle. He aimed at an armoured car he had seen several soldiers get into. A couple more were obscured behind trees with their weapons trained on him. He needed to choose quickly: the vehicle or the shooters below the trees.

Bang! There was an explosion as the rocket struck metal.

'Bashir, you're on your owwwwwwn!' someone called out.

The boy ran and dived under a tree.

Before long the helicopters were above them. The fighters lay hidden in bushes, behind rocks and under trees. The rule was to spread out, never be many men together.

Bashir lay totally still while the Americans evacuated their wounded. A jet fighter roared overhead. The helicopters flew so low he could see the pilots' faces through the thick foliage. The big advantage of summer was the leaves. The mountainous region was bare in the winter, lush in spring and completely covered in summer.

Bashir wondered what kind of weapons systems the helicopters had on board. He had heard of heat-seeking lasers; if they used anything like that he and the others were finished.

An hour passed.

The helicopters continued circling above them. The soldiers fired numerous shots towards the trees, but no one was hit.

His throat was dry. A stream trickled nearby. Bashir was so thirsty he felt he was going to choke. He had swallowed sand and clay dust. The gurgle of the stream sounded like chuckling to his ears.

They lay motionless for another hour, for two hours, three.

Abdul Manan whispered loudly that he couldn't take it any longer and was going to crawl over to the stream. 'Come on, Bashir!'

They were under separate trees, some way off from the others.

'No, stay where you are!' Bashir answered. His tongue was sticking to the roof of his mouth.

They remained on the ground while they followed the slow passage of the sun. The helicopters made several trips back and forth to pick up men and equipment, continuing to circle and taking pot shots into the trees.

Nobody risked creeping over to drink. If they found one, they would find them all.

In the afternoon, just as the sun indicated it was time for prayer, the helicopters finally left.

One by one the warriors emerged from their hiding places. Qalam's Afghans, Baitullah's Pakistanis, a few Arabs. They hadn't lost a single man! They embraced, praised the Lord and drank in greedy gulps from the stream.

That feeling! Returning to the village with the rocket launcher over his shoulder and – by the grace of God – American lives on his conscience.

The villagers had heard the shooting and seen the helicopters circling. Since none of the Taliban had returned, they had feared the worst. Now that they saw them approaching, dusty and exhausted, they welcomed them warmly. As the fighters passed the Lowara bazaar, a man called out, 'A lamb, on my tab!'

The animal was sent to a local restaurant.

Prior to this battle, few in the area had approached the Taliban. The tribal people didn't like living under anyone, including them. The war in Afghanistan was not their war. They turned away or hurried along when they caught sight of the armed men. Who was a friend and who was a foe? It was best to keep your distance.

But when the battle against the Americans started that morning, there was no doubt about who they supported. They were closest to their Pashtun brothers.

With grass stains on his clothes and twigs in his hair, on his way to eat a lamb offered in gratitude, Bashir had become a warrior.

After a few days' march the men were back in Miram Shah. Bashir ran into Sirajuddin at the mosque.

'I heard you were at the battle in Paktika, my son.'

Bashir smiled.

'Yes, I fired five rockets.'

'Who would have thought that of a little boy like you! Many invaders were killed. Over twenty, they say.'

The Taliban were not averse to inflating the number of enemy losses. The truth was they had no idea how many, if any, were killed in the fight. Several had been wounded, they had seen that. So far in the war American losses were few; they had yet to lose over a hundred men.

Large-scale ambushes were still not common for the Taliban. But it was how they would win, skirmish by skirmish, battle by battle. Small groups going face to face was their method. They had to force the Americans onto the ground. If the war was waged from the air, they didn't stand a chance.

Sirajuddin gave him a pat on the back.

'I'm proud of you, son.'

Bashir had to look away. It was too much. The warm hand on his back felt like the caress of a father.

ABC

Noor had grown. In Peshawar the organisation had been based on volunteer work. They had gathered food and clothing for the refugees in the camps, bought books with money from friends. Now Jamila had an office with employees. She had staff. She was full of hope.

She applied for funding from numerous countries and donors; the first contribution came from Canada. The goal was that every child in Afghanistan would learn how to read and write. In addition they trained women in computing, bookkeeping, budgeting and leadership.

Jamila also had a deeper motive – to work for a more equal society. That had to happen from within and by way of the most important book: the Quran. She introduced scripture lessons from a *female perspective*. To engage with the mullahs you had to meet them on their own turf, so they couldn't dismiss equality as Western heresy.

The Taliban had left Kabul and could no longer obstruct her work. Jamila could lead, debate, be involved in shaping the new Afghanistan. However, it turned out there were still men in her way. Men who wanted control over women, men who wanted to control her. Their refrain was familiar.

Where are you going?
What are you doing?

You must not.
Accept. Conform. Pay attention, you brazen woman!
The men were the same as before, the closest ones in her life – her brothers.

In Kabul, Jamila's brothers had each been given a role in the restoration of the family business as Ibrahim picked up the pieces of his properties. Bibi Sitara planted a new garden. There was enough for all to keep busy.

The house itself had to be rebuilt from the ground up, as everything of value had been plundered and ripped out. It became a home again, with soft carpets, elegant wallpaper and expensive curtains. Bibi Sitara chose a beautiful shade of green for the large living room overlooking the garden, which made the walls seem to blend in with the foliage outside. She decorated a room for Jamila, who was by now in her late twenties – the room where she would live for the rest of her life. Jamila didn't care how it looked, decor and furnishings held as little interest for her as cooking, a hassle that stole time.

She was a woman with a calling. Anything not leading to her goal was a distraction.

After persistent nagging, Noor had been given office space in one of Ibrahim's buildings. Jamila was grateful not to have to pay rent, so they didn't need to dip into the education pot. But the privilege did come at a price. Her brothers had a set of keys.

They barged in at all hours. Her brothers didn't care if they were disturbing a meeting, they just stood there looking around, casting their eyes over people before leaving again.

It was embarrassing. And humiliating.

Two of her brothers were of the opinion she shouldn't work at all; another couple of them said she could, but only from home. Just one accepted her working at an office, so long as virtue was upheld.

While Ibrahim was occupied with his own affairs, her brothers continued to trip her up. Time was on their side. All they had to do was wait until the funds dried up or their father took the offices back.

The brothers hadn't counted on the aid streaming into the country. Western donors were on the lookout for projects to back and Noor fitted the bill. The organisation had offshoots in several provinces and was soon running hundreds of small-scale educational projects, like home-schooling conducted by out-of-work teachers, and temporary classrooms in places where there were no schools.

They were soon supporting over one thousand projects. Then two thousand.

Jamila got the contract to start classes in the conservative province of Ghazni, her parents' birthplace, where Ibrahim had begun his business career in the 1940s and where Bibi had grown up dressed as a boy.

Jamila was lucky to have a rich father. He owned a mansion in Ghazni, which he rented out to relatives. When Jamila was in town she lived on her father's floor of the house. An uncle lived above with his family, another uncle on the floor below. A housekeeper was on hand to take care of practical matters.

If she'd had problems handling five brothers, she now had even more male relatives to contend with. Five times as many, in fact. In Ghazni she had a number of uncles, all had sons, and several of them again had adult sons of their own. Her cousins did not deign to speak to her directly but went through her brothers. Jamila had violated the tradition of the obedient, silent woman. The accusations flew.

'She's tarnishing our name!' they complained.

'Your sister works with infidels. She doesn't cover her face. You need to put a stop to this.'

The cousins thought Jamila's brothers were being far too timid in their response. How hard could it be?

'If you lot have no shame, have no sense of honour, then we'll put a stop to her ourselves!'

Word about Noor began to spread in Ghazni. Among those who wanted an education, and among those who wanted to put a stop to it. Mothers who wanted to register their daughters on the courses came through the door. Threats came over the phone.

One day a gang of men on motorcycles came roaring up the

street and stopped outside Noor's offices. They drew weapons and walked straight in. One of the cousins was among them. He'd had enough.

Before descending on the building, he'd put out lies that Jamila had travelled out of the country with *foreigners*, and sat alone with *men* at the office. Who knew what else she was getting up to.

The cousin claimed that Ibrahim and his sons were no longer real Afghans, that they didn't care about the family name. His plan was to escalate the conflict so that Ibrahim, as patriarch, would shut down Noor in Ghazni.

Cars began to tail Jamila on the street. She received anonymous phone calls.

'You need to wind up your activities!' her brothers implored her. 'Close the office!'

'Do you actually believe what they're accusing me of?'

No, it wasn't that they believed she was up to anything indecent at the office, but people *might* believe it if she continued to allow men there.

'Even if you were going to Mecca every time you went out, to walk around the sacred Kaaba, I still wouldn't like you leaving the house,' one of her brothers told her.

'How can we expect this country to develop with that kind of mentality?'

'I think with horror about the day when someone sees me and says, "There goes the brother of Jamila",' her brother admitted.

A woman shouldn't define a family. That was the kind of thing her brothers worried about. They wanted the world as they knew it.

Jamila tried to find a way out. Within the family she had always insisted on getting her own way. In her work life she had learned to solve conflicts by talking things through, by compromise, by chipping away at a problem until a gap opened up and then widening it, creating a space where you could find common ground. Now everything seemed closed off.

At night she dreamed she was running. Through the desert, through the mountains, in rivers and streams. Obstacles were always in her way. During the day she worked to break down barriers, at night new ones were raised.

But one thing was different at night: she ran without crutches. Sometimes she even walked on water. Other times she flew. She was weightless, but strong. Getting places, endowed with superpowers.

In reality, she was about to succumb to the pressure.

The simplest solution was to give up. Stop working, pass the baton on to someone else, admit that it was over. The pressure was only increasing – from every quarter. There was pressure at home, whether she lived with her parents in Kabul or with her uncles in Ghazni. There was pressure in public. There was pressure at work. In several places the projects met resistance from imams and local authorities. There were so many fronts to fight on.

But then young girls came by to thank her for what they had learned, before going on to further studies. In a meeting with a foreign aid organisation Jamila found herself sitting across the table from one of the girls Noor had helped to educate. What a thrill!

Close down? No, this was what she believed in, and when had life ever been easy?

But if she thought it couldn't get much worse, she was in for a surprise. The cousin who had voiced the most opposition, been the most threatening, proposed to her.

The very thought was abhorrent. She would rather die.

As the development projects were springing up, violence in the country was on the increase. Kidnapping had become a major source of income both for criminal networks and for the Taliban, and Jamila's family found themselves victims. The uncle living on the floor below had disappeared. He had been the most genial of them and had, privately of course, supported her. The kidnappers demanded a large ransom. The family had to step up and do their part. Jamila suspected her cousins themselves were pulling the strings and that she was next on the list.

Rejecting a marriage proposal from a cousin could lead to bad blood among an entire clan.

'I'll teach you. I'll show you just how I'll put a stop to it,' her cousin told her when he came by.

If her brothers couldn't do the job, then he would.

Ibrahim had had enough. Jamila was given a choice. Either cease her work for girls' education, leave the family or leave the country.

There was a fourth option.

A new proposal could offset her cousin's.

But from whom? What man would allow her to be independent? Heading an organisation, having employees, making decisions?

Given that her parents had never wanted her, a disabled person, to marry, no suitors had come her way. Well, yes, there had been one, a few years earlier.

The proposal had bypassed her family and been made via an acquaintance, who at first had not revealed who the suitor was, only informed her of his existence. Jamila hadn't been interested in marriage because she just wanted to work but had nevertheless been curious.

'Does this suitor have a name?' she had eventually asked.

It was Kakar. The Arabic teacher.

Jamila hit the roof and called him immediately.

'How dare you? You're my teacher! What kind of girl do you think I am?'

Kakar didn't give up. He proposed again. And again. And one last time.

But that was years ago. Where was he now?

The kidnapped uncle was finally set free. The family had pitched in to pay the ransom. While he had been held hostage, Jamila had grown closer to his wife. She was more open, more thoughtful than the others in the family.

Jamila told her about the cousin's threats, and about Kakar, who it turned out was a widower. She sought advice on how to communicate, after all these years, that she might now be interested. As a lifeline, she stressed. She reasoned that the newly released, more genial uncle was the only one who could convince her father to say yes to a suitor from outside.

While she waited, she drafted a list of demands for a prospective husband.

I need to work.

You cannot stop my work.

On the contrary, you must support me.

No matter what I do you are never to be a hindrance to me.

This applies regardless of whether or not you like what I do.

Jamila had never thought she would get married. Now it was the only means to break free of her family, and for them to be rid of her.

Ibrahim was sceptical. Kakar was from a different region, a different tribe completely. He was Pashtun, Jamila was Tajik. They didn't know him. What kind of man was he? Why would he want to marry a cripple?

The brothers said he was after Ibrahim's money. Besides, he'd been married before, and had children: was this really what she wanted to be – a stepmother?

Bibi Sitara thought the best thing was for Jamila to remain living in the family home. After all, that had always been the plan.

The uncle tried to make them reconsider. Kakar came from a family with Islamic scholars going back several generations. He was educated as an imam and in demand as a counsellor and mediator. His family was known for mild and traditional exercise of their religion, and one of his uncles had written a work on science and Islam.

As far as Jamila was concerned, his family was okay, the timing was perfect and Kakar was completely satisfactory.

It worked. Her father relented, her cousins vanished, her brothers relinquished their grip. The family no longer had responsibility for her. That was transferred to Kakar.

Jamila found it difficult to suddenly be so close, literally overnight, on the wedding night, to another person. She had great respect for her former teacher, but this respect created distance, imbalance and shyness. All of a sudden they were supposed to share everything. Be intimate. He had been married before; she was completely inexperienced. No, it most certainly was not a love match, she informed those who asked.

But as long as he didn't stand in her way it should be okay.

Then something unusual happened. Kakar joined Noor, began working for his wife, in the organisation she had founded. He was given responsibility for dialogue with Islamic scholars, which was important, invaluable in fact, for gaining access to the villages. In order to influence decisions they had to speak to village councils, which consisted of the region's most powerful men – always men. How were they to convince them to accept schools for girls and courses for their mothers?

It was important that what was presented did not stir up memories of the last time there had been talk of women's rights, when the godless Soviets foisted their ideas on them. Many were sceptical. Were human rights and democracy actually in accordance with Islam?

Kakar and Jamila believed so. The Taliban did not. The imams sat on the fence.

The couple worked ever more closely. They complemented each other on an intellectual and practical level. Through conversations with imams and mullahs, who often could not even *look* at a woman while they spoke, the newlyweds endeavoured to alter the traditional view on *purdah* – segregation – and on the right to education for girls. There was nothing in the Quran to oppose female education and women's participation in society, Kakar would explain in his patient manner. He quoted scripture, what the Prophet had said, and not least that Muhammad himself wanted his wives and daughters to read and learn.

They changed the name of the organisation to Noor Educational and Capacity Development, later shortening it to the acronym NECDO. Jamila had wanted to have human rights in the title but it was too controversial. You had to know where to draw the line, even she knew that. For the moment.

She relied on Kakar's patience; he let himself be pulled along by her determination.

The couple's view of Islam was at odds with daily practice in the country. Under the new constitution of 2004 men and women were equal on paper. Sharia was not referenced directly but the constitution stated that Islamic law would always take precedence. Kakar and Jamila found examples of democratic ideas in Islam whereas most people understood their faith from what their clan decreed. Local interpretations dominated. Folk wisdom and traditions from pre-Islamic Afghanistan, promoting the prerogative of men and patriarchal power, were deep-rooted.

In his first years of power, Hamid Karzai, the man hand-picked by the Americans to run the country, had been relatively forward-thinking with regard to human rights and gender equality. He was in close dialogue with Sima Samar, the doctor who became the country's first minister of women's affairs and later headed up the Afghanistan Independent Human Rights Commission. Then he began to exercise more caution. Among Western leaders he could still talk openly, but among his own people he was more low-key. None of the four female ministers he had appointed had any real power; that was still the preserve of the men in government, provincial and district governors, warlords and tribal leaders. Karzai's administration favoured traditional power structures and there was clear nepotism and political manipulation.

Formal positions of power, like ministerial posts, became a way to access the aid streaming into the country. Corruption was widespread in the ever-growing state apparatus, sucking up resources intended for development. Aid money was financing gilded taps in Dubai, the arsenal of a governor or a drug baron's armoured Land Cruiser. The aristocratic Karzai was seen as weak for old power hierarchies; tribal leaders and warlords who made alliances and broke them, were at all times granted an audience.

Thus misrule developed in the presidential palace. Owing to his indulgence, Karzai was creating a mafia state, while the USA and the rest of the West stood by and watched, turning a blind eye to the fact *the good guys* had turned into *bad guys* and even *real nasty guys*.

When Jamila and Kakar married in 2006, one in five Afghan women, and about every second man, could read and write. The couple's goal was the education of the whole of society. Jamila contacted the minister of Hajj and religious affairs and enlisted his support in the development of a training programme for imams centred around women's rights from an Islamic perspective. It was to include the right to refuse a marriage. Should a woman wish to marry, she should receive a sum of money called *mahr* that would serve as her husband's investment in her. The money would be hers to support her independence, for example in the case of divorce, which Jamila believed was a right on the same level as education or participation in politics. She wrote a small handbook containing a modern interpretation of Islam that she thought appropriate for Afghanistan, and which she assumed would be acceptable to both society and the religious scholars.

Jamila and Kakar had, over time, visited hundreds of imams. First in Kabul and Jalalabad, later out in the provinces. Jamila asked them to meet up at the study circles she organised and made them promise to speak about women's rights during Friday prayer and distribute her handbook. She hired hundreds of students from Kabul University, instructed them in women's rights and paid them from a small kitty. The students were supposed to visit the mosques where Jamila and Kakar had been and listen to their Friday prayer. Then they were to report back.

Jamila had no hesitation about approaching the imams if the students had told her their message didn't measure up. Her 'spies' also returned with moving stories. One had found an old man crying in a corner of the mosque after a sermon. The old man had approached the imam to ask why he had never said all this before.

'What you now say is sinful are things I have done. I sold my daughters in marriage. I never asked their opinion on the choice of husbands. I never allowed them to get an education. If these things are sins, then how am I to be saved?'

A new society was in the making. Jamila stressed changing attitudes. Noor was involved in advocacy work against domestic violence, for gender equality and in getting more women into positions of power.

Gradually Jamila realised there was yet another thing preventing young women from taking higher education: sexual harassment. At school. At university. On the street. On the bus. At work. Within the family. It lay like a dense and heavy carpet over society.

Some Afghan lawyers attempted to criminalise harassment but were met with stiff opposition. Jamila tried to find partners within the Afghan Independent Human Rights Commission, but they were reluctant to confront Kabul University, where there were numerous cases. She wouldn't give up, and arranged for NECDO to develop guidelines for educational institutions that she hoped to present to the new legislators.

Instead of the harassers being convicted, the female complainants were the ones punished. If the finger was pointed at powerful men, their revenge could be severe. An entire family could face punishment for a woman's allegations and threatened with reprisals if she did not withdraw them.

According to Islam, a man could have four wives. This arrangement, Jamila argued, had been established for the sake of widows, so that – with the permission of the first wife – a widow could enter into a new family and receive shelter and security for herself and her children. But the rule was exploited and bent so that a man with enough money could keep on replenishing his conjugal bed with young women. It was important to educate female scholars so their perspective could be heard, and then slowly, step by step, change Afghanistan through reforms.

Where sex was concerned, it was taken for granted that married women obeyed their husbands. Whatever the husband wanted, his wife would comply. However, the further Jamila immersed herself in the Quran and pored over the teachings of the Prophet, she came to realise that sexual relations were not one-sided. The man wasn't supposed to have all the power; it was equal.

She brought this up with her female cousins when one of them was complaining that her husband was always demanding she satisfy him in this regard.

'You're not a sex slave, you have a right to say no,' Jamila said.

Her cousins looked at her in shock.

'No, that's wrong, my mother taught us to always obey . . . '

'Your mother is wrong!'

Jamila told them what she sometimes said to her own husband: 'I don't feel like it, I'm tired, now isn't a good time.' He accepted it, as well he should.

'It's our right!'

Her cousins looked at her in disbelief. Jamila was revolutionary on many fronts, but this . . .

First She Fell for His Voice

'Why doesn't that guy get married?'

Mullah Dadullah was pointing at Bashir, who had finally grown a beard. It was a warm night, and a group of men were sitting on the veranda in Miram Shah. Dadullah was the senior military leader of the Taliban, the most powerful commander in all Afghanistan. He looked at Bashir from under thick, straight brows.

The forty-year-old had many nicknames: *the lame one*, due to the loss of a leg in battle; *the butcher*, because he was known for decapitating men. Mullah Omar had once stripped Dadullah of his command owing to extreme behaviour, but now he was needed again. You didn't beat NATO with a light touch. 'Either take the area or don't come back,' was his message when sending men out to fight.

Dadullah had a knack for quelling discord, and that was the reason he was in Waziristan, where there had of late been open conflict and blood feuds among the fighters. Moreover, he had a way with Pakistanis, and had recruited many by appealing to the notion of a common enemy and a shared future.

The other men sitting there turned their gaze from Dadullah – who even when joking looked scary – to Qalam. This was a touchy subject. Bashir had been appointed Qalam's second-in-command after a big battle in Khost Province, where he had distinguished himself with great daring and several direct hits. He had become adept at reading the course of an attack and at predicting the enemy's response.

'From now on you travel in my car,' Qalam had said after the battle. Bashir had basked in the commander's attention.

Then Qalam had demonstrated a desire to bring the nineteen-year-old even closer. He had several daughters and offered Bashir his choice of them. To offer one's daughters in marriage was not common; it was up to the suitor to ask, or in fact his mother. On top of everything, Bashir had declined.

This was beyond awkward. For the first time, the teenager hadn't done what Qalam wanted. The commander had been upset, then offended. His suggestion had been so personal. He had asked to be Bashir's father-in-law and had been rebuffed. By a fatherless boy. Word of it leaked out.

The men on the veranda held their breath. At length, one man broke the silence. He was right below Dadullah in rank.

'He just doesn't want to.'

'It's time,' Dadullah said. 'No one knows how long his life will last.'

Bashir nodded. As you did when Mullah Dadullah spoke to you.

Bashir only wanted to fight. He wanted to win, just one more time, he wanted to kill, just a little more, record another direct hit, shoot one more bullet. Be free.

Women were complex and expensive. A bride, even in the middle of the war, when human life was so cheap, cost more than a Kalashnikov. When the war was over, then he would take a wife, and not just one.

For the time being he wanted nothing more than to sit listening to the older commanders. To Sirajuddin, who called the shots in the east, Dadullah, who was in charge in the south, to Qalam and Baitullah, competing for control of Waziristan, knowing that these, the strongest among men, took an interest in him.

The Taliban had been fighting the Afghan government for five years. The pockets of resistance increased, but the Taliban still lacked an overall military strategy. In some regions they stood strong, in others they were barely more than makeshift militias. The goal was to put a structure of commanders and deputies in place, before forming a shadow emirate with a governor in every province.

Bashir fought on both sides of the border under Qalam's command. Qalam had taught him how to defeat an enemy who outnumbered you, was stronger and better armed, as the foreigners always were.

'You must be so close to the enemy that you can feel him breathe,' Qalam said. 'Face to face, then you get him.'

They had to turn their weakness to their advantage. With fewer men and lighter weapons, speed was of the essence: quickly in, quickly out.

They remained close, despite the rejection. As for Qalam's daughters, several suitors waited for an answer. The daughter of a commander was highly prized. Engagements were made and Bashir was free. Their relationship was restored to stability, he as subordinate, Qalam as boss.

One day the two of them were invited to the home of one of the younger commanders. Hamid was of solid mujahideen stock. His father, both a mullah and a fighter, had established a base in Pakistan during the war with the Soviets.

Now the women of the house had been instructed to prepare a good meal for the renowned *Qumandan* Qalam.

Hamid's little sister ran up the stairs as soon as she heard the men in the yard. She disappeared into a small room where she was hidden not only from the guests outside but also from her mother. Looking upon strange men was not allowed. She was fourteen, and no longer left the house, but she had heard of Qalam. Her father's stories about him reminded her of the heroic legends of Mahmud of Ghazni, the eleventh-century conqueror, back when her family's home town had been almost as important as Baghdad.

Now Qalam was here, walking around in her backyard.

She herself was standing behind a door.

She didn't dare go over to the window. They might see her. Oh, how she longed to just catch a glimpse of such a famous man!

She heard the men enter the visitors' room downstairs. At the same time, sounds leaked out from the kitchen, where her mother and sisters were brewing tea with cardamom seeds; guests were to be served a glass as soon as they arrived. Her brother carried the tray in. She heard laughter and had an idea. The visitors' room was on the ground floor. She could slip down the stairs, sneak out to the backyard, walk around the house and then, if her mother was busy in the kitchen and the coast was clear, she could tiptoe over to the window.

From the back door she looked around the yard. It was empty. She took a few steps outside. Gradually she drew closer to the visitors' room. She stopped by the window. The curtains were drawn, not the slightest chink could be seen.

A voice, deep and rasping — that had to be the commander. Judging by what he was saying, he was the boss. She heard her father say something and her brother answer. Then a soft trill of laughter. Who was that? The laughter drowned out a few words. A fresh outburst of laughter, turning into a warm voice floating on the air. The voice was confident. Rapid. Young. Whoever's voice it was, it sounded happy.

That was it. The fourteen-year-old was smitten.

There was a knock on the gate and she darted back inside. She hurried up the stairs, made it to the room, gasping from the exertion. Her breathing calmed down but she could not. A new feeling had penetrated her chest.

With a man like that, it sang through her head, I could be happy.

* * *

Sirajuddin Haqqani was wrestling with an ambitious plan. He wanted to capture Forward Operating Base Tillman.

The American base was in Paktika Province, on a plateau above the village of Lowara, a few kilometres from the Pakistani border. The attack was planned for the next full moon and Qalam was put in charge of it.

Usually, they operated in groups of four. If it was a larger assault eight men would be assembled. This was something else entirely: twenty or so commanders along with their men needed to get ready.

Qalam's group headed towards the border twelve days before, to reconnoitre.

On the way they ran into some soldiers from the Pakistani army. It was obvious that Qalam's men were Taliban, but the Pakistanis just said it was up to them if they wanted to cross into Afghanistan. However, they wouldn't be allowed return the same way.

'Why not?' Bashir asked.

'There're reports of a possible attack on FOB Tillman, so we have orders to close the border,' one of the soldiers answered.

Had word leaked about the planned assault? Had someone informed? Had they travelled in much too large a group?

The next day they continued towards the base. Qalam wanted to put out observers. It was important to stay out of sight because the Americans would shoot at anything that moved; there was no reason for anyone to approach this outpost unless their intentions were hostile. The area was barren; only some hardy bushes grew in the sandy soil. Not even goats grazed there.

Through binoculars, they could see that the first obstacle was rolls of razor wire. After this lay level ground, then high walls with sandbags along them.

On returning to camp, they gathered to talk. Qalam decided they should lie low and split into smaller groups. The weather was warm, they could establish several camps and stay close to the border until the night of the attack. The next day was for rest. They would gather their strength before carrying out further reconnaissance and waiting for reinforcements.

The full moon was ten nights away.

At dawn on the third morning, Qalam returned to observe the base. Through his binoculars he saw one of his own. A relative, inside the base with the Americans! He hated Afghans who had enlisted in the government army even more than the infidels themselves.

He was furious. This could not stand. He felt an urge to attack while the traitor was still in there.

Bashir was awoken by a comrade with orders from Qalam to get ready. He rubbed the sleep from his eyes, wondering what could be so urgent. There were still several nights until full moon.

'Orders from Qalam,' his comrade repeated.

What was going on? Had Sirajuddin changed the plan?

Bashir counted the men who had arrived in Lowara. Thirty-four in total. They had been told that there were several hundred government troops and just as many Americans soldiers at FOB Tillman. He argued they should wait for reinforcements and stick to the plan.

'Are you scared?' his comrade asked.

'No, but this is madness.'

'Do you fear the infidels?'

That was all needed to be said.

'Okay. Let's go,' Bashir replied.

He spoke to Qalam over the walkie-talkie to confirm the meeting point. Usually Bashir went ahead to survey the area and the enemy's routines prior to an attack. This time Qalam himself had gone to scout the conditions. Perhaps he wanted to go through plans for how they would muster and from where they would attack.

It was dark when they arrived within view of the base, and small groups were deployed so that the attack could be carried out on several fronts. Four men here. Five there. Another three a little further off. There were two observation towers on the base, Qalam told them, one high, one somewhat lower. He continued to station men at different locations; eventually eight were left with him.

They ought to have at least twenty men attacking each of the observation towers, Bashir thought. Qalam had become a great commander due to his daring, but this was foolhardy.

He looked at the commander. There were times they readied themselves but acknowledged the odds were too overwhelming. Withdrawal also required bravery.

'You stay here with the others,' Qalam told Bashir. He wanted to take a couple of men and try to get closer to the base without being discovered, to see if they could launch an assault on the lower observation post. Commanders often stayed in the background in order to have an overview, but this time Qalam wanted to go first.

'I can take the lead and cover the area,' Bashir suggested.

'Stay here!' the thin old man hissed. Bashir looked at his mentor. What had got into him?

Qalam began the approach with two men. They needed to be careful: there were usually landmines planted around the bases.

When they reached the razor wire they stopped. Qalam sat down on the ground to pray. He prayed eight *rakat*, getting to his knees and standing back up before kneeling again eight times in succession.

When the prayer was finished, Bashir contacted him over the walkie-talkie.

'Will I start the attack or will you?'

'Maybe the Americans will,' Qalam answered.

They stood in silence. No one knew what to do. Not a sound could be heard from the base. They could see the weapons systems, the lines of defence, the concrete walls and floodlights.

'Forgive me,' Qalam said. He had been quiet for so long that Bashir thought they had lost communication. 'Please forgive me.'

'For what?'

'Take the men back,' the commander ordered. 'We're calling it off.'

Bashir confirmed the order. He yawned. Now he just wanted to get back to camp and get some sleep. They trudged away.

Behind them Qalam remained standing with two men.

Then he walked towards the base.

Bashir awoke with a start to the sound of heavy machine-gun fire. It was coming from Tillman, he was sure of that. He grabbed the walkie-talkie to try and contact Qalam. No response. He tried again, and again.

Finally he got an answer.

'Qalam is hit!'

Had he gone in?

They hurried towards the base. When Bashir arrived he saw one of the fighters dragging Qalam through the fence.

A drone was approaching. Bashir managed to glance up before it slipped its payload. They were blown in different directions, left lying behind rocks, under trees, on the hillside.

Bashir was uninjured and ran over to Qalam. The commander was red hot, as though he were burning inside. Blood was running from several wounds in his chest.

A new drone approached. Bashir sought cover. Soon there would be yet another drone, then perhaps rockets. They were an easy target, too easy.

'We can't leave our commander here,' Bashir said, trying to drag him. But, lying halfway across the razor wire, he was too heavy to get loose.

'Let's cut his head off,' Bashir proposed. 'And take it with us. It's the head the Americans want.'

Qalam's head, a trophy for the Americans, he thought. One of the most important commanders in the region. Everything Bashir had learned about war he had learned from him. *You must be so close to the enemy that you can feel him breathe. Face to face, then you take him.*

A helicopter appeared.

'We don't have time!' the man next to him shouted.

Bashir quickly decided to leave Qalam and save himself. They ran, weapons over their shoulders.

Bashir sprinted so hard he could taste blood in his mouth. A thought came to him from out of the blue: 'I want to be a martyr too! May Allah take me!'

Yet he continued to run. His heart was pounding, his blood was pumping. It was as though his body knew it had to save itself while his mind longed for peace.

In a grove of trees, he collapsed by a spring. He and the others looked at one another: they were covered in blood, sand and soil. It all smeared together now as they drank and cooled themselves off with the spring water. Several men were missing. They needed to warn the others.

The petrol station at the market in Lowara had a satellite phone that Bashir often borrowed. When they arrived at the bazaar, he tapped in the numbers.

What had come over Qalam?

Hubris?

A yearning for God?

With Qalam's blood on his clothes, while the commander himself still lay in the desert sand, he was put through to Sirajuddin. Bashir told him he had a joyous message to convey.

God had accepted a martyr.

'Face to face. That was how he was killed.'

Qalam should have been buried by the end of the night, but the Americans had him. Usually they let Taliban bodies lie where they were hit to be collected by their own. But they took Qalam's corpse inside. They knew who he was. Like Bashir had said: a trophy. He had been a thorn in their side for a long time and now he was placed in cold storage within the base.

The blood darkened on his skin, congealed in his hair, stiffened his beard. The way he was killed was the way he was to meet God.

The attack had diplomatic repercussions. Not long after Bashir had called Sirajuddin, Lowara bazaar was surrounded by a detachment of soldiers from the Pakistani army.

'Put down your weapons! Surrender yourselves!'

Bashir's men refused.

The local army were in a pinch. It was obvious to the Americans that the Pakistanis must have known that the Taliban had been planning an assault. The Tillman base had complained to Islamabad on previous occasions about Pakistani soldiers who, instead of dealing with the Taliban, facilitated their attacks by allowing their fighters to operate freely. The Americans demanded Qalam's group be arrested, but the army were reluctant to attack a dozen heavily armed Taliban at a busy market.

Later in the day, members of the people's council in Waziristan arrived to mediate, mullahs and imams among them. A general landed in a helicopter to speak to Qalam's second-in-command. Bashir refused. He assumed it was a trap and that he would be flown to Islamabad and imprisoned.

In the end a member of the village council in Lowara made a suggestion.

'We'll give you twelve of our men in exchange for the fighters. They walk free, you take us.'

One by one local men stepped forward. A deal was struck. The villagers who volunteered were flown to Islamabad to show the Americans that the authorities were serious about punishing the perpetrators.

After which they were released. The situation was resolved and the war could continue.

Some time before, Qalam had recorded a video. This was now delivered to Sirajuddin. In it, the commander announced who he wished to be his successor. The cycle of fighters had to live on.

In the video he praised God, greeted the leaders and his fellow fighters, and nominated his successor – the one who would assume command of his two hundred men. In his address he said he had found the right man, one who was audacious, strong and capable.

'He is a fighter I have great belief in. May God lead him to victory.'

The youngest of them all.

Bashir *the Afghan*.

It was a tough inheritance. It coincided with the Taliban putting an improved and better organised military leadership in place. The structure was stricter and more hierarchical. There would be less leeway for rebellious commanders like Qalam.

The Haqqani Network now operated a parallel administration in Miram Shah that included courts, recruiting centres, tax offices and security forces. They lived on donations from the Gulf states and other Arab lands, as well as from kidnapping ransoms and taxation. Contractors in the area had to pay up to half of their incomes in protection money to be allowed to operate.

The new military strategy led to the Taliban, from 2007 onward, being able to carry out complex attacks on a larger scale. Roadside bombs, followed by swift ambushes and martyr operations would form a central part of this new strategy.

Nobody had recruited more men for martyr operations than Sirajuddin Haqqani and Mullah Dadullah, the man who had advised Bashir to get married because, as he told him, you never knew when it would be too late.

As it turned out, he was the one who went first. Before the summer was over, British NATO forces finally caught up with the Taliban's supreme military leader, the man responsible for the purge against the Hazaras and for ordering the destruction of the country's cultural heritage, the enormous buddhas in Bamyan. His body was to be delivered to the Taliban in exchange for five health workers. In the end it was four — the fifth was beheaded because Dadullah's corpse, with two bullet holes in the chest and one in the back of the head, was not returned swiftly enough.

Even in death he was brutal.

* * *

Bashir turned twenty and was consumed with desire for a woman.

He was engaged to his cousin, who he had grown up with in the muddy backyard at home in Mussahi, but she was not what he was after. He wanted a woman here and now, and he wanted to choose her himself.

It was quite a predicament because there weren't any young women in sight.

That was the reason mothers and sisters were endlessly going on their visits, to take a closer look at prospective brides, to make their recommendations. Bashir couldn't go to his mother; she had Yasamin waiting. He couldn't ask his sisters-in-law; they would be loyal to his mother.

He had to ask a man.

One of his closest companions was Baitullah Mehsud, a rising star in the tribal areas.

'I'll take care of it,' the young commander promised.

It didn't take long before he had tracked down a prospective bride.

'She's learnt the Quran off by heart,' Baitullah told him. Her father had taught her both Pashto and Dari. An astute and clever girl, he had been informed. But also well-mannered and docile.

She was the sister of Hamid, one of his soldiers.

Bashir liked the idea. Marrying the sister of a subordinate was better than the daughter of the boss, as Qalam had suggested. Moreover, he had already met the girl's father: he recalled visiting the home of the learned man a year earlier and had liked him straight away. That mattered – actually it mattered most – because when you got married it wasn't the girl herself that was the determining factor, it was the family.

But how was he to convey the proposal without women?

He would have to ponder that. While doing so, he was almost killed.

His group was under heavy attack from Afghan government forces with air support from NATO. Bashir got separated from the others and had to take cover in a rock crevice. Rockets exploded around him with an intensity he had never experienced. The crevice was showered with stones and gravel. This was it. His life.

When the attack finally subsided and he was making his way down the mountain, the first person he met was Hamid. Bashir saw it as a sign. Like Mullah Dadullah had said, *It's time. You don't know how long you'll live.*

That same night he told Baitullah, 'Propose!'

Galai had been born on the same day as Professor Rabbani was appointed president, in June 1992, just prior to the outbreak of civil war. Her family had fled to Peshawar during the Soviet invasion and her father had fought with the mujahideen. For him, Islam came first and he had taken responsibility for his children's education himself. But it had been impossible to hammer knowledge into his youngest daughter. While her sisters had memorised the Quran, she drew a blank. She was the last child, used to being coddled and fussed over. Aged four, when she was to learn the Arab alphabet, she refused. Her parents decided to send her to boarding school, where the discipline was stricter.

The madrasa was behind high walls. No men were allowed access. There were several dormitories, with about twenty girls in each. Thin mattresses were laid out on the floor at night and placed along the wall during the day. There they sat, their books on cushions in front of them. First they would learn the alphabet, then the Quran itself.

Galai cried all the time. She was caned across the knuckles, the bottom and the back. The body needed to be softened and tempered for the head to be prepared for the word of God. It just made her sob even more.

Her mother eventually took her out. Galai was only bringing shame on them.

So she was allowed to play a little longer. Back home again with the family, she spent most of her time with the boys. They were more fun, got up to more antics. Mostly they played with stones, large and small, competing to balance pebbles on their knuckles, throwing them, using larger ones as targets. They drew up territories on the ground and vied for land. They made obstacle courses and raced to make it over the fastest.

Happiness was short-lived, however.

Upon turning eight, she was no longer allowed play with the boys, not even allowed to talk to them. If she wanted to play, she had to make do with the girls. Within the walls of the yard.

Galai looked around her, wished time would stop. She didn't want to get older. She didn't want to grow up. There was so much sadness in adult life.

Her father had begun reading with her at home. She slowly began opening the door to learning. She liked the stories about the Prophet, about how the Quran was revealed to him, about the battles, how Islam spread. Her father taught her about the wives of Muhammad, about the first, Khadija, who was also the first Muslim, and who Muhammad confided in. Galai thought it odd that Khadija was so much older than him. That wasn't how it was supposed to be. A wife should be younger, shouldn't she? Galai had never heard of a wife being older than her husband. Furthermore, Khadija was a businesswoman, which was also strange, and had so much money, while he had nothing when they met. She couldn't imagine it, a woman being a shopkeeper.

The first offer of marriage came before she was thirteen. Her mother said no without asking Galai. Best not to ask. Her mother refused everyone who came.

'She's my youngest, I'll only let her go when I'm a good old age. Until then she'll stay here with me,' she would say.

The many offers of marriage were due to her father. Galai was a good match because of his high status. He had constant visits from fighters, and fighters had brothers, sons and cousins. Then their mothers would come, their sisters. It was never-ending, because such visits could not be declined. But the no remained a no.

A faint echo of the voice she had heard, floating out the window that spring day the year before, sounded now and then from her brother's phone.

She found out the voice belonged to someone by the name of Bashir. He would be coming to visit one day soon. She asked her brother if she could hide behind the curtains by the window upstairs, just to see.

'Please!'

'No! It could put bad thoughts in your head!'

She knew exactly what he meant.

Nevertheless, Galai stood behind the curtain. And saw.

There was a face to go with the name, a smile to go with the laughter.

Just a few days later her brother got a visit from Baitullah in Miram Shah.

'Your father is a good man. You only have one sister left. We're looking for a wife for our brother Bashir.'

Galai and his mother were sitting sewing when Hamid came home. When her brother was going to bring the matter up, Galai was sent out. With head bowed, she left the room. As was expected. Modesty was a Pashtun girl's foremost virtue.

She eavesdropped from behind the door.

Her mother said no.

It was out of the question.

When her mother heard that Bashir was already engaged back home it served to strengthen her resolve. What manner of contrivance was this? Yes, a man could have four wives, but he had to marry in the order the engagements were made. There was no way she would give her youngest daughter away to a man who didn't respect that.

Then Bashir's sister-in-law Sima, Raouf's wife, came to visit. She had been persuaded to go, without Hala's knowledge. She sang Bashir's praises. Extolled his qualities.

'I think we should ask Galai herself,' Hamid eventually said to his mother.

She could not argue with the suggestion.

Hamid went up to his sister's room. She knew what answer was expected of her.

'No . . . ' she whispered.

Inside she was shouting yes.

'Are you sure?' he asked.

'Yes.'

She sat, turning it over in her mind after he had gone back downstairs. Had she just let that man, that cheerful voice, that all-enveloping laughter, that life she dreamed about, pass her by?

Then she heard footsteps. Her brother came back in.

'I'll give you a piece of advice,' he said. 'Take him. There's no better man to be found.'

'Yes,' Galai whispered. 'I will.'

Her mother did everything she could to thwart the marriage. 'You'll be wife number two!' she warned. No matter what, the woman who was engaged first ranked higher, and there was no doubt Bashir would wed her too. Breaking off a lifelong engagement was not an option.

Galai's mother spoke from experience. Her own father had had five wives during his life; there had been arguments and disagreements from the day the second wife came into the house, and it only got worse with each new one. That wasn't the kind of life she wished on her youngest child.

'Don't marry him!' her sisters chimed in.

'You'll suffer!' her brothers' wives said.

'I'll never forgive you for this,' her mother hissed to Hamid. She viewed him as the instigator of it all.

There was a lot at stake, because they also knew that when a girl accepted a marriage proposal there was nothing her mother or her sisters-in-law could do.

Galai had made up her mind. She wanted him. She had known it from the first time she heard his voice.

Hamid called a family meeting and announced his sister's final decision. Her mother's last possible course of action was to set the bride price so high that Bashir wouldn't be able to afford it. It was set at a million afghani.

'We accept,' Bashir's relative answered.

A 'what?' escaped Galai's mother's lips.

The only person as opposed to the marriage was Hala. She berated her youngest son for having gone and found a bride himself. What was she going to say to her brother? To the others in the village? They would be held up to ridicule.

The negotiations continued. Galai's mother tried to make demands that would be impossible for Bashir to accept. His brother nodded his assent to everything until eventually she couldn't think of anything more. When the price was confirmed and Raouf was due to bring the money, it was far more than Galai's mother felt she could accept.

'Half the amount is fine,' she said.

When Bashir delivered half a million afghani, she gave a hundred thousand back.

'You'll need it for jihad,' she told him.

A date for the wedding was set.

Now finally engaged, Bashir and Galai could meet for the first time.

It was as if they belonged together. Both were sturdy, with strong arms and wide necks. Bashir had developed powerful shoulders from all the carrying; his chest was broad. Galai had wide hips and a soft stomach. They had round cheeks and, most importantly, mouths given easily to laughter.

* * *

Far away, at home in Mussahi, the evening meal had just been laid out: bread soaked in stock and bowls of yoghurt. Yasamin was sitting with her parents and siblings around a sheet on the floor. She was now sixteen, and no longer embarrassed but proud of being engaged to a great *qumandan*.

Her brother's phone rang.

She heard the voice on the other end and knew it was Bashir. He always rang her brothers, never her.

She could tell by her brother's face that something was wrong.

He hung up and told them.

A fifteen-year-old on the other side of the border had taken her place. The war made new rules for everything.

Winning Some Hearts

They were huge, the men who came strutting through the school gate. Ariana, a pale girl of slight build, had never seen men so tall. The soldiers looked around with friendly faces. They nodded to everyone and shook hands with the headmaster. Standing among the youngest pupils Ariana could see that those who held out a hand had it squeezed firmly.

Her mother, a geography teacher at the school, had been notified of the visit the day before. They had set out tables with juice and cakes for the guests, who politely declined the refreshments offered.

There were some women among the men, all wearing identical uniforms, of camouflage material in a mix of desert shades. The trousers were baggy around the thighs, with deep pockets on the sides. Very different from her father's uniform, the one he put on every day to go to work at the Ministry of Defence. That had straight legs with a crease, and the jacket was slim.

Some of the women had caps, others were bareheaded. One had straight blonde hair parted at the side, swept back and gathered in a bun on top. Others had their hair closely cropped, like little girls, while another had unruly dark curls gathered in a ponytail that danced on her back. They squatted down to talk to the children, who responded with some words in English. *Hello Mister! Hello Miss!*

A soldier covered his face with his hands before suddenly revealing it, as if they were toddlers. Peekaboo!

It was so strange for big men to play like this. She mimicked them. Peekaboo! They played tag and the children were thrown in the air by the sturdy soldiers. One had a child hanging from each arm; another let them climb up on his back.

The soldiers pulled something from their pockets. Suddenly they were wearing red noses and clowning around. The children squealed. The teachers laughed.

Some large cardboard boxes were put down in the middle of the schoolyard, forming an intriguing pile. The children flocked around as a soldier pulled a rag doll out, then another, then one more. All the girls got one each; the boys were given balls and cars. In other boxes, there were backpacks, with books and pens inside. The teachers also received gifts. Ariana looked over at her mother, holding some notebooks in her hand. Ariana peered down at the doll. It had a blue dress, brown hair, big, adorable eyes and reminded her of a character in a cartoon she had seen on TV.

Throughout Afghanistan, NATO forces launched different projects aimed at improving the lives of the people. They built roads and bridges, cleared mines, planted trees, dispatched agricultural experts to help farmers, renovated irrigation systems, constructed hospitals and clinics and – not least – filled schools with books, desks, chairs, blackboards and chalk.

The school visits were classic elements of *winning hearts and minds*, a strategy designed to get the population's support. People would not be won over by violence – no, their hearts needed melting, their minds needed liberating.

A book here, a doll there. To girls like Ariana, the American soldiers were superheroes. People grew accustomed to NATO forces in the streets, and many thought they brought a sense of security. In most areas of Kabul, and in other bigger cities, the inhabitants welcomed the foreigners and their resources.

Ariana's mother was one of them. Nadia had just finished her teacher training when the civil war broke out. Her dream of further study was shattered when she was hurriedly married off to a cousin.

That was the safest option while mujahideen roamed the streets abducting young women, her parents thought. There was fear in the air after several young women had been raped and killed; families tightened their grip.

Nadia hadn't put her teaching qualifications to use until after the fall of the Taliban. Ariana was born at the turn of the millennium and the only Kabul she knew was a city where blond soldiers patrolled the streets, entered the schoolyard and smiled.

For as long as she could remember, Ariana had been going to work with her mother. She sat quietly in the classroom; she drew, followed what was happening on the blackboard, then napped. Sometimes she played outside.

Children started school aged seven, but her mother figured that since Ariana was already there, they may as well enrol her at five. Nadia added two years to her daughter's age when she went to get her an ID card and *voilà*, Ariana was no longer born at the turn of the millennium but two years earlier.

Thus, she was the smallest in the class.

Finally, she could dress like a schoolgirl in a black dress with a white shawl, white socks and black shoes. And she loved the pens and the books. She copied the beautiful characters the teacher wrote on the board as neatly as she could.

A new world had opened up.

At the same time as Ariana was starting school, the Taliban were launching their campaign against state-run education. As more children were enrolled in schools and NATO forces handed out exercise books, the Taliban embarked on a huge effort to sabotage any teaching apart from Quran studies. Children didn't need anything other than the word of God.

The Taliban established their own education commission, which drafted rules for its field commanders. They were instructed to attack schools teaching the new government's syllabus, and where boys and girls shared classrooms. In autumn 2006, the Taliban's *layeha* – ethical guidelines – were issued regarding when an attack on a school could be authorised. The rules were numerous. First, a warning had to be issued. After that, the headmaster and teachers could be subject to physical attack if they did not comply with the demands. Rule 24 forbade anyone to work as a teacher 'under the present puppet regime as it strengthens the infidels' system'. Rule 25 stated that those who chose to ignore the warnings would be killed and the school burned down. The next rule emphasised that all religious books had to be removed before setting the fire. Schoolbooks printed after the Taliban lost power were banned.

The rules were signed by Mullah Omar, the Supreme Leader of the Islamic Emirate of Afghanistan – a leader on the run.

The year Ariana played peekaboo with the soldiers in clown noses, around two hundred schools were torched by the Taliban.

Ariana's mother was taking a degree in geography. It was her father who had insisted she specialised in one field.

'Now all options are open,' the old man said. 'Why settle for being a common teacher when you can be something more? The foreigners value education, so should Afghans!'

Ariana knew that if her mother got her degree, she could be the head of the school. That would suit her. Nadia was as strict as she was stylish. She always had her hair neatly up, with a loose shawl just covering it, when she was going to the university. Dark eye make-up lent her a mysterious gaze, Ariana thought, while her skin was lightened by foundation. No one was to notice she was several years older than the other undergraduates. Now she was to get back what the Taliban had taken from her.

The family lived in a small ground-floor apartment. When the school day was over, and her mother had taken her home and then left for university, Ariana wasn't allowed out in the backyard because the neighbours upstairs, who owned the building, didn't like children making noise. From the window, Ariana would watch how the vine outside grew throughout the school year. First sprouting small bright green leaves, then clusters of tiny berries formed. Eventually they covered the entire window, just when most shade was needed.

Ariana sat behind the vine feeling sorry for herself, until she began copying letters and forming words.

After a couple of hours her brother would come home. Then they would lie on the mattresses in the living room and switch on the TV. Their favourite show was *Tom and Jerry*, other times she saw her doll on the screen, or one resembling it. Often, they fell asleep and lay there until their parents came home.

'This was the best school day ever!' Ariana exclaimed the day the Americans had come to her school. Nadia nodded. The stationery was of much better quality than what they could buy in Kabul.

Ariana looked down at the notebook. It had a black spine and a grey hard, marbled cover. *Composition book 100 pages*, it said on a white square. She decided to write about her life in it. Starting with the best day ever.

The Surge

Three months after getting married, Bashir rang from Waziristan. He wanted to get married again. This time to Yasamin.

Things moved quickly. Three days after the phone conversation, her brother left to meet Bashir in Miram Shah. They made a deal and her brother collected a bride price of two hundred thousand afghani, half of the amount Galai's family had received in *walwar*, but then again Bashir and Yasamin were cousins.

'What kind of clothes does she want?' Bashir asked and gave him more money.

Her brother bought a red dress and arranged a wedding feast in Mussahi, which would be held without the bridegroom present. The bride would be celebrated by the women in the village, the groom by the jihadis in Waziristan.

Yasamin was prepared according to tradition. The women in the family washed her, removed all her body hair and decorated her hands and arms with swirling patterns in henna. Thick white cream was rubbed onto her face and powder applied. Her eyebrows were outlined in half ovals. Her lips coloured deep red. Eye make-up covered her eyelids; her lashes were blackened and her cheeks sprinkled with golden glitter. In the end her face was as stiff as a doll's. She wasn't going to be smiling anyway. A bride was supposed to be sad, her eyes vacant, out of respect for the family she was leaving.

Two days later, Yasamin was taken to Waziristan. Her brother, sister and brother-in-law accompanied her on the journey. They departed early, before *fajr* – the morning prayer – in a car, like normal people. If they were stopped at a roadblock by government forces, they were going to say they were on their way to Jalalabad. There they were to change cars before crossing the border.

The vehicle wound its way down towards Jalalabad, with steep mountains on one side and a sheer drop on the other. Her brother's phone rang. It was Bashir. He wouldn't be there when they arrived, he told him, he had to go on a foray.

Jihad came first.

Thus Yasamin, the proper first wife, would not be welcomed by her soon-to-be husband but by the girl who had beat her to it. She was to move into the house alone, that is to say together with, or rather left with, the other wife.

She sat on the back seat of the car, wrapped in a pale blue burka, as she was always dressed outside the house. No one could tell what she thought of the change of plan. Nor did she say anything. Yasamin had never made her own life choices. Every decision had been taken for her – the engagement when she was one year old, her lack of education, her marriage. She had never bought her own clothes, tried on new shoes or chosen anything else she might need. She was neither to look around nor to be seen.

Nor had Yasamin chosen the life she was on her way to, as a second wife. Docile by nature, she followed the path laid out by others, did as she was told and never tried to alter her fate.

The fact the Taliban had lost power and the new government were encouraging women to stop wearing the burka made no difference to her. Women in her family had always covered up. They had never attended school or worked outside the home. They weren't influenced by the Taliban, they *were* Taliban.

Though she gave no sign of it, she was nervous about the other woman. What was she like?

Her father worshipped Bashir. He had showered his nephew with love and admiration his entire life. Upon learning of Bashir's first wedding, he had assured himself and the others that everything would be fine, it was Bashir's choice and they just had to accept it. Bashir was an important commander now, of course he should have several wives, the order didn't matter.

The road was steep. Mussahi lay eighteen hundred metres above sea level and Yasamin had never seen anything other than the arid plains around the village. As they descended, the landscape shifted from barren mountain to green fields. She was fascinated by the lush countryside on the drive down to Jalalabad, known for the best fruit in the country.

They crossed the border as normal people. Her brother, who had already been to Waziristan to collect the bridal money, knew the road. They drove upwards again, into dense forest, through several villages, past roadblocks, up into the mountains, towards Miram Shah.

The car stopped in front of a gate. The courtyard was surrounded by high mud walls. Her sister-in-law Sima came to meet them and embraced Yasamin.

Next to her a figure stood dressed in a burka.

'This is Galai,' Sima said, pointing at the figure.

The two girls were standing opposite one another. They were the same height. Two meshes of blue thread obstructed their view. They peered past the woven threads. Behind the blue netting, they could make out each other's eyes.

Galai appeared strong, Yasamin thought. All that protruded from the burka were her hands. They were broad, suntanned, the hands of a peasant woman.

Galai thought Yasamin looked sickly. Her eye sockets were dark behind the mesh.

The two wives were led to the women's part of the house. They hung their burkas up on pegs.

Yasamin stole a glance at Galai. She was surprised upon glimpsing her eyes. They were sad, deeply sad. She's upset about me, she realised, something she hadn't thought of. That Galai was as troubled by her existence as Yasamin was by hers.

She felt a pang of tenderness. As though an invisible bond had arisen between them.

The wedding feast was held the following night. The date was set and it should happen at the appointed time, whether the groom was there or not.

Once again Yasamin had make-up applied, was dressed up and sat in a chair. Her painted face was stiff, motionless. Galai, meanwhile, danced and swayed through the night with the other women. She also had a new dress, in yellow tulle with gold embroidery. She had sewn it herself, in the hope of being the one who looked the best.

As soon as the wedding feast was underway, Galai had already forgotten her sadness. That was how she was. She faced whatever came her way, even if it was the most beautiful rival.

The next morning everyday life began. Together with Bashir's mother the two wives were to make food for the fighters.

Hala put them to work chopping onions and shaftal. She had them boil rice and prepare dough for the flatbreads. Bashir's mother impressed upon them the recipe for their cohabitation.

Two heads, four hands.

One thought: Bashir's happiness.

One goal: jihad.

* * *

There was one weapon Sirajuddin Haqqani realised early on that he would have to rely on to beat the Americans: the jihadists themselves. For that he needed the help of al-Qaeda. They were far more experienced in using people as living bombs and staged their first suicide attacks in Kabul in 2003, against German forces.

Haqqani called the young martyrs a gift from God. He saw to it they stayed motivated. The most well-known preacher was Qari Hussein; when he spoke it was as though something took hold of Bashir. Qari brought up the degrading and offensive treatment Muslims were subjected to, the occupation of their countries, how foreign soldiers did as they pleased, broke into homes, with no respect for women, for the elderly. He talked about how Americans burned the Quran and trampled on it. It filled Allah with wrath!

When the fighters were also filled with fury, Qari Hussein turned around and offered them the solution: the ultimate sacrifice, their blood, which in turn triggered a great reward – glory after death. 'When you die, you don't die. Because you will live for ever. And the angels will bring you whatever you want!'

Bashir felt inspired, elevated. Right there and then he longed to be transformed into a living fireball with enormous explosive power – the golden gates of paradise would open as the abyss of hell opened up for the enemy. But that path wasn't for him. The jihadists were divided into two groups. You were either a fighter or a *fedayeen* – one who sacrificed himself. Bashir belonged to the first group.

As more and more fedayeen were recruited, Sirajuddin set up his own brigade under the leadership of his brother Badruddin.

The candidates at the martyr academy had separate tuition in the Quran. Care was taken to emphasise the reward awaiting them, in order to maintain their willingness to attack.

A lot of time was spent on technical matters, like how to store the vest, which would often have been made by women in Miram Shah, how to put it on without detonating the bomb, and finally how to trigger the mechanism and kill the largest number of infidels.

Their determination was most important. Their will must not falter. Pulling out at the last moment, when everything was ready, was the worst. A suicide bomber would be tortured to death to get him to reveal everything he knew, the young men were told.

The network operated with several couriers who transported suicide bombers from place to place. If anyone was caught, they only knew the last link.

Sometimes Bashir was a courier.

For a time he lived with the suicide bombers in Logar and was responsible for sending each one out. To get close to roadblocks, the young men were often disguised as policemen or soldiers. Scouts would be dispatched to observe the place they were targeting, familiarise themselves with the routines, find getaway routes and alert them to any security forces in the area.

Bashir had got hold of several uniforms and the plan was for a boy named Sharifullah, a thin, gangly lad, barely eighteen years old, to blow himself up on a bus carrying Afghan soldiers.

They helped him put on the explosives, dressed him in trousers, a shirt and jacket, and proper military boots instead of the sandals he usually wore. When everything was ready, they blessed him and all said a prayer. Sharifullah had already recorded his farewell on video.

He was driven to Kabul and let out near the stop where the bus would soon be pulling in. At a street corner a little way off, the scout who was to follow events – and ensure motivation was maintained – was then dropped off. Sharifullah was to be watched to the end.

As he made his way to the stop, only civilians were there. Buses pulled in, but the plan was to wait to detonate until he boarded the designated transport.

More and more people arrived. From his position at the street corner, the scout saw that they began to gather around Sharifullah. The boy looked unsure how to respond. The scout went closer to hear what was being said. One man pointed at Sharifullah's shoulder.

'So you're a general, are you?'

The scout suddenly realised what all the fuss was about. They had dressed the teenager up in a general's uniform to board a bus with ordinary soldiers. An Afghan general would never take the bus. He had his own car. What a mess. The driver was called, and before the situation got completely out of hand Sharifullah was picked up.

The martyrdom was cancelled for the day.

At dinnertime they got great amusement out of the story.

'How was I supposed to know what a general's uniform looks like?' Bashir said, roaring with laughter. 'A three-star traitor as opposed to, like, a five-star one!'

Sharifullah got to live for another night, for another month in fact. When an attack was called off, the candidate for martyrdom had to wait to be reselected.

*

In one of the houses in which Bashir had stayed with the suicide bombers, there lived a teenage boy named Farouk.

While they waited for the green light from the network, Farouk was the one who brought them food and served tea. As there was a lot of waiting, a lot of tea was consumed, and Farouk made sure their glasses were filled to the brim at all times. As soon as they were half empty he threw out the lukewarm tea and poured a fresh glass.

They had been a boisterous gang, the boys had been excited, and the tea boy had hung around them while they stayed at the house.

Farouk wanted to be like them. After Bashir had delivered the boys to another courier, Farouk followed him back to the base.

Farouk's mother messaged him to send the boy home. 'Persuade him!' she pleaded.

But Farouk had made up his mind to attain eternal life.

Bashir delivered him to the camp for further training; nothing was better than that. You couldn't obey your mother if you were to win a war.

In summer 2007, they prepared Farouk to be part of a suicide team at the funeral of Zahir Shah. At the last moment, the funeral was switched to the Arg, where the king once lived. The team had no chance of gaining access there.

Bashir was assigned other duties and didn't always have an overall picture of how things went with the boys he trained or where they would be deployed. But in early 2008 he heard that Farouk had carried out his mission. He had been chosen to take part in the attack on the Serena Hotel in Kabul, where seven people were killed.

Farouk had never made it into the hotel. He had been shot by security guards outside, but as he lay bleeding on the ground he managed to trigger the detonator in his vest and take a guard with him into death.

* * *

'It is unacceptable,' Barack Obama had said during the 2008 presidential campaign, 'that almost seven years after nearly three thousand Americans were killed on our soil, the terrorists who attacked us on 9/11 are still at large.'

Obama promised the army they would get what they needed to achieve their objectives in Afghanistan – the defeat of al-Qaeda and the Taliban – and he promised voters that he would pull out the troops during his term as president.

He wanted to increase the number of men and women under arms and intensify the attacks. In December 2009, just over a year after he won the election, a plan was presented. *The Surge* would bring about the end of the terrorists. Thirty thousand Americans would be sent to Afghanistan, bringing the total to one hundred thousand. In addition to, at its peak, thirty thousand soldiers from different NATO countries and their partners.

Announcing a date for withdrawal, two years in the future, was a strategic error. It gave the Taliban an incentive to hold out, something they were good at.

Even though the most important measure was to strengthen the military effort, Obama also proposed a *civilian surge*, and promised the Afghan government greater resources to shore up the administration. At the same time he stressed that the sending of blank cheques to Hamid Karzai was finished. Too many millions of dollars had disappeared to who knew where. The honeymoon between the USA and the Afghan president was definitely over.

The plan was to fracture the connection between the Taliban and al-Qaeda, train the Afghan army, stabilise the country – then pull the troops out. To achieve their goal they needed to knock out the insurgents' haven in Waziristan. Obama renewed commitments to a strategic partnership with Pakistan, so that the two countries would stand stronger in their fight against their common enemy. The USA was granted permission to attack targets on Pakistani territory. It didn't take long for the insurgents and the local population to notice the effect of this new policy.

The age of the drones had arrived.

A drone can fly, creep along the ground or move underwater. It can circle an area for hours, take a stream of photos and relay them back to the control station directing it. The remote-controlled craft can pick up signals from phones and follow the people carrying them. The information is sent to the drone operator and the analysts who, via screens on bases far away, systematically follow suspected insurgents. They can let the drone hang in the air until the time is right. Or they can wait until there are no civilians near the man they want to take out. Drivers, bodyguards and travelling companions are not considered civilians, as opposed to women and children or random passers-by. Drone operators and their superiors constantly have to make ethical assessments: how many victims is acceptable in order to kill one bad guy.

While Yasamin and Galai chopped spring onions and spinach and tried to become friends, nowhere on earth was subject to more drone strikes per square mile than Waziristan. The drone was supposed to be the scalpel in the American anti-terror operation Enduring Freedom, which had been running since 2001. The strikes were meant to be *surgical*; you only hit those you wanted to take out. F-16 aircraft could never be as precise. They were like blunt swords compared to the scalpel.

Incision by incision, the *bad guys* would be cut away.

The production of drones increased at the leading arms manufacturers in Virginia and California. Meanwhile, women in Waziristan made roadside bombs in their kitchens. What drones and roadside bombs had in common was that they were meant to carry no risk for the attacker. The drone operator could sit in a chair at Fort Bragg in North Carolina, staring at a monitor for hours and days before making the decision to strike. The one who planted the improvised explosive device could lie back on a hillside, waiting for the foreigners before triggering it.

Operation of an armed drone over a twenty-four-hour period required roughly two hundred employees. After work they could go to McDonald's or take the kids to football. No personnel lost. And while the Taliban needed ten men for an average attack with firearms, all that was needed to place a roadside bomb was a boy and a remote control.

Drones had become the Americans' cheapest and most lethal weapon, just as roadside bombs had for the Haqqani Network. They had striking names, such as *Predator* and *Reaper*. Likewise, the Taliban named their bombs, including *Jahannam*, meaning hell, or *Omari*, after Mullah Omar, the Taliban's first leader.

There were many different recipes for IEDs. The most common contained ammonium nitrate, an ingredient in fertiliser. The USA had implored Pakistan to cease the export of fertilisers with this chemical component to Afghanistan, and its sale was prohibited in the tribal areas. But the Americans didn't achieve anything other than the Afghans finding a cheaper and almost as effective chemical, potassium chlorate, which was used in clothes manufacturing and in the production of matches. Moreover, potassium chlorate – odourless, white crystals that only become explosive when mixed with petrol or engine oil – was far easier to transport across the border.

The women had everything they needed delivered to the kitchen by Hassan, the family chemist and bomb technician.

He mixed ammonium nitrate with sugar in large containers: one part sugar to twenty parts fertiliser. The women stood ready when Hassan asked for a spoon, a ladle or anything else he might need.

The bombmaking took place at night, when the children were asleep. During the day it was impossible to keep the toddlers away and the work required concentration. They needed to be very precise in their treatment of the ingredients and in measuring the amounts. The work was carried out in darkness in the backyard, with only a small lamp on the ground between them, or inside on the kitchen floor. There was a clear division of labour. Hassan and the wife they called the engineer were in charge of measuring. Yasamin, Galai, Sima and Hala were crushers. They liked the odourless potassium chlorate best. They each sat with a mortar in front of them, pulverising the crystals with hard, rhythmic strokes. When outside, they sat in fear of drones filming them. So they always had their shawls well pulled down over their foreheads. No drone operator in America would see their faces.

The ratio of powder to oil was important. Hassan or the engineer would weigh the powder on finely calibrated scales, stir in the petrol and make a mini bomb that Hassan would go out to test. If it exploded, they continued mixing at the same proportion in larger quantities.

Hassan downloaded videos, tested out new methods and experimented with different types of explosives.

It was important that the substance was properly dried, so it was left out in the sun for a few days. If the weather was cold and there was little sun, the buckets would remain on the flat roof for several more days.

Sometimes the women would mix in a brown powder. The smallest amount made the skin burn. Once, Galai had an open wound on her finger that came into contact with the powder: she had never experienced such intense pain. 'Now I know what they mean by salt in the wound!' she said afterwards.

After everything was mixed, the final part of the operation involved transferring the explosive to a yellow cooking oil container and attaching the fuse. This casing meant the bomb had no metal components, which would register on the Americans' detectors. Bombs like this were the cheapest. A small one cost around one thousand afghani, the same as one of the family's meals.

If it was a remote-controlled bomb, an electric fuse was inserted and connected to a nine-volt battery. The mechanism would then be attached to a simple mobile phone.

When the phone rang, the vibrations would set off the bomb.

The brothers would come and pick up the finished product. The women never asked where the bombs would be used. That was the responsibility of the men.

Even though the women liked working with potassium chlorate more than ammonium nitrate, there was a certain pleasure in pouring it out of the large bags smuggled into Waziristan. 'American fertiliser,' they laughed. 'Made in America!'

Now the Americans would get the contents back, neatly packaged in a yellow plastic container.

* * *

Yasamin become pregnant first.

And was the first to lose her child.

One evening the baby started coughing. A sound like the cracking of nuts came from her chest.

After ten days of coughing, the little bundle took a deep, rasping breath, accompanied by that strange cracking sound in her chest. Then she gasped for air before lying still, staring at her mother. Yasamin sat with the girl in her arms until her mother-in-law came in and told her she was dead. The baby's eyes were wide open. It was the first time Yasamin had seen a dead child. The little girl's gaze, her eyes darkened with kohl, lingered in the room even after Hala took her away.

Asya had lived for three months.

Bashir kept a vigil over his firstborn until dawn. With his mother by his side, he recited and prayed. Neither of them cried. Nor did Yasamin. Hala had explained to her how every tear shed became a river that the baby had to ford on the way to paradise.

'The loss of a child,' Hala had said, 'increases your reward in the hereafter. You mustn't ruin that with tears. They will diminish the reward.'

Yasamin sat quietly without saying a word.

Bashir approached her.

'How are you?' he asked.

Yasamin didn't answer. She just looked at him.

'Don't be upset! If you are sad then Allah will not reward you,' Bashir said, echoing his mother's words.

'Look, dear daughter,' Hala continued, 'you've struggled for this child, carried her for nine months, cared for her since she was born. She has been chosen.'

She told her daughter-in-law how God would bless the girl's soul. In paradise, children were transformed into birds who could fly wherever they wanted. They were allowed to build nests in the lanterns hanging from the throne of the almighty, and then – when it was Yasamin's turn to enter the afterlife – the bird would turn back into a child. She would take hold of the hem of her mother's garment and not let go until she had led her into paradise.

'You mustn't ruin that by crying!' Hala repeated.

Yasamin didn't make a sound.

Bashir stood looking at his daughter, his first child. Then he whispered a prayer in each of her ears and smiled. Hala wrapped the child in a white sheet and placed her in a small casket.

Galai was the one who cried a river of tears. She had loved Asya as her own, had rocked her to sleep, had washed and changed her. It was she who had applied kohl to the baby's eyes, giving her that intense stare.

'Stop crying!' Hala scolded.

It wasn't just a mother's tears that caused problems for the child en route to paradise. Every tear became a raging torrent the baby could drown in.

The following year Galai gave birth to a son. He was named Mawia and was big and healthy, round and chubby, like his mother and father.

Yasamin was also pregnant again.

She gave birth to a son they called Misbah a few months after Mawia came into the world.

Within three days Misbah was sick. There was blood in his faeces; something wasn't right.

'Are you breastfeeding or giving him formula?' the doctor asked.

'I'm breastfeeding.'

'Maybe something's wrong with your milk,' the doctor wondered aloud.

Yasamin was instructed not to eat hard foods. Her diet must only consist of soft fare. Were eggs hard or soft? She avoided them. What about milk? No, that wasn't good for her own milk. On her next visit to the doctor she was told to cut out yoghurt too because her son was not improving.

The conversations with the doctor took place while Yasamin sat behind a curtain. Bashir was away fighting, so his brother Yaqub went in his place. Apparently something was wrong with Misbah's stomach.

A diet of green tea, overcooked rice and soup was prescribed.

One day, as they were leaving to go to the clinic, Yasamin sat in the back seat of the car with the baby in her arms. Hala got in beside her. Yaqub had just turned the key in the ignition when the old woman told him to stop the car. She looked down at her grandchild before turning to Yasamin.

'He's no longer with us.'

Once again it was Hala who confirmed the death. 'He has left,' she said.

Misbah had lived for forty days.

This time Bashir didn't stand over the little corpse smiling. While the others were looking at the baby, he was looking at Yasamin. She thought he was commiserating with her, now that she had lost a second child.

But suddenly he began to beam. His laughter erupted in the room.

'Yet another child is dead! All the more reward for us!'

'We belong to Allah and to Allah we shall return,' Hala said. 'God knows best.'

Yasamin sat in silence on a mattress under the window. Once again, no tears came. But her body had not shut down: her breasts felt ready to burst. The milk trickled out; it felt like it was running down in streams.

Her dress was getting wet. She sat, still wearing what she had put on to go to the doctor with her son. Around her there was quiet whispering.

Galai entered the room. She was holding Mawia. Big, strong, perfectly healthy Mawia.

In tears, she placed the boy in Yasamin's arms and said:

'He's yours.'

* * *

Bashir's wives took turns nursing and caring for Mawia. The women were alone much of the time. The fighting came closer. At times it felt as though they were surrounded; the gunfire was intense and the airstrikes increased.

Concentrated joy, Bashir called his wives.

On the rare occasions he was at home, the three of them would sit in the evenings and talk. He smoothed things over, alleviated concerns and told amusing stories from the front.

'You're a gift from Allah the Almighty. I love both of you.' He was never able to find fault with either of them, he added.

'Our purpose is your happiness,' Galai replied. Life felt meaningful. Cooking for the fighters. Washing their clothes. Making suicide vests.

They were following Hala's plan: two heads, four hands. One thought: Bashir's happiness. One goal: jihad.

It hadn't taken long for Galai to grow fond of Yasmin, after her initial disappointment upon seeing how beautiful she was. Galai's ideal of a woman had fair skin, big eyes, prominent eyebrows and thin lips – exactly like Yasmin. At least they were the same height, and besides, some people liked full lips and round faces, Galai told herself. Yasmin was actually far too skinny and sickly. But she was a good woman, Galai decided, modest and friendly. And inevitably, wartime life brought them closer. Their existence was accompanied by the ever-present buzz of the drones.

They would go into the yard in the morning and gaze skyward; sit down by basins to wash clothes and peer up; peel carrots and look aloft. The drones would still be there later in the day. And the next day. When they flew low they could hear the spinning of the propellers. The sound kept them awake at night.

When would they strike? Now, or now, or now? The answer was any time.

The terror affected far more people than the intended targets.

It served as a constant reminder that death came suddenly.

George W. Bush had been the pioneer of the drone war, with targeted attacks against al-Qaeda. Barack Obama normalised the weapon: no president utilised drones more, and in 2010, the year

Mawia was born and Misbah died, an unprecedented number of drone strikes took place in the Pakistani tribal areas. The objective was to take out important Taliban commanders and members of the Haqqani family, but the drone operators gradually moved on to so-called signature strikes: individuals who weren't necessarily targets but whose appearance or behaviour resembled that of the insurgents. They fitted a profile, even if their identity was unknown.

Sometimes the behaviour was easily definable: if, for example, a man fired on American troops. Other times it might be that some men were digging. Were they digging a ditch or burying a bomb? A group of people might get into vehicles with weapons. Were they fighters, or was it a family on their way to a wedding? In the tribal areas people seldom went anywhere *without* weapons, and at weddings it was commonplace to celebrate by firing into the air.

The Haqqanis ranked high on the list. A drone operator thought he saw Sirajuddin's brother, the number two in the network and the man responsible for the suicide bombers, on the screen. He showed the recordings to the CIA, who identified Badruddin by the general esteem he was met with and the many embraces he received. When the target left the funeral, and there were no civilians in the vicinity, his car was blown up. The man killed was the Haqqanis' younger brother, Muhammad, who was not known to have any connection to terrorist activity.

Another convoy slowed down by a field, the cars stopped and the passengers got out. It was dawn, they bowed on the ground to pray, behaviour the drone operators associated with extremists. Along with the adults, a dozen children were killed. It was a wedding party returning home.

The CIA recruited a network of local informers to identify targets. Rumour had it that the informants planted GPS trackers on people and cars to guide the drones. The rewards were high. The CIA were generous, perhaps overly so. Finding a member of al-Qaeda paid only too well. As in Afghanistan, there were many who secretly accused old enemies.

This led to paranoia in the tribal areas and a perpetual hunt for spies. Haqqani was ruthless. If the network thought they had captured an informant, he was first tortured to get what he knew out of him, before being beheaded or shot. Sometimes Sirajuddin ordered Bashir to be the executioner. A short verdict was read out, then Bashir pointed his pistol at the suspected traitor's head and pulled the trigger. At times they filmed the executions and put them on the web.

The fabric of the once close-knit tribal community was beginning to unravel. Life was characterised by constant distrust, not only towards outsiders, who had always been enemies, but towards one another.

In late 2010, the CIA's eye in the sky spotted a target they had been looking for. Behind high walls in Abbottabad, not far from the city's military academy, was a place the neighbours called the Waziristan house, as those who went in and out of the compound spoke with accents from the tribal areas. The house had been built by the current owner, with few windows on the floors visible from over the wall. None of the occupants had a telephone, but a satellite dish had been installed so they could watch TV. The man of the house, a fugitive from a blood feud, apparently, was home-schooling the children. The family were self-sufficient – they had chickens, goats, rabbits, a cow, beehives and a vegetable garden. They either burned their rubbish, used it as compost or fed it to the animals.

When the family had been living there for five years, American intelligence found a link between the house and a wanted courier. As time went on, they became convinced, and in April 2011 Barack Obama gave orders for SEAL Team Six to attack. The twenty-five members of the special operations force trained for the operation for months; they had even built a full-scale replica of the three-storey house.

On 1 May 2011, the national security team assembled in the Situation Room in the White House. They followed the operation, waiting to hear the words *Geronimo EKIA – Enemy Killed in Action*.

It was late afternoon in Washington and night-time in Abbottabad when two helicopters landed inside the compound. The soldiers raided the house and the man with the codename Geronimo was found on the second floor of the building.

He was standing at the end of a corridor when he was shot just above the left eye. A mere half-hour after landing in the compound, SEAL Team Six put the man in a body bag they had brought with them.

Less than twenty-four hours later, the body was dropped from an aircraft carrier. The leader of the Planes Operation found his grave at the bottom of the sea.

If Osama bin Laden had been killed in Tora Bora in December 2001, the USA could have ordered the troops home shortly after. Ten years later, his death had no effect on hostilities in Afghanistan. The war had hardly anything to do with him any more.

One night when the women were home alone, the bombing became so intense that Galai and Yasmin escaped outside and made for the wooded hills. Yasamin was in the last month of her third pregnancy. She was carrying Mawia, while Galai held her newborn, Moghaira, in her arms.

A few nights earlier, a large helicopter had landed in Miram Shah. Men had stormed out of the rear of the fuselage, the women had been told, and started shooting. The following day the locals had been met by human remains. Legs, arms, strips of flesh.

When the two teenage mothers heard several helicopters circling above the next night, they didn't know where they were going, they just ran. Galai felt heavy and tired from the recent birth. She was barefoot. Yasamin took off her sandals.

'Take them!' she said to Galai.

Galai put them on but halted after a few steps, pitying her heavily pregnant fellow wife.

They ended up wearing a sandal each. Using one foot to step over thistles and the sharpest stones.

After a few hours, Bashir's wives arrived at some tents belonging to Kochis, Pashtun nomads. They came out and saw the exhausted women.

'What's happened?'

'Judgement Day!' Galai shouted.

The women collapsed inside a tent.

'Hell has broken loose,' she gasped.

'*Kuffar!* The Americans and their Afghan traitors!' the Kochis said. 'Stay as long as you want.' The women were given bread, tea and fresh milk.

Such was life on the border.

Daytime: make food for the fighters.

At night: dash up stony ridges.

Daytime: work on bombs

At night: climb up mountains.

Yasamin looked down at herself as she and Galai lay down on the nomads' mats. Fortunately they were well covered up. She was thinking about the human remains she had stared at, the naked, uncovered, bloody flesh, and was panicked by the thought of someone seeing her like that. After she was dead. Body parts could be scattered in all directions if you were hit by a drone. She feared parts of her own body being exposed. Everything she had kept hidden her entire life.

On the Day of Judgement, when they stood in front of God and he asked, 'Why have you shown skin? Your muscles? Bones?' what would she answer then? When it wasn't her fault!

'I gave you a pretty face, a beautiful body, neck, chest, arms,' he would say. 'And in the end the infidels saw everything!'

The thought filled her with horror; she was unable to get it out of her head. 'I've protected everything I've been given . . . ' she would answer.

God's voice continued to resound in her restless sleep: 'What have you done with your body? Why have you shown it to people?'

But then her thoughts turned to Bashir. The last time he was home they had sat up long into the night. Her husband had blood on his face and his lips were dry and cracked. He had calluses on his heels and cuts on his fingers. Exhausted, he had laid his head in her lap. She had stroked his unkempt curls. They were full of dust, of earth, tiny twigs and straw.

All this, Yasamin thought, all this is mine, and so much finer than a kingdom.

On the Day of Judgement I will stand before God with my head held high.

'My husband has written history.' That's what I'll say. And the day he abandons jihad, that day I will divorce.

Best

When Ariana had learned to read, she found joy in words everywhere. First she read everything she saw along the road – street signs, posters, placards, advertisements. After that she devoured every book she could find. Gradually she became a swot. Everything had to be remembered perfectly. The joy of reading in itself was no longer enough; she wanted to be the best.

Ariana's grandfather shared her competitive nature. He had not allowed his daughter, Nadia, be satisfied with qualifying as a teacher, encouraging her to complete her degree in geography, which she had during Ariana's first year at school. The children had got used to their mother coming home late. When she finally put on her worn-out, baggy housewife clothes, Ariana trailed behind her in the tiny kitchen. Dinner on the living room floor was the best part of the day, the only time the whole family was gathered. Her father would change out of his uniform and put on a long tunic.

Karim was content with things as they were; he found change stressful. He liked his position in the Ministry of Defence, where he worked in the finance division, slowly rising through the ranks at the country's most secure workplace. The army, the state and budgets would, after all, always endure.

*

At school, Ariana was soon designated class monitor and informant. Should a teacher need to leave the classroom, she was charged with keeping an eye on the other pupils.

'If anyone talks, make a note of their name!' the teacher would say. Corporal punishment was common at the school, an ordinary state school divided into two halves, one for boys and one for girls. Generally the punishment meted out to girls was more lenient than what the boys faced: a rap on the knuckles, that was all.

Ariana never reported her friends; they were free to whisper.

'Your friends are talking!' was a common complaint.

One day she decided enough was enough. One girl she knew well had made too much noise and so Ariana took her name down.

'How dare you!' the friend hissed at her afterwards.

'I'm responsible,' Ariana replied. Integrity took precedence over friendship. With reservations. With increasing reservations. When she went to bed that night, she lay awake crying. She had broken an unwritten rule: look after your own.

In fifth grade, Ariana was officially the best in the class. Pupils in Afghanistan had large numbers of tests every term, and exams at the end of the school year. The teachers encouraged competition. The best in the class was given a prize, the worst got told off. Lists of results were hung up for all to see. There was a maximum of one hundred points for every exam. Ariana got top marks in almost every subject. She loved praise, it nourished her.

In eighth grade, a new girl joined Ariana's class.

'You have competition,' the teacher said, smiling, as she introduced Hasina to the class. She had been the best pupil at her former school.

I'll have to study even harder, Ariana thought, as she sat on the first row looking at the new rival being assigned an unoccupied desk in the furthest corner.

'I don't want to sit in the back row,' Hasina protested.

Aha, so she wanted to sit at the front. The protective instincts of the class were immediately stirred.

'You're new! Sit down there,' one girl said as Hasina was making her way to the back of the classroom.

'We don't want anyone to take your place,' Ariana's friends told her afterwards. The knives were out for the intruder, whom Ariana would soon refer to as 'my enemy'. She was touched by the newly established defences. When she got home she wrote in her notebook: what is most important to me?

Be best.
Have lots of friends.
Have nice notebooks.

The newcomer wasn't content with being second best. She believed there was something fishy going on. Maybe Ariana was getting top scores in tests because her mother was a teacher at the school.

Hasina consulted the regulations and found out that the pupils had a right to see their exams marked in front of them. She demanded that her and Ariana's papers were looked at as soon as they were handed in.

Exams were approaching. Ariana had never studied harder. She fell asleep while reading, woke up and continued. She was to sit eight exams. The first was in biology.

On the morning of the first exam, Ariana was sitting at her desk by the window. She quickly jotted down the answers. There was nothing unexpected. She knew the biology textbook inside out, but you could never be sure: might she have misread something?

'The two of you stay behind, the rest of you go out,' the teacher said, pointing at Ariana and Hasina when the allotted time was up.

Ariana had never been so nervous, it felt like the moment of truth, or even Judgement Day. Her palms were sweaty; her honour was at stake.

Hasina's paper was marked first. Correct, correct, correct, the teacher ticked beside the answers. Blue ticks all the way down the page. Then the teacher's hand stopped at a question that had two parts, each worth two points. Hasina had only answered the first.

'I didn't notice the second one! I know the answer!'

But it was too late. Hasina was close to tears. Ninety-eight points, the teacher wrote on the exam paper, next to her name.

Then it was Ariana's turn.

'Now, let's see,' the teacher said.

The pen swept down the page. Correct, correct. Correct. Everything was right. One hundred per cent right!

Outside the door, the whole class was standing waiting. Cheers erupted when they heard the result. Her classmates bought juice and cake for her to celebrate. There were seven exams remaining. Ariana dragged herself away to revise for the following day. Geography was next.

The exam was going swimmingly. Then she froze.

'In what country is Mount Kilimanjaro?'

Her mind was a blank. A complete blank. She had no idea. Was that in the textbook?

Ariana pointed surreptitiously at the question and frowned at her friends in the class. They all shook their heads. She looked over at Hasina, who was concentrating hard. With steady, flowing writing she was filling the page.

After answering all the other questions, Ariana remained sitting, looking out the window. She could see the mountains around Kabul, their presence now seeming to mock her. Was Kilimanjaro in the Alps? Should she answer France or Switzerland? Nepal? She had crammed the peaks in the Himalayas: this mountain – was it among them?

Suddenly she noticed a movement outside the window. It was a classmate. The girl quickly pulled the geography book from her bag and met Ariana with a fixed gaze. From the other side of the glass she pointed at a photo of a mountain. Ariana leaned slightly forward, just enough to read the caption.

Tanzania, she wrote in a neat hand. And submitted her paper.

This time her exam was the first to be marked. She was even more nervous than the day before. She had cheated. Perhaps someone had seen.

One hundred points, she heard the teacher say. Everything correct. But she felt no sense of relief.

Then it was Hasina's turn. She had everything correct until the teacher came to the question about Mount Kilimanjaro, and paused.

Hasina had put down Africa as the answer.

'There wasn't anything in the book about the mountain,' the girl insisted. 'But I knew it was in Africa.'

The teacher looked at her.

'Well, Ariana knew the answer, and the question wasn't what continent it was on but in which country.' Minus one point. Ninety-nine points for her rival.

Hasina hurried out, after saying said she didn't need to see any more papers being marked. The competition was over. Ariana was undefeated. She hugged the friend who had shown her the book.

'You're crazy!' she whispered in her ear.

'I wanted you to win!'

Friendship took precedence over integrity. Safeguarding the clan, the tribe, the friends, their group: this was a notion that had been drummed into them from an early age.

In Kabul it was popular to attend courses. If you had ambitions for your children, you sent them on a course. It was a way of getting ahead. But they cost money. Courses were for people of means. Ariana nagged her parents and eventually got onto an extra course in mathematics, her weakest subject, and one for English, the subject she couldn't improve in fast enough.

The quality of the education in state schools was often low. The pay was poor and many teachers had other jobs on the side. When they were absent, substitute teachers could seldom be found, so the headmaster would usually instruct pupils to take on the role. There were forty-five children in Ariana's class. It was decided that the ten best pupils would teach the twenty weakest while the ones in the middle looked after themselves. Ariana loved to teach. She persisted until her classmates understood.

One day a man came into her class, offering free courses.

Father Prem was a Jesuit priest from India. He was the first foreigner Ariana had met, apart from the soldiers who had visited her school. Prem's organisation was starting up courses in computing and English. As they were free, Ariana figured she would be allowed take them.

'Can anyone here speak a little English?' Father Prem asked. A few pupils responded with 'Hello' and 'How are you?' and 'What's your name?'

'Is there anybody who knows some grammar?' the priest inquired, stressing that it would be required to learn the language properly.

Ariana raised her hand hesitantly. When he pointed at her she held her head high and reeled off 'A noun is a person, place or thing. A verb is something you do. An adjective is . . . '

She was awarded a place on the course. It was a glorious time. Ariana learned how to use a computer. She learned how to write on it, how to draw, how to do calculations. The Jesuits had hired several instructors. Sometimes Father Prem himself dropped by in his fancy car, handing out pencils and notebooks, joking and laughing with the pupils.

Then one day he was gone.

The Taliban had abducted him.

In early June 2014, the priest had travelled to visit a school near Herat, in the west of the country. He had been warned about leaving Kabul, which foreigners commonly referred to as the Ka-bubble, but he had taken a chance. The mood in the Jesuit organisation was sombre. They feared Father Prem's chances of survival were low. He was after all a Catholic missionary, and the punishment for proselytising was death.

But he was also a treasure trove. Unlike IS in Syria, who beheaded their first foreign victim that same summer, the Taliban were more interested in getting ransom money than chopping off heads. Eight months after the kidnap, the priest was released following the intervention of the Indian prime minister.

For Ariana, now in tenth grade, the Taliban had always been something remote. Savage men fighting in the mountains, who men in uniform – like her father – would soon defeat. Her existence was composed of exercise books, reports and a boy she had just seen pictures of. His name was Justin Bieber.

She would pore over his lyrics as though studying the periodic table. Everything he sang about was taboo. Even if Kabul was a bubble the West filled with its ideas, young girls knew where the line went. But fortunately her parents couldn't understand English, so she was able to play his music loudly, without shame.

If I was your boyfriend, I'd never let you go
I can take you places you ain't never been before

Father Prem didn't return.

The computer course and the English classes were discontinued.

It was the first time the Taliban had thrown a spanner in the works for Ariana, who was now a Belieber.

Minister of Martyrs

One morning Jamila received a phone call.

'You've been nominated for the post of deputy minister at the Ministry of Labour and Social Affairs.'

'Uh, okay . . . '

'You're one of ten nominees. We'll get back in touch with you when interviews are to be held.'

The call had come out of the blue. She had never applied for any political position and was now suddenly a candidate for a role in government. It was spring 2015, and the country's leadership was marked by tugs-of-war between various wings and factions trying to get their own people in place. There was money at stake. Resources at stake. Power at stake.

Afghanistan had elected a new president the previous year. Or had they?

That was the question. Widespread vote rigging had been revealed after the first round. A large number of fake votes had been discovered in the more than twenty thousand ballot boxes transported to Kabul for inspection. The election fraud was extensive, and involved both candidates still remaining in the race: the American-educated technocrat Ashraf Ghani and the erstwhile mujahideen from the Northern Alliance, Abdullah Abdullah. The former was Pashtun, the latter Tajik. Both had run against Karzai in 2009 and lost, in an election also characterised by systematic rigging. Now Karzai was out of the picture, as the constitution only allowed a president two terms.

Jamila had been appointed to the complaints commission charged with investigating the election and the list of offences seemed endless. Many votes were declared invalid. In the first round, Abdullah had got most votes; in the second, Ghani was the winner. The Taliban exploited the power vacuum. The number of Afghan policemen and soldiers killed reached a peak.

Only after the US Secretary of State John Kerry flew in to mediate did the two candidates agree on a government of national unity with shared power. Dr Abdullah was given the title of Chief Executive. He was to be a prime minister of sorts, with responsibility for the day-to-day running of the government, and report to President Ghani, who according to the constitution held considerable authority. The two harboured a profound mistrust of one another.

Ashraf Ghani was sworn in. Relations with the US were critical for the new president. The withdrawal of troops had been postponed several times, with the previous deadline already passed. Nearly fifty thousand foreign soldiers still remained, of which thirty thousand were American. They had not managed to stabilise the country nor build up an effective national army. Only a handful of regiments were able to operate independently, without support from their allies. A withdrawal could lead to the collapse of the state and was postponed indefinitely.

While Karzai had been accused of 'wishing the war away', both Ghani and Abdullah wanted to intensify attacks against the Taliban. At the same time the two, who scarcely spoke to each other, were to run the country.

They had inherited a state on the verge of collapse. The Taliban had one of their most successful fighting seasons, IS had established itself in earnest and the security forces suffered heavy losses, with desertion rife and morale low. The economy was faltering and jobs were few. The country looked in desperation to foreign donors for fresh loans, debt refinancing and emergency relief.

Cooperation with the Americans had soured substantially in Karzai's final year. He accused the Americans of failing to keep their word and called for compensation for accidental bombings and the large number of civilians killed in the war on terror. In turn, the USA criticised Karzai for dividing power between a handful of warlords, in the government and in the provinces, and for allowing organised criminal networks to seize the country's resources. The hope was that the newly installed president, a technocrat, would change the relationship for the better.

Ashraf Ghani had been born into a prominent Pashtun family in Logar. His father had worked for the last king, Zahir Shah. Ashraf had spent his boyhood on horseback or immersed in books, until he was sent to high school in Oregon in 1966, at the age of sixteen. The freedom and lifestyle of American teenagers fascinated him. When the king was overthrown in 1973, the privileged young man was studying political science at the American University in Beirut. Here he met his future wife, Rula, one year his senior, and from a Christian family. He completed his PhD in cultural anthropology at Columbia University in New York; his doctoral thesis was an analysis of his native country's difficulties in nation building.

In the 1980s, Ashraf Ghani lectured at Berkeley in California, and in the 1990s he worked for the World Bank, which had by then begun to question its own methods: why did countries that followed their policies of liberalisation remain poor?

Through his work in the field, Ghani documented that corruption was at the root of the problem, while weak institutions and lazily conceived projects also contributed.

Who could be better placed than him to save Afghanistan from the chaos Karzai had left behind?

'I don't have any experience of working in government,' Jamila said to Kakar when she got home. 'Besides, I have so many other things on my plate.'

Over the past decade, Jamila's work had expanded in several directions. As well as her commitment to education and women's participation, she was busy trying to get recognition for the challenges facing the disabled. Just like her father, she saw opportunities everywhere. While he steadily expanded his business empire, she formed initiatives within education, women's health, civil society and psychosocial support.

In addition, she had given birth to three children: Salahuddin, who was now eight, Khadija, five, and Fatima, four. All were named after heroes of Islamic history. Khadija was the first wife of the Prophet and Fatima was his youngest daughter, while Salahuddin was the commander who repelled the Christian crusades.

'I'll take care of the children,' Kakar promised. 'This is a great opportunity for you!'

'I'm not interested,' Jamila replied.

Kakar wasn't the only insistent voice, there were many who weighed in on Jamila's future: 'At least find out what the job entails. Imagine the influence you could wield!'

Jamila was not sure. She felt constant guilt about hardly ever seeing the children. There simply wasn't time for them. When Salahuddin had repeatedly failed to hand in his homework, the teacher asked why his mother hadn't made sure he had done it.

'I don't have a mother,' Salahuddin had replied.

'Why do you say that? I know that you have!'

'No, she's her computer's mother, not mine,' the boy answered.

Kakar was the one who made sure the children got to school, picked them up and helped them with homework. His brothers made fun of him, calling him Zancho – his wife's servant.

'If you saw a woman on the street struggling with a heavy load, and she was about to collapse under it, would you help her?' he asked them.

'Of course,' they answered.

'Well, that's Jamila. Why is it manly to carry the load for a woman on the street and not relieve her of it in the home?'

Barely a week after the call, Jamila was summoned to the Arg. At the gate she was held by security. First her crutches were sent through the X-ray machine, then the alarm went off as she walked through the metal detector. She pointed out the metal device screwed into her foot to allow her to wear a shoe, and was asked to remove it so it could be put through separately. She hesitated: it felt humiliating – she wasn't even asked to do that at airports. In the end she had to relent, and when she finally made it to the president's office she faced a harsh reprimand from Ghani. Punctuality was very important to him, he stressed; he didn't like people messing up his schedule. His attitude softened somewhat when he was told of the tenacity of the security guards. Then he got down to business. He wanted Jamila to be responsible for martyrs and disabled – those killed and wounded in war.

'So, what's your plan? What do you want to achieve?'

'I'm not actually sure I'd be suited to the post of vice-minister . . . '

Ghani looked at her in surprise.

'You come here and you don't know if you want the job? People are begging me for positions and you're sitting there backing out?'

His behaviour was just as crass as Jamila had heard.

'Well, I'll be honest, I've never been in politics. I have no faction behind me and if one lacks the backing of a particular group it can be difficult to survive or get anything through at all.'

'I have your back! You can always come to me.'

'But you're going to have your hands full—'

Ashraf Ghani had had enough.

'You women are always complaining to the media that there aren't any positions for you! That no positions of power are occupied by women, and then when I offer one you won't take it!'

Jamila sat in silence. He was right. Of course he was. She nodded.

'By the way,' the president said as she was getting to her feet, 'I'll make sure you get a card to show the security guards, so they won't bother you again.'

She thanked him for his consideration.

The next day she was scheduled to meet with Dr Abdullah Abdullah. This time she had prepared bullet points. How they could best improve day-to-day life for people with disabilities, strategies they should adopt, how bereaved dependants could be helped, and how they could assist both people with congenital disabilities and soldiers who had been wounded in action.

As during her meeting with the president, several other men sat listening without saying anything. Most of them seemed to be from the Ministry of Defence.

Abdullah echoed what Ghani had told her. 'You can always come to me,' he said, adding, 'you're the only one of the candidates neither of us have argued about.'

Finally, Jamila was called in to see the newly appointed minister of labour and social affairs, a woman she knew only by name. Nasrin Oryakhil was a gynaecologist and had run an underground clinic in Kabul when the Taliban were in power. She had been informed on, dragged out, beaten and told 'to quit working and start praying'. After the fall of the Taliban she had taught at the medical faculty at Kabul University and had worked in women's health, family planning and the training of midwives and obstetricians. She was now one of four female ministers among over twenty men.

The meeting was like an efficient doctor's appointment, with a brief introduction to the tasks.

'You're the best in the country on disabilities, or so I hear,' she said. 'You have an excellent reputation.'

'But I don't have any experience . . . a ministry has huge bureaucracy, I've only worked in the voluntary sector.'

'I didn't have any experience in politics either,' Oryakhil replied. 'But I had a duty to accept the challenge when I received the call.'

'Okay, okay,' Jamila said, smiling. She would try.

This was going to work out. Two women at the top of the department was perfect.

The days were long, as were the evenings. Jamila often took work home with her, going through it like a conscientious student.

She soon discovered the department was haemorrhaging money. And it wasn't going where it was intended. She decided to make some changes.

Not knowing who exactly was responsible for siphoning off funds, she began to switch around the work tasks of the employees so they were forced to change their routines. She had, for instance, received many complaints about the director who managed pensions for the families of martyrs. She reassigned him to civil cases. This would give her the space and time to find out what was going on.

Almost immediately after the reorganisation, she received a call from the Arg.

'Why are you changing people's roles?' a man in the president's administration demanded to know.

'They're still in the same office and they still have the same positions, I've just altered their tasks.'

'You can't do that!'

She ended the call and left the changes in place. Then she got a call from the office of the prime minister.

'Why are you chopping and changing people's jobs?'

'This job can go to hell if I'm not allowed manage my own staff!' she replied. Realising her little shake-up must have stymied someone, she decided to go through all the accounts, all the budget items, all the invoices and the figures. Before she could make plans for the activities of the department, she needed to tidy it up.

While going through the register of war pensions, Jamila came across a large file containing the names of some seventy thousand men who had been killed shortly after they enlisted. Many had enrolled in the army one day, only to be killed the next; others had survived for just a few weeks. None had dates of birth, nor addresses, nor locations listed for where they had been killed. They only had a name and a bank account.

She requested more information from the section handling the pensions. Staff there assured her that everything was in order and that all the pensions went to the widows or parents.

Jamila stopped the payments immediately and informed the minister and the president's office. Not long after, she received a call from the Ministry of the Interior, instructing her to resume the payments.

'I've asked for documentation. We can't pay out until it has been reviewed,' she said.

'That's not how we do it here,' the voice on the other end of the line said. 'It'll be best for everyone, including you, that you pay out.'

There was a flood of complaints to the president about Jamila not doing her job. About her improperly withholding money.

'You're creating ill will against Ghani,' one person said. 'He won't be happy when he finds out you're the cause.'

'If the families of those fallen soldiers aren't paid, there'll be uproar,' said another. 'They'll take to the streets, kick up a real fuss,' said a third.

One morning Jamila arrived at work to find her office window smashed. Another day her desk was vandalised. On another occasion her security guard was beaten up by unknown assailants.

She still didn't authorise the pensions.

Some of the payments were inexplicable. One man was receiving bereavement support for four hundred families. Another for five hundred. Others were getting money for breadwinners who died forty or fifty years ago.

She discovered that compensation for the victims of suicide bombings far exceeded the number of victims. One of the worst attacks had been on the Abul Fazel mosque in Kabul, where seventy people had been killed. It turned out Jamila's department was paying money to twelve hundred families.

One member of parliament was handling the cases on behalf of the victims of the Hazara minority. He accused Jamila of prejudice. She saw red.

'This money belongs to the people. I need papers for each one of the victims!'

Delving further, she discovered many of the real victims had been awarded no financial recompense whatsoever. Their applications had never been registered, while other people raked in money.

Several groups came to see her about the various mop-up operations she had going on. She found out that the criminal networks each had their own protectors in parliament. The groups were from all over the country, there were generals from the communist era, there were religious men; no one was too pure to steal the state's money.

Throughout the fifteen years she had worked promoting women's rights in Afghanistan, she had rubbed a lot of people up the wrong way. The religious, the ultra-religious, the traditional, the dogmatic, the Taliban, IS, but Jamila had never been subjected to harsher threats than those issued to her from officials in government.

On another occasion, when she stopped the flow of money from the treasury into the pockets of a powerful man, he collared her in the hallway of the department.

'You've dried up my well!'

How was he supposed to pay his men now?

'That's not my problem,' she replied, and walked away.

But it would become her problem.

'Do you know what your life is worth?' asked a member of parliament who came into her office after kicking the door open. 'It's worth the price of the bomb I'm going to put under your car!' he answered himself.

'My life is in your hands,' Jamila answered calmly.

'There'll be bits of you blown into the sky if you don't sign my papers.'

'Go ahead.'

'You're living dangerously,' he said. He had two Kalashnikovs over his shoulder.

'If God has decreed that my fate is to be decided by you, then so it shall be.'

After that she checked her car every day.

Every corrupt official was part of a circuit of sons, nephews, uncles, grandsons, helpers, errand boys, sometimes a private army. If someone interfered, removed one link from the chain, the entire circuit suffered. Vengeance could be taken on a son, a nephew or an uncle of the person who interfered.

One night a bomb was thrown into the home of Jamila's in-laws. Fortunately Kakar's mother and father escaped injury, but the house was destroyed. Then armed men came to collect Salahuddin from school. They told the guards they were his uncles. Jamila had feared exactly this, that when they couldn't get the better of her they would go after the children. So she'd taken the precaution of impressing upon the school guards that only she or Kakar could pick them up. Should anyone else come, they were to call her straight away. The guards did as instructed and denied the men access. The minutes passed, and Salahuddin didn't come out, then the men disappeared just before Jamila arrived.

'One day I'll kill you,' a powerful man had said to her, right there in the Arg, surrounded by his bodyguards and hers. He was a mafia boss, from the Pashtun Tarakhil clan, and the brother of a member of parliament. This was the way of the country. There were no laws, no justice, only power. And that power was becoming increasingly concentrated in the hands of ever fewer people, while more money flooded in from abroad, into the Afghan treasury and out again.

'Pay them!' the president eventually ordered.

After Jamila had begun shaking things up and had met opposition, she had tried to get in contact with the president, who had promised to back her. But she had been unable to reach him. He was *unavailable*.

He had a wall of advisors, secretaries and spokesmen around him. To re-start the pension payments was an order from that wall.

'The money has to go to the right people,' Jamila argued.

'You must obey!' the president's man said.

Nasrin Oryakhil stepped down as minister after a year. Jamila was more alone than ever. She told Kakar she felt like a piece of meat thrown to hungry wildcats.

You've made my well run dry.
You'll be blown to pieces.
What is your life worth?

With continued threats being made against Salahuddin, she

handed in her resignation. Initially, Ashraf Ghani refused to allow her to step down.

Few accusations of corruption were made against the president personally; he had simply lost control. In contrast to Abdullah Abdullah, who enjoyed tailored suits and handmade Italian shoes, Ghani dressed in plain, traditional clothing and sandals made locally at a couple of dollars a pair.

He was called Afghanistan's micromanager, due to his penchant for getting hung up on details and scrutinising individual projects, while his associates helped themselves and ran the country on his behalf. He became increasingly isolated inside his inner circle of advisors, who told him how things on the outside were looking.

Everything had a price. Loyalty, access to people in power, political position. Criminal syndicates and drug barons, kidnappers and highway bandits, politicians and officials sucked the country dry, while Afghans' villas in the Gulf or in Turkey grew ever more luxurious.

But the ship had sprung a leak. Soon it would sink. Still no one worried, because the hole in the hull wasn't in *their* part of the ship.

After two years, Jamila swam to shore.

'In two years,' she said, when she was finally free and able to spend an evening with Kakar, 'I haven't even managed to get two minutes with the president!'

Whose back he was covering, the world would soon see.

Trapped

Suddenly a hood was being pulled over his head. He felt his breath against the dense fabric. His hands were tied behind his back. He closed his eyes and opened them again. It was just as dark.

They had him now.

Bashir was arrested a block from home. He had just taken a right-hand turn to drive out of the neighbourhood towards the city centre. His brother Raouf sat beside him in the passenger seat.

The power struggle within the local leadership in Waziristan had become so fierce and paralysing, with internal killings and subsequent acts of revenge, that Bashir and his brothers had decided to go home to Afghanistan. They had first left for Khost Province, bordering Pakistan, where Bashir had set up a base and led twenty or so small and medium-sized groups that operated countrywide. Some he acted closely with; others were more independent. The targets were the same as before: Afghan government forces, foreign soldiers, international organisations, the president, the vice-president, the defence minister, provincial governors, district leaders, departments, staff at the Arg, chiefs of police, police stations . . .

The Taliban resistance was financed by the support of donors abroad, the drug trade and extortion. Bashir was involved in the kidnap of wealthy Afghans. The hostages were often taken to Waziristan, where the authorities couldn't find them. Unlike petty criminals, who also abounded, the Taliban were in no hurry. If they kidnapped you, you were in for a long time. The criminal cartels were quicker to release or kill you.

When the net began closing in on Bashir in Khost, he changed his identity and relocated the entire family to a house outside Jalalabad.

Goodbye, Bashir, son of Mullah Wasir.

Welcome, Sor Gul, son of Muhammad Amin. A humble travelling salesman.

This morning, he and Raouf were on the way to the market. The two brothers had always been each other's closest companion and they looked alike: the same unruly curls, round face and heavy build. In character they were quite different. Raouf was mild-mannered, his little brother the commander.

Bashir saw a white minibus approach and presumed it was one of the private buses without fixed stops that picked people up along the road. When he drew up alongside the vehicle, a car pulled out in front of him, blocking the road, and a man pointed a machine gun out the window. The adrenalin pumped into his bloodstream.

'Stop!'

American commandos emerged from the bus. More vehicles arrived, pick-ups, a small van, boxing them in. Instinctively, Bashir looked for a way out. His brain told him: you are trapped.

A couple of Afghan soldiers demanded to see their papers. The brothers handed them their fake ID cards. One of the soldiers mumbled something and tapped in a number on his phone.

'. . . but the reg of the vehicle is the same as you gave us,' Bashir heard him say to the person on the other end of the line.

Then the hood went over his head, and everything went black. The brothers were bundled into a car and told not to speak to one another.

Bashir had no idea where they were being driven. The car stopped and they were ordered out. They were taken into a building and led to separate interrogation rooms. Bashir's hood was pulled off. They were at the airport in Jalalabad.

'*Mawlawi* Bashir,' the interrogator said. The honorific was a religious rank above mullah, but below imam.

He didn't reply.
'We know that you're Mawlawi Bashir.'
'No. I'm Sor Gul.'
'Do you call yourself Mullah Bashir?'
'No.'
'Imam Bashir?'
'No.'
'Commander Bashir?'
'No.'
'Doctor Bashir?'
'No. I'm Sor Gul. Travelling salesman.'

He would deny everything. He couldn't talk about anything, he had to deny, and keep on denying. He wasn't going to admit who he was or what he had done. Then they would have him. Then they could pressure him, and he might give himself and others away. He knew that. He had interrogated prisoners himself. He knew what torture did to people.

The last time he had been arrested was twelve years earlier, in 2005. Unlike now, they hadn't taken his fingerprints, so they lacked concrete evidence of who he was.

Over the radio, Bashir heard a man talking, asking something in English. When the conversation was over, the interrogator looked over at his colleague. There was a piece of metal pipe on the table in front of him that Bashir was doing his best to ignore. Right after the conversation over the radio, two Americans came to collect him. The hood was put back on. He didn't know where they were taking him, he just trudged off between the men. They walked down a corridor, down some steps and outside. A light breeze was blowing. They were probably on the runway. They walked some distance. The men stopped. 'Up!' they said. 'Stairs!'

They followed him up the aircraft steps and strapped him into a seat.

'Where are we going?' Bashir asked.

No one answered. He knew the Americans took prisoners either to the military base at Bagram or to Pakistan. He feared it would be Pakistan. Then he'd never get out. They'd beat him to death. He knew far too much that the Pakistani authorities wanted to know. The few jihadists who had emerged from Pakistani prisons were utter wrecks. Backs broken, feet mangled, arms deformed, teeth knocked out. Bashir sat there with the hood tightly over his head, restrained in the seat. He had never been so afraid.

Sweat trickled down his neck. The air conditioning started up, blowing straight at him, and he sent a kind thought to whoever had put it on. They flew for a long time, too long. He prepared himself for Islamabad. *Bashir the Afghan* was going to be tortured to death by Pakistani intelligence.

The plane door was opened and as they led him down the aisle and out, he felt cool, clean air and a slight breeze. Kabul, it had to be Kabul! He felt a surge of gratitude. The only thing he wanted now was to be put in a prison in his own country, no matter where. He wanted to be at home.

Inside the prison complex they removed his hood. They fingerprinted him, scanned his irises, measured his height, weighed him and gave him a number: 747. Afterwards he was taken to a shower room. He was told to remove his clothes and given a palmful of shampoo. Then they turned on the water. Before he rinsed off all the lather, the jet was turned off. Bashir refused to go out as he was still covered in soap. Irritated, the guard pressed a button, the water came back on and he rinsed off properly.

They gave him new clothes. Trousers with a drawstring waist and a shirt, both green. Shackles were fastened to his ankles, his hands were tied together and he was led to a cell. The latrine was the first thing he saw, then the mattress. On a shelf there was a copy of the Quran. Again he felt thankful. The infidels providing prisoners with the word of God wasn't something he would have imagined. The room had three hatches in the wall, and a reinforced glass door that the guards outside could see through but he could not. A surveillance camera was on at all times.

Bashir lay down on the mattress but couldn't sleep. He took down the Quran and began to recite. But instead of concentrating on the verse, he found himself overtaken by other thoughts. What fate had he been ascribed? Why had Allah allowed this? Did he want him brought here? Was this both the end and the beginning?

He lay tossing and turning, dozed a little, and after a while lost track of time and didn't know if it was day or night. It was pitch black around him and there were no windows. Suddenly he heard a voice calling to prayer. He got up, washed in the jug of water left out and began to pray. When he had finished and gone back to bed, he heard another *azan*. A little later a third call to prayer. No one knew what the right time was. While he lay thinking about that, a man came in to explain the prison's rules and routines.

'The first rule is that if there's a knock on the door, you get to your feet and walk slowly backwards towards the lowest hatch.' The man pointed at the hatch, which was now closed. 'The shackles will be placed on your ankles.' After that he was to move sideways so his back was facing the next opening, which was slightly higher up, where his hands would be tied. 'Then you move to the door and bump it with your behind to open.'

Out in the corridor, earmuffs would be placed over his ears and goggles over his eyes so he could not see or hear. Food would be delivered through the third hatch in the cell door. He was to take the tray and return it when he was finished. If he didn't want to eat, he was to leave the tray where it was and the guards would collect it. While the man was explaining all this, Bashir was allowed to test out what he had been told. He walked backwards towards the hatch where they chained his legs, before moving to where they tied his hands, and then he tried to bump against the door with his behind.

He was taken to see the doctor. There he was instructed to undress for a full medical examination. Bashir refused to remove his underwear.

'You can chop me up into a thousand pieces before I'll strip naked.'

He was spared the indignity. This was going all right. So far everyone had treated him well. He was checked for scars, bullet wounds, abrasions and cuts. Bashir turned out to be remarkably unscathed for a militant jihadist. After the visit to the doctor they brought him to an interrogation room. In the first interview he was asked about his family, his father's name, his brothers, uncles, aunts and mother.

'You say you have three brothers,' the interrogator said. 'But your brother says there are eight of you.'

Bashir knew immediately that they were testing him. Raouf and he had agreed on telling it like it was, that there were four brothers.

'My brother must have taken leave of his senses,' Bashir replied. 'There are only four of us.'

One of the Afghan interrogators said he was a lawyer and began talking about his career and how, among other things, he was an expert in seeing through lies.

'Good,' Bashir responded. 'Having such an education means you must be able to read. It says who I am on my ID card.'

In the end he thought he had managed to convince them that they had arrested the wrong person. It had gone so well. The interrogation was over and he was returned to his cell.

Was this the American way? All so pleasant and friendly. He mustn't allow himself be deceived. They were the enemy. The Americans had occupied his country and now they thought they could punish him for defending it. Who gave them that right?

After a few days he was given back his own clothes and handed in the green pyjamas. As did Raouf, who he hadn't seen since they arrived. With their eyes covered and their hands bound behind their backs, the brothers were led to a vehicle and driven to a new location.

With that they left Little America with its neatly laid out barracks. They left congeniality behind. Now they were headed to the real Afghanistan, their own country.

There were other prisoners in the vehicle. The brothers exchanged a few words with each other. Bashir stressed they shouldn't mention Mussahi, so as not to put people in danger. They should say they were from Jalalabad.

'I'll say I only have one wife,' he added. He wasn't going to mention Yasamin and her family in Mussahi. Only Galai. 'Galai is my only wife and I have two sons.'

The vehicle stopped. A chill went through Bashir when he heard where they were – Riyasat 90, the interrogation centre of the Afghan security services. They'll recognise people like us straight away, he thought. The 90th Directorate was something quite different from the Americans' room service.

Riyasat 90 was located in the district of Shash Darak, close to the Ministry of Defence, the American embassy and the headquarters of both the International Security Assistance Force and the CIA. The international contingent closed their eyes to what went on there.

This was where confessions were extracted.

The accusations against Bashir the Afghan were numerous: terrorist activity directed at the authorities, kidnapping and extortion, a major assault on the Ministry of Defence, subversive activities against the Afghan security services, attacks on police stations, army divisions and NATO bases. He would deny everything. He would be the quietest man ever inside the gates of Riyasat 90.

On the first day the interrogators listed all the groups he led in the provinces of Logar, Paktia, Paktika and Khost. Several men had signed statements saying they had been abducted by him personally, taken to Miram Shah and held prisoner until their ransoms had been paid. In addition he was accused of planning and organising suicide bombings, of kidnapping two professors from the American University, of being behind the shock attack on Daoud Khan Military Hospital and an armed assault on Police Station Number 2 in Kabul.

The Directorate of Crime described him as one of the leading commandants in the Haqqani Network.

He denied everything. Including who he was.

It was his only option.

To the Afghan state it was subversive activity. To him it was a struggle against a foreign occupier. To the regime it was terror. To him it was holy war.

The punishment if found guilty, he knew, could be nothing but death.

The investigators spent a lot of time trying to get him to admit that he was Bashir, son of Mullah Wasir. One day they showed him a photo of the husband of one of Galai's sisters.

'Who is this?'

He looked at the picture closely and said, 'I've no idea.'

'Your brother-in-law has told us all about you. He confirms who you are,' the interrogator said.

Bashir just shook his head.

'You're haji, you've been to Mecca, you've worked with the Saudis, it's unbecoming for a haji to lie,' the interrogator said. Bashir had in fact never made the pilgrimage to Mecca, he hadn't had time, but a few years earlier he had paid the mother of one of the Saudi jihadists to do it for him. Seeing as she had walked around the sacred Kaaba with Bashir's intentions in mind, he put haji in front of his name. But he hadn't actually been there, so this investigator didn't know *everything*.

'I have another photo,' the interrogator said. 'And now, by Allah, you have to answer truthfully.'

It was a picture from Waziristan, taken a few years ago. On seeing it, Bashir grew a little nervous. There were many familiar faces there. How had they got hold of it?

'Is this you or is it your brother?'

The photo showed Bashir with a big smile on his face. He remembered the occasion well. It was after a victory on the battlefield. Ah, may Allah guide whoever took this picture!

'I don't know who that is.'

'Well, it looks like you, or is it your brother?'

'It's neither of us. I don't know.'

When they brought him back to the cell he was worried. He lay down on the floor – unlike in Bagram, where he'd had a mattress, there wasn't even a blanket here. They gave him too much time to think, to turn things over in his mind. Towards nightfall some of the interrogators entered his cell. One of them walked directly towards him. Bashir got to his feet, ready to defend himself. The man stood right in front of him and put his hands inside Bashir's tunic.

'What are you doing?'

The man *tickled* him. The men laughed, and eventually he had to give in and laugh along with them. Were they trying to make him smile like in the photo they'd been so obsessed with?

The next day one of the investigators asked if he could tie a *lungi* – a typical Pashtun turban. Bashir demonstrated he could, wrapping it and tying it as you were supposed to. The investigator asked him to put it on. Then they took a picture of him with a mobile phone. They produced an older photo in which he was wearing a turban and placed it beside the picture on the phone. The turban was wrapped in exactly the same way. Bashir pointed at the screen of the phone and said, 'That's me. I don't know who that other guy is.'

Sometimes the deputy chief of the 90th Directorate stopped by. The questions were largely the same and Bashir denied everything. His interrogators grew weary and threatened to arrest a relative to take his punishment. They had sent photos of him to all the provinces to verify his identity. Districts were already getting back to them, confirming it was him.

'How can they know me better than I know myself?' Bashir merely responded.

One day he was led into a long narrow room where a number of investigators were sitting, and again the deputy chief was present. There was a file marked 'Baiat Mawlawi' on the table in front of him. *Baiat* means oath of allegiance, and the Taliban swore allegiance to new leaders when they were initiated. He was asked about his time in the tribal areas, as well as his relationship to the leaders of the Taliban. He denied having any connection to the leadership.

After he finished, everyone in the room turned their attention to a TV mounted on the wall. A video from Waziristan began to play. Bashir appeared on the screen.

'I am Mawlawi Bashir and I swear allegiance to Mullah Mansour.' Mansour had become leader of the Taliban in 2016 following the death of Mullah Omar.

'Well?' one of the investigators said triumphantly.

'What kind of idiot doesn't accept his own video?' said another.

A third took out a sheet of paper and a pen.

'Sign here confirming you're Bashir.'

Bashir took the pen. 'Execute me if I'm Bashir,' he wrote.

One night they wouldn't let him sleep. Guards took shifts sitting in his cell, refusing to let him close his eyes. When his head drooped they hit him.

The next morning he was brought to the interrogation room. After a while he fell asleep in the chair. Then he was told to stand while questioning took place. The only breaks he was given were in order to pray. Prayer they respected.

After a week of sleepless nights and a total of fifteen days since his arrest they made good on their threat to arrest a relative. 'Muhammad Khan, do you know him?' they asked.

It was his nephew Sifat's alias.

'Hmm . . .' he prevaricated.

'Your nephew is here. If he confirms your story, we'll let your brother out.'

Sifat was fifteen years old and not privy to what his uncles had agreed to say, should they be detained. They hadn't imagined they would arrest a minor. Bashir sat in his cell pondering what to do. He knew new arrivals were placed in the corridor until given a cell, so following morning prayer he asked to go to the toilet. The directorate didn't have an en suite latrine like at the Americans' place.

Bashir looked around. His gaze swept over Sifat, lying sleeping in a corner of the corridor. When he came out of the toilet his nephew was still asleep. Bashir was escorted back to his cell. He had to try again. He waited until the shift changed. He banged on the door.

'Stomach ache, stomach pain, I need to go to the toilet, quickly!'

he shouted, and was allowed go again. Sifat was awake. The prisoners were sitting facing the wall so his nephew couldn't see him. Bashir had to get his attention. He bellowed as loudly as he could that he only had one wife. 'My name is Sor Gul. I've only got one wife!' he proclaimed. The guard stared at him, asked what kind of nonsense he was spouting. 'You don't know Bashir. You've never heard of him!' Bashir carried on.

When he passed his nephew on his way back from the toilet, he said, 'I've two sons. I have only two sons. Mawia is the eldest.'

Had Sifat heard him and understood?

Bashir demanded his soldiers be sharp and cunning. Sifat was neither of these things. After a while he banged frantically on the door again, complaining of diarrhoea. His nephew was still sitting facing the wall. As Bashir went past he repeated the same sentences aloud, so they would stick in the mind of the fifteen-year-old.

'I've never been to Mussahi in my life!' he added.

The guard probably thinks I've lost my mind, Bashir thought. He was still worried that Sifat hadn't understood: his nephew had shown no sign at all of having done so. He knocked on the door for a fourth time, asking to be allowed to go to the toilet. His nephew was in the room with the latrines when he entered.

'Did you understand?' Bashir whispered.

'Don't worry,' Sifat replied. 'It's all in here.' He pointed at his head.

Late on the Friday night of his second week without sleep, while Bashir was waiting to pray, a guard entered his cell. He was told to accompany him to the interrogation room. There were several men there when he arrived.

'How many wives do you have?'

'One.'

'What if you have two?'

'I have one.'

'Your nephew says you have two.'

'I only have one.'

The investigator got up and struck him hard across the face. No one had laid a hand on him until this point. 'How many wives do you have? How many wives do you have?'

'One. One!'

Bashir's hands were, as usual, bound behind his back. He was blindfolded and marched to a room on the floor above. Once there they tied him to a chair. Some men entered.

'Don't say a word. Just listen to the conversation,' one of them said.

Sifat was there. They were questioning him. 'How many wives does your uncle have?'

The boy took a while before answering in an almost inaudible voice: 'Two.'

They continued asking questions. He continued answering.

'Do you know . . . ?'

'Yes.'

'Where did you meet . . . ?'

'There.'

Bashir wanted to scream at his nephew! He opened his lips to say something but was struck across the mouth. Then in the throat. 'Shut up!'

Bashir could feel his lips bleeding. It was difficult to breathe. His mouth filled with the taste of blood. He made a sound.

'Don't speak!'

'I wasn't speaking, I just couldn't breathe,' he protested.

Someone hit him in the face, others struck him across the body.

'Admit that you are Bashir or things will turn out badly for your nephew.'

'I'm not Bashir. I'm Sor Gul,' he answered.

They beat him with something that made him groan loudly. He felt a metal bar hit his side, then his ribs, then his feet. The bar struck the soles of his feet with such force that the skin cracked.

The blows felt like someone was ripping the flesh from his body. What kind of instrument was this? He had never experienced such pain. The blindfold slipped down and he saw that his hand was black, as though it had been burnt. Then he understood: they hadn't been beating him; they'd been electrocuting him. It had felt like blows but it was electric shocks. They continued. More questions, more false answers. He tried as hard as he could not to scream. When they put the electric prod to his head it felt as though someone was ripping the pupils from his eyes.

He began to count. Four, five shocks. Then a question. Four more shocks. Then a question. Three more, a short pause, then a question again. He counted to twenty-eight. Then he passed out.

The next night they came for him again. And the next night. And the one after that. These interrogations were the worst. That was when they hit hardest, when they were most worked up. On one occasion they didn't take him one floor up but one floor down, then down another and out into a yard. They pushed him into a car and drove to another building. Bashir hated the feeling of having no idea what was going to happen to him. They took him down to a basement. There, two men bound his feet while others stood ready with metal pipes.

The lead interrogator asked, quite calmly, for him to confess.

He refused.

They hung him upside down. They beat him until the blood ran from his feet down over his stomach, across his chest and onto his face. The pain was unbearable. Bashir yelled: 'I'll confess!'

They stopped hitting immediately and took him down from the hook he was hanging from.

'On two conditions.' Bashir looked at them.

'Conditions?'

'Yes. That I speak to the deputy chief of Riyasat 90. And that my brother is released.'

When they took him back to the first building, Bashir wasn't able to walk. He collapsed on the floor. Two guards grabbed him under the arms, a couple of others lifted his legs and they carried him to the car. Back in the interview room, one of the torturers told him to write down on a sheet of paper that he was Bashir and that he confessed to everything he was accused of. Then he would be allowed to sleep.

Bashir insisted on seeing the deputy chief.

'Will you confess?'

'I set conditions!'

They carried him out to the car. Back to the other building. They can't beat me any more, Bashir thought, not if they want me to live. He felt his whole being was disjointed. But they did begin hitting him again. I'm going to die now, he managed to think prior to losing consciousness.

They left him lying on the floor. From far, far away he heard the voice of someone calling to morning prayer. A man approached.

'What are your nephews' names?'

'Nasrat, Umar, Hekmat . . . '

He was delirious. They were the names of the smallest boys at home. The man called someone on the phone and said, 'Bashir has confessed. Come and pick him up.' Bashir passed out. When he came round he couldn't get up, but at the same time lying down was unbearable. The pain cut through him. His whole body ached. He lost consciousness again and came round to the torturers yelling at him. He began to throw up. This is what hell must be like, he thought. He turned on his side and brought up the contents of his stomach.

'The deputy chief is waiting in the room next door,' one of the torturers said.

Bashir's clothes were covered in vomit, mucus and blood. They carried him to a bath, turned on the tap and washed him. Shampoo was applied to his hair. Once the blood was rinsed off, he noticed his head and hands weren't as badly injured as his feet. They helped him up some stairs and into the room where the deputy chief was supposed to be. But he wasn't. Two officers were there instead. They expressed their surprise over his ongoing failure to confess and told him they would wait until he admitted his crimes.

'Do as you like. I'm not confessing.'

He fell to the floor. Every time he tried to get up, he passed out.

He had never fainted before. Up to now life had been child's play. A couple of the torturers made a move towards him, metal pipes in their hands. No, he couldn't face being beaten again. He wasn't able to take any more. He said he'd talk.

'I was in Waziristan for nine months. I met the caliph and the whole Haqqani Network. I'm a commander in the Taliban.' He paused, before pulling himself together. 'But . . . I'm not Bashir. I'm Sor Gul . . .'

Then he collapsed on the floor.

One day two Americans showed up to the interrogations. He hadn't seen any Americans since being transferred from Bagram, even though he had the feeling the questions asked came from three different masters: the USA, Pakistan and Afghanistan.

One of them was a well-built man with a blond beard who spoke Pashto.

'*Assalam aleikum*,' he said.

'*Aleikum assalam*,' Bashir answered. 'You're American but you look like a mullah,' he said, smiling, though the foreigner's clothes were Western enough.

'We have your confession,' the American said.

'No, you don't,' Bashir replied. 'You have this,' he said, displaying his feet in the open sandals. They had cuts and open wounds that had become infected and filled with pus. Up along his legs his skin was bulging and black, blue, red and yellow.

The American turned away. Probably not the sort of thing he's supposed to see, Bashir thought.

'I'm a simple man from a small village, a salesman, my name is Sor Gul. I'm neither Talib nor terrorist,' Bashir said. 'I'm haji.'

The American looked at his feet again, the wounds on his face, the bruises, the cuts.

'If you stay here, you won't survive,' he said. 'Do you want to come back to Bagram?'

Bashir wanted that.

The two Americans talked among themselves. Bashir caught a few words. He thought he heard something about the Taliban and

Haqqani, General Miller, and then one of them used the word for *negotiations* in Pashto.

After five months at Riyasat 90, Bashir was transferred back to Bagram. It was Eid, the end of Ramadan. All the prisoners were brought a good meal. Food had been scarce at the directorate, and now, alone in his cell, he didn't know whether to eat or sleep first. He fell asleep with his hand in the rice bowl.

For three days he did little other than sleep, only waking long enough to eat and pray.

At Bagram there was no physical violence, no torture. The Americans had saved his life, that was how it felt.

One day his mother came to visit. They embraced. Ah, it was good to see her! But he realised straight away that something was wrong.

'I know it already. Just tell me everything,' he said.

But he knew nothing of what she was about to relate.

Both of his elder brothers were dead.

Hassan had been killed in a drone strike a month and a half after Bashir had been taken into custody. A drone had also done for Yaqub six months later.

The brothers had always insisted on one of them being at home with their mother. Now she had no one. Two dead, two locked up.

Hala told him what she knew. Hassan was killed in the Kharwar district of Logar Province. His troops had been under heavy fire and split into groups to repel attack from a larger force from several sides.

'God knows how the Americans knew! They bombed each group, in different places, at the same time!'

Hassan and the men with him had barricaded themselves inside a house. 'He fought to the end and became a martyr,' Hala sobbed. Bashir cried too.

Ah, Hassan. The eldest who always behaved as though he were the youngest. Always so happy and carefree, a fighter from when he was a teenager, never far from the opium pipe. What a sweet life they had shared!

His mother had brought a photo for him. A martyr picture. Hassan lay dead and pale with his chin bound up, on a bed of roses. The flowers had been photoshopped in. A cotton swab had been placed over one eye. He glowed like a prophet, an earnest, peaceful aspect to his face, waiting for an angel to take him to paradise.

The mood in the house had been so morose, Hala decided to arrange an engagement, the best thing she knew. She thought it would cheer up Hassan's eldest son if he became engaged to Yaqub's daughter. He was fifteen and she was twelve, so they would have to wait for the wedding, but they could celebrate the engagement in a big way.

She began to cry again, because then Yaqub was killed!

The drone had got him when he was in a car travelling from Charkh to Kharwar, near to where Hassan died. That was all she knew. His body had come back in three pieces. Bits of him had been blown off. But his face was almost in one piece.

She produced a photo of Yaqub prior to his burial. His skin hadn't been lightened digitally like that of his brother. His face was covered in cuts. The tip of his nose was missing. There was a depression between his eyes. His skin was bloody – martyrs were not supposed to be washed. He had a pearl-encrusted *kepi* on his head, and wrapped over it, and the rest of his body, was the white sheet he was to be buried in. One eye was covered, the other closed. There was some cotton wool in his mouth. Around him lay a wreath in many colours, like the ones a child would receive when he became hafiz and had learned the Quran off by heart. The wreath had bright pink, intense yellow, purple, green and blue tassels, to make it easier to spot for the angel who would take him up to the wonderful, eternal afterlife.

In May of the following year judgement was handed down.

The trial had lasted several days. Alongside Bashir in the dock sat Raouf and Sifat, now sixteen. They had each been appointed a defence lawyer, but none of them thought they did very much. In any event, Bashir had decided to represent himself.

He was led into the courtroom, past the judges' bench. He received a blow when he caught sight of the papers laying there.

'Execution Order' was written on one of the sheets.

He was aware of the penalty. But still, seeing it in black and white. Was it his? Probably. He only hoped it didn't apply to Raouf as well. Then his mother wouldn't have a single son left.

One of the judges began reading the reasons for the sentence.

'Mawlawi Bashir is one of the Taliban's top commanders and is accused of engaging in terrorist activities against the authorities, and the kidnapping and extortion of foreigners and wealthy individuals. He was responsible for and involved in attacks on the Ministry of Defence and other public buildings. He controls numerous armed groups in Logar, Paktia and Khost engaged in subverting the activities of the authorities and the security forces.'

The row of judges sat in silence while the evidence was presented.

'In a video the accused confirms his membership of the Taliban and that he swore allegiance to Mullah Mansour following the death of Mullah Omar. His brother Raouf also appears in the video.'

Bashir was charged with a series of kidnappings. The judge listed some of these.

'Haji Muhammad Gardizi confirms that he was abducted by Bashir personally in Logar and taken to Miram Shah and a sum of one and a half million dollars was demanded for his release. Several other businessmen confirm being kidnapped and subjected to blackmail by Bashir. He is also found guilty of the kidnap of two university professors in Kabul. A number of murders and executions were carried out by Bashir personally, like the murder of Mohamadullah, Son of Nazir . . .'

The list was long. He was convicted of an attack on a hospital, on a police station and of being behind numerous suicide bombings.

The charge sheet also contained operations he had not got around to carrying out.

'When Mawlawi Bashir was arrested it was discovered that, together with Sirajuddin Haqqani, he was planning a suicide bombing of the military academy in Kabul. To this end, he had received twenty thousand dollars for the purposes of planning and the acquisition of equipment. Fortunately, this attack was averted due to his arrest.'

The sentence was then read out.

'We, the panel of judges of the prison court at Bagram, sentence Sor Gul, known as Mawlawi Bashir, to one year of prison for possession of a false ID card. In addition, he is sentenced to five years in prison for membership of a terror organisation.'

A further twelve years were added for the kidnap of a businessman.

The judge continued reading.

'For subversive activities, you – Mawlawi Bashir – are sentenced to death by hanging.'

The Great Game

Bashir was no longer in solitary confinement. After his sentence was handed down, while he waited to be hanged, he was moved. Now he shared a cell with a dozen others. He was still Sor Gul: it was best to exercise caution, you didn't know who might inform on you. In prison everything could be bought and sold.

The first thing Bashir got himself was a mobile phone. A tiny model, easy to conceal and requiring little battery power. Phones were forbidden and there were no sockets in the cell, but charging was available for a fee. If you gave the phone to a guard along with a few thousand afghani, you got it back fully charged. The guards were also the ones selling the phones.

Finally, he could keep in touch with his militias again and – if there was enough battery – his family.

No one in his cell knew about his death sentence.

'The trial was postponed,' he said whenever someone asked what everyone wonders about in a prison: what are you in for and how long did you get?

In time, when the death sentence was upheld on appeal, he said he had been given five years. He had no desire to stand out, he just wanted to be seen as a nice guy who performed his religious duties. In this way he could get on with things with minimum disruption. Because the war continued. There were battles to win, people to kill.

*

At the same time, on the outside, high-stakes politics were taking place. Afghanistan had become a very expensive quagmire. With air support Afghan government forces might win battles, but they couldn't win the war. There was no solution to be found on the battlefield because there were too many like Bashir – men who would never give up.

'A bleeding wound,' Mikhail Gorbachev had called the war he inherited. Enduring Freedom had been taken over by the third American president.

When Donald Trump became president in 2017, he led the USA down new paths. Afghanistan was no exception. He didn't want to persist with Obama's plans for withdrawal and negotiation. He wanted to win. Preferably quickly and without American casualties. During Trump's first year in office, his army carried out more airstrikes than in any previous year, and a threefold increase on 2016. In August 2017, the same month Bashir was arrested, Trump was adamant the USA would remain in Afghanistan until they had defeated both al-Qaeda and IS. 'The consequences of a rapid exit are both predictable and unacceptable,' he stated.

But within a year he had grown weary. Trump appointed two old hawks – the deeply conservative John Bolton as National Security Advisor and CIA chief Mike Pompeo as Secretary of State – and told them to fix Afghanistan. Trump decided to bypass President Ghani, who he called a 'crook', and speak directly to the Taliban. For the job, he appointed a third old hand, Zalmay Khalilzad, who had been ambassador to Afghanistan under George W. Bush. He had been pulling the strings since the summit in Bonn in 2001, and during Karzai's years in power was called the Emperor of Kabul.

The special envoy knew Ashraf Ghani well. Both being sons of the Afghan elite, they had been sent to high school in the US in the 1960s, and while Zal was working on his PhD in political science at the University of Chicago, Ashraf was submitting his own in anthropology in New York. Their relationship had always been more of a rivalry than a friendship.

Trump's orders were clear: make a deal with the Taliban!

In October 2018, two months after Bashir's death sentence had been handed down, Khalilzad went to see the man he had known for over half a century. They met in the Arg in Kabul, where Ghani resided with his wife and his personal library of seven thousand books, but without the ability to form coalitions, make compromises or communicate with those he disagreed with. He was quick to anger and prone to confrontation. Staff were frequently replaced while the circle around him grew ever smaller.

Ghani had prepared a PowerPoint presentation for the meeting.

He pictured himself sitting on the same side of the table as the USA, with the Taliban across from them. Khalilzad dismissed this as unrealistic. The Taliban had been demanding to speak to the USA alone for a decade. Internal peace negotiations between Ghani's government and the Taliban could take place after the American withdrawal, he told him.

Just as when they were teenagers, there was mutual dislike and mistrust, yet they were hostage to one another.

The formal negotiations started in January 2019, in Doha. When and how the US and NATO would be pulling their troops out of Afghanistan was at the heart of the talks. The two parties had to agree on a ceasefire. The Taliban were to guarantee no terrorist groups would attack during the process. Afterwards the Taliban were to negotiate a power-sharing agreement with the Afghan government.

The conversations went back and forth. The Taliban agreed not to attack the international forces, but a formal ceasefire wasn't on the cards. Their fight against the Afghan regime had to continue as before: that was an internal affair that foreigners had nothing to do with.

Criticism of the Doha negotiations came from many sources. The Taliban delegation were viewed as the softer men in the movement. The lead negotiator, Sher Abbas Stanikzai, was so modern that he even took his wife out to restaurants.

Khalilzad, who had worked in Republican administrations since

Ronald Reagan's presidency, advocated that the Americans temper their demands if they hoped to get the leadership in Kandahar to ratify any agreement, as they were far more dogmatic than the Doha delegation. One of the Taliban's founders, Mullah Baradar, was flown in to meet the US chief negotiator, a sign that the leadership were taking the talks seriously. Baradar's life was also intertwined with that of Khalilzad. In 2018, the latter had managed to negotiate the release of the mullah from a Pakistani prison, where he had been sitting for eight years, after being arrested at the instigation of the CIA. In Doha, they met in Baradar's luxurious suite with a view over the hotel swimming pool. Women in bikinis lay tanning on sun loungers or splashing about in the pool.

'You must feel like you're in heaven,' Khalilzad joked, alluding to what the Quran taught about afterlife for jihadists. Mullah Baradar made a beeline for the window and drew the curtains.

The talks hobbled along through the winter, in plenary sessions, in hotel rooms, on messaging services like WhatsApp and Signal. Khalilzad was pulling most of the strings while his old rival Ghani complained about being sidelined. The ceasefire proved an impediment to progress. The Americans continued to demand the Taliban laid down their arms across the whole country. The Taliban continued to refuse. Instead, in early 2019, they made a counter demand: they wanted several thousand Taliban prisoners released from Afghan jails.

A few days after the initial demand, the draft of the agreement was changed. The Taliban wanted five thousand of their men released from captivity.

As the Taliban were advancing new demands, Jamila Afghani flew to Qatar. The USA and the Taliban had taken a break in their talks and representatives of civil society had been invited to the Gulf state to speak directly to the Taliban. Jamila had been selected as one of eleven women among fifty or so men.

She was dreading it. Jamila had never met anyone in the Taliban. When they were in power in the 1990s, she had lived in Pakistan, and when she returned to Kabul they were gone. Or rather, they were still there, only in the form of an ever-present threat, like suicide bombers, car bombs, or rocket attacks on the loya jirga. Put simply, they were the enemy. Now, at forty-three years of age, she was going to meet them face to face.

The idea behind the direct dialogue was to discuss how peace could be maintained after an agreement was signed.

The first evening, Jamila sat on the bed in her room unable to get up. Not because her foot was in pain or she was without her crutches. Something else was paralysing her. Horror. Too much bloodshed. She couldn't face meeting them. An inner struggle played out. She told herself: you've been chosen to convey the voice of Afghan women, and to speak for those who have endured tribulation and loss. You must dare to meet your nemesis.

She looked at the time. She was late. The dinner had already begun. She collected herself, stood up, checked in the mirror that her hijab – subtle, light brown – sat as it should.

Everyone had taken their seats when she entered the dining room. A group of men in turbans were sitting at the first table. There they are, she thought.

'*Salam*,' she mumbled, while looking around at the other tables for a vacant chair.

'*Wa aleikum assalam wa rahmatullahi wa barakatuh*,' the men replied in unison, some low, others loudly. The Taliban had chosen the respectful form – *May the peace, mercy and blessings of Allah be with you* – while she had used the shorter version, suggesting either informality or impertinence. She should have said assalam aleikum and was annoyed at herself as she made her way between the tables, feeling everyone's eyes on her. She headed for a vacant chair next to Fawzia Koofi, vice-president of the *wolesi jirga*, the lower house of the parliament, who herself had survived an assassination attempt by the Taliban.

Before getting to her seat, Jamila noticed one of the Taliban had stood up and was coming towards her. What did he want? Was he going to chide her, say something nasty because she had failed to show respect? All sorts of thoughts raced through her head. Why was he following her? As she reached the empty chair and took hold of the back rest, she heard the turbaned man behind her.

'Sister, is everything all right? I see you have problems moving, does your leg hurt?'

She gasped. He gestured to the place she had chosen.

'Will that chair be comfortable enough for you? Shall I find you a better place?'

Jamila put her crutches aside and made to sit down. Unsure whether her voice would carry, she just nodded briefly.

'I'm at your service: if you need anything please let me know.'

She nodded again.

'What did that Talib say to you?' Fawzia asked.

'He said he'd find me a better chair . . . '

She sat, feeling disconcerted. This ran counter to the image she had of them. Something was amiss.

The next morning, Jamila awoke and saw she had several missed calls. They were from a relative in Ghazni who had lost a son the previous week. Afghan government soldiers had mistaken him for a member of the Taliban and killed him out in his field.

Jamila returned the call.

'They're at the hospital! They're wounded! More were killed!' the older woman cried.

That same morning the Taliban had detonated a car bomb outside the offices of the intelligence service in Ghazni. As well as a dozen people being killed, close to two hundred had been wounded, including several children in a neighbouring school.

Two of them were the sons of the man killed in his field.

'You're in Qatar, you're sitting down with the Taliban,' the boys' grandmother cried on the phone. 'Ask them, "Why are you killing us?" Make them stop!'

It felt hopeless. The Taliban sitting here talking about peace, while at the same time killing schoolchildren in Afghanistan!

The tears were still welling up as she entered the meeting. It was held in a large hall. The wallpaper, curtains and carpet were in light, delicate pastel shades with golden threads. The two parties were to sit in a semi-circle facing each other.

She found it difficult to pay attention to the introductions. When it was her turn to speak, she put aside the speech she had written in Kabul.

'I want to tell you a story,' she said. 'About two boys who have never known anything but war.'

She told how they had lost their father the week before. Nevertheless, they had turned up to school every day since. Because they wanted to learn, they had to learn, because now they were the two oldest in the family.

'But this morning, while we were preparing to sit here and talk about peace, you' – she nodded in the direction of the Taliban – 'detonated a car bomb in Ghazni. You wanted to strike the security forces, and gave no thought to children, Afghan children, whom this peace is for, also being killed. The two boys, the sons of my relative who was killed, have been wounded. Their condition is uncertain.'

She took a deep breath.

'Why are you killing us?'

She paused.

'Why?'

She looked directly at the Taliban.

'You call yourselves an *Islamic emirate*! And you . . .'

She fixed her gaze on a couple of young men who were advisors in the Arg.

' . . . call yourselves an *Islamic republic*.'

She surveyed the assembly.

'But where is *Islam* in this? What does this word that you both use mean?'

One of the Taliban wiped his eyes with the end of his turban.

They all knew what it meant. This word that both sides lay claim to meant surrender and submission.

*

After Jamila had made her presentation, it was time for a break. She felt clammy and anxious, and disappeared out to the toilet to calm down. After taking a breather she went back to the hall, but her unease quickly returned when she saw a Talib on his way towards her at the tea table.

'Sister, you are right,' he said. 'You moved me to tears. My heart wept.'

'If you mean that, stop killing us. Stop this meaningless violence!' she replied.

'I'm set on peace, but we have many challenges—'

'Whatever! It's in your hands!'

She was so upset she wasn't even able to look at the man.

Discussions with the Taliban continued after the break. Fawzia Koofi told them how her husband had been imprisoned by the Taliban and how she herself had been harassed.

'The last time you were in charge, women were beaten for not wearing burkas,' she said. 'What is your definition of appropriate covering for women now?'

A Talib answered.

'According to our understanding of Islam, the shawl you're wearing over your head is sufficient. We have no problem with that. But should other women choose to follow our Afghan tradition and wear the burka, then we have no problem with that either.'

The Taliban were disciplined, both in answers and behaviour. At mealtimes, breakfast included, they came together in freshly ironed garments, with their turbans wrapped in the same style, the end of the material resting on their left shoulders. They were like a well-drilled troop. Today's exercise: diplomacy.

Jamila's group was more diverse. People talking right and left, moving in and out of meetings, talking on the phone, texting. Compared to the men in the turbans, they seemed disorganised and chaotic. In addition to the activists and Ghani's men, some warlords, or their children, had places in the delegation. Among them were the sons of Dostum and Atta Noor, who had grown up as heirs of their own little fiefdom in northern Afghanistan and had as little in common with Jamila as the Taliban.

The Taliban troop included a young man in a pearl-embroidered hat who listened attentively and found references to what was said during the meetings. He produced the correct version of a UN communication, an Amnesty report, or an analysis undertaken by the American Congress.

The atmosphere in the room was bitter.

'You've killed my father, you've killed my brother, but I'm here to talk to you,' Matin Bek, one of Ghani's advisors, said. There were also harsh words from Nader Nadery, a close associate of the president and long-time member of the Afghanistan Independent Human Rights Commission. He called the men sitting across from him terrorists and murderers. Bek and Nadery ate breakfast with Khalilzad the following morning, and Bek was cross: 'Please, for God's sake, the Taliban are not in favour of negotiations, they are not in favour of a political settlement. They're really on a victory march!'

Calmly and patiently, the men in turbans tolerated all censure. Like Jamila, Bek also had doubts that these men were the real Taliban. Perhaps it was just diplomatic theatre. To get the deal done and take power.

Before travelling home to Kabul, the Afghan delegation had a meeting with Khalilzad. He emphasised that as far as the Americans were concerned there were four important aspects to the peace negotiations. US national security. Counterterrorism. Ceasefire. Power sharing.

'When negotiating this deal with the Taliban,' Jamila asked, 'what picture do you have in your mind for how Afghanistan will be? And where in this picture are the women?'

'*We're* making the frame,' Khalilzad said. '*You people* paint the picture.'

Back in Kabul, each person who had been in Doha was invited to the Arg. President Ghani wanted all the details.

A number of those who went to the presidential palace mentioned what Jamila had said about the explosion in Ghazni that had injured her young relatives. They called her speech 'effective' and 'wonderful'. It had made the Taliban cry, one of them told Ghani.

When it was Jamila's turn to visit, she met an irate Ghani.

'You should have said to them, "What are you crying for? Dry your eyes! Stop the killings!" Did you say that? Did you say that?'

His forefinger was quivering.

'Why are you pointing your finger at me?' Jamila asked. She was no longer his vice-minister and didn't need to answer to him. This man who had never been there when she needed him, the man who had promised he had her back.

'From now on,' Ghani said, his anger undiminished, 'anyone travelling to Doha needs authorisation from my office. We can't let all kinds of people with their own separate agendas go. Everyone needs to present our national agenda. We must show that we stand together. Everyone needs to have the same agenda and it needs to be approved by me!'

'The president wants to control every single person in the country,' Jamila complained to Kakar afterwards. She watched the negotiations from the sidelines. Before going to Doha, she had thought the government was relatively strong, but after seeing how well organised the Taliban were, she was becoming anxious.

The Afghan president was, as usual, preoccupied with the smaller picture and began compiling a list of who could travel. He ticked the names he approved and crossed out the ones he didn't like. Only people who proactively supported the government would be allowed go. Jamila heard, via a colleague, that after looking over the list he sent it to his wife, who made further adjustments. Jamila was frustrated by the regimentation Ghani, once ostensibly a liberal, had introduced. She had to stand firm. Her role was not to take sides.

Prior to the meetings in Doha, Jamila had believed the Taliban could perhaps secure a quarter of the seats in a coalition government, maybe a third, but now she realised that their power resided in their patience, in endless time. They were unwavering. They never stopped halfway, preferring to win big, or lose big. They would never accept an equal distribution of power. If they got most of the ministerial posts, how would Afghanistan look then? Would it be winner takes all, like during the talks in Bonn, when the Taliban were excluded after being defeated on the battlefield?

Jamila was often in meetings in Kabul with foreign diplomats and organisations. The mood had changed.

At the American embassy it was as if they had had enough. 'We're bringing in money but how long are we going to keep doing that? Why can't you manage to build anything up?'

They're right, Jamila thought.

On the one hand. On the other hand, they're not. The foreign donors were also responsible for who they had put their faith in.

She had met Mike Pompeo twice in Kabul. He hadn't even tried to be diplomatic.

'We've injected money, we've put vast amounts of dollars into Afghanistan,' the Secretary of State said. 'We've given you time, time to change the system, but the corruption only increases, and now our taxpayers are asking, "Where's our money going?"'

'When is someone considered of legal age, at eighteen, right?' he added. The USA had been trying to raise them for eighteen years. It was time to stand on their own two feet. 'Afghanistan is the responsibility of the Afghans. We've done our bit.'

Women's rights – that was their own responsibility. Human rights – they'd have to take care of that themselves.

The slogans about supporting Afghan women had vanished. About granting girls access to education. About freedom and democracy. Donald Trump was at least honest, Jamila thought. America first.

The Doha talks continued over the summer. The Americans demanded a halt to the conflict; the Taliban refused. What about an armistice in some provinces, Khalilzad suggested. The US could begin their withdrawal from there and the war could continue in the rest of Afghanistan. If the Taliban attacked the Afghan army the US would step in, but they wouldn't initiate an attack on the Taliban themselves. The commander of the US forces, General Austin Miller, argued the proposals were too constrictive to operate in. They also needed to be able to engage Taliban who were planning an attack.

Khalilzad went to Kabul and showed a draft of the agreement to Ghani, but failed to include all the details, fearing they would be leaked. In any event, the president didn't like what he saw and produced his red pen. Neither Pompeo nor Khalilzad paid any heed to the corrections. Donald Trump had told them not to take any notice of him anyway.

At the end of August 2019, the Taliban accepted the draft and promised not to attack NATO forces. 'If one American dies after the deal is signed . . . the deal is off,' General Miller told the Taliban envoys.

Trump wanted to invite the Taliban to Camp David to sign the agreement, but a car bomb went off in Kabul on 5 September. A dozen people were killed, including an American major.

The peace agreement was called off with a tweet from the president: 'If they cannot agree to a ceasefire during these very important peace talks, and would even kill 12 innocent people, then they probably don't have the power to negotiate a meaningful agreement anyway.'

But Khalilzad managed to salvage the deal by arranging the release of the two professors Bashir was convicted of abducting. They were being held hostage by the Haqqani Network in Waziristan and had been prisoners since 2016. In exchange Ghani had to release three men, two of whom were at the top of the network's wish list: Anas Haqqani, Sirajuddin's bespectacled younger brother, and Mali Khan Haqqani, his uncle.

The agreement between Trump and the Taliban was signed on 29 February 2020.

The USA were to pull their forces out within a year. The Taliban were to enter negotiations with the Afghan government to create a lasting peace.

The Taliban's supreme leader, Haibatullah Akhundzada, issued a statement from a secret location. The agreement was a victory for all Muslims, he claimed.

The day after the signing, Trump rang Ghani to talk about power-sharing with the Taliban.

'We're relying on you to get this done,' Trump said, because the deal was 'popular among the American people'.

'It's popular among my enemies as well,' Ghani retorted drily.

'Call me if you need anything,' the American president said in conclusion.

Two days later Trump rang Mullah Baradar.

'You guys are tough fighters,' he said. 'Do you need something from me?'

'We need to get prisoners released,' Baradar said, but Ghani wouldn't cooperate. Trump responded that he would have Pompeo pressure the Afghan president.

That spring, the Taliban delivered a list with the names of five thousand prisoners they wanted released before the conversations about power-sharing could begin.

On the list was Sor Gul, alias Mawlawi Bashir, alias *Bashir the Afghan*.

Among the five thousand, Ghani's people rejected the release of several hundred men: kidnappers, drug traffickers and convicted terrorists. Bashir's name was also on that list.

In May 2020 just under a thousand prisoners were released.

The Taliban were unshakeable: all five thousand or no negotiations.

They knew the Americans needed to pull out with heads held high. So instead of pressuring the Taliban, Trump leaned on the Afghan president, whereupon Ghani finally responded: 'If you want to leave, then leave, no hard feelings.'

The harsh truth was that the Afghan regime's survival was completely dependent on the money and military might of the USA. Since 2001 Afghan forces had been supported by their bombers, rockets and drone strikes. Now they were left to fend for themselves.

For a long time Ghani refused to release the prisoners who had been sentenced to death. In the end he found an Afghan solution. He convened a loya jirga to determine the fate of the most problematic of the Taliban. In August 2020 the assembly approved the release of all of the prisoners.

First Raouf and Sifat, sentenced to twenty-five and five years respectively, were let out. They went straight to the house in Jalalabad, where Hala arranged a huge celebration. But their happiness was short-lived. After just a few days local Afghan forces stormed the gate. They beat Raouf until he lay bleeding on the ground, brutally searched Sima when she wouldn't let go of her husband, then dragged him into a car and drove away.

The news reached the prisoners yet to be released. Yes, Ghani had freed the five thousand, but only to arrest them again.

Eventually eighty prisoners remained. Those considered the most dangerous.

One of them was Bashir.

On a hot August day the guards finally came to collect him. An officer took his fingerprints for the last time, handed him a written copy of the verdict, on which Bashir had once written 'do not agree' next to his signature, and then he was given a brand-new certificate of prison release.

A brother in arms was waiting outside with a car.

Bashir didn't go home. They weren't getting him that easily.

My Heart Will Go On

The old man looked at them with a steady gaze. He was very sick; perhaps this was the last time they would be in his company. Around him the lilacs were in bloom. The purple flowers the area was renowned for had just opened. They were sitting on the veranda where branches of a large apple tree hung above them.

'My dream,' the old man said, 'is for one of my grandchildren to become a judge.'

Baba Musa had grown up as 'the judge's son'. His father had served on the bench under Zahir Shah, but since the fall of the monarchy no one in the family had achieved the same heights.

'You're the sharpest,' he said to Ariana. He was barely able to lift his forefinger. 'You can do whatever you want.'

Her grandfather was an ambitious man. When his own children were small, he used to sit all four of them down on the floor, every night except Fridays, light the lamp and dictate something to them. His wife, who was illiterate, would put out nuts and serve tea. The children didn't do any housework. 'No, no, all of you shall learn,' she would say. 'Go and read, I can manage the house.'

When she was a child, Ariana's mother had been envious of her cousins having fun outside. After the dictation was finished, they would go through all the words and crown the winner. If anyone made too many mistakes they had their knuckles rapped.

Strict, but open-minded. Girls should achieve great things, Baba Musa believed.

He hadn't liked how hard it had been on his daughter, constantly having to up sticks because the army were posting Karim to different places. Until his son-in-law was finished moving around, Nadia, Ariana and her siblings would live with him and his wife in the country, he decided. And so it came to pass. Soon, Karim's itinerant lifestyle was at an end.

Baba Musa himself worked as a tax collector. People greeted him respectfully when he passed on the way to the mosque. But he had never become a judge like his father.

Ariana had just finished secondary school. She nodded.

A judge? That wasn't something she had ever thought of. She had considered becoming a teacher like her mother. After all her courses in English the headmaster had asked her to teach a class. There would be sixty pupils, and she was to be paid three thousand afghani, or around thirty pounds, a month. She loved it. Entering the classroom, all the pupils' attention on her. Saying *Good morning!* and being greeted with of a chorus of *Good morning, Miss Ariana!* in return.

But her dream was something else entirely: to pack a suitcase, say goodbye to her family, set out on a journey. Ariana wanted to experience other countries, ways of living, methods of learning, seize the opportunities that came her way. In her diary she wrote how she viewed her life as a book. She needed to follow the plot as it unfolded, not stay put while others turned their pages and moved on.

Her father had become stricter as the security situation in Kabul deteriorated. Every week more bombs exploded, and Karim would rather his daughters stayed at home. Ariana wasn't allowed take any more courses and that caused her worry. She had to get top grades in the final school exams. She needed courses in chemistry, physics and mathematics. Everyone took courses, everyone was talking about their courses, or so it felt. Eventually he relented, as long as she wore her school uniform. She was mortified. The others dressed in jeans or leggings with baggy T-shirts, some with tight belts round their waists. Why was her father so strict? She had seen photos from the 1980s of her mother when she was young, dressed in short skirts to her knees, with bare legs and white socks. On her head she was wearing . . . nothing! In some pictures her mother's hair was curly, in others it was straightened, with hair clips and a side parting. Boys and girls had attended the same class, even shared the same desk. Why hadn't that time returned?

Nadia had started school under the communists and had finished during the rule of Dr Najibullah, her grandfather's hero, who had been executed and hung from a lamp post when the Taliban took power in 1996.

Following the fall of the Taliban, her grandfather had quickly become a staunch supporter of Hamid Karzai, of the Americans, of NATO, and now of Ashraf Ghani. He still remembered when Afghanistan had been open to the world, back when the country had been a monarchy, and now he welcomed all Western support. There were no two ways about it. The country needed modernising. He had worn a suit and tie all his life. Only on Fridays, when he was at home all day, did he put on the soft cotton tunic shirt and the wide pants.

'What rank now?' was her grandfather's opening question every time they came to visit. Ariana could hardly wait to answer, but her older brother was supposed to go first. He never did well in school, coming in around twentieth place or worse. Her sister did better, often in fourth or fifth, once third. But it was Ariana who excelled; she retained first place throughout her school years.

'Splendid,' Baba Musa would say. 'Brilliant!' And then he would take each of them in turn for a ride on his motorcycle.

But now he was dying.

Towards the end of the evening the refrain was no longer 'You can do whatever you like.' Ariana's grandfather fixed her with a steady gaze and said, 'You must apply for law school. Someone needs to revive our name!'

Getting into law school was tough. She needed to excel in the entrance exams to get a place. Not everyone had to strive as hard.

Admission could be bought, and places were reserved for the sons and daughters of important men.

The university in Kabul was the preferred choice. Even though Ariana expected to finish among the best, applying to study in the capital carried the risk of not getting in at all and thus losing a whole year. It was easier in the provinces. She ended up applying to a university near her grandparents. Then she could stay with them some weekends, and go home to her parents for others.

Ariana passed the entrance exam with flying colours. Baba Musa just managed to celebrate her achievement before his death.

The university was situated on a large plain with mountains on three sides and desert on the fourth. Her father stopped the car when they got there and helped carry her suitcase. He had been against the whole thing. With all the suicide bombers, fighting, kidnappings and the growth of the Taliban, how safe would his daughter be here all alone?

An elderly guard took the suitcase and was about to lead her inside. The pale, petite girl couldn't hold back the tears any longer.

'Don't worry, you'll make loads of new friends,' the old man assured her.

The girls in the hall of residence all looked like they were best friends. For the first week Ariana hardly spoke to anyone and counted down the days until Friday.

That changed quickly. Soon she didn't want to leave at weekends. She had landed in the best place in the world, sharing a room with five other girls, each with their own dramas, passions and trifles. She became active in the association of law students, took advanced computer courses and got a job on student radio. Two days a week she helped make programmes, taking questions from listeners and preparing competitions. After a while she also went on air. She took part in a workshop on conflict resolution and peacebuilding and discovered the many ways to participate in society. She soaked up knowledge. She felt so good. Ariana loved life and life loved her.

She got a smartphone. There was free Wi-Fi and computers on

loan, and when all the reading rooms were closed, classes were over and the discussion groups had finished, the roommates sat on her bed watching movies on the small screen of her phone. They saw *Titanic*. They saw *Top Gun*, they saw *Spider-Man* and *Pride and Prejudice*, and dreamt about everything they had yet to experience.

Several women had approached her mother to ask for Ariana's hand on behalf of their sons. But her mother had rejected all of them, even her own sister. Ariana was going to study, as Baba Musa had wished.

One day in the canteen, where she always arrived starving for lunch because she hadn't had time for breakfast, a classmate called out to her. She told her, excitedly, about a competition called the Jessup. It was open to law students worldwide; they were given problems to solve, and the final was to be held in Washington DC! All the finalists would gather at a hotel there to compete in teams of four. To take part in the competition you first had to pass a test.

'When's the test?' Ariana asked.

'Now! It starts now!'

'Well let's go then,' Ariana replied.

They found the room where the test was to be held, entering as the doors were closing behind them. A five-page test was handed out.

'Take five minutes to peruse the questions,' the teacher said. 'After that, those of you who don't think you can manage to answer them can leave. It's up to you.'

Ariana looked through the test. They were complicated questions. When the five minutes were up, she lifted her head to survey the room and saw that most of the students were leaving. She began the laborious process of answering. Some parts she managed while others were unfamiliar. The results were posted the following day. She had the third highest points total and became a member of the 'Jessup community'. From universities all over Afghanistan, teams were set up to compete for a place in the final.

The first task in the contest was to represent a country accused of engaging in war crimes. Ariana was to defend the accused.

She thought it the most interesting thing she had ever done.

The four members of her team, herself and three boys, eagerly awaited the result. In the end they made it all the way to the national semi-finals, where teams from across the country spent a long weekend together at a hotel.

Ariana noticed that people knew who she was. At one event she was asked to read a piece she had written at a workshop arranged by the American Peace Center, a club of sorts that arranged seminars, meetings and classes in English. The title was 'The Value of Knowing English'.

She prepared for days. On the morning of the speech, she was so nervous she was shaking, but when she went up on stage it was as if someone flicked a switch. She felt energised, knew what she was going to say. She looked around, was aware of behaving naturally.

'Speaking one language is like knowing one person. If you learn a world language, it's like knowing the whole world! You can travel everywhere, talk to everyone . . .'

She knew the speech struck home; she knew she had made a good impression. Relieved and happy, she received applause.

Afterwards she felt everyone at university knew her name.

'Of course, you're Ariana!'

'Here comes Ariana!'

'So nice to meet you, Ariana.'

She even got a call from one of the instructors in the IT faculty. He congratulated her on the fantastic content and delivery, and asked where she had learned to speak such beautiful English.

She didn't quite know what to answer.

'Your English is really good. I was impressed,' he said.

'Everyone in the room was impressed,' she replied, unexpectedly sharply.

He laughed. 'Absolutely. They were. I was one of them.'

He said he had tried to get her number. 'I've seen you many times,' he told her. 'I've noticed you walking by my window. I'd love to get your address. We can be in touch.'

'I'll have to think about it,' Ariana said, taken aback, before she gathered herself. 'No. I don't want any contact with you. I don't know who you are.'

'Well, you have my number now. Get in touch any time, ask me whatever you want. Text me. Call me.'

She shook off the unwanted attention and turned to what she wanted more of: everything around her that was seething and teeming – student life, laughter, the big wide world just outside. She was bubbling within.

Tonight they were going to watch *Titanic* again, or a few episodes of *Stranger Things*.

On the bus at the weekends, when the girls from Kabul were going home, she acted as DJ, playing Justin Bieber and Beyoncé. In the end they would all be singing *My heart will go on, and on, and on, and on!* from *Titanic* at the top of their lungs – even those who hardly knew a word of English – until someone intervened, wanting to play their own music, as most on the bus preferred Indian or Afghan songs.

But Ariana was looking outward.

Part Three

Collapse

When Nadia awoke just before six her husband was still fast asleep. Birds were chirping in the backyard and the roar of traffic could be heard far off, otherwise it was quiet.

August had been hot. Sand dust saturating the air, sticking to the skin and settling like a clammy layer on the body. The oppressive heat eased somewhat at night but the nocturnal cool evaporated while they slept.

Nadia turned over in bed as the day's chores forced themselves into her mind. She converted the stress she felt into organising tasks into lists, which became bullet points in her head. Several of her classes had exams, and to allow each group time to sit the tests she had arranged for quick changes between the appointed time slots from early morning and throughout the afternoon.

She got up and made tea, fetched yoghurt from the fridge and took out yesterday's bread. The exam for eight and ninth grade was to begin at eight o'clock. Tenth grade was scheduled to start at eleven, while the younger pupils would have tests after lunch. Karim was snoring peacefully. She woke him with a pat on the cheek, and took a uniform from the closet, where four identical ones hung along with a dress uniform. Karim was in the process of putting it on when Nadia stuck her head into the bedroom and told him to get a move on. They slurped some tea and had a few bites of bread. That would have to suffice.

Nadia took a quick look in the mirror as her husband opened the front door. A thought crossed her mind. She took a few steps back and opened the closet. *I need to dress properly today.* She grabbed hold of an abaya – a wide, full-length robe to be worn over clothes, so that the forms of the body were concealed.

The conversation from the previous night was lodged in her mind.

Outside, Kabul was beginning to wake up. Shop owners pulled up shutters, chairs were placed outside a teahouse. Melons loaded on the back of trucks awaited buyers; carts were laden with piles of apricots.

Nadia was the principal of a school in the neighbourhood. The walk to and from work was her sanctuary. Then she couldn't do anything else. Her breathing had become heavier with the years and she was already sweating. Soon the sun would be beating down.

The smell of freshly baked bread followed her from one bakery to the next. Widows, some by war, were sitting on the ground outside, many with small children clinging to them. Beggars always wore burkas, which were otherwise rarely seen in the city centre. Poverty was all around her, and many more were teetering on the brink. Several public sector workers hadn't been paid in a couple of months; teachers' salaries were often late. Nadia cursed those who directed the funds into their own bottomless pockets while the hands sticking out from the burkas remained empty.

Classes had been cancelled for months due to the pandemic, but at last the school had reopened. Many pupils had been sitting at home for an entire year. Finally, they were going to learn something again!

After hanging up the abaya in her office, she went to the classrooms where the exams were taking place. She put her head around the door to check everything was all right, nodded to the teachers and lingered a little. It felt so peaceful, surveying all the girls sitting there writing.

* * *

There was a banging at the gate.

Someone was hammering on the metal. A short pause, then the banging resumed. At the same time Bashir's phone began to ring and vibrate, the screen lighting up. He continued snoring, oblivious, but Galai heard it. Half-asleep, she gave him a push.

'Take it.'

She shook Bashir and placed the phone in his hand.

A voice yelled on the other end.

'We have conquered Jalalabad!'

Bashir sat up. Galai listened to everything being said, as she always did when somebody rang Bashir. When he was released from prison the year before it was like getting him back from the dead. She now guarded him like a lioness.

'Hurry! The caravan is moving on!' the talib on the phone yelled.

Bashir dressed quickly.

He was often vague about where he was going, and when he didn't say she didn't ask. Now he told her: 'We're headed towards Kabul!'

He mumbled a quick prayer, grabbed his rifle and left.

Galai felt a pang of anxiety. The news of the last few days had been joyful but that didn't mean they would always be. But she said nothing.

Outside, his friends were waiting with the engine running. Bashir jumped in.

The car slipped into a convoy carrying dishevelled soldiers with scraggly beards and scruffy tunics. The long line of vehicles had been travelling for ten days. Men were sitting on the beds of trucks or squeezed together in cars with the windows open. Clouds of sand whirled around them. Some wore sunglasses, others were wrapped in shawls, covering their faces except for a narrow slit for the eyes.

They were on their way.

To Kabul.

To Kabul!

Many of them had never been to the capital. The majority of the Taliban came from the south and east of the country. Several in the convoy had not been born the last time the Taliban governed the city. For them Osama bin Laden's Planes Operation was the stuff of legend and not of their time. They drove at full speed through the desert landscape, past villages, bazaars and vendors selling tea and grilled meat on skewers. They had mountains on either side, close enough to reach out and touch the rough rock with the left hand and far off on the horizon on the right side, gleaming in the morning sun.

After a while they could make out the checkpoint at Sang-e-Neveshta, between the provinces of Logar and Kabul. The rust-coloured structure loomed like a triumphal arch, welcoming them to Kabul. From there it was an hour's drive to the outskirts of the city.

Thousands of Taliban soldiers were approaching from several directions.

The police at the checkpoint quickly realised how outnumbered they were. There was nothing to do but lay down their weapons and raise their hands above their heads. They didn't even have time to flee.

Not a shot was fired. The border forces had been caught unawares. Bashir and his friends took over the checkpoint and let them go. They were obeying orders from the top: amnesty was to be granted to all those who surrendered without a fight.

Neither Bashir nor the other Taliban had expected that the road to Kabul, in the middle of August 2021, would lay completely open. Everything had happened so fast. Only a week had passed since the first of the country's thirty-four provincial capitals had been captured. Even the Taliban were surprised by – and unprepared for – how quickly things had moved.

The other order from the emir had been to 'stand by for further instructions before advancing'. So, they stayed where they were, by the huge gateway to Kabul. The bearded men were slipping into their new roles: from terrorists to traffic policemen.

* * *

As Hala was about to prepare breakfast at home in Jalalabad, she saw they were out of cooking oil. She sent out Yaqub's son, Hamza, with some housekeeping money she kept in a tin.

Her grandson returned with good news and bad news.

The good news was the same as Bashir had received a few hours earlier. Their city had been conquered by the Taliban overnight without a shot being fired! Hala and the grandchildren, who were home alone, hadn't even noticed.

The bad news was that he hadn't had enough money for cooking oil. The price had shot up yet again.

'Fourteen hundred afghani?' Hala groaned.

But they needed oil, so the old woman fished out four more hundred-afghani bills. God help us. The boy was sent back out.

After a while he came running back with a big container of cooking oil, the same type in yellow plastic that they'd used to make roadside bombs in Waziristan. Hamza rushed into his grandmother and showed her the message he had received on his mobile, the only smartphone in the house. It was a photo.

Bashir was smiling broadly at the camera. Behind him was the captured frontier post. And behind that, at the foot of the mountains, the village Hala had not been in for years: Mussahi.

Around his neck, her son had a big wreath of plastic flowers in vibrant, cheerful colours. Who had given it to him, she wondered. In his hands he held his rifle tightly.

Hala recognised the smile. The smile of victory. She shed a tear and said a prayer for her sons, the two who were living and the two in the hereafter.

* * *

Karim was on the bus to the Ministry of Defence. The journey took almost an hour due to the chaos of Kabul traffic. It was pure anarchy, with everyone trying to wind their way past one another, go round the side, slip back; otherwise, you didn't move. Police stood at junctions directing the traffic, the officers stopping cars or waving them on, but for the most part their whistles were ignored and the fastest had the right of way. With every new roadblock put up, every new blast wall built, the streets grew narrower and the pavements disappeared. The walls were a defence against suicide bombers, they protected embassies and departments, the university, banks, private schools and the houses of the wealthy, and were often painted with optimistic messages about democracy, equality and progress.

After making his way through security, Karim sat down at his desk not quite knowing what to do. It was twenty years since he had been a soldier. At the very start of Enduring Freedom he had been sent to Helmand Province to fight the Taliban. But Nadia's uncle had intervened and ensured he was reassigned to a desk job in the accounts department. There he had been trained to set budgets and calculate inventory, shrinkage and surplus. He had risen through the ranks, in fits and starts, to desk colonel.

While he sat behind a desk, where meticulous order reigned, the country was falling apart. Nine days earlier, on 6 August, the Taliban had seized control of the city of Zaranj, the seat of power in Nimruz Province in the south. It was the first district capital to fall since the Taliban intensified their attacks on the government forces in early May. The following day the northern province of Jozjan fell. The fighting had been fierce. Government forces had held out for a long time but were eventually forced to retreat.

The previous Sunday, the province of Sar-e-Pul had fallen. On the same day, Takhar fell. There the Taliban opened the prisons, thus replenishing their ranks with thousands more soldiers. War is war. The wealthy Kunduz Province resisted for a time but following heavy losses on Bloody Sunday, government forces pulled back from the city centre, then to their military base and finally to the airport. Now the door to the mineral-rich north, indeed to all of Central Asia, was open to the Taliban.

Each loss felt like another cut to Karim's own body. Defeat in each province, one after the other, was painful. But he told himself that each piece the Taliban took was the last. They wouldn't conquer the rest. Then yet another piece was overrun, and he thought that *it* would be the last.

Colleagues in the finance department had backed each other up throughout the week, assuring one another their analyses were correct. Of course the Americans had control – this was just part of their plan. They had agreed a peace deal with the Taliban last winter, a deal the Afghan president had done his best to slow down. Ashraf Ghani hadn't been interested in any negotiated power-sharing, and now he was being punished for it. The Americans were probably allowing the Taliban to take some provinces. It must be part of the deal, so that they would be able to negotiate on an equal footing. The Americans must have given word to the different army divisions to retreat, given that several provinces had fallen without a fight. Yes, that must be it.

Then there came another cut. Then a couple more.

The day after Bloody Sunday, Samangan Province fell. The next day local authorities confirmed that Farah in the west was taken and the Taliban raised their flag in Baghlan. Badakhshan had been captured four days previously. The next day Ghazni capitulated, and the entire local government fled to Kabul. On the same day, Herat, the country's third largest city, fell.

The knife was being driven further in, twisted; the blade was deep in the innards of Afghanistan, slowly gutting it, that was how it felt. Bit by bit the republic was becoming an emirate.

It wasn't about equilibrium or balance of power. What they were looking at now was something else. How could the army lose Herat? A man in Karim's office reassured the others that there must be a plan, everything would turn out all right. The northern provinces still held. There was Tajiks living there, as well as Uzbeks and Hazaras. Of course, the Taliban wouldn't get any further north. Negotiations would soon be called for; a political solution would be worked out and a new interim government formed.

The USA and NATO had spent billions of dollars training and equipping the Afghan army. On paper the army had three hundred thousand men under arms, while the real number was barely a third of that. Military officials cashed in the pay of so-called ghost soldiers, and sold the weapons, ammunition and rations these shadows had been issued.

On Thursday evening, the Taliban entered Kandahar. Then they took Helmand. Over the weekend they conquered the provinces of

Badghis, Ghor, Uruzgan, Zabul and Logar. Several of them without a fight. Then Mazar-e-Sharif fell.

'What is left now?' Karim and his colleagues asked.

When they'd come into the office that morning, they learned that Jalalabad had fallen. There were hardly any more cuts to take. Apart from the Panjshir Valley and the mountains of the Hindu Kush.

But in Kabul, the Afghan army provided security, they assured one another. The capital was under the government's control.

Then the telephone rang.

* * *

Kakar turned the key. For one last time, Jamila looked at the brown front door with the golden handle, peephole and extra security lock. A plastic dust curtain kept out the swirling sand that blew into all the buildings in Kabul. Kakar and the children carried the luggage as Jamila trudged down the steps.

They would soon be back. She had to come back. There was so much left to do, but the threats had increased. Despite her resignation as minister, the Tarakhil clan had not relented after she caused their well to dry up. She and Kakar had decided months ago that they had to get away, but it had taken time to sort out the education programmes and the library they had put together in their cellar, filled with Islamic knowledge. Moreover, her father was ill, and one of her brothers wanted her advice on a matter. So, they had postponed leaving, then postponed a little longer, and then some more.

Eventually they had booked tickets for a flight to Istanbul on 15 August. Their bags were packed with the intention of returning, although perhaps not in the immediate future.

The traffic was almost at a standstill. There was tension in the air as the Taliban advanced ever further across the country. It had pained her when her home town of Ghazni fell, and she had been shocked to learn that Herat, one of the most progressive cities in the country, had negotiated safe passage for the Islamists in exchange for them not attacking the city.

*

Six weeks earlier, the Americans, quietly and under cover of darkness, had left Bagram – the epicentre of the USA's war on the Taliban. They had taken the heavier weaponry with them and left the rest behind. Ammunition had been destroyed beforehand, but everything else remained; the scheduled departure had not been revealed to the Afghan authorities. The local commander at Bagram didn't know that the forces would be leaving on the night of the first Friday in July.

Twenty minutes after the last flight took off from Bagram, the electricity went off, as it was programmed to. The base, about the size of a small town, with swimming pools, a cinema and a Burger King, lay in complete darkness. The blackout was the signal for criminal gangs, who never slept, to go in. Looters broke down the gates, scoured the barracks, tents and hangars. The Americans had taken the keys of the vehicles, but the fridges were still full of Coca-Cola and energy drinks.

In Washington the next morning, Joe Biden, the fourth president in charge of operations in Afghanistan, bemoaned the amount of goodwill. 'I want to talk about happy things, man,' he told reporters, finding their questions too negative. After twenty years the Afghan people would have to run the country themselves.

The remainder of the forces would be withdrawn by the end of August, Biden had promised. But they could hardly pull out now that the Taliban were making such rapid progress, Jamila thought as she bade farewell to her city through the car window. That same morning the president had posted assurances on Facebook that the army would keep Kabul safe.

* * *

Every morning at nine o'clock, Ashraf Ghani held a staff meeting. This Sunday was no different.

The president had become an increasingly isolated figure after the signing of the Doha Agreement in February 2020. His gatekeeper and – in his own eyes – possible successor, was Hamdullah Mohib. Three years earlier, Ghani had appointed the thirty-five-year-old as national security advisor, despite him having no military background. However he had ample experience of Ghani, having worked for him since the election campaign in 2009, when Ghani won 3 per cent of the vote.

Within the walls of the Arg, the president had arranged for his young aide to live in a house next door to his own. Mohib's children played in the president's garden and his wife became friends with the president's wife, while he built up a young, well-educated and eloquent administration who found winning the war on social media more satisfying than paying attention to the losses in Khost and Kandahar. Under Mohib's leadership, thousands of fake accounts were set up on Twitter and Facebook with one purpose: to promote the government and attack the critics, in a country where few of the inhabitants had access to the internet. Mohib was known for asking people granted an audience with his boss 'not to be too negative'.

In the early hours Mohib had participated in a group chat on Signal with the chief intelligence and security officials in the country. The news was only getting worse. In addition to the provinces that had fallen, reports were coming in that the Taliban were just outside Kabul. Members of the capital's police force had abandoned their posts, as had soldiers and security guards.

At the same time as Mohib entered the presidential palace, the US chargé d'affaires, a stone's throw away, realised that security around the Green Zone – where the Arg, the American embassy and several other official buildings were situated – had collapsed. The diplomat consulted with Washington and subsequently ordered the immediate evacuation of all remaining American personnel at the embassy. For fear of leaks reaching the Taliban or IS, he neglected to inform the Afghan president that his palace was no longer secure.

That same morning, Zalmay Khalilzad met his counterpart Mullah Baradar at the Ritz-Carlton in Doha. The mullah promised the American envoy that Taliban forces would not enter Kabul. Khalilzad raised the subject of a ceasefire. Baradar didn't deign to answer.

When Ghani was informed at his nine o'clock meeting of

Baradar's assurances he commented drily that he viewed both the mullah and the American envoy as unreliable sources.

Up until that point Ashraf Ghani's main concern had been how to move his book collection in the event of having to vacate the palace. At about eleven o'clock he met with a diplomat from the United Arab Emirates to discuss a possible evacuation. They sat in the garden. The morning was already hot. The diplomat promised he could have a plane ready and waiting the next day. Above them they suddenly heard a swarm of Black Hawks that had taken off from the helipad at the American embassy. Outside the palace, shots could be heard. Ghani's bodyguards swiftly moved the president back indoors.

Around noon, Mohib and Ghani were sitting in the library. They agreed that Rula, the president's wife, should travel to the UAE as soon as possible. She got a seat on a scheduled flight that same afternoon. Ghani asked Mohib to go with her, to follow the talks between Khalilzad and Baradar. He wanted his trusted aide to be present when they were discussing the fate of Kabul.

At approximately one o'clock Mohib received a text message. Khalil Haqqani wanted to speak with him. This was followed by a call from a Pakistani number. The voice on the line simply said 'Surrender!'

When Mohib protested, saying that first they needed to negotiate, the man repeated the message and hung up.

At two o'clock Mohib arrived to escort Rula to a helipad behind the palace. The two of them were to be transported to Hamid Karzai Airport to catch their flight.

* * *

A smell of sweat lingered. The air was hot and thick. Narrow streaks of sunlight fell into the room between the curtains. It had to be late in the day. Ariana propped herself up and switched on the ceiling fan, grateful the electricity had been restored. August had been merciless, dry and scorching. She heard her father's footsteps. Odd – shouldn't he be at work?

Not caring about waking her sister, she put on Justin Bieber's 'Stay' and turned up the volume to drown out the fan.

I get drunk, wake up, I'm wasted still
I realise the time that I wasted here!

There were several unread messages on her mobile – ah, so her friends must have continued chatting after she fell asleep. She would take a look through the thread, but first she had to lie down and close her eyes for just a little longer.

She hummed along to the music. The mobile lay beside her, blinking.

I feel like you can't feel the way I feel
Oh, I'll be fucked up if you can't be right here . . . oooooooh!

Suddenly her father was standing in the doorway. He was buttoning up a tunic he had just changed into. Why wasn't he at work?
He looked at Ariana, then at her little sister who was still dozing.
'Turn off that music!'
Ariana grudgingly lowered the volume.
'The Taliban are right outside Kabul!' he cried.
'What?'
Her father stood there, at a loss. Then he went back out.
Zohal sat up in bed.
'What's going on?'
Ariana checked her phone. All the messages were about the same thing. Taliban. Taliban. Taliban.
But surely it couldn't be that easy to take Kabul? All the soldiers, the helicopters, the roadblocks, the Americans. Her father was a colonel in the army. He should know.
'Dad!'
But her father was on the phone.
The Taliban? Ariana had been born in the last year of their rule. She had heard of their repression, the floggings and stonings, but

they had seemed at a remove. It had practically taken place before her birth. Besides, they had lost. She knew they had banned TV and music. Her sister Zohal could never do without Turkish soap operas, and it was hard to imagine life without Netflix and Justin Bieber.

No, it was impossible, nobody wanted the Taliban here in Kabul. The entire population would revolt against them. People would gather in the streets to protest. The week before, she had been to a bowling alley with some friends. They had rented a lane, taken along their own music. There had been a group of boys in the next lane, joking around. It had felt exciting and illegal. She recalled her parents' stories about sport arenas and cinemas being banned. Her friends had just seen *Far from Home*, the latest *Spider-Man* movie, which was showing all over Kabul. No, this had to be just rumours. Kabul would never allow it. Besides, the Americans were taking care of them.

Her mother came home. Her face was blotchy from crying.

'I had to call off the exam,' she said. 'The first class managed to finish, but I cancelled the rest.' She looked at her daughters and burst into tears.

Karim had alerted her when he left work.

'Nadia! The Taliban are on the outskirts of Kabul!' he had shouted into the phone. 'Go home!'

She had gone to the window of her office, which had a view over the whole district. Everything was the same as usual. Car horns honking. Fruit vendors calling out. An ice-cream truck driving past. Then she had walked into the corridor. It was completely quiet, and in the classrooms the only sound was the scraping of the girls' pens on paper. It couldn't be true. She would wait and see, let the pupils at least complete the exam. They had so much catching up to do after a year of school being closed; calling off an exam now was the last thing they needed.

Hostilities had been going on in the country since before these girls were born. For them it had meant being unable to visit relatives in areas where there was fighting. At the same time, they had lived in peace of a sort in Kabul, the only shadow being terror attacks and suicide bombings. The last year and a half, since the peace negotiations in Doha, had been the most violent period since the extremists had been driven out twenty years earlier. The Taliban's takeover, of rural areas in the east, then the south, and subsequently the west, had happened so gradually that people had continually adjusted to the new normal. A skewed normality – the Ka-bubble.

Nadia went down to the entrance of the school. Pupils who had shown up for the second exam shift were standing close together, chatting while they waited. What was she to do? Send them home?

She checked her mobile. Several sources were reporting the same thing: the Taliban were coming.

She straightened up and told the girls that the exam had to be postponed and asked them to hurry home. For security reasons, she said. Then she went into the classrooms where the first shift was finishing up. She asked them to hand in their papers and go straight home.

She set out quickly herself, while wondering if all this was real. The pavements were just as packed as before. Had she overreacted? Been wrong to cancel the second exam?

Back home she and Karim each sat with their phones, reading text messages. Ariana and Zohal came in to join the rest of family, who were gathered on the mattresses along the walls of the living room. Sheer curtains with imitation gold leaf hung in the large windows. Outside there was a balcony where Karim grew dahlias, deep red like blood. Their apartment was a short distance from the city centre.

'Taking Kabul won't be easy, will it?' the eldest brother asked. He had always been the most cautious of the siblings and kept largely to himself. 'Will there be heavy fighting?'

Karim made no reply. His entire section, and everyone else at the ministry, had simply gone home, taken off their uniforms and put them away. The army divisions had done the same.

He himself had changed into the uniform of the people – the tunic – within minutes.

So who would take up the fight?

* * *

Mohib stepped into the helicopter after the president's wife, still thinking about what the head of the presidential guard had said.

'I want you to take the president with you.'

It was uncertain which and how many of the bodyguards would remain loyal, should the Taliban enter the palace.

Mohib asked the pilots to await further instruction. Rula remained in her seat while the young head of national security went back to the residence. There he found Ghani and took his hand: 'Mr President, it's time. We have to leave.'

Ghani wanted to go upstairs to collect some of his belongings, but Mohib feared that for every minute they tarried more people would figure out they were leaving. Panic could break out; the guards might mutiny.

The last time the Taliban had taken over Kabul, they had lynched the president, castrated him, tied his battered corpse behind a car and driven him around the Arg before hanging him from a lamp post.

The president went with Mohib.

On arriving at the helipad there was an argument about who would travel. The pilots said each helicopter could take six passengers. Twice as many were already squeezed into the president's aircraft.

Several of his closest associates were still inside the Arg when the pilots started the engines. One was on the phone with Khalilzad, discussing how they could manage to put a ceasefire in place, as the president's helicopter took off and flew over the palace gardens, where gardeners struggled to keep the plants alive in the dry summer heat.

* * *

On arrival at Hamid Karzai Airport, Jamila and her family joined long queues of people. Why was everything moving so slowly? The first security check was conducted outside the fence. The guards scanned both people and their luggage, before frisking them again prior to their entering the terminal building. Once inside, they finally checked in. The heavy suitcases were placed on the conveyor belt, disappearing into the airport, before the passengers went through yet another security check after passport control. Exhausted, Jamila sat down in the large concourse with its panoramic window over the runway.

She had placed her crutches beside her and was sitting glued to the screen of her computer, her fingers on the keyboard, while the children played on their phones and Kakar checked the news.

'This doesn't look too good,' he said to Jamila.

Delays were announced over the speakers. Apparently, their morning flight was now an afternoon flight. Jamila heard a commotion and turned to look. A group of smartly dressed men came running up the steps. She discerned several people she knew, ministers, vice-ministers, men from the president's administration. They raced across the floor of the terminal, flanked by their security teams, who were shoving people out of the way, until they reached the gates for the planes bound for Istanbul and Islamabad, the next two flights scheduled to leave.

What where these men doing here?

She turned her attention back to the computer screen, continuing to write instructions she had forgotten to give to her office.

Finally, their flight was called. Jamila packed away her computer and, with difficulty, got to her feet. The whole family moved at her pace towards the counter, but upon reaching it they were stopped by armed men and relieved of their boarding passes.

Passengers who had already boarded were dragged from their seats. The men with the guns won yet again.

The flight for Istanbul took off without Jamila and her family.

The mood was sombre in the taxi home. Jamila looked around. There were no policemen on the streets. All the security forces had disappeared along with their military vehicles. Even the traffic police were gone. It was a city without protection.

She gasped for air. It was boiling hot in the car and difficult to breathe. A leaden feeling had settled in her stomach.

Back at the apartment word reached them: the Taliban had taken the city.

The evening was spent burning papers. Documents, letters, books, notes, contracts, photographs. There wasn't time to separate family snaps from pictures that could put someone in danger. Photo after photo, face after face vanished in the flames.

Then she received a text message from a colleague: the president had fled the country.

He had betrayed them. Her and all of Afghanistan.

The Victor

Jihad had marked most of Bashir's life.

Death, more than anything, had shaped him.

Audacious, astute, self-reliant were the characteristics his own people used to describe him. Stubborn, wilful, controversial said those who observed him at a distance.

Over two decades, he had risen through the ranks. When his superiors were killed, he had taken command of their men. Each fighter could apply to serve under whichever commander he wished and, if he wasn't found wanting, join their group. Should he be killed, another who was willing to die took his place.

That was how the Taliban won the war.

They were outnumbered in combat. Their armoury was inferior. They had a fraction of the money. But they had something that the strongest army in the world, and the world's most powerful military alliance, could never have: men who went gladly to their deaths.

Martyrs took up more room in Bashir's stories than the living. They walked again in the heroic legends.

Walid, he's gone now, but he used to say . . .

Qasim was so slow, until he took the bullets, so that we could run . . .

When we found Latif, his body was in one piece and he smelled of musk . . .

And Sharifullah, who put on a general's uniform, he . . .

The men talked about the highlights, not everyday life. They spoke of the great victories and also the gruesome defeats when Allah took a whole group, but rarely about the boredom, the hunger, the lice, the longing.

The men often sat talking well into the night. They drank tea and watched videos from battles. They passed around footage from the bodycams of American soldiers as they met their deaths, material that had found its way onto the internet. They showed one another photos of fresh decapitations. They saved the images of the body parts of fedayeen, all very young, from attacks carried out by IS. Several sequences were set to music. Trucks, Humvees and tanks driving over IEDs and exploding featured frequently, recorded by the person on the hillside setting them off. They had recordings on their phones from when they themselves fired rockets from orchards or wheat fields. The sudden peace resembled a holiday of sorts, where they could talk about the war, think about the war, plan the war, because there would be another, wouldn't there?

Bashir had been engaged in destruction for twenty years. His bullets had hit warm, living bodies. His bombs had exploded, raining brick, chunks of concrete and rebar on people on the street. He had prompted others to blow themselves up. Always with one goal in mind: maximum possible destruction.

Now he found himself unable to gain a foothold in this vertiginous time when everything he knew had come to a standstill. The fighting had subsided. The bullets remained in the magazine. No one needed his orders.

The army of terror had become the authorities. They were the ones supposed to build the country. Did he have it in him, to build something up?

'Peace building' was how the Americans, after a while, had described what they were doing. 'Nation building', the Europeans had termed it. Now it was the Taliban's turn to build. Did *they* have it in them?

If you sought answers back in history, a swift descent into civil war was the most likely outcome. The cycle of changeovers in power, one government superseding another by violent means, was the standard.

So it seemed best to look forward.

'Unemployed,' Bashir would say if anyone asked what he was doing. But that was pretence – once a commander, always a commander.

In the period following the capture of Kabul, he had received job offers from the new authorities, as thanks for services rendered. He hadn't found any of them appealing.

Twice he had been summoned by the man who had received him before he was combat-ready, served him tea on the veranda and given him responsibility for the keys to the weapon depot – the caliph himself.

Sirajuddin Haqqani – the mastermind of the Taliban's military strategy in eastern Afghanistan, the man behind most of the suicide attacks against the international forces – was now minister of the interior, and thus remained one of the most powerful men in the country. When he was appointed, barely a photo of him existed. The US authorities had posted two pictures of him on their website Rewards for Justice. In one, a woollen shawl covered most of his face, but his profile suggested pronounced features, a mass of black hair and bushy eyebrows. The other was a computer-generated image of how he was believed to look. He was described as having 'a light complexion with wrinkles'.

The Haqqanis had built themselves up as a counterforce to the circle around the late Mullah Omar. Throughout the war they had largely pulled in the same direction and submitted to the senior leadership.

Now they were to rule the country together. At the top sat the Taliban's emir, Haibatullah Akhundzada. He had inherited the title *amir al-mumineen* – commander of the faithful – from Mullah Mansour, who had been killed by an American drone strike in 2016, three years after he succeeded Mullah Omar.

The emir had sent his own son to his death as a suicide bomber and was a reclusive figure who seldom left Kandahar. He allowed others to take the spotlight when victory was announced in August but issued a statement that the Taliban would follow international laws, treaties and commitments unless they were at odds with Islamic law.

'In the future, all issues of governance and life in Afghanistan will be governed by the laws of holy sharia,' he said and congratulated the people on their liberation from foreign rule.

Sirajuddin Haqqani remained on the FBI's most wanted list with a bounty of ten million dollars. He was one of the reasons the US had frozen access to most of the country's assets.

How were you to punish terrorists who became ministers? By boycotting them? By starving the population? Several of the members of the new government were on sanctions lists. It made negotiations difficult. Afghanistan's previous governments had deposited nine billion dollars – huge amounts of the central bank's reserves – in Western banks. The money was now frozen so that the new authorities could not access it. The Taliban called it theft.

With or without these funds, the country needed governing and Sirajuddin had to put together a staff. He wanted men he trusted in the provinces. Now, while peace was still warm, he sought to bring any troublemakers into the fold.

The month after the takeover, Bashir was sent for. It was the first time he and the caliph met since the victory. They thanked God for allowing them to live to experience it. Since the Almighty had willed it, they could now humbly begin on new tasks.

What kind of posting would Bashir be interested in? Sirajuddin offered him a range of positions. Was there a particular province he wanted? Logar, perhaps, close to the village of his birth? Or something further east, towards the border with Waziristan?

Bashir was noncommittal, said he was unsure.

The caliph made a concrete proposition.

Bashir turned it down.

One month later he was summoned again.

He refused for a second time.

Sirajuddin was annoyed. 'This is my decision, not yours! I'll send you where I want.'

Bashir sat in silence. An administrative role was not part of his plan. Especially when such a position only brought problems. There was no money, people weren't getting paid and the further into the winter they went, the more people would be feeling the pangs of hunger. No, governing this peace was not for him.

Their ties from the war meant he could sit there quietly and not obey the order. They shared a powerful bond. Bashir had been fourteen and Sirajuddin thirty when they met for the first time.

Bashir was given a warning, nonetheless. There was to be no doubt about who was in charge.

'Next time you're summoned, you'll go where I send you,' Sirajuddin insisted. Bashir nodded faintly.

If it had gone as the caliph wished, he would now be a district governor or a chief of police in some province. But Bashir preferred to follow his own plan. Should that coincide with Haqqani's then all well and good; if it didn't, he would sit quietly until the storm had passed and hope he got what he wanted.

Peace presented challenges for the family too, such as where they would live. Bashir's people belonged to the Husseinkhel clan, a branch of the larger Ahmadzai tribe. In Jalalabad they were strangers. But he didn't want to live in the countryside, in Mussahi, as his mother wished. He wanted to stay in Kabul and was on the lookout for a house.

The extended family now comprised more than thirty people. At the top was the matriarch, Hala. After her came Bashir and Raouf. Between them they had three wives and fourteen children. In addition, they were responsible for the wives of their dead brothers Hassan and Yaqub and their children, and some of their sisters' sons.

One day a friend called to say he had found a house he thought Bashir might like. He offered to take him to look at it. They drove far outside the city centre, out to where the tarmac ended, where car wheels spun in the mud when it rained and the tyre tracks dried into deep, hard ruts. They drove past shacks selling clucking hens and yoghurt from large pails. Others sold nuts and dried fruit, fizzy drinks and canned goods from Pakistan. All sorts of people lived here, but who exactly, should you lose your way in the streets without names, it would be hard to find out. From the outside, only high mud walls and heavy iron gates were visible. No ostentatious façades, no nameplates, nothing to reveal the owners.

Halfway along a narrow street they stopped beside a grey gate with peeling paint.

When Bashir's companion opened it, it was as though the gate to heaven swung open. Across a tiled courtyard lay a lavish villa.

It was pale pink and extended over three wide storeys. A mint-coloured balcony ran along the first floor. The railings had oriental motifs and the beams were painted in light pastels. In several of the windows, some arched, others rectangular, mirrored, violet glass had been fitted so no one could see in. In front of the glass was a carefully made wooden lattice. The house was a cross between an Asian pagoda, an oriental palace and a Greek temple. By the entrance stood Corinthian columns with gold-decorated capitals.

Three wide steps led up to the entrance. The risers were mint green, while the treads were a mosaic of marble tiles in pastel shades. The ceiling above the steps was decorated in silver patterns. The wide door, with floral carvings, was of dark wood.

Above the door, on a panel of pink reflective glass, *Mashallah* had been carved. The Arabic expression meant *God has willed it* and was to ensure the evil eye could not see in, thus preventing demons from entering. It also helped guard against jealousy.

'Borrow it as long as you like,' said Bashir's friend, who had taken ownership of the house. A politician had lived there previously. Where was he now?

The friend shrugged. In America, maybe. He had disappeared along with the traitors.

*

The family moved in not long after. Soon they had made the house their own.

Outside the front door now lay a jumbled heap of footwear covered in dried mud: worn-out sandals, boots with tears, lopsided slippers — most of them small, some large.

It didn't seem to go together, the expensive mosaic and the muddy trainers, the mirrored glass and the scruffy sandals. It was like the owners of the shoes had taken the villa hostage.

It was war booty anyway, and the nicest house Bashir had ever had.

Just borrowing it, he told people.

The member of parliament might have appropriated it himself — those people stole everything they came across, Bashir's friends said. Perhaps they were right, it wasn't always easy to tell what was bought and what was stolen in Afghanistan. There were only two hard-and-fast rules. Winner takes all. Nothing lasts for ever.

Aside from God, everything was transitory, and just now, with victory secured, it was Bashir's house. Like the white Land Cruiser he now drove. Gift from a friend.

Outside the gate, in the dusty little street, two young men with rifles were posted, indicating an important man lived within.

At the end of the road was a small workshop that sold dreams. A kite-maker made frames from thin plastic and sticks, with a string to hold. From there the children could run over to the plain on the other side of the road, which in spring had a faint greenish tinge, but the rest of the year was as dry as a desert. If the wind was good, the kites would whirl and fly, or break loose and disappear into the sky.

But the children in Bashir's house weren't allowed play with kites. They had other things to do.

Lost

Ariana wasn't allowed out.

Except for her mother, who sometimes went to buy groceries, everyone stayed at home. Her father was the most fearful. Karim was afraid the Taliban were out to get him, that they wanted to exact revenge on the traitors – the ones who had worked for the Afghan army, who had killed so many of their brothers. Karim hadn't killed anyone, but he had ensured those who had received their wages. Where did that place him on the list for revenge?

He spent most of the day staring into space. Initially he had talked about the National Resistance Front based in Panjshir. After a while he didn't mention it any more, he almost stopped talking altogether. What was there to say?

Ariana's mother was at home because her school had been closed. She hadn't been back since sending home the girls who were supposed to sit the exam. Some primary schools opened a couple of weeks after the takeover, but many stayed shut. The Taliban said they would open all the schools again when security allowed it. Nadia was waiting for word.

Ariana's oldest brother was at home because the company he worked for had shut down operations.

One sister sat at home because her biology studies never started up again.

Her other sister was staying home because the dentist's office where she was doing her practical training sold its equipment and closed its doors.

Her fourteen-year-old brother was at home because the female teachers could no longer teach teenage boys.

Her youngest sister stayed home because the teachers at the primary school weren't showing up for work. That was also the reason for her youngest brother being at home.

Lastly, Ariana was at home because the university was closed. It didn't meet the requirements for division between the sexes.

The academic year was soon over anyway, as autumn was coming to an end. All state schools were closed from mid-December to the vernal equinox – *Nowruz* – the Persian New Year. Most schools were simple mud buildings without any heating, so in the winter it was too cold to learn.

The days – and the mood – in the apartment grew darker.

Late one afternoon, Karim went up onto the flat roof of the building. Up there, they dried washing on clotheslines and sometimes children came to fly their kites, as the wind was good. On this day Karim took the stairs alone. He passed the small room on the landing where he usually kept his dahlias over the winter. Pots and buckets were stacked in a corner, a trowel thrown in a basket. He couldn't face tending to flowers, something that had given him so much pleasure, when everything else was meaningless. Anyway, the dahlias weren't the reason he had come up.

Karim put down the heavy petrol can he was carrying. Outside, by the door to the stairwell, stood a large empty oil drum.

He felt a sadness unlike anything he had ever experienced. Before there had always been hope. No matter what happened, he had always had dreams, or a purpose. Now he had nothing. But fear.

He walked back down the stairs.

In the bedroom he opened the wardrobe and took out the five uniforms. Every year they were given a new one, sometimes he had worn them out, other years they had piled up. Now they were a danger to him. The Taliban had begun their second round of raids. They had already been to the apartment once, searching for weapons. Karim had handed in the gun registered in his name at the Ministry of Defence.

When they came, one had asked his youngest son, 'Where's your father's gun?'

The seven-year-old hadn't answered. The Talib had held up his own weapon.

'Like this,' he had said. 'Where is it? Show it to us or we'll put you in prison!'

They had relented when Karim had implored them to leave. He had young girls in the apartment, he said, it was undignified, and he had already turned in his gun. But before leaving they had asked for the bathroom. They wanted to wash as it was time for prayer. He had shown them. They had entered one after another and washed. Then they had got on their knees in the living room to pray.

They could return at any time. He had heard about one man who was beaten senseless because the Taliban had found uniforms in his closet.

'We served our country,' Karim grumbled to the colleague who told him about it. 'Now we're nothing.'

Karim had been born in 1969 and had enlisted in the army during the rule of Dr Najibullah, to whom he had pledged allegiance. He had learned to shoot, to defend his country, even though he had ended up far from the battlefield, at the accounting office.

He had also learned how to respect his uniforms and take good care of them. Now he carried all five up the dusty stairs, opened the narrow door to the roof and walked over to the oil drum. One after the other he threw them into it, pouring petrol over them before setting it alight.

He stood staring into the flames. When Nadia came up, he hid his face in his hands. He had worn his country's uniform for over thirty years. He was burning his identity. It disappeared in the blaze.

Fear came over him again. Soon darkness would fall. Perhaps

someone in one of the other buildings would see what he was doing.

He picked up the last one and stood there with the black parade uniform in his hands. It was supposed to last his entire life, only to be used on special occasions: when you received a medal or an award, for a retirement ceremony or on Independence Day, when Afghanistan celebrated liberation from the British in 1919. It was a crime to burn it.

He threw it in.

Now both Nadia and Karim were crying.

Soon the lump at the bottom of the oil drum was no longer recognisable as four green and one gold-buttoned black uniform.

Karim went back down to the apartment and fetched documents and certificates from the ministry. Exam papers, course diplomas, photos of the class – everything went into the oil drum.

But he had saved one item: the three stars sewn onto the epaulettes of his dress uniform. He had cut those off, unable to commit them to the flames. Everything else might be burned to a cinder but no one was taking his rank from him.

A few weeks after descending red-eyed from the roof, Karim had received a call from the Ministry of Defence. The Taliban wanted him to come in. There was something regarding the computer system that they were unable to figure out.

Should he go and help the Taliban, who had moved into his office? Did he dare? What if they locked him up? Did he dare to refuse? They knew where he lived. They hadn't *requested* he come in; it had been an order. He had no choice. He had to report the next morning.

It was the first time he had been outside on the street since the middle of August, almost two months previously. The weather was fresh, some leaves were yellow, others had fallen. Karim had dressed in a tunic with wide trousers underneath.

Walking the same route as he had on *that day* was unbearable. Not only had he lost his job, but he had also lost his self-respect. Who was he without the army at his back? What was the head of a family without an income?

Arriving at the ministry, where he used to just flash his ID card and be waved through the barriers, he now had to submit to a search.

'They called me an enemy,' a colleague had told him on the phone. Like Karim, he had been ordered to come in to fix something for the Taliban. 'I asked why they were being so rude, so rough. I said they couldn't treat me like that.'

'That's not for you to decide,' the Talib had responded and struck him in the face.

Karim's colleague had been so upset that he reported the guard higher up the system.

After listening to what he had to say, the superior had looked him in the eye and said, 'You should be grateful we didn't kill you!'

The only reason they didn't, they said, was because of the general amnesty. But he was more than welcome to lodge further complaints if he didn't value his life.

With that in mind, Karim humbly allowed himself to be frisked. He was escorted up the stairs he had ascended thousands of times before, to the floor where he had always turned left, down the corridor, in through the wonky door, and saw the desk where he used to sit. Everything belonging to the army had been torn down. Flags and emblems of the Islamic emirate were hung up in their place. The Taliban walked around in the corridors with bandoliers and weapons. The desks were mostly empty.

He was told to fix the spreadsheets in the computer system.

From then on, he would be ordered to come in once a month to make an inventory for the last thirty days.

The Taliban had better things to do.

Their father was like a different person.

In the early days he had just sat staring vacantly into the middle distance. If they brought him tea, he would forget it. He ate slowly and very little. Sometimes he spoke to colleagues on the phone, exchanging horror stories they had heard. But mostly he just sat there. Until he awoke as a tyrant.

From early morning to late at night he ordered his daughters and wife around.

Get me a glass of water!

I want tea!

Boil me an egg!

Put out some nuts!

Apricots!

Fetch my cushion!

Plump my cushion!

Get me a blanket!

Where are my glasses?

Where's the remote control?

Get it!

I want to sleep, switch off the light!

Often when they sat down to read, watch a movie, listen to music or just chat, new orders would be issued. They were so fed up with him. They were so fed up with one another. They began to yell. Everyone began to yell. Their mother too.

Why are you just sitting there?

Go clean the kitchen!

But I just cleaned the kitchen, Ariana could answer.

Go to the kitchen anyway!

What are you doing on your phone?

Who are you talking to?

Who are you texting with?

The Netflix password Ariana had got from a friend at university still worked. When she put on headphones and watched *The Queen's Gambit* the world around her disappeared. She turned the volume up to full and was suddenly the heroine of the series. Or when she watched the last season of *Stranger Things*. Then she had superpowers like the girl called Eleven.

Then her lost future didn't even exist.

*

One day in autumn an aunt, living in a small town in the neighbouring province, telephoned. She was a widow with several children and had applied for financial aid from a local organisation. She had been granted assistance but had to come to Kabul to collect the cash herself. She had no idea how to get around the city and asked her brother, Karim, to accompany her. The office she was to go to was in the neighbourhood of Shahr-e Naw.

'That's right beside Yummy,' Ariana said when she heard the address. Ah, Yummy! She felt a pang at the thought of her favourite place, with its white plastic tables and red benches, where she and her friends had sometimes treated themselves to a meal. Yummy had the most delicious snacks: chicken nuggets, chips and hamburgers. They had sat there with straws and greasy fingers, looking out the window, thinking the world was growing ever larger for them. It was – until those men came out of their caves and down from the mountains and ruined everything.

'Ariana can take you,' her father said. Ariana looked at him, shocked. Was she to be allowed to go out?

It would be the first time since *that day*.

She put on an abaya, a black headscarf and a Covid mask over her nose and mouth. That should do it. She was standing ready when her aunt came.

Arriving at the address, they stood in front of a large five-storey building. They were taken upstairs by a guard, passing a door that said NECDO, before being shown into an office on the floor above. The walls were covered in posters.

'Free education for all!' one said. 'Women have the right to work!' proclaimed another. She spelled out the letters of the organisation's name in English – Women's International League for Peace and Freedom – WILPF.

There were several women sitting at a long table, talking. Some of them had their heads covered, others did not. Women were walking in and out of the offices, carrying papers, leaving laptops on the desks, talking on the phone, throwing on a headscarf and hurrying out.

What kind of place was this?

Ariana heard her aunt say her name falteringly, and was surprised when she was actually given the money she was promised. Ten thousand afghani. The older woman looked at her with tears in her eyes. But Ariana's thoughts were somewhere else entirely.

She wanted to stay.

How could she make that happen?

The old Ariana, the one who grasped every opportunity that came her way, woke up. She plucked up courage.

'I'm very good at English. I was the best in my class. I won . . .'

The woman who had handed her aunt the envelope with the money looked at her with a kind expression.

'I need a job,' Ariana said. 'I can translate, I know how to use a computer – could you take my name? Maybe you have a small part-time position? Anything, really.'

The woman wrote down her name and phone number.

On the way down the stairs, Ariana thought about some of the posters hanging side by side with the creed: 'Participation for women in the peace process!' 'Stop climate change!' 'Justice for the disabled!' She had read on one of their flyers about the need to mobilise men for the advancement of women. Females were not the only ones who should be involved in the struggle. It was a human right. Every person should have equal rights.

A revolutionary thought.

Of course, they didn't need her.

As the weeks passed, the thought of having asked for a job grew embarrassing. Seriously, what kind of opinion did she have of herself?

The family had almost gone through all of their savings. Meat was off the menu. They had stopped eating chicken. Potatoes, rice and bread was the daily fare. Carrots and cabbage, the cheapest food at the market in autumn. But they had salt, some spices, and they ate their fill. All the same, they all had an empty, hollow feeling within.

One day the woman who had taken her number called, not to give her a job but to offer her a course. Ariana didn't quite understand what she meant; she mentioned something about *mental peace and stress management.*

A psychosocial course, she called it. Would she like to attend? It was to last for five weeks, and all the participants would have their bus fare covered. The course was the idea of the head of the women's organisation – Jamila Afghani.

Ariana said yes on the spot, before her parents had the chance to refuse. Anything was better than sitting at home. She would have to contend with her father later. It was too dangerous, he would say. The Taliban could steal her away and marry her off to one of their soldiers, then the family would never see her again. He had heard about that kind of thing.

Strangely enough, she was allowed to go.

She was going to attend a *course* again!

She had something to do on Tuesdays, for two hours, for the next five weeks.

About two dozen women of all ages were sitting around an oblong table. They wore typical middle-class attire. Some in skirts and suit jackets, others in dresses, a number had belts around their waists; they weren't dressed in tents, like the new rulers wanted them to.

At the end of the table stood a full-figured woman in a tight, short dress over a pair of jeans. Looking at them from under well-pencilled eyebrows she introduced herself as a psychologist.

The participants looked at the energetic instructor with resigned expressions. These women had been teachers, lawyers, economists, who overnight had gone from an active working life to being confined at home.

The psychologist asked how they *felt*.

It was like triggering an avalanche. One by one they began to tell their stories. About fear. Hopelessness. Poverty. *I feel so weak. Life is meaningless now. My son is sick. He needs to see a doctor. I have no money. My life is over. I was a criminal prosecutor, in terrorist cases. I put members of the Taliban away. I was a teacher. The school is closed. The girls have been* sent home. *I worked for an American company; they pulled out. I was left behind. I was studying for a masters. Can't continue. Even if the university opened, how would I afford the books? My parents are at home too. Everyone in the family is at their wits' end.*

Those who had children talked about them. What would become of them, of the schoolgirls, the female students? Concern for the children eclipsed everything else when an entire family had lost all their income.

It was Ariana's turn. 'I'm so disappointed,' she began. 'I had one semester left of my law degree. I want to be something, or I *wanted* to be something. Now I have lost my goals. I try to concentrate on other things, but I'm not able. All I can think about is what I've lost. I don't believe they'll open the universities to us again.' She looked up at the psychologist. 'No matter what I do, university is all I can think about.'

When everyone had told their story, there was an air of exhaustion in the room. The psychologist sat quietly for a few moments, calmly surveying the red-eyed women.

'Can you forget about all this for one minute?'

They looked at her sceptically. 'We could try,' one of them said.

'Close your eyes. Imagine you're outside. In the fresh air with nice weather. In a lovely spot. With beautiful scenery. Trees. The wind is blowing through them, rustling the leaves. Take a deep breath. Breathe slowly out. Inhale the fresh air down into your lungs. Exhale through your mouth. Stretch your arms above your head. Spread your fingers out . . . '

They all had their eyes closed.

'Once more. Stretch your arms above your heads. Splay your fingers. Make a fist. Open your hand. Open your eyes and stand up!'

They continued with the stretching exercises until the psychologist asked them to sit down.

'Let's start again. Tell me about your problems. We're going to talk very calmly now. You need to think positively. Believe that everything is going to work out. That you'll get your job back. That life will be the way it was before.'

The breathing. The lungs. Muscles. Tendons. It was a whole. The stomach. Neck. Hands.

Life as they had known it was gone. But the Taliban were not going to stress them out.

Exile

A thin layer of ice lay over Alta. Clear as water, so translucent you didn't see it before you lay there, flat on your back. The snow had fallen in a light sprinkle from the end of October. A white blanket settling softly over the mountains in the west, before covering the plains, the pine forest, the town and the wharf. Then, during the first night of November, everything melted, first down by the sea, then further towards town, where the meltwater turned to ice and lay invisible on steps and paths. Such are the caprices of the Norwegian winter before it makes up its mind. When the temperature hovers around zero, the moist air from the Arctic makes every surface mirror-smooth, so that only the natives, those used to black ice before the onset of real winter, can manage.

Jamila Afghani was doomed to fall.

She solved the problem of keeping her balance by not venturing outside. It was no great sacrifice. In fact, she had never left her house without a clear objective in mind. A necessary visit, an important meeting, a pre-planned journey. Although there were many of her parents' customs she had not made her own, certain rules for living were so deeply embedded that she didn't even think of them. The idea of taking a walk, just to get some air, was not something she could relate to. Moreover, in Afghanistan, going out was not to be taken lightly. A woman walking around aimlessly was enough to get rumours circulating. Where was she going? What was she doing? Did she *want* to be seen? Was she trying to entice someone in particular? Or just being demonstrative? In Ghazni, it didn't take more to ruin a woman's reputation than uncertainty around what exactly she had been doing outside the home. Even in Kabul, going out was associated with danger. Listening to accounts of what might happen to young girls *out there*, just beyond the gates of the house, were part of growing up. By instilling fear rules become easier to comply with, bans more logical and easier to observe.

Jamila had always had to weigh up the risk by leaving her house against what she could achieve. As a young girl she endured the harassment and the insults, as a young woman she ignored the threat in in men's looks, then came the dangers of being caught in crossfire, of getting kidnapped, wounded or killed, or more specifically, as she began to raise her voice, that someone would make good on the threats they had made against her.

On this November morning, she sat barefoot in her new house in a little town far above the Arctic Circle, watching people slipping and sliding past the window. The morning light was bluish; the sun had still not risen even though it was ten o'clock. By the end of the month the sun would disappear completely, they had said. It would be gone until the spring.

She rocked in the chair. She was safer than she had ever been, but her existence felt more barren than at any time in her life.

Exile.

The safest place can be painful to live in when it's not yours. Not only had she left behind everything she owned; an entire world had been lost. The light in Kabul was so different; yellower, more subdued, somehow. Yellow from the fine sand that weightlessly became a part of the air, or greyish from the smog, never blue and ice cold like here. The colours, smells, tastes, everything was foreign. The house they had been allocated had no colours beyond brown, black and white. Apart from the bathroom. That had green tiles. Sometimes she went in there just to look at the tiles. They reminded her of something.

She ought to get a carpet. That would soften it. Moreover, she liked sitting on a carpet. She preferred eating her meals on the floor, like at home. The dining table was angular and foreign; the family looked at one another in a different way from when they sat in a circle around a pot.

Alta seemed as hard and angular as the dining table. Not a spot, not a blemish, barely any sound. People spoke in low voices, not calling out blessings nor curses. The pedestrian street downtown was covered in scrubbed grey slates. Like in a palace, an ice castle.

But who was she here?

On the form they were asked to fill out on arrival, she was supposed to tick boxes for what kind of job she could be interested in. The choices were numerous.

Cleaning.

Cooking.

Mechanic.

Electronics.

Retail.

Work with children.

Work with the elderly.

She had been pulled up by the roots. But it was as though her new homeland wouldn't allow her to sink her own roots into the ground and let them grow. No, they wanted to put down different roots, so an effective cleaner or a kind orderly would sprout up.

Exile. A smooth surface and a ragged, bloody underside.

The shock had not yet worn off. It lurked within her. Losing everything had happened so quickly. She could feel the tremble of loss within. Exile is losing control, being deprived of the familiar. No matter how dysfunctional her life and her country had been, it had been hers.

Part of her believed she ought not to have left. Should she have stayed? She spent hours a day on her phone. Her voicemail was full of desperate messages.

Help me get out! Put me on a list! How can I get a seat on a plane? Visa! Ticket! Out, out, out, out!

She listened to the messages at double speed to get through them all – despairing voices, women she knew, women she didn't know, some nameless. All sending long voicemails full of anguish.

She had turned in her passport upon arrival. It was now with the Directorate of Immigration in Oslo. Norway owned it, and she would get a new identity card. An Afghan passport, what was that worth today? It was painful. The passport had been an essential part of her life for so many years. She had visas for eleven countries inserted and stamped on the pages. The passport had once meant something, had granted her freedom and acceptance. Now it was gone. Whenever she was issued with new travel documents they would allow her entry to every country except one: Afghanistan. If she were to travel there, she would lose the right to live in Norway.

They had taken her to the police station in Alta.

'The system won't let me register you,' the woman behind the counter had said. There were some technical problems with her case, she was told. She had been in the country for almost three months and she was still nobody. Invitations flooded into her inbox from all over the world. The UN in New York asked her to describe women's lives in Afghanistan. She was invited to Stockholm, Vilnius and Istanbul. She had to turn everything down.

The process of obtaining new travel documents was on hold because the system couldn't register her fingerprints. She was therefore without any papers. When the issue of fingerprints was resolved, she would be issued with a residence card within a week, the person at the Alta Centre for Integration and Competence had explained. Then she would receive a social security number, which would enable her to get a bank card, thus allowing her to board a flight – a domestic one at any rate. In the meantime, she held meetings on Zoom around the clock. Afghanistan was three and a half hours ahead, the office in Geneva was in the same time zone as Alta, and towards the afternoon New York woke up.

She had accepted positions in her home country because she believed she could make a difference. All her life she had held that belief. Leaving had been a tough decision. She had even taken the country's name as her own. She called herself Jamila Afghani – *The Afghan*. When she had married, she did not want her father's or her husband's name, preferring a surname that neither denoted ethnicity nor clan. Her whole identity was built up around Afghanistan.

For a week, they had tried to get into the airport. Every morning they had locked the front door and left with less and less luggage. Every evening they had to turn back. Along with thousands of others they waded through a river of sewage, over barbed wire, trapped in the crowd.

The Americans were guarding the airport, preventing them from entering; they, the inhabitants, were being kept back by them, the intruders. She felt they were trampling on her identity, on her human dignity. How could they ever have trusted the Americans? She had sat in government, participated at the negotiations in Doha, been invited to speak to the UN Security Council. She had warned against what had eventually unfolded: women being sidelined in the peace process, civil society being overlooked. Western diplomats and politicians had many fine things to say about women, democracy and participation, but what did that matter when they were wading through excrement to get into an airport in their own country, while they, *the internationals*, were sitting safe and sound in their offices making action plans?

It was humiliating.

Ten days after the Afghan president had fled, the family finally got seats on a military transport plane to Oslo. They were placed in a camp along with other evacuated Afghans: human rights advocates, military interpreters, embassy employees. Within the first forty-eight hours after arrival, it was decided where everyone would be settled, without any attempt being made to place people where they could be useful or continue their work.

Alta is among the world's northernmost towns, with twenty thousand souls, high mountains to the west and the large Finnmark plateau to the east. The place has salmon rivers and reindeer, sawmills and power plants, a dairy, a library and a swimming pool. It has polar nights in winter, with the northern lights occasionally flaming up the sky, and in summer it's eternal day. And it was incredibly slippery.

Jamila and the family had arrived with the clothes on their backs. At the reception centre they could choose from donated clothing. Now they went around in various types of traditional Norwegian knitted sweaters, but they still wore their shoes from Kabul. Jamila owned one pair. She only wore them out in public. Indoors she went barefoot. It was easier to keep her balance.

She had experienced a strange feeling on arriving at the house on Church Street. It reminded her of something. From childhood. Everything was different, of course, the smooth parquet flooring, the wood-burning stove, the fireplace, the kitchenette, the spacious living room, but the windows faced the same way as home: towards the mountains.

It was the tiles in the bathroom that had made tears well up in her eyes. They were the same green colour as her mother had chosen for the walls in her childhood home.

Some doors had been kicked in, their handles broken off; lone asylum seekers had lived there previously, men who had fled from God knows where and must have been angry and frustrated.

She understood why. Without knowing them. *Exile.* Smooth on the surface, sore, ragged and bloody underneath. Roots aren't ripped up without pain. It was understandable that a few doors might suffer.

Opposite the kitchen window was a white church with a high, narrow steeple. The children had tried to go in, but it had been locked on each occasion. When darkness fell, the view changed. The graves around the church began to light up. There were candles in glass jars on the snow-covered gravestones, and bright LED hearts hung on some of the crosses. Other headstones were covered with fairy lights and shiny wreathes. The entire graveyard came alive at night.

Her son had been upset when they were settled by a graveyard. 'So many dead people right next to us,' he complained.

'Death!' she replied. If any place was filled with death, it was where they came from. 'This is where we survive.'

When the house was quiet, when the children were at school, when her husband had left for his Norwegian language classes, she sat with her back to the graveyard, went online and called up Kabul.

The doorbell rang. It was Helene, a tall, cheerful woman from the Centre for Integration and Competence.

'Didn't you get the message?' she asked Jamila, who was standing barefoot in the doorway.

'About what?'

'You have an appointment with the career advisor. At twelve!'

Jamila switched off the computer and went to the bedroom to change. She found the block that kept her foot in place inside her shoe, pulled it on and attached it to her knee. Out in the hallway she sat on a stool, struggling to put on her other shoe.

'You should have a shoehorn!' Helene exclaimed.

On the slippery steps outside the house, she added, 'And crampons on your shoes.' She helped her down the steps and into the car. 'And spikes for the crutches,' she mumbled to herself.

Jamila should get in touch with the Technical Aid Centre, Helene explained, and seek funds from the Norwegian Labour and Welfare Administration for spikes for the crutches. Helene gave her the rundown on the application process as she gripped the steering wheel and navigated her seven-seater car down the winding road to the centre.

When they got there, the careers advisor greeted them cheerily and mentioned that the interpreter was ready. Upon arrival in Alta, Jamila had let it be known she did not need a translator, as she was happy to hold meetings in English, and not in Dari, Pashto, Farsi, Arabic or any other of the interpretation service's languages.

'The interpreter is for me!' the career advisor laughed when Jamila again pointed out she didn't need translation. The career advisor wasn't that confident in English and would rather speak Norwegian.

They sat down in one of the classrooms. Floor-to-ceiling windows afforded a view over the fjord. The mountains were bathed in a pink glow. This was where Jamila would receive help to build her career, to integrate into Norwegian society.

Cleaning.

Care work.

Cooking.

Perhaps shop work might appeal?

'Crampons,' Helene had said. 'Spikes for the crutches.'

To stop her from falling.

But Jamila was already off balance.

Time for Tenderness

Bashir sat propped up against a golden cushion, listening. The flower stems entwined behind his broad back. Life was good. His stomach bulged beneath his tunic; his cheeks were round like those of a toddler. His curly, shoulder-length hair was shiny, his beard unruly. Over his tunic he had a waistcoat and he wore a brown, round-topped cap with a rolled-up rim.

It was time to receive people.

An assault rifle lay next to him. It was a Krinkov, designed by Mikhail Kalashnikov but shorter than his famous namesake; daintier, easier and quicker to take up, perfect for the drivers of armoured cars and helicopter pilots, who had less room to handle the long Kalashnikovs.

The Krinkov, almost like a machine gun, with a foldable stock, first came into use after the Soviet invasion in 1979, quickly gaining trophy status as an Afghan only took possession of one in victory. The rifle also acquired a certain cachet due to it becoming Osama bin Laden's favourite firearm.

Bashir's lay there on the cushion. Not that he needed it at home, but where else would it lie?

He was sitting on the top floor of the pink villa, in a bright, rectangular room with large windows on three sides, like a conservatory, set back from the roof terrace.

Guests entered by an external staircase so they would not see the women of the house. The steps led up to a balcony between the first and second floors, from where they were shown to the internal stairwell, and they ascended the last flight inside, before emerging onto the terrace, which took up half the roof. From here there was a view over the whole garden below, the houses around, and towards Kabul. At the windows, divided into oriental patterns by wooden latticework, hung thin light blue curtains, tied up in plump knots so as not to be in the way of those sitting against the walls. In one corner there lay a pile of folded blankets, for guests invited to stay overnight. If they were many, they slept in the open, on the terrace outside. Apart from the textiles, the room was bare. This was the men's world.

Bashir was a good host; in the kitchen the stove was on from early morning. Visitors who came to Bashir to seek advice, to make plans or share gossip complicated life for the women, who were constantly being told to leave the garden or stay away from the windows. His small nephews, who acted as messengers, often forgot to let them know when the coast was clear, so the women would sometimes sit inside for most of the day. They complained about this to Bashir, who quickly came up with a solution.

Beside the parking area, on the other side of a pergola with grapevines that had yet to bear leaves, was an unused plot of land. He would build his own guest house on that spot.

No sooner thought than done. A few days later a group of young men in sand-coloured tunics were digging in the garden. It was unfamiliar work; the men were used to handling weapons, not spades. They were stiff in their movements, digging clumsily, spilling earth. It took time. But no one in Bashir's house was unduly stressed: they were still revelling in victory.

Bashir had already begun to decorate the new guest house in his head. He would need a soft carpet, covering the whole floor. He looked at interior design websites online. Should it perhaps have some shades of blue?

At present, Bashir was sitting in the conservatory listening intently, eyes fixed on the man speaking. The only discernible movement was his hand holding the prayer beads. One by one he let the pearls pass between his fingers.

On the floor were glass cups, filled to the brim with green tea, and between them a plate with nuts, raisins and dried peas. A small bowl of toffees had been placed in front of the two visitors. They sat with their legs crossed, facing each other.

It was one thing having command of a thousand men in war; it was quite another being responsible for them in peacetime. Now everyday life had been thrust upon them and they turned to their old commander for advice. Men who had lived among men, employing violence as a method, had returned home to be fathers and husbands. They sat there, in small, draughty houses, without money, without jobs. War's way of dealing with things lay closest to hand.

Violence was easily resorted to.

The two visitors, an older man and a younger one, sat on their respective mattresses and presented their cases in turn.

One of Bashir's fighters had beaten up his wife during a row. Her wrist had been broken. The woman was the sister of another of Bashir's soldiers, who avenged himself on his former comrade by doing the same to his own wife, who was the first man's sister. You could say the men were even. They had both injured their wives, the other's sister.

Bashir was sweating. Another typical day.

'I can't picture a general in America having to solve his soldiers' everyday problems,' he complained to his friends. 'When the war is over for America, it's over for the generals too, don't you think?'

Yes, they thought so. That was probably how things worked in America.

But this was Afghanistan. Everyone and everything was connected. People being so tightly woven together was a strength, but also a weakness. They brought honour or shame on each other, happiness or unhappiness. No one was just one individual.

The men, sitting with their glasses of tea, each represented their respective abuser. The younger one was the brother of the first man who broke his wife's wrist. The older one was the father of the wife beaten in revenge. Neither of them wanted to back down.

This mustn't escalate, was Bashir's assessment after having listened to both. Retaliation was no solution. He sweet-talked the men into a meeting between the families to reconcile matters. If that didn't take place, they were to return to him. They expressed their gratitude and praised God before leaving. The next visitor, who had been sitting outside, waiting in the autumn sun, could be sent in.

It was an older man, who had been under Bashir's command at one time. His son needed an operation. The old fighter had no income and no money for the private clinics carrying out procedures in Kabul, while the public hospitals had no room for his son. They were full, he had been told.

Bashir promised to send one of his men. An operation was something he should be able to arrange with a little pressure. After twenty years in the field, he had friends everywhere.

Next!

A lawyer, a cousin of one of Bashir's soldiers, entered. He was representing a Turkish woman who for several years had run a construction company in Kabul. Under the former regime, she had loaned a man half a million afghani, close to six thousand dollars. Now he refused to pay it back. What was she to do?

Bashir considered the matter, enquired as to the identity of the debtor and said they could mention this visit to him as leverage. He believed a woman's place was in the home. But she was Turkish, and no one owned her, so he let it go. She should get her money back: it wasn't right to be deceived by an Afghan.

'If he doesn't pay up, I'll respond with a show of force,' Bashir assured the lawyer.

That was the type of pressure one would rather avoid.

The lawyer thanked him. Bashir let out a deep breath.

Enough appointments for today. Some of Bashir's men had come to eat lunch. They embraced before throwing down their handguns and

Kalashnikovs. Only the two youngest placed theirs neatly against the wall by extending bipods from the barrel.

Jamal and Muslim, still treating their weapons with reverence, were Bashir's bodyguards and errand boys. They ensured the car always stood ready outside, took messages for him and generally kept an eye out. A man who has killed will always have enemies.

Jamal was a striking teenager with dimples and shiny curls; he wore a desert-coloured tactical vest with pockets bulging with ammunition. Three glow sticks that could be cracked to use as a light source were fastened to a loop. On the chest it read 'Afghanistan Special Forces'.

His comrade Muslim also walked round with an enemy scalp in the form of a pouch that read 'Enduring Freedom'. Taliban soldiers had a style all their own. Something stolen, something won, something borrowed and something found. American uniforms were combined with woven shawls and keffiyehs. Others wore tunics and wide trousers. They had rings on their fingers, bracelets and gold watches. On their feet they alternated between captured military boots, Pakistani trainers and plastic sandals. When visiting, whether at someone's home, a ministry or a police station, all footwear was removed and placed by the door. Now, those who wore socks took them off and tossed them in the corner.

No self-respecting Talib went anywhere bareheaded. One of the lunch guests had a black turban, another a white one. A couple wore embroidered Kandahar hats decorated with glass beads. One sported a baseball cap with sunglasses perched atop over a shawl, and another was wrapped in a *patu*, a thin woollen throw. Bashir had his *pakol*, the round-topped woollen hat, pushed high up on his forehead. He took out his phone and tapped on the camera function to look at himself on the screen. He studied his face, raising his chin, examining his teeth, checking his eyes and his hairline.

Farid, the oldest and broadest of the men, sat in a large camouflage jacket, chuckling at his vanity. A pair of handcuffs dangled from his black submachine gun. As the longest-serving man under Bashir, he could get away with that kind of thing. He gestured at Bashir's freshly ironed tunic.

'You're dressed in black?'

Bashir gave him a sheepish smile.

'Like a boy!' his friend added. They all laughed. Adults didn't wear black. They dressed in white, if they could afford it, in light grey if they wanted to appear serious, and in increasingly dark hues of brown, depending on how often they could afford to wash a tunic. But black – that was something only young boys wore.

Bashir now grinned. He had a particular reason for dressing as he had. He continued to examine his appearance.

The men laughed.

'Teenager!'

He smiled. With a pause in the war, it was time for new love.

Bashir was to meet the man who, if all went according to plan, would be his new father-in-law. The third one.

It had all started when a group of fighters were gathered at a house in Mussahi. Bashir had mentioned aloud, to no one in particular, that he wanted to marry again.

Obaidullah, a Talib from the village, who was both a mullah and a fighter, hadn't said anything, but his thoughts had turned to his daughter. He had already married off her older sister, now it was Mariam's turn. She had just turned sixteen.

Perhaps it was written in his eyes, because a couple of weeks later Farid rang him and said he would like to come by. Farid had, by this stage, already dispatched his wife to take a look at the girl. She had inspected her and voiced her approval.

Now it was Farid's turn to be served tea. He sat with Mariam's father on the mattresses by the glowing stove in the middle of the room. Obaidullah listened to what he had to say about the famous man.

The fact that the suitor already had two wives was of little concern, Obaidullah himself had two wives and that worked out fine. Together they had given him nineteen children, so a man like Bashir wanting to have a third was only reasonable.

But Obaidullah didn't say that. He said he would have to discuss the matter with the girl's mother, his second wife.

She thought Bashir was a good man. But they had to ask Mariam.

Everyone in the village knew who Bashir was. Mariam had heard stories about him growing up. He may have fought all over the country, but his roots were in Mussahi.

The girl said yes straight away.

'But you'll be wife number three, don't you want to give it some more thought?' her mother asked.

'It's fine as long as I don't have to live with the other wives,' Mariam replied.

'He is old, in his mid-thirties, does that bother you?'

'No, I don't mind. He's a good man,' she answered.

Now, some weeks later, Bashir was a little on edge. He had yet to meet the girl but had heard of the teenager's beauty by word of mouth. Tonight, as he was to meet her father he wanted to look his best, so he would just have to put up with his friends' jibes.

The proposal was being kept within the group anyway. Mariam was the little sister of Jamal, the striking soldier with the tactical vest – his bodyguard.

For the time being, Bashir's men knew more than Hala and his wives. He was dreading having to tell them. Especially his mother. It was the second time he had found a wife himself. She was going to be angry. And Galai and Yasamin . . . he would have to think of some way to placate them. Well, he would cross that bridge when he came to it. It was easier to ask forgiveness than permission.

A long plastic sheet was rolled out on the floor between the mattresses. Steaming dishes of *qabeli palaw* – rice sprinkled with oil and thin, glazed bits of carrot and raisins – prepared by the women of the house, were placed beside chunks of lamb and bowls of parsley and spring onion.

The men used their fingers to pinch mouthfuls of rice and picked up bits of meat with pieces they tore from the large, still-warm flatbread, which Hala and Yasamin had baked. The sound of the men eating replaced their chitchat.

Bashir wore a Bluetooth earpiece. It lit up now and again with a blue light under his curls and a conversation ensued. Matters, both important and trivial, interrupted mouthfuls of food. One minute it was about a new mediation meeting, the next about some equipment he needed, before he got worked up about the key to the Land Cruiser going astray. The remote-control fob was missing. A new one would cost eight hundred dollars, he was told. 'Find one for two hundred,' he ordered.

After the meal, Bashir and Farid sat twisting their fingers together. Afghan fighters are naturally close to one another; most of their day is spent with other men. When they sat like this, full after eating, several of them stroked and cuddled, patted one another on the thigh while talking, or played with one another's hands.

These men, sitting wriggling their toes after the heavy meal, were Bashir's most trusted. They would follow him no matter what he asked of them. He knew that. He had spent a lot of time on home decor and it was beginning to get to him. A restless thought was starting to take shape.

Jihad wasn't over.

Jihad would never stop.

The blood of a holy warrior ran in his veins.

He hadn't been completely honest with Sirajuddin Haqqani. Now that the caliph had become minister of interior affairs, he wasn't going to support Bashir's plans. Sirajuddin wanted order and calm in the country, to demonstrate to the world that he had control, while Bashir had not finished fighting.

He had his eye on the east. He had kinsmen in the tribal areas. They shared the same idea: they wanted to Talibanise Pakistan. When the time was right, they would overthrow the infidels' regime. They would not give up until it fell, just like Ghani's castle in the air. They had liberated Afghanistan, now it was time to set their neighbour free.

Building peace was not for him. First everything not in God's image had to be brought down.

In spring, when the buds appeared and the fighting season began, he would leave.

In spring, when the sun warmed again, everything would happen. The wedding. Flowering. A new war. Allah's angels would still be watching over him.

Ah, life was smiling.

He took out a packet of dental floss from his pocket. One of the men rubbed at his glass eye. Another let out a cough. Outside the afternoon was growing dark.

Do You Want to Meet the Taliban?

In Alta, the polar night had descended. The lights in the cemetery beyond the kitchen window flickered at all hours. Sometimes they saw shadows there, figures tending pillar candles by torchlight or changing the batteries in fairy lights. Batteries didn't last long in temperatures of thirty below zero and needed checking if a lamp was to continue shining for the dead.

The days had begun to get shorter until the sun had disappeared completely at the end of November. Mid-morning, a few shreds of light could be discerned. Rays from below the horizon, where the sun was to be found, reflecting faintly. Salahuddin and Kakar found it fascinating; Jamila thought it was awful. Khadija and Fatima dealt with the phenomenon as they did with most things in life, it was just something that happened, that's how it was now – before they disappeared into what mattered: new friends and the iPad.

Sometimes the northern lights blazed in the sky, fluorescent yellow and green, red or purple. Salahuddin and Kakar would go outside to observe the celestial performance. It was frighteningly beautiful, but offered no warmth. The wind from the mountain plateau had brought a chill into the house. The floors were cold, almost freezing by the front door, and though the radiators were running red hot they were unable to heat up the draughty house with the panoramic windows. There were two fireplaces, one in the living room and one in the dining room, but where would they find firewood?

It was so insurmountable, everything.

As the new semester started in January, there were no more excuses: Jamila Afghani had to attend the Norwegian language course. She had been granted an exemption in the autumn. The family had arrived late in the semester and she'd had so much to do in dealing with her organisations in Afghanistan, so she'd had her course postponed until the new year, while Kakar had attended from day one. He was an eager student and enjoyed a classroom environment. As a teacher in Arabic, he had a great interest in grammar, word inflection, syntax, rules and exceptions. The course became a lifeline at a time when the world as he knew it had fallen apart. He adapted, just as he had always done for Jamila.

Immigrants intending to seek permanent residence had the obligation of three hundred hours of language tuition. Lack of attendance was not taken lightly. You could not come to Norway thinking you had more important things to do. If someone wanted to continue their work for basic human rights in their homeland, they must do it in their spare time. The main activity for a refugee was Norwegian classes. It was like a job, from eight in the morning until three in the afternoon, with homework in the evenings.

It was dark from when they got up to when they went to bed. There was a similar gloom in Jamila's mind. She thought about all the things she would rather be doing than learning Norwegian words. She felt her energy was being misspent. That she should have remained in Kabul.

How she longed for her city! The people, the office, the view towards her mountains.

One night, Torpekai, the deputy head of WILPF and office manager in Jamila's absence, called her. She said they had run into a brick wall. A number of the programmes had come to a halt. They were unable to contact the authorities.

It was hard to get used to the Taliban being in power. After a while it became imperative to meet them. The organisation needed permits to be renewed in order to continue with their aid and education projects. Torpekai was worried about breaking both written and unwritten rules, which might be used as a pretext to close down the office. She had even taken the step of hiring men. Something they had never done previously. After all, it was a women's organisation. Except for the guards at the gate, they had prided themselves on filling all the positions with women. Now everything had changed. The Taliban didn't receive female visitors, they didn't reply to enquiries from women. Fortunately, they had found some nice young men who adhered to the organisation's procedures. Torpekai and Soraya, her deputy, were still the bosses in the office, but for all errands outside the building they had to send a man to get anything done.

The whole family left the house at the same time each morning. Khadija and Fatima plodded off to the local school in new pink jackets, padded trousers, reflective tags and lined boots. Down the road they met a classmate. They quickly got used to walking unaccompanied. In Kabul they never set foot outside on their own.

Salahuddin disappeared in the opposite direction, towards the secondary school, while Jamila had been provided with transport to the Norwegian class, which was down by the fjord, and Kakar went with her. The driver was the refugee service's factotum, Abdul. He had arrived as a refugee from Syria some years previously. '*Æ elske Alta*', meaning 'I love Alta', was the first thing he taught them. 'You need to get a wheelchair,' he said to Jamila, in Arabic, on seeing how she struggled on the ice. 'My wife got one,' he said, adding however that she had even more difficulty walking than Jamila. Abdul and his wife had small children, and he insisted there was no better place on earth than this town. He reeled off all the things it had to offer: the good people living there, the welfare granted, the northern lights.

The girls finished school at around half-past one. Salahuddin came home around three o'clock. Being home alone was not something they had experienced before. Jamila could see how the girls were thriving. Friends called to ask them to come and play, to go sledging, to build snow castles, and they came home black and blue from ski training, with eyes shining and snow crystals in their hair.

The whole family had been invited to go dogsledding. The social worker from the town council showed them photos of her huskies. She said Jamila would sit on warm reindeer hide inside the sleigh, while the others could drive the dogs themselves, have the wind in their faces and race across the plateau, before lighting a fire, making some coffee and just thoroughly enjoying themselves.

Jamila gave her a perfunctory nod. This wasn't for her. Kakar and the children could go.

But perhaps the Competence Centre could arrange a less intensive language course? Was it possible to cut down the hours? In Afghanistan things happened every day and she had to keep up, take part in online meetings and answer emails from colleagues. There were reports to write, conversations to have, and the time differences between Kabul, Geneva and New York were the same as before.

The less-intensive course was for people who couldn't read or write, the woman with the huskies informed her. 'The class would be completely unsuitable for you,' she said.

After classes were done for the day, it was time to make dinner. Jamila hated cooking: it was time that could be spent on other things. She had always felt that way. Now it was taking what little energy she had left. She had pains from repetitive strain in her back, shoulder and in one hand. There was a delay in getting a doctor's appointment. X-rays had been taken when they were waiting for relocation to Alta but she had been registered with the wrong social security number so the images could not be retrieved. As far as Jamila understood, they didn't want to take new pictures because the old ones were in the system somewhere. They were trying to sort it out, she was told, but the weeks passed.

'I'm so tired, in so much pain, and I still have no appointment to see a doctor,' she complained to Kakar, before taking a few more painkillers and settling down to do her homework.

'*Æ elske Alta*' was not part of the lesson.

At the end of January Jamila received a telephone call. It was from the Norwegian Ministry of Foreign Affairs.

A woman informed her of a meeting to be held in Oslo. They wished to invite representatives of Afghan civil society and, well, possibly, the Taliban.

Jamila straightened up in her chair.

'What's on the agenda?' she asked.

'For the moment there is no agenda,' the woman answered. It was the Afghans themselves who would decide the content of the meetings. She emphasised that the potential meeting had to remain secret until it took place.

Jamila felt confused. What should she say? 'Possibly' the Taliban would come?

Until given permission, the woman impressed upon her, she was not to tell anyone about this conversation.

'OK,' Jamila said.

She called up Torpekai straight away.

'Of course you have to go!' she cried. 'No one listens to us here! If the Taliban are really going to Norway, you must meet them!' Maybe she could make some headway there, the office manager hoped.

Jamila called up the woman in Oslo to say she was interested in attending the meeting, in case there had been any doubt about that. She received an email, but it didn't tell her much more. Again it was stressed that she must not share this information with anyone until she received confirmation the meeting was to go ahead.

It didn't take long.

Two days later, Jamila and Kakar flew to Oslo. Jamila had asked the office in Kabul to write her a speech as, right there and then, she had enough to deal with packing crutches, shoes and insoles, a few large shawls and what Salahuddin referred to as her baby, her laptop.

From the airport they were driven to Holmenkollen. There, among the skiing trails in the forested hills surrounding the capital, the meetings were to take place. There had been much debate among the Afghan diaspora in Norway regarding the propriety of meeting the Taliban. Some believed it could be viewed as recognition, others that dialogue was the only way to influence them.

When Jamila stepped onto the flagstone floor of the lobby at the Soria Moria Hotel, her eyes brimmed with tears. Standing in front of her she saw women she knew well. Mahbouba, Masouda, Nazifa, some of whom had travelled directly from Afghanistan. They hadn't seen one another since before the evacuation; now they sat down on a sofa waiting for their room keys. It hadn't occurred to Jamila just how deeply rooted these women were in her heart. They had all been struggling for years, in different ways, for the same thing: women's participation in society. It was as though hope sprang anew at the very sight of them.

'Does anyone know what's on the agenda?' one of them asked.

Everyone shook their heads.

'We provide the space,' one government official told them at dinner. It was up to the Afghans to decide what they wanted to talk about. The following day they would have the opportunity to confer before meeting the Taliban delegation the day after. Apart from this timeframe, the Norwegians were leaving the discussions and their content up to the Afghans. It was their meeting.

That same day a private jet took off from Kabul airport. The Norwegian Ministry of Foreign Affairs had wanted to keep the flight low-profile, but the spokesman for the Taliban's foreign minister put up several photos on Twitter of the turban-clad delegation sitting in the cream-coloured interior. *The special flight*, as he called it, had sixteen seats, six beds and Wi-Fi. The first person to comment on the tweet was a Norwegian woman: 'Remember that this flight is being paid for by Norwegian WOMEN and men. With our taxes. Norway is rich because both women and men work. Furthermore, women and men have equal rights in our country. Try to learn something while you're here!'

The representatives were from a broad background and there was great diversity in opinion and priorities. Some were positive to the Taliban; others were virtually at war with them. Jamila occupied the space between the extremes, as usual. The most important thing, she believed, was to establish a dialogue, then try to move forward from there. She had no illusions but was focused on the art of the possible.

One man seemed to support the Taliban, in Jamila's opinion. Another, who had worked under Hamid Karzai, agreed with everyone. 'Watch out, or you'll end up seeing eye to eye with the Taliban too!' they teased him. A woman from the arts sector loudly voiced her disapproval of what she termed the normalisation of terrorists.

The fourteen Afghans spent the entire day inside, discussing the form and content of their meeting with the Taliban. At ten o'clock at night they had finally managed to agree on the proposal they would put forward the next day. They were going to ask the Taliban to set up a commission to revise the constitution as well as to invite discussion on how it might be changed. This would take a year or two, the group estimated. Until a new constitution could be enacted, there ought to be a transitional government put in place. Following this, elections would have to be held.

Unlike the Taliban delegation, they did not form a cohesive group; there was no natural hierarchy, so who would speak at the meeting? Eventually they agreed that each of them would be given the same amount of time to introduce themselves and put their views across, while one of them would ensure the time allotted was equitable. They decided to do their utmost to address the Taliban in a diplomatic manner.

*

That night, Jamila hardly slept. She was dreading the next day, the clamour, meeting the Taliban. Their leadership had previously declared that they didn't believe in elections, in democracy, that sharia sufficed. So how was this going to play out?

The Taliban were at breakfast when she and Kakar came down. They all sat together, like in Doha, before strolling over to the buffet. A large painting of snow-covered trees dominated the wall behind the coffee pots. In the picture the sun was rising behind some huge spruce trees, their branches weighed down by snow. A bullfinch looked on from a snow-laden bough.

The representatives of civil society were first to arrive at the meeting, sitting down along a table with their name cards set out, as though for a negotiation. The walls in this room were decorated with images from Norwegian folk tales. Some of them were quite suggestive, like Theodor Kittelsen's *Fairy Dream*, in which a naked blonde fairy entangles a man in her transparent veil. The Taliban had to be careful where they looked.

The delegation filed in, wearing tunics over wide cropped trousers, most of them in turbans, and nearly all with long beards.

Even though Jamila had steeled herself, the sight of Anas Haqqani, Sirajuddin's younger brother, was disquieting. Why had they sent the worst ones? For her, the Haqqani Network were terrorists; their very name gave her a jolt, after all the suicide attacks and car bombings they had carried out.

She was nervous. There was so much pent-up anger.

The senior official in the group, the Taliban's foreign minister, gave the opening address. Jamila's shoulders tensed; she was dreading the first interruption.

'We have many faults, we have made many mistakes,' Amir Khan Muttaqi, seated with his back to the white winter landscape, began. 'We weren't ready. We were placed in that situation when the last president left,' he continued. 'We were expecting to have some share of power, but all the responsibility was placed on our shoulders all of a sudden, for which we were not ready. This has been very difficult for us, so help us! Give us advice, tell us your thoughts.'

The speech eased the mood somewhat. Jamila looked around. She was the only one who had brought her laptop to the meeting and wrote down everything that was said.

The foreign minister had struck a conciliatory note, poured a little water on the flames. Now it was their turn. Each of them would get five minutes to talk about one topic, the only way to cover everything. The grand old dame Mahbouba Seraj had suggested not spending time on how women should dress and leave the burka aside, as that would risk swallowing up all the time. They needed to talk about power. About the constitution. About elections, not clothing.

Where Jamila was seated meant she would be the last to speak. For her, the most important matter was girls' right to education, at all levels. She had resolved to employ the Taliban's own language and terminology – to show them respect, but also to get their attention. She wanted to show the new authorities that their mutual faith left room for more than they currently permitted.

'No religion, no ideology, no law or constitution can close the door on the education of girls,' she began. 'It is beyond all reason.'

If the Taliban truly cared about Afghans, about the future of the country, she said, this was where to act. And act now. 'The Prophet said it was everyone's duty to learn. "Seek knowledge, even if you have to go to China," it says in a well-known hadith. The Prophet makes no distinction between boys and girls here. By what right do you?'

At this time of year the schools were closed for the winter, the spring equinox marking when they opened again. This was too late! After the Covid lockdowns, after the disruption when the Taliban took power, pupils were lagging far behind.

'What are you waiting for?' she asked. 'You could open the schools in the south in February, it'll be warm enough.'

She watched the Talib responsible for education. He had not thought of that! There were many provinces where schools could soon reopen. The very thought made her impatient.

'Afghanistan is our country,' she said. 'And our collective responsibility. But you are the ones in power. How long are we going to fight about this? Let everyone go to school!'

The foreign minister and others took notes as she spoke and made follow-up comments. Anas Haqqani sat quietly listening. He hadn't said a word throughout the meeting. She remembered how he had been released to get the negotiations between Trump and the Taliban back on track, in exchange for the kidnapped professors.

At lunch, which was without seating arrangement and name cards, she saw Haqqani sit down with his delegation; he gently greeted those on either side of him, spoke in a low voice. Jamila observed a member of her own group, a woman from Herat, approaching him. She pricked up her ears. The woman told him she was experiencing problems with the local Taliban in her home province. They wouldn't allow her to work, and they were harassing women in her organisation.

'Here's my phone number,' Haqqani said, scribbling some digits on a piece of paper. 'Call me when I'm back and tell me what I can do to help.'

The Norwegian facilitators had ensured the buffet was halal. With a cook from the Middle East, everything was in the best of hands. There was rice and lamb, chicken and chickpeas, food they were all accustomed to.

Kakar, who had not been present at the meeting, also took the opportunity presented by the joint lunch. The Taliban had stopped NECDO handing out food and blankets. They had initially been allowed to distribute the items, then been informed that the Taliban were to receive half of everything. His colleagues in Kabul had called him when they heard he would meet the Taliban in Oslo. 'Please ask them! They won't listen to us here.'

Kakar went straight over to Haqqani and took the matter up with him. The powerful man promised to sort things out.

After lunch, two hours were set aside for debate. The Taliban responded to some of the proposals raised. They're actually communicating, Jamila thought. Maybe this was what was needed to open a dialogue.

Both sides agreed that communication needed to improve. The majority were also critical of the USA, which had yet to unfreeze a large part of Afghanistan's bank reserves. Still the representatives from civil society stressed that Western countries had to impose conditions on the payback to push the Taliban in the right direction.

When Jamila had met the Taliban in Doha two years previously, they had come across as more human than she had imagined. Now they seemed even more accommodating. The debate was rounded off with the participants sharing their thoughts on how the meeting had gone, and the Taliban had gifts for everyone: a box of saffron from Herat.

Jamila's slow pace in exiting the room allowed her to have one last word. She approached the foreign minister.

'This in in your hands,' she told him.

He nodded and said he had taken her words on board.

'You are the leaders of the people now,' Jamila went on. 'So you need to care about us!'

Did they? Did they really care about the people? She wasn't sure.

They had listened in the meeting but what had they actually promised?

The most specific part of their joint statement was that the participants recognised that cooperation was the only solution to the problems facing Afghanistan.

During their conversations the Taliban had suggested that the schools would be open for everyone in March. Or had they?

On the flight back north the couple's optimism started to falter. A creeping doubt lay just below the surface.

Would it be like Doha, when the Taliban fooled everyone?

'It's like they've realised it's not so easy to run the country,' Kakar said.

'Killing is easy, being killed is easy. Governing fairly is something else. There's no magic wand,' Jamila replied.

They crossed the Arctic Circle. Outside the windows it was pitch black. She felt a sudden darkness creeping within her. In Oslo she had been someone. She had been important. Tomorrow morning it was back to the language course.

Back home she saw on Twitter that the Taliban had put out another photo of their private jet. They called the meeting a success.

'We shared the stage with the world,' the foreign minister said, before flying back to Kabul to rule exactly as before.

Rector Redbeard

There was an uneasy peace in Kabul.

People kept their heads down. Adapted. Waited.

No one could relax. Usurped power can be wrested. No position was safe.

On the streets the fighters ruled over shawl and beard. Once a bombmaker, now a policeman. Once a terrorist, now a law enforcer. Men in turbans went door to door. The imams imposed punishments. Holy warriors waited for positions. What was the reward for twenty years of armed struggle?

The reward was slow in coming. There was no money. Jobs were offered without pay. People took them anyway, on the off chance they would be first in line when the treasury was replenished.

The population were freezing. They were hungry. The snow that had fallen softly on cement walls and barbed wire around New Year had been shovelled into hard mounds, more black than white.

Many stayed indoors. Those sitting the most quietly of all were the people who had lost everything but still had one thing left to lose: their lives. The prosecutors who had accused the Taliban, the judges who had sentenced them, the torturers who had tormented them and the special forces who had killed them. Those who hadn't made it onto the evacuation flights were desperately trying to find a way out.

The Taliban knew who they were. Some of them were already

dead. The names and addresses of the guilty in the former justice system were easy to find. The records had been left behind in desk drawers and filing cabinets when those who could save themselves fled. The new forces of law and order could knock on their door at any time and drag them into the street. The amnesty declared by the Taliban was full of holes.

One can lie low for a while, but not for ever.

The Taliban had time. They were in no rush to kill. Not right now. In this grey, cold winter, no one knew for certain what the Taliban's true colours were. The senior leadership in Kandahar rarely expressed themselves publicly, scarcely showed themselves. The administration in Kabul had enough to govern day to day, filling the country's highest positions with fighters.

They had fought, suffered, sacrificed. They had lost brothers, fathers, sons and limbs. They had beaten the strongest military power in the world. Now they would do as they pleased. Because they deserved it.

* * *

'Put on something nice. We're having guests!'

Ariana looked at her mother in surprise and then down at herself. She was wearing a pair of loose trousers and had thrown on her sister's plaid shirt over a cotton sweater. Her long chestnut-brown hair hung loosely, cascading over her shoulders.

'Who's coming? Why do I have to dress up?'

'Someone from back home.'

'Relatives?'

No, they weren't relations, but the visitors were from her parents' province.

The course on mastering stress had finished. They were to take what they had learned and apply it to daily life, the psychologist had said. Ariana spent every waking hour with her parents and six siblings. The course turned out to be zero help against the irritation that had spread out like a heavy, itchy blanket over all of them.

Ariana didn't bother changing from her sister's soft flannel shirt just because her mother was having guests, but she did cover her head with a shawl.

When the intercom buzzed, her mother went down to welcome the visitors. Three women, one older and two younger ones, came up the stairs. The usual greetings and blessings followed. Her mother didn't seem to know them very well; they talked about common acquaintances as though they were strangers. Ariana and Zohal were asked to serve tea. They put out biscuits, raisins and nuts.

'Sit down with us,' her mother said when Ariana had poured tea for everyone. The new year had got off to an ice-cold start, and as they were having guests a generous amount of wood was burning in the stove in the middle of the room. Usually they sat wrapped in heavy, woollen blankets and put hot water bottles underneath. Now the fire crackled cosily.

However, Ariana only sat for a few minutes before excusing herself. The women were from a farming family. They talked about how much land they had. What their house looked like, about the fruit trees in the garden, what they cultivated in the fields. Ariana wanted to get back to Netflix. Her little sister stayed.

Not long after, Zohal came into her room.

'They're talking about you,' she said. 'And about him.'

'Who?'

'They were saying stuff like, "We have a son. A real gentleman . . ."'

Something darkened within her.

Now she understood. They had come for her.

This had happened to so many of her friends in the last few months. Parents had lost their jobs and the household budget had tightened. As it had for them. And she was already twenty-one. Tears began welling up. Several of her friends had been married off in a rush, before finishing their studies – girls with completely different plans for their lives. After that she had lost contact with them. She wasn't allowed to visit them now that they belonged to other families, and they didn't come to see her.

Zohal told her the three women were the mother, sister and daughter-in-law of the magnificent specimen.

Everything within her resisted this. She wanted to study, wanted to learn, to work, travel and live by herself. She wanted to be free!

She refused to come and say goodbye when her mother called out to her.

'Since when are you so rude?' her mother asked.

'I'm not interested.'

'He has lots of land!'

'I'm even less interested!'

'We've heard so many nice things about him.'

'He's not my type.'

'Don't talk like that.'

'I am not interested. I need to finish my studies!'

She heard how hollow it sounded. There were no studies.

'Forget university,' her mother said. 'The Taliban have no respect for education anyway. It's better if your father and I find a good match for you. For you and your sisters.'

She'd had one single semester left for her law degree when the Taliban came to power!

Ariana felt belligerent. A good match for you. The words whirred through her head. For you and your sisters.

Her parents had grown up under communism. People went on dates then, so she had heard; they sat in the cinema holding hands, she imagined. They had received an education and now they were suddenly throwing out everything they believed in to 'secure their daughters' futures'.

'The Taliban might open the university . . .' Ariana said, more in hope than belief.

'That's not going to happen,' her mother said. 'There's no point in even thinking about it!'

Something had changed within the family. Something fundamental. Even so, she had thought her parents would listen to her where her own future was concerned. They used to reach decisions through discussion. Not any longer. Suddenly she was no one. She, who had always been the golden girl.

Her parents, who cursed the Taliban and hated them intensely, had without noticing been Talibanised. The Taliban had crept into their minds, into their subconscious. Her purpose in life was to marry, not to be happy.

'Maybe they'll open . . . ' she tried again.

Overnight, she turned restlessness into patience. She insisted on a wait and see approach, while her parents went on about the hurry. Marrying her off had suddenly become their number one concern. They put her teenage sisters' fate in her hands. If she didn't marry soon, it would be difficult to find a man for Zohal, who actually wanted to be a biologist, and Diwa, who had hoped to become a dentist. They had never talked like this before. They used to allow their daughters to dream. They had let them believe they could be something other than merely married.

Every day they sat squeezed together in the apartment they became increasingly isolated from one another.

All the while using firewood sparingly. All the while conserving food. A life on the back burner with compassion switched off.

The Taliban were operating on a low flame too. They made do with patrolling the streets and not much else. The whips weren't to be seen, the rods under wraps. The much-feared purges had yet to materialise. The Taliban settled some individual scores, but the general population were left in peace.

'Maybe they'll improve,' Ariana said, trying to drop a hint. 'They might loosen up.'

Her parents continued to pressure her. He really was a good match; his family were well off and he had a good name.

'I can see now that they don't care about me,' she wrote in her diary. 'Maybe they never really did. They just keep saying the same things over and over. They've become so hard.'

After keeping the man's family on tenterhooks for so long, she had to say yes, her parents argued.

But she had already said no!

'They're waiting for you,' her parents replied, as though they hadn't heard her. 'Marry him and you'll have a good future.'

No, no, no!

One day her mother showed her a photo of him. He didn't look that bad. Not handsome but not terrible-looking either. He was around ten years her senior. He had finished school, her mother told her. In other words, no higher education. A marriage like that would never work out. After all, she had nearly finished her degree, was practically on her way to being a judge. Her mother believed that kind of thinking was futile.

'The Taliban aren't going to reopen the universities,' she repeated. 'What's more, you don't need them to because you'll never get a job anyway,' she continued. 'But we need money for food now.'

Amid all this they were indoors all day.

Going out was dangerous, her parents said.

The Taliban are stealing young women, they harped on. For their soldiers.

You need to make up your mind!

I have made up my mind!

You don't know what's best for you!

The first time someone asked for Ariana's hand she was in her final year of secondary school. One of her teachers had approached Nadia on behalf of her son. Neighbours had also asked. Her mother's only sister had asked. She had just one son and thought it would be so nice to have her niece in the house. Such things were not uncommon. Ariana was a beautiful girl, clever, sociable and capable. Even her friends had put forward their brothers for consideration. Over the years Nadia got used to lines like 'We saw your daughter at so-and-so's wedding, and we were thinking . . . ' Both mother and daughter had rejected the offers. After all, she was going to make something of herself.

Until now.

The cold weather was releasing its grip when, in mid-February, the Taliban issued a statement: 'The universities will open in ten days.'

'It's too risky,' her father said.

'But I have one semester left!'

The campus was in a troubled region, her father argued. The Taliban were engaged in mop-up operations there. And who was going to pay? For the books? For the accommodation? For food and transport?

Karim himself was in a deep depression. Mornings were difficult. Getting out of bed for nothing. For a life indoors. As a former colonel in the Ministry of Defence, he was among the despised. Someone who could never play a part under Taliban rule. In the beginning he had hidden away, but not any more. They weren't looking for him. He was too insignificant. They let people be, let them understand they were being left to rot. That was the punishment for choosing to work for the Afghan government. He could sell tea on the street, or push around a cart of carrots. But he could never be an officer again.

'And afterwards, what happens then? When you're finished?' he asked Ariana, like he was talking to the air.

Why doesn't my father speak *to* me? Why doesn't he look *at* me?

Ariana lowered her head. Looking away herself, she asked in a low voice: 'Dad. Please. Let me go back to university.'

The day the universities reopened Ariana sat at home crying. What if the Taliban clamped down again and this was her last chance? That they allowed women in for this one semester to recover the frozen funds before closing everything. Completing her studies now would mean getting a degree, then maybe she could go abroad, take a masters.

It was absurd that the Taliban had actually reopened the university but her middle-class parents refused to let her go. They went on about the risks, never about the danger of not going, of not completing her studies, let alone about the risks of marrying their daughter off to someone they hardly knew.

She rang up a fellow student. There had been forty girls in her class.

'There're only three of us here,' Sauda whispered the day after lectures resumed. 'They're going to suspend classes unless more show up.'

'What's it like there?' Ariana asked.

'It's so quiet. There's hardly anyone on campus. Where is everyone?'

They were at home like Ariana.

The next day Sauda called to say two more had arrived. They had wanted to see what the situation was. The day after one more came, then another couple. A week passed. The university didn't get caught in the crossfire from any battles. The bus ran as usual. None of the girls suffered any physical abuse. The place was peaceful. Sauda told her that only those who registered by next week would be allowed complete the course.

'By the way, one of the teachers was asking about you.'

'What? Who?'

'Not one of ours, he's from a different faculty. Lectures in computing, I think. He asked where you were, wondered if you were coming back. He said he knew you, that he'd spoken to you. And seeing how he's on the staff I just told him I didn't know but that you might be back next week.'

It must have been the guy who had called her after the talk she had given about the value of learning English. Creep. Chasing around after her like that.

One more semester and she would have a law degree. Taliban or no Taliban, she had to see it through!

'Unless more of us turn up, no one will be allowed to complete the course,' she told her parents. 'They'll close it down as we'll be too few.'

Finally, they allowed her to go.

The campus was bare and empty. Students went directly to where they were supposed to be, then back again. The girls, who had used to dress in tight jeans and colourful T-shirts, were covered in full-length black gowns. The boys, who had worn stonewashed jeans and sharply cut hairstyles, wore tunics and let their beards grow.

The Taliban had guards stationed to ensure boys and girls didn't speak to one another.

The morning Ariana arrived, the female students were called to a meeting in the large lecture hall, which was in the agriculture faculty. The head of the university was going to give a speech. When everyone was present, heads covered so not a hair was visible, the rector entered.

He was dressed in a light-blue tunic and a black turban, his huge beard dyed red with henna. When their beards began to grey, many Afghan men chose to dye them either jet black or reddish. His was almost orange.

The previous rector had fled. According to rumour, he was abroad. Adding to his academic qualifications. His replacement was one of the old lecturers in Islam and sharia.

He opened by reciting from the Quran. Then he embarked on his speech. It was threatening. I should never have come, Ariana thought.

'We've fought twenty years for this!' the rector exclaimed. 'Finally, Afghanistan will be ruled by the laws of Allah.'

To attain this, the students had to follow university laws. Ariana took notes.

'You are not allowed to have smartphones.

You are not permitted to speak to teachers in private.

We will punish you.

You must wear the Islamic hijab.

You are not allowed to wear new clothes. They are to be old, well-worn, and no clothing that can attract attention.

Speaking to boys is forbidden. As is the sending of texts.

We will punish you should such contact be discovered.

Make-up is prohibited. It makes girls look brazen.

Those who look brazen will be sent home.

Perfume is not permitted. It's not good for you. It can attract someone.

Wandering around on campus is not allowed. You must go straight to the lecture hall.

And just so you know, guards will be monitoring. In places you don't know about. We have guards you will not see. Watching closely.'

How could this happen? How could life have taken so many steps backwards? She felt like screaming.

The rector continued.

'We no longer have any health services. There's no point calling for an ambulance if you become ill. Don't pretend to be ill. It's a sin and a disgrace. Should you not follow these rules we will punish you. The prison isn't far away. It's right by the university. If you disobey us, or God's laws, we will send you there. For a few days to start with. That will help you familiarise yourself with the rules.'

He didn't bat an eyelid when he said it.

Prison?

White sheets of paper with quotations from the Quran had been stuck up above the blackboard. The red-bearded man raised his forefinger. 'We're keeping an eye on you now. Last week we didn't. You are not allowed sit on the benches outdoors. Or on the grass. You must go straight from the auditorium to the student residence.'

There were new rules there too. Despite the inner courtyard of the dormitory being surrounded by four high walls and only girls being present, they couldn't go there any more. Nor were they permitted to leave the building after midday prayer began. They were only allowed on campus from eight to twelve, when they had lectures or classes, and to proceed directly to their destination.

'Anyone who fails to comply will have no university, no place to sleep, no learning, they can go home!'

Afterwards, Ariana whispered to her friend:

'We can't put on make-up, but he's allowed to dye his beard red!'

Visiting the Dead

Peace is not for everyone.

As winter was coming to an end and Bashir had been resting at home for a time, he was growing restless. War's momentum, that impetus to push ever more, ever further, fighting on several fronts, had formed him. He began to miss old friends.

'Sightseeing!' he laughed. He was going to visit the liberated areas that he had only seen in times of war.

Nangarhar, Paktia, Parwan, Logar, Kapisa, Paktika, Khost. Bashir set out in the armoured Land Cruiser with his bodyguards and a bunch of friends. Two cars were filled up with men and weapons, vests and blankets. They visited brothers in arms, living and dead. At the homes of the living they ate grilled meat with thick slices of raw onion and chillis. At the graves of the dead, they recited prayers.

One day he went to the house of a Talib who had helped him when he was imprisoned. Samiullah had already been inside for five years when Bashir was transferred to his cell after being sentenced to death. The young man was a dedicated believer and often led prayers among the prisoners. He also knew the routines about the buying and selling of services, which guards were easiest to bribe, how to send messages out and have answers smuggled in.

Bashir was above him in the Taliban hierarchy and the two of them gloated when they learned about the threat Bashir's men had sent to Mohib, the president's security advisor: if Bashir was hanged, Mohib wouldn't survive the day.

Samiullah was also the one who prayed with Bashir when he lost yet another child. After Yasamin's first two children died, she gave birth to a son and a daughter who both lived past infancy. One morning, while Bashir was in prison, the women were preparing breakfast at home in Jalalabad when Yasamin noticed her daughter was missing. She was busy kneading flour into a dough, so she asked their five-year-old son to find her. The boy returned, saying 'Mama, she's in the bathroom.'

Yasamin glanced up. 'Well fetch her then.'

'I can't,' the boy replied.

Yasamin got up from the floor and went to the little bathroom. Inside, her daughter was head down in the large drum they stored water in. She had clambered up and fallen in. She was not yet two years old.

Yasamin said nothing to Bashir. But he learned of his daughter's death from Raouf, who had heard it from his wife.

Bashir phoned Yasamin and said he wanted to speak to the children. She put their son on the line. After chatting with him for a while, Bashir said he wanted to talk to his daughter.

'She's sleeping,' Yasamin said.

'Wake her!' Bashir responded.

'She's not very well . . . '

'I want to hear her voice.'

There was silence on the other end of the line.

Yasamin, who always obeyed, always complied, could not meet his demand.

That night Bashir sat with Samiullah and prayed for his dead daughter. Bashir and Yasamin had lost three of their four children.

The two men shared a cell until both were released as part of the Doha Agreement in the summer of 2020 and returned to their respective areas to carry on the struggle. A year later, a few days after the president had fled the country, Samiullah went to the airport, where the evacuation was in full swing.

It was his last chance to kill Americans. Their days in Afghanistan were numbered.

Bashir left his bodyguards outside when they arrived at Samiullah's house in a village in Logar Province. He only brought his best friend, Farid.

'May I die for you!' Samiullah's mother cried. 'He loved his friends so much . . .'

She was overcome with tears.

The men were led upstairs in the modest dwelling, into a room with turquoise walls. Light shone in from a large window that almost reached the ceiling, covered by transparent white curtains. The two friends each sat in a corner, placing their weapons beside them on the light blue mattress.

'Your friends have come!' the mother sobbed. 'Oh, my handsome martyr! Allah would not let me keep you!'

Now both jihadists cried. Farid was the first to regain some composure and speak. 'Dear mother, be grateful that your son is a martyr. He will be happy on Judgement Day. The Almighty didn't want us. Your son is fortunate. He has been chosen!'

'But he died before so many of our wishes could be fulfilled!'

'Allah chose, dear mother. Samiullah fought hard for the victory, giving us our new government,' Farid continued.

Samiullah had joined the Taliban in his early teens. To the dismay of his parents, he had dropped out of school and become a fighter. He hardly managed to get involved in the fighting before he was arrested. His mother believed some relatives had informed on him. They had worked for the government and feared landing in trouble because of him. Giving information to the authorities was most convenient: it meant your own back was covered.

'Seven years and four months he was imprisoned,' the mother said. 'His father died while he was there, then he was released, and then . . . !'

'This kind of death is rare, glorious. Not everyone is lucky enough to be a martyr,' Bashir interrupted.

A small boy entered with *waziri chai* — cardamom tea with hot milk — and set down a large plate with thick slices of cake. Bashir and Farid offered variations of the same sentiments over and over, while the mother dried her eyes.

Samiullah would receive his reward on the Day of Judgement. He would help her into paradise. This was the best kind of death. Her son was brave, the bravest of them all. 'So how can you be sad?' Bashir asked.

'That's what my son said,' she replied. 'If I am martyred, don't cry for me. My mother is strong, he told his comrades. As a widow, she is both a mother and a father to me.'

'Yes, he said the same to me in prison!' Bashir exclaimed. 'And remember what I told you when you came to visit him there? That you needed to find him a girl as soon as possible. And you did.'

Three months prior to Samiullah going to the airport to kill Americans, he had wed the fifteen-year-old his mother had chosen.

'Where is she now? Did you marry her off to one of your other sons?' Bashir asked. Samiullah had two older brothers, and it would have been customary for her to become wife number two for one of them.

'We married her to my stepson.'

This was the son of her dead husband's second wife.

'Is he older or younger than Samiullah?'

'He's fourteen.'

'How wonderful that you married her to him!' Bashir said.

'Yes, I just couldn't let her go. I chose my stepson so she would stay in the house.'

A widow must first continue living with her in-laws. After a waiting period of three months, called *iddah*, to make sure she wasn't pregnant, she could be married off to a relative of the deceased.

'Do not be sad, dear mother, now she is his wife. Where else could she go?'

'Yes, you're right, it was the only way.'

Bashir wanted to know more about what had taken place at the airport. The Americans had coordinated the evacuation with the

Taliban, who had given their men orders that no shots were to be fired. Samiullah had defied these orders.

'It was just after the Taliban had entered Kabul – the next day, I think. He came home around two in the afternoon, had a nap in there' – she gestured behind her – 'then he got a call asking him to go to Kabul. He washed and said he'd return around breakfast time. At dawn, just before morning prayers, he rang me. He said that Kabul was quiet, the prison was empty, the prisoners freed, that he was grateful Afghanistan was finally to be governed in accordance with Islam.' She took a deep breath. 'Then he left for the airport. I don't know, I wasn't there, but they say he shot at the Americans and they returned fire. He was martyred there. They say he killed two Americans.'

The door was ajar. Three teenage girls sat listening in the hallway. One of them was the young widow, who had lived just three months with Samiullah. The two others were his younger sisters. The girls shrank back when the old woman caught sight of them, but she let them remain sitting there.

'It felt as though someone cut out my liver when I heard he had been killed. There was weeping in all sixty houses in the village!'

Bashir knew the attack had failed but said nothing. No Americans were killed at the airport until IS exploded a bomb ten days into the evacuation. If Samiullah's motives were unclear, the family myth shone on: the martyr took two infidels with him into death.

Next to the reception room, another door stood ajar. It led to the bedroom where Samiullah had taken a last nap in the conjugal bed. Now his stepbrother had taken over both the bed and the girl.

The round bed took up almost all of the floor space. The light-coloured cover on the headboard was still in its plastic packaging, as though no one had quite allowed themselves to make use of the bed.

'You are fortunate,' Bashir said to Samiullah's mother as he made ready to depart.

He slipped a wad of notes into her hand. She protested mildly but kept the money and cried a little more.

Bashir had to get a move on. There were so many martyrs.

Outside the cows lowed. It was time for milking.

Clouds of dust rose behind the two vehicles driving at high speed across the barren desert of Logar Province.

Bashir had always had great faith in Latif. He was smart, strong and well-disciplined – Bashir's most important criteria when choosing his men. If those who came to him were very young, he had one additional criterion: they shouldn't be too pretty. Bashir didn't want people to think he was running some sort of harem. He had developed a nose for who would work in a team and in a fight. Latif was one such man.

'You need to pay closer attention to who you take in,' Latif had said after being with Bashir for a few weeks.

'Oh?'

'You didn't check any of my references. You handed me a weapon straight away. I could have killed you.'

Bashir laughed at the reprimand. 'I've got my eye on you the whole time. I have men observing you. The entire group is watching you. In addition to all those you don't see, who are also keeping tabs on you. Are you happy now?'

'I just don't want someone to betray you,' Latif mumbled.

He had been killed by the only enemy the West and the Taliban had in common – IS.

They called themselves IS-K. The K stood for Khorasan, the historical name for the region that covered large swathes of Central Asia, Iran and Afghanistan. IS were established in Afghanistan in 2015, when they were at the height of their power and still ruled their caliphate in Iraq and Syria. In Afghanistan, they attacked international forces, the army, Shia Muslims – and the Taliban. They were frustrated members of Tehrik-e-Taliban Pakistan, an offshoot of the Haqqani Network and al-Qaeda. The rift and split was part of the reason Bashir had eventually left the tribal areas.

IS was a rival he did not need.

Jalalabad in Nangarhar Province had become their heartland, and when a friend of Bashir was tasked with leading the fight in a district where IS stood strong, Bashir offered him his best men. In his opinion, their leaders needed to be killed, their people taken control of and their Salafism undermined. For IS-K, the Taliban were not orthodox enough. They put tribal law before Islam, wore amulets and healed with magic. Furthermore, they allowed the Shias to live and were too close to the Pakistani intelligence service.

The Taliban managed to drive IS-K out of some districts around Jalalabad. But at a price. Latif was killed in an ambush.

Now his sister was asking for help. She had called several times, sounding increasingly desperate. Rambling about an engagement, she had seemed afraid.

He was rarely contacted by a female: mediation was the domain of men, even though most conflicts pertained to a woman. Occasionally her life was at stake. Spilling blood was the last resort to wash a family clean. Bashir always tried to avoid that, as problems seldom ceased with the taking of *one* life. It began to spiral.

He had little desire to go but was conscious of Latif's sacrifice and the responsibility he had taken on for the families of his men.

Soon after Latif was killed, his father died. Consequently, Latif's mother and sisters had moved in with some relatives. The lack of a man in the family rendered life exposed and vulnerable. Bashir had been asked to come when the relatives were away so the sister could speak freely.

The sun was still high. High walls in squares and rectangles were spread across the desert landscape. They hid mud houses, livestock, most likely a well, some fruit trees. Within the walls extended families lived.

Bashir, driving the Land Cruiser himself, turned off the road and followed some tyre tracks towards a brick wall a little way off from the main settlement. Stones and sand surrounded the high wall. He slowed down. A gate was opened. A few metres inside the courtyard stood a covered woman.

Malala was thin as a rake, with high, angular cheekbones, large deep-set eyes and a wide mouth. It was four years since Latif had been killed; the grief no longer played on her features as it did with Samiullah's mother. It was resigned, dimmed.

Bashir was shown into the visitors' room.

'Tell me everything, quickly, because I can't stay long,' he said. 'I have to get to another martyr's house.' He was served tea, leaned back against a cushion and set his expression to show that he was ready to listen. Malala sat on the floor in front of him.

'Almost three years ago a woman visited my mother. She came on behalf of her brother, who wanted to marry me. He was rich, owned numerous properties, sixty shops, two hundred *jeribs* of land, had a well-paid job, several university degrees and a lot of gold. Moreover, he was young and handsome.'

This man was sent from heaven, her mother said. Life was hard, she and her daughters had entered their relatives' house as servants, far from their own home district. Her only other son had injured his hand in battle and had fled to Turkey.

The old woman was captivated by the thought of a wealthy son-in-law. It would solve all their problems. Malala, who was eighteen at the time, wanted to meet him but that was against tradition. 'You won't accept your own mother's opinion?' Malala was scolded when insisting on seeing the suitor.

Malala's dream was to train as a midwife. She decided to set a few conditions before accepting the proposal, to see what this man was really like. He had to accept her going to school and allow her to work. In addition, she wanted a high bride price – *walwar* – so her mother could have a better life, and a large dowry – *mahr* – which included clothing and items for herself.

The suitor, via his sister, accepted everything.

The engagement was entered into by proxy. They met for the first time two months later.

'I nearly fainted,' she told Bashir, speaking quickly and nervously. 'He was forty-five, at least! I said to myself, you can't make fun of people's age or appearance, but I swear, he is not a good-looking man. Still, he's probably a good man, I thought, as he'd agreed to all the conditions, and Mum really needed the money. On his first visit, while my mother was in the kitchen, he said he'd like to come over now and again. I could make him some tea and be with him.' She spoke in a low voice, faster now.

'When I refused, he became upset. He asked why. Was I saving myself for someone else? 'We're Pashtuns,' I said, 'it's not our custom to leave a fiancé alone with a bride before marriage.' But he continued to pester me. Eventually I let him come one day when no one was home. He was so kind, until he got what he wanted from me.' Now she was almost whispering. 'Then he changed completely. He said he wouldn't accept any of my conditions after all and that I couldn't do anything about it, since I had, well, had . . . He had had his way with me. He said that from now on I had to do everything he commanded, and that he would come to me whenever he wanted. "If you don't let me come, I'll break off the engagement and make your life hell," he threatened. And now that's the situation I find myself in.'

'Where does he live?' Bashir asked.

'Over there. They have a good view of our house as their place is a little higher up.' She pointed out the window in the direction of the dark mountains where nothing grew.

Her betrothed was in Ghazni at the moment, but his house had eyes. As Bashir was listening to Malala's story, the man's brother sent his son over to check who had come to visit. The boy approached Bashir's bodyguards outside the gate.

'Who are you? And why are you here?' he asked.

Jamal and Muslim waved him away. 'The commander's wife is visiting the women of the house,' they said, as they had been instructed to. The boy headed home.

'He fooled us,' Malala went on. 'Did I mention he's already married? His sister had told us that beforehand, so I'd accepted it. As he was willing to let me study, I thought it was all right. But here's the thing: he won't pay the agreed price, he won't meet the conditions, but he still wants to marry me. For almost two and a half years I've been saying, "First you need to pay what you promised, then we can marry." The clock is ticking. Oh, you should have seen how I looked two years ago, I was plump and beautiful, now I'm gaunt and old . . .'

'If he can't afford it, he can't afford it,' Bashir said. 'But if you behave yourself now, he'll see it as a favour and repay you in the future. He will show you gratitude.'

'I've been good to him for two and a half years! Have you heard the saying: if you respect someone wise, they will in turn respect you, but respect a swindler and he will never value you?'

'If you postpone this any longer or insist on him breaking off the engagement, he'll make life miserable for you,' Bashir replied. Only a man could break off an engagement, and if he did the woman was already sullied. 'This is my advice: get married. If he comes here and takes you by force, and says "this is my wife, I want her in my house", no one can tell him not to. It's his right. There's no court in Afghanistan you can appeal to,' Bashir said. 'Only he can do that.'

'But, brother, I've already explained to you how he tricked me.'

'This isn't Europe, it's Logar,' Bashir said, and explained the rules in sharia regarding *nikah* – marriage.

Malala interrupted him. 'But I agreed to marry him because he accepted my conditions!'

'You are entitled to a dowry,' Bashir said. 'If he doesn't produce the items and clothes he promised, you are within your rights not to marry him. But that has nothing to do with sharia, it's about *Pashtunwali*.'

'He says he wants me without paying, and I can't do anything about that since he's already taken possession of me.'

'Well, that's where you made a big mistake. There's nothing I can do to help you now. You made this blunder yourself. You shouldn't have let him near you. You should have said, "First fulfil the requirements, then I'll do as you say."'

'So you're taking his side? He tricked me!'

'I'm not taking his side. I'm describing Pashtun culture.'

'You're just like him! You don't let your daughters go to school! But when your wife gets sick, do you want a male or female doctor to treat her? A female, of course! If girls aren't educated, where will you find doctors for your daughters in the future? And how are your children to be born safely if no midwives are trained?'

'Do you talk back to him the way you're talking to me now?' Bashir asked. 'Even if a man curses his wife, or wife-to-be, she has no right to answer back. Saying one thing will lead to another. She is to obey! And as for this village, no girls go to school here, as you well know, so how could you believe he would accept that?'

Perhaps he had been a little tough, so he became more conciliatory. 'Sometimes I quarrel with my wives, say harsh things, and they respond in kind. It's normal between man and wife. By the way, would you like to see a picture of my fiancée? My third wife?'

'I'd rather you listened to me!'

Bashir handed her his phone all the same.

'She's not even pretty!' Malala exclaimed. 'You want a well-behaved girl from a good family. You want nice things for yourself. As do I. If your wives don't do as you say, you complain. I also complain when my husband-to-be doesn't respect me. But I'm poor, I'm weak, I have no power.'

Malala sat upright on the floor in front of Bashir as she spoke.

'I know you through our brother,' Bashir said. 'Latif was a brave mujahid. God be with him. He wouldn't have liked to see how you're all living now. Without a man in the house, people will gossip. Particularly now that your fiancé isn't on your side. No one will dare wed you nor your little sister. My advice to you is get married. You can't continue to live here without a man.'

Malala's mother entered with more tea and cakes. She had the same high cheekbones as her daughter, and deep eyes that were almost blind. The haggard woman in her late forties was even thinner than her daughter, and since her son and husband were killed had been taking strong medication for anxiety, which made her lethargic.

'Oh, *Mawlawi saib*, dear Bashir, my son is a martyr!' she cried.

'Why don't you ask your other son to return and look after you?'

'I have, but he refuses.'

'Surely he could send you money from Turkey?'

That had been the plan, but they had hardly heard from him and he had never sent anything.

'You are family. How can he, as the only man, abandon you like this? Tell him to come back! You can't go on living like this for ever. You have another daughter. Who is going to marry her if Malala breaks off the engagement?'

The mother began to weep. Bashir thought for a moment. There was another solution.

'Leave this place! Go somewhere your fiancé can't find you! None of you can stay here if this drags on. This isn't even your village. Living here alone, just women, it won't work.' The mother lowered her head. Bashir turned to Malala. 'The only way to be rid of your fiancé is to leave. And the only place you can hide is in Kabul.'

'How are we supposed to afford to live in Kabul?' Malala asked.

Bashir said he could sort out a place for them, but it needed a man. The brother had to return from Turkey.

Malala didn't care for any of the solutions he outlined. 'Put us on a plane to our brother!' she begged.

Bashir rebuffed the suggestion. 'I don't want that kind of life for you.'

'Latif was martyred four years ago, and who has been here to help us since? Nobody! You've only spoken to me once!'

'Have we only spoken once?'

'Conversations over the phone don't count! No one has helped us!'

'I swear,' Bashir said, 'that all the extra money I have goes to the families of martyrs. It's not from official coffers, it's from my own pocket. I have refrained from visiting for the sake of your honour. People would have spread rumours about you. And don't say I haven't helped you. I've sent money. Keep in mind this is Afghanistan, you must live in accordance with the culture! You need to either leave or marry that man.'

'What's the punishment for defrauding someone?'

'What do you think?'

'A bullet in the head.'

'If you need a gun, tell me.'

'Can you speak to him?'

'My advice: love your fiancé, then it'll turn out well for you.'

'If that's your advice then I have no choice but to take my own life. You, my brother, do not stand by me, even though you have power.'

'Listen to me . . . '

'No, I won't listen to you. One bullet is enough to solve all my problems.'

'It's late, I need to go,' Bashir said, and got up. He had honoured Latif, had offered his sister advice, enough was enough.

Malala stayed on the floor. Her mother bid Bashir a subdued farewell. He slipped a roll of banknotes into her hand, as he had done for Samiullah's mother. Now he had to be getting on, to a third martyr.

The dead did not wait.

Eclipse

The school should shine. The classrooms, lecterns, desks, everything that had been locked away since the Taliban took over was going to gleam. The spring sunshine would soon flood through the windows. It was too much work for the cleaning staff alone, so the teachers pitched in. Nadia brought her daughters to help. Only Ariana remained at home to study for her exams.

The school year began after *Nowruz* – the first day in the solar calendar. Colourful flags and decorations were for sale from carts and stalls. Those who could afford it invited guests and prepared feasts to celebrate the arrival of spring. The Persian New Year had for long been a public holiday in Afghanistan. But two days before Nowruz the Taliban issued a decree stating the celebration was un-Islamic. Civil servants were informed they would be docked a month's pay should they fail to turn up at work. From now on the country was only to have two celebrations annually: Eid al-Fitr and Eid al-Adha. The Prophet Muhammad had said that all heathen festivals should be replaced by these. Birthdays, Mother's and Father's Day, Independence Day – and Nowruz – were cancelled.

But the Taliban's power wasn't as absolute as before. Ribbons in spring colours were still being sold from the carts, while the stalls offered bags of *haft mewa* – a mixture of dried fruits and nuts soaked in water and sprinkled with cardamom.

More important were the clothes to be worn the following

day: the school uniforms. For the girls it was a mid-length or long dress, depending on age, and a large white shawl to cover the head, shoulders and chest. For the boys, a classic tunic with wide trousers beneath.

Nadia had purchased a new bell for the school as the last one was rusted to pieces. She liked the sound of the new one and was looking forward to the pupils filling up the narrow area outside the school building when it rang.

She hung up lists of names on the doors of the classrooms. In the office she had copies of them, an overview of the teachers, the subjects they taught, the addresses of the pupils and their parents and guardians. Everything had been noted down, ticked off, crossed out, changed around and rearranged. The organisation of the first day of school had been one huge jigsaw. Finally, she had put it all together. If the pupils came in three different shifts, it would work out.

Nadia's school had pupils from first grade all the way to final grade, divided into classes of fifty. The classes had been mixed, but now they had sent the boys to another school and taken girls in return. The same with the teachers; male teachers had been transferred to boys' schools, while Nadia had hired several women.

She had prepared everything over the course of the winter, without knowing for certain whether the schools would reopen, and for whom. Nadia had complained to Karim, saying she wanted to return to teaching. Then she could just come to work, teach and leave again. As principal she felt the weight of responsibility. The system was cumbersome to say the least. Getting answers was difficult, instructions were vague, everything took ages, until the Taliban suddenly issued a decree with new rules.

In mid-March, a week before the schools were to open, the Ministry of Education invited all the headteachers in Kabul to a meeting. On the way in, the men were directed to seats in the front half of the hall, behind which was a cordoned-off area, and the women were shown to the back rows.

The head of the education board, Mullah Khitab, stepped up to the podium. His name meant 'one who holds speeches and sermons', and it was certainly something he seemed to enjoy.

After quoting at length from the Quran and holding forth on the sacrifices made by the Taliban for over twenty years, the warnings and admonishments began.

'No matter what you do, or where you go, God, the Almighty, sees you! When you do a poor job, when your work is sub-standard, he notices. When you slack off, he notices. When you cheat, he notices. When you accept bribes, he notices.'

Nadia was fuming. The schools were opening in a week, and he chose to begin this way!

'Many pupils left school under the previous administration without any real knowledge. We will change that. We need to improve the standard of teaching. Children will receive the *correct* doctrine. You must all work hard!'

To achieve this, society needed to be steered in the direction God had pointed out.

Mullah Khitab dedicated a long time to clothing and covering up. What teachers could wear, how the pupils should dress. All females had to cover their heads and bodies.

Purdah – segregation – was the next topic. Men could no longer enter girls' schools; this included fathers. They had to drop off their children outside the gate and could not meet the female teachers.

A lengthy admonition followed on the treatment of school property, chairs, tables and blackboards. These belonged to the emirate and needed to be taken proper care of.

Previously such a meeting would have been held in Dari, which was the language of the authorities. Now everything was communicated in Pashto, a tongue Nadia estimated less than a quarter of the people in attendance used at home. But it was the language of the Taliban and took precedence at official meetings.

Nadia had feared the Taliban would introduce a new curriculum, that they would replace science and mathematics with Islamic teaching. Mullah Khitab didn't mention that, other than to say they were preparing a new syllabus.

When a woman raised her hand, Khitab said no questions were being taken and neither was it allowed to ask any.

Nadia felt dejected. At prior meetings like this one, the female principals had been heroes, and had visible roles on panels and in debates. They had been cheered. She had been so proud the first time she had been appointed as headmistress; it had given her such a sense of importance. Now she was seen as a speck of dirt.

Nadia had circled the date on the calendar in red. At four o'clock on 23 March she was already awake, excited about school starting and nervous about everything being in place.

She put on make-up, did her hair, fastened a shawl over her head with pins and covered her clothes with an abaya. Mullah Khitab hadn't said anything about colour, but she wanted to be on the safe side, so she chose a black one with a simple pattern of black pearls. At dawn she slipped out the door.

The first thing she did when she arrived at the school was to make sure the microphone was working, and sound was coming from the loudspeakers. She was going to hold three speeches, one for each shift. Some pupils were to read poems, others to recite from the Quran.

The secondary school girls were to start first. A few of them began arriving a whole hour before classes were due to begin. Nadia heard the voices rising and falling out in the schoolyard. She looked out; they had ironed their dresses, shined their shoes, washed their shawls. They were ready. She was ready.

The new bell rang at seven on the dot. The microphone was switched on.

'Welcome, dear pupils!'

Nadia looked out over the white headscarves and expectant gazes. She felt a tightening in her throat. They'd done it!

'You must all work hard. Take school seriously. You've lost a lot of time, six months gone now and a whole year during the pandemic. This is the time to put in an extra effort!'

The girls stood looking at her with serious expressions.

'We've washed everywhere! Make sure you keep the classrooms clean. Look after the school, it's yours. Treat it as you would your own homes. And the best part: we have new books for you. Everyone will get new books. Handle them with care, others will be using them after you.'

With Mullah Khitab in mind, she asked the pupils to respect the dress code. Only black dresses and white headscarves were allowed, nothing else, no patterns, nothing that shimmered, no subtle hues in the material. If that was the price to pay for the Taliban to allow them to learn, then so be it.

Each class followed the teachers into the building. Nadia went upstairs to her office. She plumped down onto the soft black desk chair.

'I'm a hero! We did it!' she said to herself.

She sat there enjoying the moment, leaning back, swivelling a little on the chair. Her office was on the top floor. One wall had windows with a view over Kabul. There were rooftops, aerials and clotheslines as far as the eye could see, all the way to the hills where the poorer neighbourhoods began rising up, and beyond them, the mountains.

The telephone rang. It was the principal of the boys' school she had exchanged pupils with. They had got to know one another well, and swapped gossip, tips and experiences. She greeted him happily and wished him all the best on the new school year.

'I'm so relieved,' Nadia said, before he interrupted her.

'But have you opened?'

'Yes, we started the first shift at seven, full attendance, everything went wonderfully—'

'Do you know anything more?' he asked, cutting her off again.

'What?'

'Someone said the girls' school weren't going to open after all.'

'Don't kid me around now!'

Nadia was annoyed. It was no time for jokes with everyone so on edge.

'Everything is all right. The girls are here and they're staying here. I need to prepare for the next shift.'

She ended the call and hung up. But the feeling of contentment had evaporated. What had he meant, exactly?

The principals in Kabul had their own group on WhatsApp. She took out her mobile. Unread messages filled the screen. She scrolled down, tapped on a message. Read it. Read it again. Checked others. The thread was chaotic. Lots of emotional outbursts. No one knew for certain what had happened or was going to happen. Some messages referred to a tweet the Ministry of Education had put out that morning. Others claimed the message was fake.

A voice message from a spokesman in the Ministry of Education had been forwarded by several people in the group. Nadia tapped on it.

'*Assalam aleikum!*' the voice said. 'How are things with you, dear principals?' he asked in a friendly tone.

'This message is for the principals at the girls' schools. Classes from seventh grade to twelfth grade will have to wait. All is not ready. Wait for further instructions!'

She listened to the message again.

'We will notify you again when the schools can open. This is from the Ministry of Education.'

She played it one more time. When the schools can open? They had already opened.

She sat stock still, glued to her seat. The office was spinning. She focused on the floor, with its red carpet. Everything went red. A feeling of despair welled up within her.

The first class of the day was halfway through. The teachers were probably well under way with the lesson, or busy handing out books. Maybe they were informing the pupils about the new school year, what they would be covering, how they were going to make up for lost time.

What was she going to do?

She remained sitting.

No one knew anything yet. Not the teachers nor the pupils. She could just refrain from saying anything, hope it was a misunderstanding. She checked her mobile again, waited for someone to write that it was a mistake, that they should ignore the whole thread.

There was always the hope that . . . no! Inside she knew. It was true.

The sky was blue, not the usual light grey. Spring was here. It was blossoming. Everything was serene. The school was silent. The cooing of pigeons could be heard from the roof and outside, far below, the hum of the traffic.

She listened to the voice message once more.

Then she stood up. She walked out of the office and down the corridor towards the nearest classroom. She knocked on the door, opened it and entered. The girls got to their feet when they saw her. She glanced at the chalk writing on the blackboard. The teacher had written up the timetable for the year. The pupils had just opened their notebooks and picked up their pens.

How was she going to tell them they had to go home?

No, she couldn't bring herself to do it. Couldn't bear to. She didn't say it. She just stood there. Then she beckoned the teacher over, brought her out in the corridor and said what had to be said in a quick whisper. 'You can tell the pupils yourself. I must inform the other classes.'

The teacher grabbed her by the arm, as if to hold her back. Nadia twisted loose and walked on.

'We've been given an order,' she said in the next classroom.

'We've been given an order,' she said in the third one.

'We've been given an order,' she told the fourth teacher.

She continued until she had visited every classroom. Then she went back to her office and shut the door. She leaned on the desk and hobbled over to the chair. She slumped down in it.

There were several missed calls on her mobile. She turned it off silent and rang back the first number, a male principal.

'What's happening at your place?' he asked.

When Nadia tried to answer no words would come. She tried to say something but began to sob instead.

'It'll all work out!' he said, trying to comfort her. He talked and talked; he was also nervous. 'I'm sorry. I'm so sorry about this. I can't believe it. What's happened to us?'

When he hung up, one of the teachers supposed to be working the afternoon shift called.

'Is it true?'

Then she heard the girls in the corridor.

Why?

What's happening?

Why are we going home?

Now?

But we just got here!

Eventually the teachers had to shoo them out. Then they came to see her. They wanted answers.

Why?

So late? The same day?

Who decided this?

When did they decide?

Everything was ready, all the announcements . . .

Nadia didn't know any more than they did. She tried to think and remembered that a statement had been issued that at the official opening of the schools at the Ministry of Education, women would not be allowed to attend. She hadn't given it much thought, that was just the way the world had become, and she wouldn't have had time to take part anyway. But this was something completely different.

Three women entered the room with their daughters in tow. They were angry and wanted answers. The daughters, all pupils at the school, stood behind them, crying.

'We need to leave this country!' one of the mothers said. 'Here they just want us dead.'

'I'd sooner be killed than live like this,' one of the pupils said.

Two girls in tenth grade came in. They hadn't gone home yet. They looked imploringly at her.

'Dear headmistress, will the school open again tomorrow?'

Nadia looked at them and shook her head. She could not speak any more.

On the way home she felt like shouting: why are you doing this to us?

But she didn't.

She, like most women in Afghanistan, had never expressed an opinion in public. It remained, fermenting, within her.

Arriving home, all she felt was emptiness. There were no tears left. Her heart also felt hollowed out. Her family had already heard. Social media in Kabul was full of baleful eyes and videos of weeping schoolgirls.

In the late afternoon her sister-in-law, the widow of her late brother, called. She lived in a small town in Parwan Province. Deeply upset, she related how the Taliban had stormed into the school.

'They poured into the classrooms and began hitting the girls. The teachers, who had only just been told to send the girls home, begged them to stop. "Let them walk out themselves!" they shouted, but the Taliban continued dragging and pulling, pushing and berating them. They struck my daughter across the arm with a rod – she's still in pain!'

Suddenly one of them began shouting: 'Take off the socks! Off with the socks!'

'And do you know why?' her sister-in-law almost shouted. 'The Taliban's flag is white. The socks were white. And the wearing of – walking on – a sacred colour is forbidden. Then you're dishonouring Islam, insulting the Taliban . . . '

The line went silent. There was nothing more to say.

* * *

Far away, north of the Arctic Circle, a woman was walking around her house in tears.

She was crying while waiting for the kettle to boil. While placing a teabag in the cup. As she made her way to her chair. As she put her crutches on the floor. When she sat down. And when she got up again. Most of all, while looking at the screen of her laptop.

Jamila hadn't believed it at first. The tweet from the Ministry of Education had to be fake. Someone just wanted to sabotage the start of school. After all, the minister himself had said all week that everything was fine.

Towards evening, after weeping over all the pictures from her homeland, the videos of stunned girls walking home, she took to social media herself:

'What is the Taliban's problem with girls and women??' she wrote. 'Today, when thousands of girls arrived at the school gates after months of waiting, had they remembered the hijab?? You have made a mockery of religion. Have you an answer to all these tears? The oppression can't go on.'

Everything she had fought for seemed to be petering out into nothing.

Jamila sat slumped in the soft leather chair. The snow still lay in drifts several metres high, but the days were bright, making the snow crystals glitter. In Kabul, night was approaching.

She had to do something; they couldn't give up. She rang Torpekai.

'We have to protest!' she said.

'Yes!' Torpekai replied. She had spent the day consoling her granddaughter, who had been among those sent home.

In Alta, Jamila's girls had learned to ski, they went swimming at the pool, were in a mixed class at school, learned to set their own boundaries, to be on their own, to be with others. For them, nothing changed with this dreadful day. But how damned you were to be a girl in Afghanistan!

She had believed, at the meetings in Oslo, that the Taliban had listened, had understood what she and the others had to say. After talking to the foreign minister, she got the impression he believed in education for all. He had used the word *zhmena* – promise.

Had he fooled them, or had he lost the battle?

* * *

The decision had been made in Kandahar the previous night. Word was sent to the Ministry of Education in Kabul an hour before midnight.

Three days earlier, amir al-mumineen had called a meeting. The leadership council had been in attendance, the entire government travelled down from Kabul, and a couple of dozen Islamic scholars, men close to the emir of the faithful, were also there. The meeting was scheduled to last for three days.

Did the Taliban's top leader want a shake-up of ministers? Make some strategic changes? Infighting had been a feature of the organisation over the preceding months.

As leader of the movement, the emir had absolute authority. When he decided something, no one could go against him. To influence a decision, you had to do so before he ruled on it. The Taliban was a movement based on consensus. They tried to reach an agreement satisfactory to all; this was part of the reason for their resilience and longevity. While the government in Kabul was responsible for the day-to-day running of the country, the leadership council in Kandahar – *rahbari shura* – advised the emir.

The reopening of the schools had been under debate for months. For outsiders, the process had been just as impenetrable as usual, but this time the Taliban had divided internally. They had discussed it on their own patch, within their own faction, closing their eyes to the possibility of others in the movement not agreeing.

The minister of education, Noorullah Munir, had operated independently of the emir when he planned a full school opening. As had foreign minister Amir Khan Muttaqi when he made his promise in Oslo.

It was as though they expected the emir would give way. Seeing as they had stated it publicly, both to the population and to potential international donors, without censure from the leadership, they could assume everything was all right. At the same time, it was known that the emir was personally opposed to female education. Nevertheless, he was expected to act in accordance with the view of the majority, which was to allow girls to attend school, at all ages. Since the minister of education didn't hear anything, and the emir was not approached by the minister, the preparations continued without approval from the highest level.

The government could have taken up the matter months before with the council of Muslim scholars in Kandahar, who exercised great influence over the emir. They could have raised it with clerics across the country, to give impetus to swaying the emir's decision.

None of this was done.

Neither the emir nor the leadership council were consulted.

So when conservatives at the Kandahar meeting began to argue against teenage girls being allowed to return to education, the more pragmatic element were unprepared. They had assumed everything was fine since the emir had made no protest. Until now. Three days before the schools were supposed to open.

One day passed.

Two days passed.

The day before the schools were to reopen, the meeting was still in progress.

One front, consisting of two dozen influential scholars, wanted to issue a fatwa that girls over primary-school age could not return to school. For these men, the idea that marriageable girls would be going to school for everyone to see, even if fully covered, was as disturbing as it was provocative.

Other scholars disagreed. It was contrary to the purposes of Islamic teaching not to allow both sexes to study at all levels.

'If anyone has a different opinion based on sharia, I'm prepared to have that debate!' the education minister was reported as saying at the meeting.

Most of the government were included in his group. While hard-nosed on other issues, interior minister Sirajuddin Haqqani, deputy prime minister Mullah Baradar and defence minister Mullah Yaqub, son of Mullah Omar himself, supported the opening of schools for all. As did the foreign minister, who had appealed for international recognition in Oslo.

But they were unprepared. They were engaged in other matters, in their own power struggles, there were so much else to clarify and settle in the space of the three days, so there was no real opposition to the most conservative voices on the matter, no organised push-back.

Thus, the emir, following his heart and in line with his convictions, backed the powerful minority, a small circle of ultra-conservative imams.

Kandahar defeated Kabul.

During the night, the phones rang off the hook at the Ministry of Education, where few had imagined the long-awaited school opening was in jeopardy. The fateful tweet had been posted in the early morning, in a country where many were without electricity and far fewer were on Twitter. It had been sent out as the girls, oblivious to events, pulled on white socks, fastened their white shawl and checked the mirror one last time to make sure the pins were holding it in place.

* * *

Three days later the hall of Jamila's office building in Kabul began filling up. On the green wall-to-wall carpet, covered by a kilim in orange and red, stood a lectern. A sheet of paper was taped to it, reading 'Schools must open NOW!' And underneath in Pashto, 'Education is our human right!' Below that, in Dari, it said, 'Girls in school make for a bright future!'

Jamila and Torpekai had decided the press conference would take Islam as its basis. Female education mustn't be construed as a Western notion – after all, it wasn't. For that reason, they had invited several female Islamic scholars – *ulema* – who argued their point with the Quran in hand.

One of them was Zeynab, a university lecturer in her thirties who had worked closely with Jamila for a long time. She wore a beige shawl, which covered her head and most of her upper body.

'Can those who know and those who do not know be deemed equal?' she asked, quoting from the Quran.

No, not according to God. He said the wise should rule. And if girls are not granted education, how are they to become wise? What the Taliban had done went against the Quran. Islam was the only religion in the world with a holy book that opened with the word *Iqra!* Read!

'The importance of everyone reading is emphasised in our sacred texts,' Zeynab continued. 'When Gabriel appeared to Muhammad, he says no fewer than three times, "Read!"'

The shawl, draped gently over her form, moved every time she stressed a point.

The scent of perfume pervaded the room. A dozen journalists, mostly women, had turned up. In the rows of seats sat teachers, school principals, scholars and activists.

'Look at Muhammad's wives. How Khadija guided him! And no one memorised and passed down more of the Prophet's teachings than Aisha! And Salama, she saved over three hundred hadith from oblivion. And Hafsa, who was constantly asked for help in solving problems! In Afghanistan there are many people, learned men among them, who don't think girls need an education. But according to Islam, this is wrong! As an educated woman I have a responsibility to fight for women's rights.'

Zeynab pressed her thumb and forefinger together and surveyed the gathering.

'Allah says it is our duty to seek knowledge. Preventing us from doing this is akin to preventing a Muslim from fasting. Or stopping us from praying!'

Several people spoke and finally a schoolgirl went up to speak her mind.

'We waited patiently. We counted down the days until spring,' she said. 'Three times, you've deceived us. First last autumn when you said that girls would return to school in the spring. Then in Oslo, where you flew in a private jet and enhanced your status. And now you try to fool us into silence by saying "wait for further instructions!"'

The fourteen-year-old glared into the cameras.

'We're not going to wait any longer! Open next week! We're not going to accept any excuses!'

But the leadership in Kandahar had other matters to consider. The day after the conference, the Ministry for the Propagation of Virtue and the Prevention of Vice announced a new decree: women who were 'not too old or too young' were to cover their faces and entire bodies when in public.

And the best burka, the decree suggested, was to stay at home.

Four Dresses and a Mobile Phone

The almond trees were blossoming with tiny pink flowers around Bashir's house. Green leaves were sprouting on the vines. Growth was taking place inside the house too. Both his wives were due to give birth in the summer. Galai was furthest along.

Yasamin, who felt embarrassed about everything to do with pregnancy, and bodies in general, hadn't had the nerve to tell Bashir she was expecting. She waited until he saw it himself. Then she hid her face in her shawl and giggled. She rarely looked directly at him. Like her mother-in-law, she lowered her gaze when her husband spoke to her.

She had given birth to six children, of whom three had survived. Obaida, who was born in Waziristan, was now ten. He was a bright, kind boy. Seven-year-old Muhammad was almost deaf and commanded very few words. One of his ear canals was fused. Some sound was audible in the other, but not enough for him to hear clearly. He would have preferred to stay close to his mother but instead spent all day upstairs with the other children who were old enough to read the Quran.

Muhammad was a constant source of worry for Yasamin. One night Bashir was awoken by her crying and when he asked what the matter was, she managed, between sobs, to utter the boy's name.

'He can't hear, he can't speak, what will happen to him when he grows up?'

'Muhammad will be fine. Allah has a plan,' Bashir assured her. 'The deaf are the most holy. When they read the Quran, the word of God goes in and stays there.'

Muhammad was the most affectionate child and knew where everything was in the house. Mum's slippers, her shawl, her handbag. If something belonging to Galai was in Yasamin's room, or vice versa, he put it back where it should be.

Galai had five children. Mawia, the boy they had both looked after in Waziristan, was the eldest. After a few months Galai had called a halt to him being breastfed by both. She explained to Yasamin that while she was nursing, she couldn't get pregnant, and it was time she had another baby of her own. That child was Obaida.

As could be seen outside the front door, where all the shoes lay strewn, the house was full of children. But inside they were seldom to be heard, apart from the smallest.

There were no toys in the house. Toys only made noise. And led to arguments. So the children played with what they found: an insole became a car, a sock was rolled up to a ball, they raced slippers against one another. The toddlers exulted in striking the floor with a spoon, they fought like lion cubs or played hide-and-seek in the laundry piles.

Galai's youngest daughter, Hoda, was an imaginative child, creating patterns on the carpet with nut shells from a tray. The four-year-old formed dolls from napkins, figures she would play with before unknotting them and making new ones.

Most of all she liked hiding away in a corner, all by herself. Gathering everything she needed, she held her own tea party. With her back to the room, she poured water into cups and bowls, mumbling, talking, laughing softly, pouring back, drinking, smacking her lips, smiling to an invisible guest, whispering some more.

There were lots of wonderful nooks and crannies in the house. When you stepped in, below the Mashallah inscription meant to protect those within, you first entered a large hall with a ceiling some four metres high. Several doors led out of this hall. The first to the right was to Galai's room, which was simply furnished, with mattresses along the walls and thick cushions to lean against. She shared it with Bashir every second night. The other nights he was with Yasamin.

The division was strictly adhered to, and it was Bashir who kept track. It could get complicated because Yasamin had lived in Jalalabad longer than Galai and liked to stay over with her parents in Mussahi, so he had to include those weeks, fortnights and weekends in his calculations.

When he was released from prison, after waiting three years for his death sentence to be carried out, Galai was granted the first night, seeing as he had been with Yasamin the night before his arrest. This was the kind of thing one could sit working out while in a cell.

Yasamin had a smaller room across the hall. She hadn't done much with it either. A carpet on the floor, mattresses, cushions. That was it.

Sima's room next door was quite another story. Their sister-in-law had decorated her room like an oriental harem. A large, soft double bed with a purple velvet covering dominated one end. Huge cushions lay on top, and a dust ruffle hung down along the sides. Several layers of sheer curtains, in gold and royal blue, hung in front of the windows, and a golden sofa sat shimmering opposite the conjugal bed.

Sima also had a cabinet. For the most part, items in the house were stored in cardboard boxes, bags, suitcases or in big piles. It was as though they hadn't quite moved in. A chest of drawers, clothes hangers, what use were they? It wasn't like they would be here for ever. But since Sima had a cabinet, it kept filling up. The nice piece of furniture with the glass doors was actually intended to be a vitrine, but two of the shelves were now filled with shoes. It had become medicine cabinet, safe, wardrobe and cupboard for important things.

The family's engagement bouquets, household mementos, were displayed on top of it. The bouquets, made from fabric or plastic, were wrapped in cellophane so as not to get dusty, but now the sheeting had become somewhat brown.

Only the newest bouquet was shiny, the flowers still bright. It was also the biggest by far. Ostentatious, Galai thought. The women in the house were in complete agreement on that.

The bouquet belonged to the *intruder*, who had yet to appear.

A wide staircase led up to another hall, where the previous owner's ornaments revealed a penchant for excess. One wall was papered with the trunks of birch trees, another had a jungle motif, a third featured a waterfall, while the fourth was a bunch of roses.

In the room that had been the politician's living room, daylight came in through full-length windows along two walls. His deep armchairs and dark, solid tables were pushed against the wall.

Now it was Bashir's madrasa. He had started his own, so his children didn't need to mingle with their peers in the neighbourhood. Everything was kept within the family, including the teacher. Hasibullah was the son of Bashir's oldest sister, the only one of the surviving siblings who remembered their father, Mullah Wasir. She was seven when he was killed, Bashir just three months. She counted herself lucky that her nineteen-year-old son had also become a mullah. Hasibullah was a big, rather flabby boy who had studied the Quran under a renowned scholar in Pakistan. He didn't allow any nonsense or slovenliness from his smaller cousins.

The children sat on the floor with their backs against the soft furnishings, and a cushion in front of them. Their legs were crossed. None of them glanced up if someone came into the room; they knew what the punishment would be. The book lay open on the cushion. They memorised, some mumbling, others singing. Each of them found their own style and voice, some chanted out loud, others were barely audible. While reciting, their upper bodies swayed back and forth, back and forth. That made it easier to remember. Because that was the goal, to become hafiz, one who knows the word of God off by heart.

They would first learn *qaida*, the basis – the alphabet, grammar and the small symbols denoting pronunciation. The youngest children, the four- and five-year-olds, sang the alphabet over and over.

Their fingertips followed the letters from right to left in tattered booklets that had been handed down. After that they would progress on to *nazira* – the correct pronunciation and the rules behind recital.

The tone was what mattered, the rhythm. They had yet to get to the meaning of the words. Only later would they learn the contents of the book, and after that they would learn to interpret it, not to mention follow it. That would be easy, as they already knew the message subconsciously. It should already have penetrated their minds, in the way the Archangel Gabriel had revealed the Quran to Muhammad.

Now and again the children would get to their feet and go over to Hasibullah to ask about a sound, or as they got older a word. Sometimes he would call them over to him, other times he just walked around the room with slow, heavy steps.

Mostly he sat with his legs crossed at the end of the room, his back against a sofa, watching what went on. He had a wooden box in front of him filled with the scariest items: a flex, small rods, a cane, some cables and a whip. Failure to learn fast enough, or lack of concentration, meant a taste of the contents of the box.

The methods were manifold. The simplest was a rap across the knuckles. But being hit with a cane or a hard rubber hose on the soles of the feet could also help jog the memory. One of Hasibullah's methods was to weave a pen between the fingers of someone not learning quickly enough, one finger over, one finger under, one over, another under, and then squeeze their hand as hard as he could. Then they learned. Sometimes he made them lean over the back of a chair and he flogged them across the backside.

He had Bashir's support in all of this. Violence awoke the mind. Bashir used the word *torture* when describing what he had been subjected to when he learned the Quran as a little boy. 'Torture always works,' he said. All over the world, in fact, which was why it was so widespread.

For every new verse the children learned, they would go back to revise the previous one, and then the one before that, building line by line. This was the way Bashir had learned. First – with a pure mind – learning by rote.

Throughout their entire childhood religious knowledge was all they were taught. If the boys did, as adults, want to become doctors or engineers, that was fine. As for the girls, God's words were enough.

The children spent most of the day in the living room. They were woken before dawn to pray. Afterwards they were given some tea and bread, and would sit down at their cushions to read. At around eight o'clock they had a breakfast of egg and yoghurt, before continuing to read until eleven. They then slept for two hours, the boys upstairs on the mattresses with Mullah Hasibullah, the girls in a room downstairs. When they awoke, they ate lunch before carrying on memorising.

From four o'clock to half past five in the afternoon they could do as they pleased. The boys liked to go and play cricket on the plain. Until they were about nine years old, the girls were also allowed to run around and play outside. The flock of children leaving the house, running at full speed across the yard and out the gate, gazes fixed firmly forward, was a sight to behold. They looked neither left nor right, terrified of someone stopping them, asking them to take down clothes from the line or help carry a barrel. This time was theirs!

At six o'clock they would be back, legs crossed, the cushion in front of them. If they fell asleep, they were hit hard. So they didn't drift off again. They continued to recite until nine, then it was time for supper and evening prayer, before they could close their eyes and dream. About whatever they wanted.

Only the small children were downstairs during the day.

'Do you want to go upstairs?' Galai asked Hoda, who was sitting in the corner hosting her tea party.

The four-year-old shook her head vigorously without turning around.

The women laughed. Earlier that morning Galai had pulled

down Hoda's pants to show them the red streaks. The little girl had long, swollen marks on her backside from being lashed by Hasibullah.

'I sent her up to the madrasa yesterday and when she refused to sit down, he took out the whip.'

They all laughed again and shook their heads. That was how it had to be.

'Do you want to go up again?' Galai teased.

Hoda had stopped playing. She sat stiffly, her back still turned.

'Will I walk up with you?' her mother continued.

Hoda ran and hid behind the curtains, to howls of laughter from the women sitting on the floor. As well as Bashir's wives, Sima and some of Hassan's and Yaqub's daughters were present. The teenagers were mothers now. They nursed their babies or fed them morsels of bread or biscuit soaked in tea. They themselves ate pieces of a golden baked cake.

Hoda stood completely still behind the curtains where the morning light flooded in. If she stayed like that, motionless, they might forget about her.

Her mother persisted. 'Do you want to go up?'

'I don't want to, I don't want to! Wallah, I swear to God! I don't want to!' Hoda shouted back.

The women laughed, then went on chatting.

After a while Hoda crept out. She crawled across the floor, as though trying to make herself less noticeable, and nestled against her mother. She sat there quietly listening to the adults, before reaching out to take a piece of cake. Galai clicked her tongue against her palate. A clear no. Hoda withdrew her hand. She lowered her head, embarrassed at being caught trying to take something that wasn't for her, then shuffled back to her corner.

Just like the cake, the conversation was for the adults.

'What can we expect from her?' Galai wondered aloud. 'She seems so demanding.'

When winter had been at its coldest, and the only warmth was to be found under the blanket, she had noticed something wasn't right. She could sense it.

'Is there someone else?' she asked Bashir.

'Is there someone else?' she had asked again, the next night they slept together. And the next. And the following morning. 'Is there someone else?'

Only a month after the engagement did he finally tell her.

'I'm getting married after Ramadan.'

Galai was inured to worry, yet still she was unprepared. She was the one among the women who figured things out, who fixed and arranged, who had oversight and control. The only thing she couldn't control was what Bashir decided. Her tone was tough, even Bashir yielded to Galai – or, that is, he did as he liked, but dreaded having to tell her things he knew wouldn't please her.

'If it makes you happy, then I'm glad,' she managed to say.

Then she cried for a month.

Because she was not enough, because Bashir looked elsewhere, because she would see him less often. Regardless of a man's right to have four wives, it was a blow, a cause of deep sadness. But not a bad word crossed her lips. Not until Bashir showed her a photo of his newly betrothed and asked Galai if she thought the sixteen-year-old was pretty.

Galai studied the picture on his phone. The girl had a cute, doll-like face, a small, pointed chin with a rather sizeable double chin and deep eyes with long dark eyelashes.

'Even a shoe will look pretty if you apply that much make-up!'

Bashir had to laugh at that. As did Galai. But she had little doubt that the girl had no gumption.

What was Bashir going to give for her? What were her demands?

In a country where one was defined by marriage more than anything else, this was certainly a hot topic of conversation.

They're demanding a million afghani!

Jewels and dress material.

A mobile phone.

But the primary condition Mariam had set was not to live with the other wives.

This was a big ask. He would have to start another household. Bashir was among those in receipt of a salary of sorts from the Taliban. He got half a million afghani, around four thousand pounds, a month. That was to cover house and home, vehicles, guards and martyrs. In spring 2022 he started up a business buying and selling properties and cars, to keep his lifestyle and still afford a new wife.

The plan was to secure an apartment for the teenager. Yasamin, who had just turned thirty, and Galai, who would follow suit in the summer, would go on living at the villa. Bashir would go back and forth between the two properties. He had wanted to have everyone under the same roof, that would have been easiest, but he had agreed to the condition. Now he was considering the neighbourhood of Mikrorayon, where low-cost, prefabricated blocks of flats erected by the Soviets in the 1960s still stood. These concrete-panelled apartments, known as *khrushchevkas*, were constructed all across the Soviet Union and its allied nations and pervaded Kabul. They had running water, electricity and central heating. The problem was that Mariam and Bashir couldn't live there alone, because what was she to do when he was away? The erstwhile commander would never allow her to be on her own, not even in her own apartment. That would be frowned upon. Therefore, one of his sisters-in-laws would have to move in, either Hassan's wife, or Yaqub's, along with their children. Because Bashir was going to be away a lot, especially in the fighting season. Or rather, he might be away a lot in the fighting season.

The prerequisite for having several wives was that they were all treated equally. This had been a chief concern of the Prophet Muhammad. For Bashir's part, that meant spending every third night with one of them.

Mariam believed that practice had to change. She told her sister that she thought he should be with her more since he had spent so many years with the two others.

Bashir's new fiancée had lived a sheltered life, had never attended school nor learned to read or write. In contrast to her fifteen-year-old sister, who was envious of girls who were allowed go to school, Mariam had never shown any interest in anything intellectual. 'Women don't need it,' she said.

She had yet to meet Bashir when he gave her the best present a teenager could get: a mobile phone. A brand-new smartphone with a purple rubber cover. Though she couldn't understand the letters, she could look at the pictures, and Bashir filled it with photos. Of himself.

One name and one number were saved on the phone. His.

She kept the phone underneath her dress. Or attached to a band around her waist. It was there when she woke up, when she went to sleep, when she sat with her sister waiting for the sun to go down and new pictures to come. The screen became the centre of her existence.

After a while she became a dab hand with the camera and its features. She filled up the phone with photos of herself. Hundreds of pictures, soon a thousand. No one else, not even her sister, was allowed to enter the photo archive. Only Mariam and her fiancé lived there. In time she began sending Bashir photos of herself, heavily made up, wearing dresses he had sent her. In profile, from the front, from behind, close-up, full-length, sitting, standing, at all manner of angles.

Mariam had asked for four dresses and received three of them, one green, one yellow and one pink. The fourth, in magenta, Galai was busy sewing. It had been her own suggestion that she would sew a dress for the new wife and decorate it in a pattern of her choosing.

Hala had made a scene when her son eventually told her he was engaged again. For five days she refused to eat. But tradition compelled her to attend the girl's engagement party. Mariam's parents had invited the women of the family to their house in Mussahi.

Mariam's home was humble. Several of the windows were smashed but taped up to hold the glass inside their broken frames a little longer. Now, with the arrival of spring, the farmyard was mostly mud. On the way from the front gate, Hala and her daughters-in-law had to step from stone to stone to avoid the slushy ground. The house itself lay so deep in mountain shadow that the winter ice around it had yet to melt.

Clothes were hung to dry in the trees. Mariam was one of nineteen siblings. Long and short trousers, sweaters and small vests usually adorned the backyard. At the front of the house was a large patio, and a lot of the cooking was done here, with water they fetched from a well.

Hala was already angry when she arrived but events soon made her livid. Music was played – *haram*. There were drums and people dancing. Neither did Hala approve of Mariam being dolled up in a low-cut dress. But worst of all, the rule about being of shy and modest appearance was broken. Mariam joked and laughed, was loud, and wiggled and swayed her hips on the dance floor.

Except for the obligatory greetings, Hala didn't say a word to her new daughter-in-law during the entire party. Yasamin didn't talk either. Galai scarcely spoke. They attended. They were there. They stuck it out.

The three women left as soon as they could. Everything had gone wrong, as far as Hala was concerned.

But if this was what the apple of her eye wanted, then so be it.

* * *

The engagement didn't impact on everyday life in the pink house. The wedding wasn't until after Ramadan, which ended in May, so they didn't need to worry about it yet.

There was peace. They could relax.

They had been through so much together, the war, the imprisonment, the dead children. Their sufferings were over. Still, things were more exciting before, Galai thought. Back when the kitchen was filled with batteries, wires and oil containers, when their reward in heaven amassed, when they knew they would ascend more steps on the ladder to paradise with every bomb they made. Now there was little reward to claim, and more women in the house than there were chores. They got under one another's feet, were listless. It was almost difficult to get used to this new peace and quiet. It wasn't as though Galai and Yasamin never had any disputes. They would express their irritation by slapping each other's children. 'She hits mine, I hit hers!' Galai would laugh. After any period of conflict, they would stop talking for a time – until they were back on speaking terms again, and an air of contentment again pervaded the house.

Galai served as an information bank for the women. She had a smartphone that could connect to the internet, and was a fast reader. She kept up to date with new decrees, like the school ban for teenage girls, new rules about covering up and the travel ban – you couldn't fly or go on a longer journey unless accompanied by a male relative.

'Makes no difference to us,' she said. No one in the house sent their children to school anyway, and the women hardly left the house, and never unaccompanied. 'But I do feel sorry for the girls who actually want to go to school and won't get to finish,' she added.

'And how are we to have female doctors if they're not allowed to continue school?' asked Yasamin, the family member who had most dealings with male doctors. Men often blamed women when infants became sick, like the doctor in Waziristan who had argued that there was something wrong with her milk when her son was dying. Or the one in Kabul who said her seven-year-old was hard of hearing because she had breastfed him with his ear in her lap. A child should be nursed with their body at a ninety-degree angle, he had told her.

Yasamin couldn't help but think how nice it would be to go to a female doctor.

Bashir himself was a middling sort of Taliban in that regard. He didn't mind other children going to school but wasn't going to send his own. His house – his castle. His children – his rules.

While the women sat chatting about this and other matters, Galai would usually be working on something. Being the seamstress in the family, she had sewn cushions, mattresses, curtains and clothing. Now she sat with the dress for her husband's fiancée, made to the girl's ample measurements: a short, slightly plump girl – the Taliban's ideal figure.

On a cushion in front of her, Galai had placed a bowl with white, light blue, pink and silver pearls. One by one, she threaded them with the needle, creating a wavy pattern all along the hem. They gleamed brightly against the purple material. The needle passed in and out through the pearls. Galai's design would flow around her legs.

At the very bottom of the skirt she embroidered small pink and light blue stars. In the centre of each star were tiny silver chains, with two tiny oval shapes linked in. From above they looked like minute handcuffs.

The neckline. The bodice. The skirt. The waist.

There would not be one place on Mariam's body that was not first touched by Galai.

The Runaway

One day a runaway arrived at the house.

She was brought there from Police District 15 by one of Bashir's former fighters. Abdul Jalil would rather spend his time interrogating suspected IS supporters, so he decided the best way to get rid of her was to call Bashir. The case was then out of his hands, leaving him to concentrate on more important matters. Crime in Kabul was on the increase. As the gangs realised that the Taliban were not enforcing law and order by the cutting off of hands and feet, they carried on with the same activities they had engaged in under the previous regime. Robbery and car theft were on the rise, as well as extortion and kidnapping. The biggest threat, however, was IS. Not a week went by without them blowing up a target in Kabul. The victims were mostly members of the Hazara minority, the crime scenes often their mosques. To the extremists, Shia Muslims were infidels.

The runaway herself looked Hazara, Abdul Jalil thought. She wore an abaya but no burka. Her head, neck and chest were covered by a black shawl.

Omar, one of Bashir's nephews, opened the gate when they knocked. The girl was so slight that she was almost hard to spot standing in black among the men who had brought her. The nephew asked them to wait in the courtyard while he went to inform the house. The women gave up Galai's room so that Bashir could receive the runaway in private, while they gathered with the youngest children next door, in Sima's room.

The girl was shown to a mattress, and she quickly tucked her legs under her so only her toes protruded. She had beautifully shaped eyebrows that ended where the shawl began, narrow eyes and prominent cheekbones. The skin around her eyes was almost white and was the only part of her face not covered in angry red spots.

Her voice was barely audible when she answered Bashir's questions. Her name was Rawda and she was eighteen years old.

'Please, don't send me back to my parents,' she said. 'They will cut me into small pieces.' Slowly, one finger at a time, then the arm, followed by the toes, then the feet, slicing them little by little, she would later tell Galai: that would be her father's punishment for her running away from an arranged marriage. That was how she would die, until there was no living part of her left. It wouldn't be the first time someone had been killed in this way within her extended family. A beautiful funeral was always arranged afterwards, where relatives gathered and wept over an unfortunate teenager who had stumbled and fallen into a well.

Bashir told her not to worry, he was not going to send her anywhere.

'Tell me what happened, otherwise I can't help you.'

With her eyes fixed on the floor, she began to relate her story. She stroked her fingers against her bare toes while she spoke.

About a year ago her parents, who were not Hazara but Turkmen, decided she was to be married off to a cousin. She was about to finish secondary school, while her cousin, who lived in the countryside, had never gone to school. Marrying him would mean moving into her uncle's house, and she knew that he beat his wife and children. He was well known for having a bad temper. A daughter-in-law would be bottom of the pecking order. Furthermore, the cousin they wanted to marry her off to wasn't 'pure'. He ran around chasing girls, harassing them on the street.

She spoke in a low, monotone without any facial expressions, as though in an interrogation. She would rather die than marry him, she said. Something she had also attempted.

The engagement had been arranged without her approval ten months ago. The following day she had drank a bottle of Whitex, a household bleach, in the hope of leaving this world. But when her brother came home, he had noticed the strong smell and forced her to throw up. She lost consciousness and woke up in hospital, feeling as though she was going to burn up inside. The pain was everywhere in her body. She couldn't swallow, couldn't speak, every breath she took was agony.

When she was discharged after a few weeks she still couldn't eat. She drank only milk, which eased the burning pain somewhat.

But the engagement was not called off, and after a time her cousin's mother and sister visited with sweets and a scarf, thus sealing the marriage deal. The next day, when no one else was at home, she shut the front door behind her and fled, determined never to return. Without any plan, she trudged from the outskirts of Kabul towards the city centre. After a few hours walking along roads with heavy traffic, she left the poorer districts she came from and strayed into one of the richer areas of the city. One street was full of beauty parlours and high-end shops with sumptuous bridal dresses on display in the windows. She went into a hairdresser's, not the largest or most fancy, but a simple small salon. They were about to close for the day. She quickly explained that her father would kill her, that she had run away from home, and asked if she could sleep there for the night.

The women who worked there said she could, but suddenly Rawda got a bad feeling. What if it wasn't a hairdresser but a brothel? What if they wanted to sell her! She ran back out the door. Arriving at the park in Shahr-e Naw, she slowed down. She took a look around before entering and sitting down on a bench. Then she broke down in tears.

Before long a young man approached her.

'Why are you crying, sister?' he asked in a gentle voice.

She told him about having run away from home. He had stood at a respectful distance and said she could stay with his mother. He had an elderly mother and an older sister, and she could live with them and feel safe. His mother would treat her like a daughter. She had a big heart.

As darkness fell, the character of the park began to change around them. Women disappeared from the streets and groups of men began to gather. She followed the kind young man.

At the apartment she was given an ultimatum.

'Marry me or I'll turn you over to the police. I'll tell them you're a prostitute,' he told her. Being handed over to the police under the previous regime, Rawda emphasised, was like being delivered to brutes. Bashir nodded while moving his prayer beads through his fingers, one pearl at a time.

For about a year Rawda lived with her new husband. Then one day he left for Iran. She stayed behind with his mother and sister. Once he departed, she was treated like a slave; when the women went out, they locked her in the house. They told her she was ugly, that was the reason she had not managed to hold on to her husband, and they should never have got mixed up with someone of her ethnicity. One day her mother-in-law said, 'Get out! I'm so sick of you!'

Rawda had nowhere to go and asked to stay one more night. At dawn the next day she set to work on her chores, in the hope her mother-in-law would change her mind, but when she had finished with the laundry her mother-in-law approached her with a knife: 'Out! Out! Or I'll stick this in you!'

That was ten days ago.

She ran until she came to a hospital. She walked through the gate. No one appeared to take any notice of her. At night, she slept in different places on the hospital premises. She spent days and nights there, until the guards told her she couldn't stay any longer. 'I've nowhere else to go,' she pleaded. 'I can clean, do anything at all.'

The guards rang the local police station. Some soldiers came and collected her. She called her mother-in-law and asked to come back but when she handed the phone to one of the Taliban, the elderly woman told them they mustn't trust her. Her son had divorced her because she had been unfaithful.

That was a daunting accusation. The Taliban's punishment for infidelity was flogging if you were unmarried; if married, it was death by stoning. But there was also severe punishment for a false accusation.

The police took her back to her mother-in-law's.

'My son caught her red-handed five times! She's no longer welcome in my house!' the woman screamed.

A neighbour appeared and said that Rawda was never out of the house, so that accusation didn't hold up. She was taken back to the police station, where she remained for three days.

In the meantime, her mother-in-law obtained divorce papers from her son in Iran. He had also recorded a video she showed the Taliban. In the video he introduced himself by his full name and stated whose son he was.

'I want to divorce from my wife, Rawda. I wish to divorce because I've seen her three times with other men. Twice I forgave her, but not the last time.'

He went on to say the words that had to be repeated three times to carry out a divorce: *Talaq. Talaq. Talaq.* I divorce. I divorce. I divorce.

This had occurred the night before.

'Commander Bashir will decide what is to happen to you,' the police in District 15 had told her.

Bashir thought for a moment before saying: 'Don't share your story with anyone. I will find a good man for you. One of my soldiers.'

Rawda sat looking down at the carpet, pulling the dress she was wearing further down over her long, wide trousers.

'Just say you have run away from your parents because they wanted to marry you to an abusive man with no respect for Islam. Do not mention that you've been married and divorced!'

She nodded slowly.

'Only your new husband can know the whole story. You will have no secrets from him. But nobody else must find out.'

He said she could stay at the house until he found a husband for her. She couldn't get married for three months anyway, the period the Quran commanded so they could be sure she wasn't carrying a child.

Bashir told her he would ask his wives to assume responsibility for her but under no circumstances was she to tell them her story.

Several of Bashir's soldiers wanted a wife but getting married was expensive. Parents required money for their daughter, in addition to the clothes and items the bride demanded, and ideally gold and jewellery. The soldiers mostly came from poor families and since the Taliban didn't pay their soldiers, a bride was something many of the young victors could only dream of.

Now Bashir had a giveaway bride on his hands. He would have to think carefully. Who was most deserving of her? To whom did he owe a favour? One of his closest friends had served nine years in prison, three of them with Bashir, and he had yet to have a son. He was married already but his wife had only given him a daughter before he was put in prison, and there had been no children since. She was getting old, so the husband had a lot of catching up to do.

Bashir would offer the runaway to him.

That same evening Galai managed to extract the whole story from the newcomer, promising the girl that she would not tell anyone.

Galai was the only one of the women who spoke proper Dari, Rawda's tongue. Rawda didn't understand Pashto, the language of the rest of the house, so Galai became her sole channel and interpreter.

Right after she got the girl to disclose her story, Galai found out through Omar who Bashir was planning to offer her to.

The man had accepted on the spot.

When Bashir was out of the house the next day, Galai called the man's wife, who was as yet unaware of her husband's forthcoming engagement.

'She's run away from two husbands . . . '

Galai told her everything she knew.

'I just thought I should let you know. She's been sleeping rough at a hospital and a police station. I don't know if you want to have someone like that in the house . . . '

She certainly did not.

Galai had a suggestion. Rawda had said she would prefer to live in Kabul. One of the reasons she didn't want to wed her cousin was, Galai surmised, that he was a farmer, and that she didn't want to spend her life cleaning out a barn and milking cows.

'She wouldn't exactly be of great help to you,' Galai emphasised. 'Tell all this to your husband, and kick up a fuss, then he'll decide not to take her on – he won't want the hassle.'

Galai hadn't been able to prevent her own husband's third engagement but given the opportunity to help a sister – one of their own – she was quick to act.

The woman on the other end of the line blessed Galai for having warned her.

'Think nothing of it: we'll put a stop to this.'

The man rang Bashir the same evening and called off the whole thing. 'Give her to someone else,' he said.

It was better to find someone who was unmarried.

Enayat was chosen. He had spent seven years in prison, had no money, no wife, and lived on the outskirts of Kabul. Enayat was a handsome young man. It was a shame he wasn't married.

He wanted to see the girl.

The following night he was outside the gate. It was almost eleven and the house was quiet. The children old enough for Quran school were asleep; they would be woken before the first rays of the sun. Even the infants and toddlers, who often didn't go to sleep before their mothers, were silent. Enayat came alone, without a mother or sister, but this was an unconventional betrothal.

Bashir had asked Rawda to change her story slightly, or rather condense it.

'If the two of you agree, I can see to it the engagement is arranged as early as tonight.' Bashir's status as *Mawlawi* meant he could put them on the first step to marriage.

He told her to say that she had been married off against her will, that her husband had turned out to be a drug addict and had later moved to Iran. She had fled back to her parents, who forced her to marry her brutal cousin, and then she had run away.

Rawda nodded. Galai followed her up to Sifat's room and told her to sit and wait for Enayat to arrive. The women of the house gathered downstairs in Sima's room while the young man was led up to the first floor by Bashir, who closed the door of Sifat's room behind him. Rawda and Enayat greeted each other, their hands on their hearts and a faint nod. They sat on mattresses several metres apart.

No one heard Galai tiptoeing up the stairs.

In springtime the windows were often left open, as they now were in Sifat's room. Bashir's wife stole halfway around the balcony on the first floor and crouched below the window.

'I know your story,' she heard Enayat say. 'Bashir has told me everything. You don't need to say any more. I have no issue with your former life.'

Bashir insisted Rawda relate the story all the same. It was best if he, as the matchmaker, knew what she told the young man, to avoid any misunderstandings later.

Enayat was tall and slim, with regular features, wavy hair and pale skin, which Rawda found attractive.

When she had told him the new version of her life, it was Enayat's turn to tell her about himself.

'I'm not wealthy. I have many debts.'

'That doesn't matter,' Rawda replied. 'I'm ugly. And I'm divorced.'

'You're not ugly!' Enayat protested.

'You're free to find someone else. I would understand if you didn't want me,' she said.

'Bashir is like a father to me,' the young man answered. 'If he has chosen you for me, then he knows best.'

Galai propped her legs against the mint-green railing, now in darkness, and listened.

Enayat asked if she had any contact with her family. She confirmed that she did not. He said that although he could accept her past, his parents would not. They needed to come up with a version of her story he could tell his family. He already had a suggestion in mind.

'I can tell my family that your husband was a mujahid and that he was martyred. They wouldn't like me marrying a divorcee.'

Rawda nodded her assent. That was a story she was more than happy with.

But what would they say about her parents, the reason she no longer had any contact with them?

'I can say they're dead,' Rawda said.

Now Enayat nodded. Rawda suggested a cover story she could easily remember and relate, since the events had actually taken place, only that it had involved other people. 'I had an uncle and aunt who died in a car accident when their daughter was five years old. I can say that *I* was the little girl: knowing as much as I do about her experiences as an orphan living with her uncle, it would be easy for me to talk about. And then we could say that my uncle tried to marry me off to someone I didn't like, and so I ran away.'

'It's convincing,' Enayat replied. 'That's what I'll tell my mother. By the way, did I mention we don't have our own house, that we rent? Is that okay?'

It was settled.

But Rawda felt a familiar, chilling sensation surge up inside. That she was ugly. She thought about her spots, which she had heard would disappear when she turned eighteen but hadn't. She thought about her nose, which had been broken when she had been thrown down the stairs. She looked at her hands, covered in burn marks, from the times her mother had pressed red-hot spoons, heated on the fire, against her skin. Of course his mother and sister wouldn't accept her.

She had a sinking feeling. The judgement she feared most was a mother's condemnation. She had never felt any love from her own mother. The mother of the cousin she had been matched with was wicked. And the mother of her husband who went to Iran turned into a monster when he left.

What was it about mothers that made them so cruel?

Her train of thought was interrupted by Bashir, who had been sitting chatting to Enayat. Now he wanted to say a prayer, after which he recited some verses from the Quran, and Rawda and Enayat were pledged to one another.

All that remained was for the agreement to be confirmed by his mother and sister.

Galai sneaked away from the window and tiptoed quietly down the stairs. Soon all the women in the house knew what had transpired in Sifat's room.

That night, Rawda began to eat again.

When she went to bed, she thought about Enayat. His face was behind her eyelids. It smiled at her.

The Boys Are Coming!

To become a judge, you first had to take a bachelor's degree. This last semester, Islamic law was on the curriculum. Ariana's class had learned about the Quran as a legal text, and how it had replaced pre-Islamic tribal law. They were taught about Muhammad as a lawmaker, and how one knew his statements were authentic, and therefore true. There were many criteria concerning who had passed what down to whom, and how reliable the sources were. Ariana learned about legal proceedings, trials and the criminal justice system, about blood feuds and blood money. She studied laws around marriage and the dissolution of marriage, about children, inheritance and distribution thereof. The class learned the difference between *hudud* and *tazir*. For crimes punishable under the principle of hudud, the punishment was specified in the Quran. These might pertain to infidelity, but also false accusations of infidelity, the consumption of alcohol, incest and other serious crimes. For offences in the tazir group, the court decided on the punishment, and judges could exercise their own discretion.

Ariana found it exciting. This was a part of her history, of her society, and she liked the logic of the system. Moreover, it was a relief to immerse herself in a subject after months of anxiety.

At the end of the semester came the exams. There were nine this time – one for each major topic. After handing in their papers on inheritance, an important issue in sharia, Ariana and her friends were standing on the steps outside the exam hall waiting for everyone to finish so they could all walk back to the student residence at the other end of the campus, to study for the following day's exam.

'What did you answer about whether a father can inherit from his son?' one of them asked.

'He's the first in line to inherit if the son is unmarried, then comes the mother,' a girl answered.

'Oh no, then I got that wrong!'

'This exam was really hard . . . '

They stood, carrying out their post-mortem, quizzing one another, conferring nervously.

'If he has no children himself and both parents are living,' Ariana said, 'the father inherits two-thirds and the mother one-third. If he has children, and his mother is dead, then the father will inherit one-sixth of what he owned.'

'What did you put down for the question about distribution of inheritance if the son had several wives still living?'

An old feeling returned, one Ariana had almost forgotten: the ambition to be the best. The tingling in her body in the moment she thought she had answered incorrectly, the relief when she realised she had the right answer. The dream of submitting a perfect exam paper: the unattainable was always the goal.

Two guards approached.

'Get out of here!'

Had they lost track of time? One of them checked on their mobile. No, they still had a *right* to be on campus, it wasn't the boys' time yet.

The Talibs, guns over their shoulders, continued to shoo them away.

'Get off the university grounds!'

As if they weren't students there! And resided on campus. The five girls remained standing. They had a right to be there. It was their allotted time. Here they were, studying Islamic law and order, and these thugs were going to tell them where they could and couldn't stand. It was insulting. They had the knowledge, but *they* had the power.

When the guards had almost reached the group of girls, Ariana noticed people had begun to gather in front of the main building. Was a meeting taking place? More proclamations?

She glimpsed the rector and some others from the administration. A convoy of cars drove onto the campus.

'Clear off! The boys are coming!' the Taliban shouted. They yelled something else, that the girls didn't catch, about someone else coming, and when they drew close, the guards snarled, 'Get out of here, the governor is arriving!'

It really was the provincial governor stepping out of a car, a big, solidly built Talib with a black turban and a large stomach.

What was he doing here?

Ariana's friends told the guards they had to walk past the main building, where all the men were assembled, to get to the student residence. The guards jostled them against the wall and told them to stay out of sight until the ceremony had finished.

The *ceremony*?

'It's the graduation ceremony!' one of the girls gasped. 'For the boys!'

Ariana froze. The graduation party!

She remembered the students' festivities the previous year. Flowers, ribbons, flags. Speeches, juice, cakes. How they had been looking forward to their own ceremony. The thought of it hadn't even entered their minds this semester, just like they had suppressed everything else that hadn't come to pass.

They stood silently, waiting for their path to clear. It was as though they were rooted to the spot. No one said a word, they just stood looking at what was taking place. They had all learned the same but only the boys' efforts were to be celebrated.

The boys were wearing mortarboards. Some had flowers in their hands. They were taking pictures of one another, smiling, standing in groups taking selfies.

Ariana closed her eyes. All she wanted was to have a hat like that and be photographed.

She would finish among the best in her year. Now she just wanted to cry. Having worked so hard, laboured to understand the old texts, put so much effort in her notes, jotting them down with different coloured pens, and then for the Taliban to come and take everything from her! Even though she knew there was no room for educated women in Afghanistan at the moment, she wanted to be the best. Moreover, she wanted her degree conferred on her with pomp and circumstance, and selfies.

Now they were being reminded that they were only there on sufferance.

'This is the worst thing I've ever experienced in my life,' Ariana said. *This* had made a deeper impression on her than anything she had experienced since the Taliban took power.

University had been the most important thing in her life, and the most beautiful. One of her friends had tears in her eyes. 'When you know you've given your all, and no one is there for you,' she said.

They nodded.

'And you don't know what's going to happen to you,' Ariana added.

The five girls standing against the wall were all barely twenty years old. They were top law students. They were only halfway through their exams, but it was already over. Not one of them, absolutely none of them, they knew, would ever be what they had dreamed about: a judge, a prosecutor, a defence lawyer, a business lawyer.

Ariana later wrote in her diary:

'We have no worth. No one values our efforts. We are nothing.'

* * *

Potatoes with bread. Mashed potatoes baked into bread. Rice with bread. Carrots, turnip or cabbage, occasionally yoghurt, all according to what was in season or on offer. Without Karim's income, and due to delays in payment of Nadia's salary, the fare was meagre.

Ariana had always enjoyed cooking. If she hadn't pursued law, she would have liked to have been a chef. Now she sought out recipes for dinner with few and affordable ingredients.

Her father's mood had improved. A few nights in a row, he had been on the phone. That was unusual: generally he would take a nap after dinner, only appearing again just before bed. These phone conversations lasted a long time. He sounded lively and engaged, a different tone in his voice, more like his old self.

Ariana asked her mother who he was talking to. 'Oh, just an old colleague,' she answered.

One evening, after they had eaten their potatoes with bread and a couple of spring onions, her father said there was something he wanted to speak to her about.

She recognised the look in his eyes. An imploring look. Asking her to be understanding and amenable.

'You have a new suitor.'

She felt her heart sink. She looked at him, said nothing.

'It's someone from the office. A colleague. Or rather, his nephew.'

So that was what had him so energised: the prospect of marrying her off. Finally, her father was *in demand*. And it was she, his daughter, who could link him to the life he had lost.

This colleague was higher up in the hierarchy. His nephew had also worked for the military in some capacity, as she understood it. She didn't enquire any further, but he had apparently been working in the local administration in a small town in some province or another and had lost his job when the Taliban came to power. He was out of work, but that was temporary, her father said. Or as permanent as his own unemployment, Ariana thought. A miserable fate he shared with millions of other Afghans.

'What sort of education does he have?' Ariana asked.

Her father was not sure. He had completed secondary school at any rate, he said. Ariana sighed. This was never going to work; it was never going to happen.

Her parents continued bringing up this nephew.

What was this really about? It was all about her father, she reasoned. Suddenly something happened in his life. He had got a call. He had something to focus on, to discuss, to negotiate.

She tried to avoid the topic. Every time her parents mentioned the subject, she refused to talk about it.

'No, I won't get married!'

They attempted to persuade her. She went on dismissing the idea.

Who would hold out the longest?

They couldn't force her. She herself had to utter the words 'Yes, I will.'

That was not something she was going to do. They showed her a photo of him.

'Not my type,' she said flippantly.

'Don't be cheeky!' her mother snapped.

They attempted fear.

'You'd be safer if you were married, with the Taliban you never know . . .'

Then time pressure.

'You've just graduated. You'll never be as sought after as you are now. In a year you won't be as eligible.'

They appealed to her sense of responsibility.

'Have you given any thought to what will happen to your sisters if you don't get married? People will start to wonder — what's wrong with that family?'

Finally, they grew suspicious.

'Is there someone else? Someone we don't know about?'

'I'm not ready to marry anyone!' Ariana yelled.

It continued all through May.

Towards the end of the month, her father began to talk as though the engagement had already been agreed. He chatted away on the phone, not caring if she was in the room and could hear.

'She can live with us in the village initially,' said the person on the other end of the line. 'For the first month, anyway, and after a few months we can buy a place in Kabul, or maybe not buy, but rent.'

How was that possible? Renting a place in Kabul when you had no income? Live with them in the village first? It was obviously a trap – they'd never let her out of there.

Karim said they must, in any case, hold the wedding at a nice hotel in the city.

While her father was sitting at home, her mother had her hands full at the school because the primary age pupils were attending as usual. She had more responsibility than she had resources. The female secondary school teachers, who no longer had pupils, often stopped by her office. Were they going to get paid now that they no longer taught? Nadia didn't know. She tried to find out from the Ministry of Education. But it was impossible to get a straight answer from them. 'We'll let you know' was their only response when she called to enquire.

Every day the teachers ticked an attendance sheet – perhaps the secondary school teachers could do likewise? After the Taliban took over, salary payments had been even more unstable than under Ghani. The World Bank had financed the education and health sectors in the country, and now it had tightened the purse strings to force the Taliban to respect human rights and include more women and minority groups in government, and, not least, to allow all girls to receive an education. But the sanctions adversely affected ordinary people, squeezed between the Taliban leadership and the international community determined to teach the Islamists a lesson.

Nadia had been appointed principal in January 2020, but then Covid had come, and the Taliban after that. She had not, therefore, managed to register herself as she was supposed to. The deadline would soon pass. She would then be occupying the position illegally. In which case, they could replace her with whoever they liked.

The Taliban had become a bureaucratic nightmare of permits and exclusions if authorisation was lacking. She needed the signature of Mullah Khitab, the man who had given the principals a tongue-lashing the week before the schools were to reopen, to get her papers approved.

On arrival at the Ministry of Education Nadia was stopped by a Talib at the entrance. 'Wait over there,' he said, pointing across the road. Was she supposed to stand there like a beggar of some kind? Not even allowed to stand on the same side of the street as the ministry. She had turned on her heel, thinking she would try her luck tomorrow. But the next day she realised she had no choice but to wait; she needed the principal authorisation. So she stood there, an authoritative woman with responsibility for hundreds of pupils, while the guard was a simple yokel with a gun. That was how she saw it. At the end of the day, when she approached him again, he just said, 'Leave it here' and pointed to a counter.

Why hadn't he said that straight away? But then she realised no one had been manning that counter all day. She couldn't deliver her papers into a void.

On the third afternoon, along with the others who had assembled hoping to see the mullah, she was finally hustled inside. Several were on a similar mission to her own. Everything came to a halt without a signature from Mullah Khitab – the keystone in the system – who could approve or invalidate.

They were taken to his enormous office, the walls with large sofas and small tables. She had been in the office before, under the previous regime, and couldn't see that anything had changed apart from the sign on the door. And that they had to remove their shoes prior to entering.

The mullah was behind a large desk and seized the opportunity to reprimand the school employees.

They had all, the entire profession, been guilty of creating a mood of hostility against the Taliban.

'I can see it in your eyes, I can see you don't like me,' he said. 'Here in Kabul I can even see it in the eyes of the schoolchildren. You're responsible for that! You're responsible for the attitude of the children! You haven't been doing your jobs! You must teach the children to love the Taliban. You yourselves must love the Taliban! You hear?'

Everyone nodded. They all needed a signature.

'Furthermore, from now on only Pashto is to be used in school,' he said from behind his beard. 'Not Dari. Everyone must learn the language of the Taliban.' They nodded again. All of them *had* to have that signature.

The mullah waved the men forward first, then the women. Nadia could hear his voice echoing in her head on the way out, but she had got what she came for. Everything was in order, for the time being. She exhaled, then took a deep breath and tensed up again. Now she was off home to her husband and seven children. Home to the depressed family.

The solidarity between Nadia and Ariana when the Taliban had shut out the secondary-school girls had ended. Back then her eldest daughter had been the one to console her mother to keep her from falling apart. Now, with the advent of this new suitor, it was as though their ties had been cut, mother and daughter had drifted apart, were almost alienated, or worse still, hostile towards one another.

Eventually Ariana agreed to meet the suitor. The family had a good reputation. There was no baggage. He was a good man, apparently. Her father and his colleague talked and talked.

Ariana still thought the idea of him buying a place in Kabul sounded like wishful thinking when he had no job, but maybe his family had some money saved. Usually the family of the groom bore the expense of the wedding: everything from the bridal dress to the banquet was supposed to be paid for by them. But the colleague let it be known that they did not want to spend money on a large wedding. Right, her father had replied.

What did this man have on her father, exactly?

And what was she *worth*?

She had never dreamt of a large wedding feast, but with the suitor's family being so stingy, she got the feeling she was being offered at a knockdown price. She resolved to talk to this nephew herself; she needed to find out what he was like, so she allowed her parents to give him her number.

She spent all of the next day dreading the call. But it didn't come. Nor the day after that. He didn't phone. Not even on the third day.

A week passed. This was the worst that could happen: he had her number, they had been allowed to speak without their parents present, and then he didn't call. Did he not dare to? Did he not want to? He was a grown man and he let his parents do the talking for him!

It was communicated via his mother that he would prefer to meet in person. It was agreed, without Ariana having any say, that he would come with his mother and sisters the following weekend. But his mother fell ill and the visit was postponed.

Why didn't he call himself?

Oh, life wasn't supposed to be like this!

One day Ariana came home from a friend's to find her mother and father looking sheepish.

'We've had some visitors,' Karim said.

Had the colleague's nephew been there without them letting her know?

Her father had been the only one at home when there was a ring at the doorbell. Three women were standing outside. They introduced themselves, and he called Nadia. She had to come home from work; he couldn't very well entertain these women on his own. They waited in the visitors' room until Nadia arrived. Then they got straight to the point.

'We're here about your daughter,' the eldest of them said. 'My son teaches computing. At the university. That was where we got your address from.'

She told them about her son and made a marriage proposal on his behalf.

Nadia didn't quite know what to say. They were in the middle of considering another proposal, after all.

'Ideally, we would like it to happen as quickly as possible. And if you're not interested, we'd also like to know quickly.'

They had agreed to come back the next day. To get a closer look at Ariana.

'I can guess who it is,' Ariana said. She remembered the teacher who had called her up and been so gushing in his praise of her English and had asked her classmates about her when she hadn't turned up for the first few weeks of university. It had to be him.

'So Mum, what do you want me to do? You and Dad have promised me to another, and now this guy suddenly pops up? What do you actually want?'

'We couldn't know these others would come. They're better.'

'I don't want either of them!'

'You have to at least let them see you now that I agreed to it,' her mother said.

The following afternoon the women returned to take a look at Ariana. Her mother asked her to get dressed up. She refused and met them in worn-out lounging clothes. The computing teacher's mother, sister and auntie were nice enough. They spoke to her in a familiar way, as though expecting to be on the same wavelength. At the same time, they all watched her movements closely. The sister was a midwife and the aunt was a teacher, as was another sister. The women and Nadia hit it off. Ariana sat with them for a quarter of an hour, but the visitors stayed until evening.

When they left, Nadia went straight to Ariana's room.

'What do you think?' she asked. 'This guy or the other one?'

Her mother looked so happy, and before Ariana could answer said, 'He has a master's in computing from India!'

'I prefer this guy, I think,' Ariana replied. 'I don't know, I've never met him. Maybe he's better, who knows?'

'I'll talk to your father,' Nadia said.

The colleague's nephew seemed to be out of the running. But Karim would have to deal with that.

'I mean, he has a job, and it's better to be with someone who's working than someone who isn't,' Ariana reasoned to her sister afterwards. 'He might not be great but he's better than the alternative.'

When the women returned the following afternoon, they asked: 'What do you say? Will you accept?'

Nadia said that Ariana would have to meet him first. She was the one who was going to decide. A meeting was arranged for the next day, at a restaurant in the city centre.

Mahmoud was slight, barely taller than her, with narrow shoulders and thin hands. He had a pointy face, with regular features. Unfortunately, he had lost most of his hair.

Nadia wasted no time when she met her prospective son-in-law.

'What goals do you have? What do you want to achieve in life?'

He wanted to study further, he said. But above all he wanted to support Ariana, no matter what she chose to do. 'Anyone can take a bachelor's degree,' he said. 'It's better to have a master's.' He could help her with that.

Ariana stressed that she wanted to live in Kabul.

'We'll live where you want!' he said. 'I'll make sure you have a good life. If you wish, you can work. I'll get us a nice place. We can decorate it ourselves. You decide how it will be.'

Ariana had never had a boyfriend, had never held someone's hand; her only experience of romance was from films, soap operas and the world of pop lyrics.

Mahmoud did most of the talking, speaking all the time in fact.

'And the wedding, Ariana can also decide. She can choose the wedding hall, where the engagement party will be . . . Ariana will decide everything,' he said.

'Ariana is very special to us,' her mother said, 'So—'

'Well of course she is! She's very gifted, I know!'

'How do you know?' Ariana asked, a little coquettishly.

'I know everything about you.' He smiled. It was the first time he addressed her directly: he had been speaking to her mother nearly all the time. Ariana figured that was how it was supposed to be. What did she know?

'I will do everything for her, everything she wants!' Mahmoud promised Nadia.

The suitor wanted an answer by the day after.

Nadia asked Karim what he thought.

'You decide,' he said.

Despite her father having to make the difficult call to his colleague, for which he could expect a good deal of abuse for making a fool of him, he recognised that Mahmoud was a better candidate.

Ariana thought so too.

They met the deadline. The next day her parents agreed to the engagement, just four days on from the three women turning up unannounced on their doorstep.

The engagement dress was sent to them the following day. It was dusty mint with silver patterns, low-cut and short-sleeved. Also in the package were an extravagant necklace and earrings, and a diadem. It had small tear-shaped pearls that glittered against her forehead.

Mahmoud would bring the ring himself that same evening. He turned up dressed in a navy pin-striped suit with a patterned tie and a matching pocket square. The men in his family were with him, his father, uncles, brothers, and they were entertained by Karim in one room while Nadia played host to the women in another.

The engaged couple met for the second time.

Five days had passed since the three women had rung the doorbell. They would all soon be family and the chemistry between the two sets of parents was good, at least.

Now Ariana and Mahmoud had some time to speak on their own.

'You've no idea how much I wanted this to happen! How often I've stood by my window waiting for you. When I saw you walk past me at the university that first time . . . I was totally knocked out. After that I stood by the window in my office looking out for you. I began to recognise your schedule, knew when you would be walking past.'

'Oh, I had no clue . . . how is that possible? I haven't even seen you.'

'No, I mean, I was in my office, how could you? I didn't even know your name. I gave thanks to God when you went up to the podium to give your lecture, because then they announced your name. As soon as I found that out, I was sure I was going to find you, and then I called you up.'

He spoke incessantly, repeating the same things, only in slightly different ways. How he had stood at the window, peering out, hoping, longing, without even knowing who she was. And now!

'I want to show you the world,' he said. 'I want to . . . '

I want to . . .

I want to . . .

I want to . . .

Out of the Shadows

One spring day Bashir had a prominent visitor from Pakistan. His guest, who had come up to the roof by way of the exterior stairs, was the shadow governor for the tribal areas in Waziristan. In much the same way as the Taliban had once controlled districts in Afghanistan while the traitors were in power in Kabul, the Islamists in Waziristan had a parallel leadership council, courts and armed forces. They copied the official district government, but they operated in the shadows, in wait, in secret.

Bashir sat on the nominating committee for the leadership of the shadow government, whose long-term goal was to overthrow the Pakistani government. The organisation Tehrik-e-Taliban Pakistan (TTP) had gathered jihadists of all stripes, including IS.

The governor, named Gohar Wazir, was newly appointed. He was a man of slight build with a narrow, lined face and was dressed in green combat fatigues. On his head he wore, like his men, a felt hat that looked like a large muffin cup: flat on top, with curved ridges around it and the felt covering his ears and the nape of his neck. This type of pakol was common in Waziristan but otherwise was not seen on any other military group.

Gohar Wazir was a taciturn man. He'd come to thank Bashir for his support and make plans. While Bashir constantly tried to lighten the mood with anecdotes and stories, the shadow governor stayed quietly with the business at hand. Details of who else he had met in

Kabul he kept to himself. It was well known that Sirajuddin Haqqani had been a close associate of the TTP, but now that he was minister of the interior, he had a different role.

The group was the largest military organisation fighting against the Pakistani state. The Taliban victory in Afghanistan had been a boon for them; they were finally safe in the entire tribal area, on both sides of the border. But they weren't satisfied by having power there: the TTP wanted to take over the whole country. In the wake of the Taliban signing the peace agreement with the USA in February 2020, soldiers flowed to them from several organisations, including three supported by al-Qaeda. At the same time, many men had drifted over to IS-K. There was a steady transfer of extremists between the two groups. The reasons for the switches were ambiguous, or murky. They were often to do with relationships on a personal level, or concerned power, and partly direction.

Bashir was fired up. A new jihad, no less. With the long-term goal of installing Taliban rule in Pakistan.

When would the time come? Whose support could they enlist? How many men were certain? And, not least, what was the view of the Taliban leadership?

Relations with Sirajuddin were delicate. The minister of the interior knew about Bashir's continuing role in the TTP. At the same time, he didn't want any problems with their powerful neighbour in the east; they had enough difficulty with the outside world as it was.

As yet, everything was unclear.

There was still snow in the mountains. The plan was to launch their attack in the holiest of all months, because during Ramadan they would get maximum assistance from Allah. All those killed for jihad during Ramadan could expect double the reward in heaven.

Bashir has been given the honour of naming the planned attack.

It would be called *Al-Badr*. The full moon. That was also the name of the Muslims' first victory over the Quraish tribe at Medina and marked a turning point for the Prophet Muhammad on the battlefield. Back then, as now, the fighting took place during Ramadan.

Bashir didn't need an entire army, he needed good men. And the checklist was the same as always: they had to be smart, brave and strong.

He knew enough people, they just had to be aware that he was recruiting. He had barely got started.

He played the messages on his mobile to Gohar and the others. A man's voice on one, saying, 'I'm ready. Call me, there are a number of us.' Another voice on the next: 'I tried calling you. Just to let you know, I can get fifty men. We're ready.'

It was certainly easier to recruit nowadays than it had been twenty years ago, when NATO came along with their overwhelming firepower and the Taliban saw their men being mown down when the bombing waves just went on and on.

'But we didn't give up and with Allah's help we won!' Bashir said. He picked up his Krinkov. 'This was made by an infidel!' he exclaimed. 'Somewhere in the Soviet Union. It was brought here to kill us. Now it's mine. It's not about weapons but about who's using them. And here we are, Afghani mujahideen, unbeaten.'

'Tell them about your Krinkov,' Farid challenged.

'Hehe, do you want to get me killed?' Bashir asked.

The story he sometimes told when asked was that the rifle had belonged to Osama bin Laden. The Saudi had been in a battle in the Zazi region of Paktia Province when an Arab fighter had taken the weapon from a dead Soviet soldier and given it to Osama.

Osama had kept the Krinkov until he carried out the terror attack against the USA. Then he presented the rifle to a talib. That fighter had been killed and the Krinkov was passed on again.

'Then I got it,' Bashir explained.

'Who from?' one man asked.

'How?' asked another.

'A friend gave it to me as a gift, that's all.'

They sat there on the top floor, each with their glass of tea. Everyone grew silent, immersed in their own thoughts. From the large veranda outside there was a view over the large garden and of the guest house that was taking shape, brick by brick.

Behind the house, clothes were hanging out to dry: dresses, trousers and jackets, along with carpets. At the very end of the property there was a swimming pool, filled with rainwater. The mosaic tiles along the edge were cracked, the blue paint on the walls was peeling. A tyre, a couple of lengths of rubber hosing, some scraps of timber and clothes that must have been blown off the line, were floating on the surface. A semi-submerged bicycle was swaying around, the air in the tyres preventing it from sinking to the bottom.

The visibility diminished gradually from the brownish surface down to the mud.

What lay hidden on the bottom could not be seen from the roof. From here one had a view, but to discover what was stirring one needed to dive into the depths.

Like Bashir. He had to go down into the mud. Back to the war.

The Women and the Caliph

From May the sun no longer dipped below the horizon. The Arctic summer was a time of eternal light, but the sun didn't warm Jamila. In June she put up blackout curtains in order to sleep.

In Afghanistan, everything was growing darker. A darkness had also descended upon her because *there*, in her homeland, was where she was. That's where her attention was focused, it was from there that she was waiting for news.

The battles were being lost one after another. The schools were not reopened for the older girls. The travel restrictions remained. Women were not allowed go further than seventy-two kilometres from home without a male guardian. An edict on covering up had been introduced and women did not return to the workplace. As regards the authorities, experience had been replaced by incompetence. Some ministries had taken into consideration women's loss of income when they were let go. They were asked to send a male relative to do their jobs. *Any male relative.* In Alta, Jamila fumed and swore.

At the same time, she was filled with guilt for having left her country. Perhaps she could have accomplished something. Maybe had some influence. Instead, she had left them in the lurch. She often regretted her choice. The much-feared mass arrests of activists and politicians hadn't come to pass. The Taliban's amnesty had held. Some of the women who had protested by displaying banners and chanting slogans had been jailed, and they reported harassment and abuse while inside. But public demonstrations had never been Jamila's domain. Her work required discussions, cooperation and compromise. It was difficult to engage in from Alta.

Living in a small, frozen town complicated life. Norway demanded so much of her, the language course, career guidance, follow-up regarding integration, yet didn't give her what she really needed: the missing X-rays. The pain had spread to her entire body, but she couldn't face wasting more time on the impenetrable bureaucracy of refugee health.

She would rather spend the time with her baby – the laptop. So many emails and statements to compose, so many meetings, discussions and seminars to participate in. It was frustrating, because the activists, experts and politicians who had been cast aside spoke within their own bubbles, with one another, but never with those in power.

How could they do something that led to change? It annoyed her that the Taliban showed up every time they were invited abroad, be it Oslo, Abu Dhabi or Doha, and were willing to meet diplomats and UN envoys in Afghanistan.

The foreigners smiled politely at the men in turbans. Some of them took selfies and posted them on Twitter, where they expressed concern about developments and emphasised that they had raised the issue of human rights.

The Taliban smiled back and tightened their grip.

Jamila decided to write to the UN delegation in Kabul to complain that they were not doing enough to pressure the Taliban. They held meetings, on a daily basis, with representatives of a government who continued their inhumane policies. The international community was allowing itself to be wrapped around the little finger of the Taliban, who refused to meet those really involved: Afghan women.

Jamila asked for help in arranging a meeting with the powers that be. The meeting had to be face to face, the women themselves needed to set the agenda and do the talking. Why should UN and Western diplomats speak on behalf of Afghan women when their own voices were strong enough? She asked and encouraged all the women in the office to write similar letters to the UN delegation.

A few weeks later she received a call from Kabul.

'Where's your deputy? We can't get hold of her.'

Jamila's deputy was in Iran, without a phone signal. A representative from the office was urgently needed. The Taliban leadership had agreed to meet with five women. Three had already been picked; Jamila could choose two more.

The meeting was to take place the following day. Oh, if only she could have gone herself!

Jamila got in touch with Zeynab, the devout university lecturer who had delivered a fiery speech against the Taliban at the press conference about the school closures. Zeynab's life consisted of teaching and praying. Women's liberation was her calling. She belonged to a group of female scholars who went far further than their male colleagues in speaking out against the Taliban.

In addition, Jamila wanted to invite an older activist. Soraya had grown up in the 1960s and described her adolescence, with short skirts and without a veil, as the best years of her life. Back then Afghanistan was a good place, she reminisced. She had been a teacher most of her working life, and was well schooled in religion, an advantage when facing the Taliban. She came across as a traditional, maternal Pashtun woman, perfectly cast for the meeting, because she was also direct and not afraid to speak her mind.

Both women said yes immediately.

Jamila sat in Alta, Zeynab and Soraya in Kabul, talking via computer screen. They decided to focus on women's participation in society, in the workplace and in the leadership of the country, and to demand that schools were opened to all. They didn't know who they would be meeting. Jamila guessed it might be the minister of education or his under-secretary. It could also be Muttaqi, the foreign minister who had headed the delegation in Oslo.

'Don't be afraid!' Jamila said.

'I'm not afraid,' Zeynab said. 'I have God with me.'

'So have I,' Soraya responded.

'Good. Be confident, but friendly. Use traditional turns of phrase when you speak, and, whatever you do, don't employ English words or international aid expressions! This is Afghans meeting Afghans. Listen to what they say, refute their arguments and remember to provide evidence for everything you say, but try to incorporate some old proverbs if possible . . .'

The meeting was scheduled for nine o'clock the next morning, and the women turned up well in advance. They were taken to a guest house at one of the Taliban's ministries and asked to wait. Besides Soraya and Zeynab, a former vice-minister of health and two female activists were there. Soraya noticed she was trembling slightly. She had never spoken to anyone in the Taliban leadership and said a quiet prayer. A man collected their phones and placed them in a box while the women were shown to some soft armchairs. They sat well covered with face veils and headscarves. Soraya was about to text Jamila to let her know that everything was fine, when she remembered she had handed over her phone.

Then they heard footsteps in the corridor. The door opened and a group of men in flowing white clothes and black turbans entered, a broad-shouldered man at the front. His beard covered most of his face and pitch-black hair curled down over his ears. The men behind him backed off slightly as he approached the women.

His eyes were deep set, almost in the shadow of his eye sockets, below a pair of bushy brows. He didn't look at them as he made to sit down. Once seated he delivered the Islamic greetings, still without looking at them, and they answered in kind before he said in a calm voice, 'I have come to listen to you.'

It was Sirajuddin Haqqani.

*

Few people had caused more blood to be spilt than him. This was the man behind most terror attacks in Kabul, who had established mass production of roadside bombs, run his own martyr academy, manipulated, motivated, extorted and killed.

Few people had a better understanding of how to win power and keep it. Some months after he was appointed interior minister, he held a memorial service for the relatives of suicide bombers at the Intercontinental in Kabul, a hotel he had ordered an attack on some years earlier. In the lavish tribute to the martyrs, he thanked their fathers, who went home with a new set of clothes and ten thousand afghani, as well as the promise of a plot of land.

His followers were to feel seen and recognised.

In March, while inspecting a parade of new recruits to the police academy, Sirajuddin Haqqani finally allowed himself to be photographed in public. He no longer hid from the authorities; he *was* the authorities.

The former vice-minister, a doctor, was the first to speak. She outlined the catastrophic healthcare situation, talking quickly and clearly. Many faithful Muslims had hoped the Taliban had changed, she said to Sirajuddin, who still looked down or to the side while she spoke. Many had hoped the Taliban would bring improvement after years of corruption and mismanagement, she continued, but the policies were headed in the wrong direction and there was a severe shortage of healthcare workers, especially women, because of the restrictions, segregation and postponed salary payouts. Furthermore, they were lacking equipment, medication and vaccines. The experienced doctor stressed that the Taliban's hostile attitudes towards women was in effect a demonstration of hostility against half the country. 'Why do you treat us as outcasts?' she asked.

The interior minister sat silently in his chair. He acknowledged the shortages at clinics and the scarcity of doctors in the countryside. He promised improvement, in general terms, and lamented the lack of resources, but blamed it on the West for having frozen the funds.

The next woman to speak criticised the exclusion of women from working life.

Haqqani continued to look down. A man next to him took notes.

The third woman concentrated on the patriarchal power structures. Why were there no women in government or in other positions of power?

Zeynab's entire face, apart from her eyes, was covered. Over her abaya she was wearing a cream-coloured hijab. Both the way she had tied it, and how she held her head, gave the impression of a conservative Muslim. Unlike the other women, who looked directly at the interior minister while speaking, she sat, like him, with her face turned. But her voice was strong and clear.

'I say this without fear. Because what I say is the truth. I am prepared to accept all consequences. This is the voice of the women.'

She was heeding Jamila's advice: be confident!

'You are making a grave mistake in pushing us aside, a mistake that first and foremost is a danger to you yourselves. It will lead to your downfall. What you are doing goes against God, goes against the Prophet, peace be upon him, goes against Islam. The blame lies squarely on your shoulders, and you will have to answer to Allah on the Day of Judgement.'

Haqqani was clearly irked by the accusations. He turned towards his men, who raised their eyebrows slightly, but none of them said anything. Zeynab was looking down at the table as she spoke.

'You know well what it says in the first verse of the Quran,' she said, addressing Haqqani although, again, both of them were gazing at the tabletop. 'God's first command is: Read! *Iqra!*'

From the way she recited the Quran, the references she brought forth, no one could be in any doubt that this was a learned woman speaking.

'Why does *Iqra!* come first? Because for God, learning comes first! But you say hijab first, then learning. That's in the wrong order. God did not reveal the verse about covering up for another *eighteen years* after telling us all to read! Only in the fifth year after the

Prophet, peace be upon him, travelled from Mecca to Medina did the advice come on covering up, in verse thirty-three of the chapter *Confederates*. For men *and* women. And he told *both* men and women to dress virtuously and guard their gaze!'

Sirajuddin guarded his gaze.

The Quran commanded men in *The Light* to virtuous behaviour. *Tell the believing men to lower their gaze and guard their chastity. That is purer for them. Surely Allah is All-Aware of what they do.*

Women were given the same message in the next verse, when they were told *not to reveal their adornments* and *draw their veils over their chests*. Despite God treating men and women equally, demanding modesty and proper behaviour from everyone, the Taliban only imposed these practical limitations on women, which led to job losses, exclusion and the interruption of education.

'What you're doing is not only wrong according to Islam, what you're doing is a great atrocity against Islam,' Zeynab continued. 'You're causing people to hate Islam. You're making Muslims turn away from religion because they associate it with you.'

What she said made Sirajuddin Haqqani lift his head and look at her. It was as though the harsh words rendered her an equal.

'*Wallahi*, by God, I had no idea that women in this country were so strong,' he interrupted, turning to his men. 'I had no idea such knowledgeable women existed among us. I'm impressed!'

'Let's talk in concrete terms,' Zeynab went on. 'We cannot disagree on God's first word. But you have circumvented the rule. You have closed the schools for the girls in secondary and up. You have made it harder for women to study, and to use what they had previously learned. Female students are being harassed by your soldiers on university campuses. You refuse to allow women to learn but demand that women must cover up? No, this is not a good way you have chosen.'

'*Bismillahi rahmani Rahim*, in the name of God, the beneficent, the merciful,' interrupted Haqqani again, 'we have made a great mistake not including you earlier, by not having you take part in decisions.'

Zeynab was not finished.

'Yes, what you're doing is terrible. And Allah does not let terrible leaders survive long term. If you fail now, you will push the country into a hundred-year-long civil war, which it will take another hundred years to emerge from. Open the schools for everyone. Let us work. Let us travel,' she said, eyes fixed on the table.

Haqqani had raised his head.

'I was in favour of opening the schools, I wanted it done,' he said, defending himself. 'But powerful forces were against it. Threats were made. We chose to refrain from opening the schools so no lives would be lost. We acted out of concern for the girls' safety.'

'That argument was also used the last time you were in power,' one of the women said. 'The girls' own safety.' She went on to object to the Taliban constantly changing the explanation. The classrooms weren't ready, there was resistance among the population, there was a shortage of teachers and now once more the old argument about safety. The difference between the Taliban in the 1990s and the Taliban of today, she continued, was that 'now you break your promises. Back then you promised nothing.'

'Listen to me. I tried . . . ' Haqqani protested.

Before his hands were folded calmly on his lap; now he used them more actively. The men around him shifted in their seats.

Soraya spoke up. 'Another misunderstanding in regard to the Quran,' she said, 'is that you misinterpret counsel and compulsion. Covering up was advised in the time of the Prophet on the grounds of safety. If the woman wished it. The same goes for the hadith that specified a limit for how far women could travel alone in his day – again, a recommendation for their own safety. Back then seventy-two kilometres was the equivalent of three days' journey by camel. In hidebound fashion, you have retained this limit.'

'I will have word sent to the airports that women can fly without a guardian,' Haqqani suddenly said.

The women looked at one another. This meeting was taking an unexpected turn.

A man entered carrying tea and sweets. Soraya was already

annoyed by her face veil, and even the Taliban didn't demand women of her age wear one. She removed it decisively, putting it in her bag – how else was she supposed to drink tea? Zeynab kept hers on.

'I'm trying, I promise, you need to be patient,' Haqqani repeated.

'How long are we supposed to be patient?' Soraya asked.

'We need time to bring changes. You give us strength to govern, you are scholars, you are doctors. We have listened. Now you must trust us. And there's one thing I'd like to ask you, and that is to tell the sisters who are protesting that they need to stop. It's not dignified. How come you don't prevent your sisters going out into the streets like this?'

Why is he pointing the finger at me, Soraya thought. Moreover, the Taliban had never viewed women as equal members of society, never respected them, why should they trust him now?

'It says in the Quran,' Soraya replied, 'that when your rights are violated, you have the right to protest. We're crying out because you are violating our rights. Be our brother, show us respect, and people will cease. Listen to us, sit with us, because we have something to say to you. But if you don't listen then we'll continue going out on the streets.'

Sirajuddin Haqqani was becoming bombastic.

'You have opened my eyes. You have opened my mind. I want others to experience what I have experienced today. It pains me to think I have neglected such wise people. We shall hold a loya jirga of scholars next month. We'll ensure that women can also participate. Female scholars are better at explaining than men! You are our sisters. We need one another. Not allowing you to talk to us has been a great mistake.'

He continued showering them with compliments.

You're all so wise.

You're so intelligent.

I didn't realise women could be so knowledgeable.

Then he had to leave. He asked them to remain with his staff to formulate more specific proposals. They stayed for another couple of hours, then were served lunch, and after the meal Haqqani returned. Following behind him were men carrying five large boxes. 'Afghan handicrafts,' he said.

One of the men opened the lids.

Soraya looked down into her box. Inside lay a black velvet dress, with broad white lacework running lengthways in strips along the skirt, and thin pink, green and midnight blue borders at the very bottom. On the chest was a lively gold and orange zigzag pattern. As she stroked the rows of thin brass coins and small silver beads on the front panel, some round, some tear-shaped, there was a tinkling sound.

The fit was far too slim for her, she saw that immediately. My daughter can have it, she decided before closing the lid.

Upon leaving the guest house and having their phones returned, Soraya saw she had several missed calls from Jamila. She quickly called her back.

Jamila gasped on the other end of the line. 'I was so worried! No one's been able to get hold of any of you all day!'

The five women looked at one another. They were filled with the words and promises of the powerful man, standing there with his gifts – like hostages of his insistent compliments, his position and his powers of persuasion.

The manipulator. The motivator. So pleasant, so pleasant. This was the man who had coaxed young men into blowing themselves up for something *he* believed in. The man who had let explosives rain down on his enemies. The man who, through his guile, his charisma and his friendly, intelligent conversational style had for over twenty years waged war on democracy, on women's participation in society, on freedom and equality.

Be patient.
Wait for word.
Sit tight.
Then you will be heard.
Then I might meet with you again.

They went their separate ways, to different parts of Kabul, some on the back seat of a car, others on a bus. Each with their boxes in their laps.

Neatly packed, with a tight band around the middle, the valuable dresses lay in darkness. Inside, the clinking of silver beads in the shape of tears.

Running Up That Hill

It began with Ariana getting a little bored.

Mahmoud wanted to talk all the time. Monologues. About how the apartment should be, what kind of furnishings they ought to have. Curtains or blinds? Which colours did she like? Light hues or dark?

'We'll find a place close to your parents, okay, wouldn't that be good? They're incredibly nice, I feel like I've always known them, I was considering buying them a gift. What do you think? Maybe a pair of sandals for your father. Do you think he'd like that? What kind of sandals? I'm sure I can find some nice ones. And what about your mother, what do you think she'd like? A shawl, perhaps, what are her favourite colours? And for us, we need to buy crockery and cutlery, towels and bedding. What do you like best? Cotton? Silk? Is white the nicest?'

He called her every night. She began to dread the conversations.

'I'm tired, I have to sleep.'

'Tired? It's only nine o'clock!'

'I'm getting up early.'

'Aw, just talk to me for a little while,' he pleaded. 'Can't you stay up a little longer? I'm looking for an apartment in a nice area. It's not easy to find. Have you any preference about what floor to live on? It would be nice to have a balcony, I know . . . '

If only Ariana had been interested in building a nest! Then everything would be perfect. After all he was a good man, wasn't he?

She forced herself to sit calmly and listen. Gradually she started doing other things while he was talking. Searching for a document on her laptop. Putting him on speakerphone so she could scroll through other messages or check Instagram while he shared his thoughts. She would get up, tidy her room, put away clothes. A sense of unease took root. This wasn't how it was supposed to be, was it? Why were these conversations so hard to endure?

She challenged herself to find positive aspects to him. Objectively, he had many good traits, but those which she *liked* were pitifully few. Compelling herself to listen to him was one thing, accepting him and her fate was something else entirely. *She was going to spend the rest of her life with him.* It was scarcely a week after the engagement and the thought gave her palpitations.

'I think you're better off finding someone you like,' she told her little sister, her only confidante among her siblings. Zohal nodded in agreement, that would be best.

'It's not a good idea to force yourself to like . . . ' Her throat tightened. It was the first time since the engagement that Ariana cried.

She had kept the growing anxiety within: after all, she was the amazing daughter who could do anything. Even now she checked herself and said, 'It'll be fine. I'm sure it'll all be fine, things will work out.'

Zohal searched for words but found none.

'He's so slow. Everything has to be turned over and looked at from every angle and discussed endlessly,' Ariana continued. 'I like people who just do things and then say, "Come and take a look!" But on the other hand, why the big hurry with the apartment . . . why is he rushing to get that done? Couldn't we just be engaged for a while and live separately? I'm worried that, when he finds an apartment, he's going to say, "The rent is already being paid, we need to get married fast!" I feel that's his plan – to get married quickly, and the apartment he's on about is the key to a swift wedding.'

Ariana's parents were for their part besotted with their future son-in-law.

'They say he's an angel, oh, they like him so much more than I do! I've realised why: it's because he seems to belong to the same generation as them. They're so similar. He's younger than them but he thinks like them. When he turned up with that gold ring, Mum was all "Look, a gold ring, he's a good man! These are good people!" His family brought dried fruit and biscuits and she exclaimed, "Oh, look what they brought, these are good people." When she heard he had five brothers: "What good people!"'

Mahmoud rang every evening. He was suffocating her with all his nattering. With his fussing, his nestbuilding, and his constant refrain 'I'm doing this for you, just tell me what you want, I will do everything you ask, I will . . . I will . . . I will . . . '

'He just talks and talks, even if I tell him I have something to do. And when the monologue is over, he inevitably asks, "What do you think?" That isn't how two people converse, is it?'

Zohal shook her head. What should she say? Should she say what they were both thinking, that this wasn't going so well?

Fortunately, she did have some important things to do. She was going to receive her degree certificate.

The last weeks at university had grown steadily grimmer. If the female students went to sit down on a bench they were chased off. If they displayed a lock of hair, the guards threatened them. The campus that had at one time bustled with life had become a stony waste. The emptiness exposed all of the imperfections, the litter blowing around, the weeds sprouting up between the concrete. The students walked around in fear after a boy was beaten senseless with rods because he had stopped to talk to two female classmates from the previous year. Afterwards he was thrown into a car and taken to prison as the rector had threatened.

Her dream had been that her parents hired a function room at a hotel for her graduation, so that she, Baba Musa's brilliant grandchild, could shine. She was going to stand with a mortarboard atop her head and be photographed, and then the world was going to open up: studies abroad, a career, prizes, conferences. Instead, she was on her way to the Ministry of Education to pick up her certificate by herself.

The man at the counter refused to hand it over.

'None are being issued.'

'But we were told to collect them here.'

'Nobody's getting one, it's been decided.'

'Why not?'

'When the world recognises us and sends us our money, then you'll get your degree certificate!'

Western countries were still withholding payment of nine billion dollars belonging to Afghanistan. Seven billion of it was frozen in the USA. President Biden had touted the idea of half of these funds going to the victims of the 9/11 attacks, something which not only provoked the Taliban but the majority of Afghans. Were they to bear the blame and the burden for bin Laden's terrorist acts twenty years earlier?

Afghanistan was an outcast and Ariana was a pariah in her own country. The Taliban made sure they punished those they believed were deserving. Among highly educated young people the movement had little support. For the Taliban the logic was clear: the withheld billions meant that people were starving, that the schools had to remain closed and that the Ministry of Education lacked ink for the printer.

'The world recognised the republic, the most corrupt of regimes, but not our emirate,' the man at the counter said. 'Until they do, you'll just have to wait for you degree certificate.'

Ariana's relationship with her mother fluctuated between annoyance and regret, hostility and reconciliation. They were bound together by many things, but one thing more than any other: teaching.

Mother and daughter grieved over the girls not being allowed to continue school after sixth grade while the Taliban urged patience. How everyone should just wait for word – the minister of education had said they would 'soon get good news', but it seemed increasingly like an empty promise. The excuses were ever-changing, first the closure was on cultural grounds, then it was due to a lack of space to separate the classes, then a teacher shortage, and after that simply that everything wasn't in place yet. The authorities weren't going to allow girls into secondary school this year, they just had to face that.

Nadia was principal of the largest school in the neighbourhood and many of the girls lived nearby. But she never saw them any more. Sometimes she ran into their fathers: they worked in shops, at the market, drove carts, swept the streets – people in all kinds of jobs lived in their area.

'Let's teach them here!' Ariana suggested one day. 'We can start a home school!'

Their apartment block had a basement room of which all the residents owned a share. It was seldom occupied, except when some of the neighbours gathered the children for Quran recital on Fridays. Ariana suggested they could use that.

Her mother looked at her. She thought about it for a minute before exclaiming:

'Yes, we can!'

Zohal joined them, Diwa joined them. Some of Nadia's teachers who had been sent home also joined. One of the women's husbands worked for a firm that could get them paint at cost price. They bought tins in a light pink colour and set to work with wide brushes on the walls and on the beams holding the building up. They hung up lace curtains in the small basement windows and laid down carpets. Nadia brought a whiteboard and a marker from school.

Teaching was to take place every weekday between two and five in the afternoon. Ariana would take charge of English and Dari. Nadia was tasked with geography. Zohal and Diwa would instruct the girls in science, and a couple of teachers from the school would cover mathematics and Pashto.

They had not expected Karim to be the one to try to stop them.

'Are you insane? Do you want the Taliban at our door?'

'The Taliban haven't forbidden the teaching of girls,' Ariana argued, 'as long as they're segregated. And men are not allowed in here!'

'It's too dangerous,' her father reproved her. 'For *me*. When the Taliban come, it won't be for you. They'll ask, "Where's your father? Where's your brother?" They don't take women who violate the rules, they take their husbands. You're putting me in danger.'

'What about the girls sitting at home? Have you thought about *them*? Their whole future is on the line if they don't get to learn.'

Her father was always the one who was most scared. He was constantly assessing risks and prioritising safety above all else. The last year had led Ariana to see him more clearly. Her father was unable to see the big picture. He complained but took no action. She had always viewed him as wise, reliable and kind, but now she felt he was proving to be a little man when it mattered.

Her father despised the Taliban, but he didn't understand that this was a part of the resistance! Ariana wasn't taking to the streets with placards, she had started a school. Her mother wasn't sitting in fear behind her principal's desk, she had got hold of a whiteboard. No one knew what risks they were taking, but when the idea was first suggested it was impossible not to put it into effect.

This time they weren't listening to the patriarch. They finished painting. When everything was ready, they needed to find a way to gather the pupils. How would they let them know? Through word of mouth?

They hoped that Nadia's status as principal would offer the families a sense of security, so at least some would dare to send their girls. Nadia suggested they inform the primary school pupils about the offer.

'Do any of you have big sisters who were sent home from school?' she asked when the small girls were gathered in the schoolyard early the next morning.

Several of them raised their hands.

'We're opening a small school in our home. Lessons are starting up tomorrow.'

She gave them the address.

Would anyone come? Would their parents allow them?

*

One hundred girls turned up.

It was as though the neighbourhood was composed solely of girls aged from thirteen to sixteen who had finally emerged from their caves.

The girls proudly stated their names, addresses, ages, what year they should have been starting. They were animated, excited; many of them hadn't seen one another since that day in March when life collapsed.

Ariana put girls from different years into her English class, otherwise the timetable wouldn't work. To get an idea of the levels of proficiency she invited the girls to have a conversation, and asked if any of them wanted to tell the class a little about themselves. Lots of hands were raised. The girls she pointed to stood up, gave thanks to Allah, then began to speak. Most of them had to take breaks to cry.

They had never put their traumas into words before.

They were unprepared for the effect that saying things out loud would have on them.

It had been drilled into all of them that school was the golden gateway, by fathers who were streetsweepers, who sold bread over counters, by mothers who couldn't read a recipe.

They were going to have a better life.

But they had lost all control over their lives.

'There're too many of them!' Karim said. He had not been able to stop the school, but he insisted on limiting it.

'So who shall we send home, then?'

'Keep half of them,' Karim said. 'Or thirty, at the most. Send the rest home!'

'When I look at their faces,' Ariana said, 'when I see the sparkle in their eyes – how can I tell them there's no room after all? Papa, I just can't!'

The days passed. The Taliban never came. Not to their door nor to the other places where mothers and unemployed teachers had started up home schools.

This was the new Taliban. Who turned a blind eye.

Moreover, this was a different population. Who wouldn't give in. This was the difference twenty years of education had made compared to the last time the Taliban had power.

Hardly any young women with Ariana's level of education covered their faces in Kabul, even though the rules demanded it. Many wore make-up, or let locks of hair show, even though the recommendations were otherwise. They put on an abaya but left a button open. If they were chased out of a place, they returned the next day. If they weren't allowed to continue their studies, they found an alternative way to learn.

That was what this boiled down to. If they didn't find these gaps in the system, they would lose themselves.

Nadia was pleased to have three of the teachers from school on board. The girls' own teachers. The reunion was tearful. No one was paid, no one had money, they did it for the girls, they did it out of self-respect, they did it for their country.

When teaching was finished, they were let out in groups of no more than ten at a time, to avoid a hundred girls flooding out of the building all at once. The classes Ariana held in the low-ceilinged, pink basement room were a glimmer of hope. They were hours where she was able to forget what was causing her anguish. The new man in her life.

He was in love. She was fed up.

He wanted to hold her. She wanted to be free.

It wasn't working out. It wasn't going to work out.

She had accepted him because she had believed, for a moment, that he was probably a good choice. Better than the others. But now Mahmoud was buzzing in her ears, scratching out space in her head, and she just wanted him out.

Breaking off an engagement was no small matter. Yet Kabul wasn't like the countryside, where it was unheard of, and engagements amounted to mini weddings. Ariana reasoned to herself that the engagement period should be a time to find out if the two of you were compatible or not. It was a probationary phase. What was the point of an engagement otherwise? It was still possible to pull out of what she realised was the biggest mistake of her life.

After they were married it would be too late. Getting divorced under the previous regime had been difficult; under the Taliban it was impossible. She had studied this, she knew this. Thousands of separations granted just before the fall of the republic were all invalidated by the Taliban. Women were forced to return to their abusive husbands. The courts no longer heard divorce cases or countenanced accusations of violence within marriage. The Ministry of Women's Affairs had been superseded by the Ministry for the Propagation of Virtue and the Prevention of Vice. The Afghanistan Independent Human Rights Commission was closed down. The Special Commission for Women was closed. There was nowhere to lodge a complaint. Your husband was your guardian. If you were in a marriage, you were locked in.

But an engagement wasn't legally binding, it was a verbal agreement between families. It wasn't until you entered the contract of marriage – nikah – that you were bound hand and foot by the pact.

The question was who she should tell first. Her parents or her fiancé? Since her parents had been the ones who made the deal with his family, they were the ones who had to break it, she figured.

She was dreading it. The days passed.

Netflix had just released season four of *Stranger Things*. How she loved that series; she had devoured the other seasons while at university. Her roommates had curled up in her bed while she translated the dialogue. Fortunately, Ariana could still access her friend's Netflix account. To be on the safe side she downloaded all seven episodes onto her phone.

She switched off the light, plumped some cushions to make herself comfortable and watched the first episode. Finally, the world was reduced to the small, glowing screen and the sound in the headphones. When it finished, she gobbled up the second episode. The third she watched almost in a trance.

She resolved to get up. She had to save some. There were four episodes left. And she needed to break off the engagement.

She texted instead of calling him.
'We need to talk! I can't go on like this.'
'What's going on?'
'I don't want to marry you.'
'Don't plunge my world into darkness!'
'I can't take it. I want out.'
'I'll do anything for you. Just tell me what you want.'
'I want you to break the engagement.'
'I love you. You can ask me for whatever you want. I'll do anything for you.'
'Then I'm asking you: break off the engagement.'
'Don't ruin my life!'
'Don't ruin *mine*!'

She suggested they meet the next day at Cafeteria in the city centre – a safe place for both groups of girls and couples. 'I don't think I can,' he said. 'I think I have to work.'

God, he nattered away on the phone for hours, yet he couldn't meet her to talk properly.

She texted him again the following day. 'We need to meet and talk!'

But he had discovered that, yes, he did have to work.

She figured she would give him a little time. He didn't strike her as very strong, and he was an all right guy, so it was unlikely he would insist on marrying her when she didn't want him. Besides, he deserved better than her, someone who would appreciate his words and his household plans.

In the meantime, she had to speak to her parents. Her mother first.

'Mum, I'm not ready!'
'It'll be fine. This is just a phase, dear.'
Then her father. He exploded.
'Don't even think about it! Do you want to destroy our name?

Do you want to ruin things for your sisters? People will laugh at us! He's a wonderful man, the best you could get.'

Her father needed time, Ariana knew. He was often prone to short temper, then would give in. Like when he wouldn't allow her to return to university and then he let her go after two weeks, or when he refused to permit them to open a home school but relented about that too.

She went to bed, thought about watching *Stranger Things* but decided to save it. Like Max in the series, to shut the world out she put 'Running Up That Hill' by Kate Bush on repeat instead.

She spent the whole of the next day in her room, listening to music on her headphones. She didn't notice her mother had come in before she tapped her on the shoulder and asked her to come out for a cup of tea.

She got up reluctantly and followed Nadia.

Mahmoud was sitting in the living room.

She gathered herself and said *salam* like a sulky adolescent.

'Mahmoud has found an apartment,' Karim said. 'Very close by. He wants you to come and see it.'

After what she had written to him the previous evening! After he had told her he needed to work! He had found an apartment . . .

She couldn't bear to look at him. She stared at the floor, felt an icy hatred surge up within.

'Mahmoud wants you to take a look,' her father repeated.

'I'm not interested,' Ariana said. 'I don't want to look at anything at all!'

She left, went to her room, lay down on the bed and wept.

When Mahmoud had gone her father came in.

'You're behaving like a child. This is so embarrassing for us.'

'I don't want to get married. I don't want this to happen.'

'You can't cancel it! You committed yourself to him by saying yes to the engagement: there is no way out. I have asked him to arrange everything that needs to be arranged.'

Then her mother entered. 'How dare you act so disgracefully!

Do you want to bring shame upon us, destroy our lives? This isn't some game, it isn't pretend or something for fun. You must accept this. You have no choice.'

'I don't want to marry him!' Ariana sobbed.

'Stop crying!' her mother scolded.

'Why won't you listen to me?'

'Because you don't have anything logical to say! I didn't want to marry your father either. But I did. I did! And you're going to do this! The wedding will take place within a month. So save your tears!'

'But I hate him. I can't live with him.' She sat up on the bed, looking directly at her mother.

'Does it mean anything to you whether I am happy or not?'

'No,' her mother answered. 'Your happiness means nothing to me.'

Ariana gasped.

It felt like the end. It *was* the end. *They didn't care about her.* Her whole life, her whole childhood, everything came crashing down. In that case, she had nothing more to say to them. She forced out the only punishment she could aim at her mother.

'If you make this happen, I'll never speak to either of you again. Ever! It's your choice. You can destroy my life or you can set me free.'

Her mother gave her a hard look. 'No one does that kind of thing in our family.'

If only she could wake up from this nightmare!

The following evening, on her way from her bedroom to the kitchen to make some tea, she heard her father on the phone. She stopped to listen. She could tell by his voice that he was talking to Mahmoud. His tone was jovial, man to man.

The conversation was drawing to a close. She froze where she stood in the hallway.

'Yes, yes, just buy everything you need. No need to wait. Everything is confirmed on our side!'

Her father sounded in high spirits. He asked her fiancé to find a wedding hall.

She entered the living room as her father was hanging up.

'The lease is signed,' he said, giving her a challenging look. 'Everything is agreed. The wedding will be in a few weeks.'

They were both desperate. Ariana wanted out. Mahmoud wanted her in.

In her diary she wrote:

He doesn't listen to me. A week has passed since I said I didn't want him. He's never listened to me, I see that now, neither when we talk or text, he just pretends to listen, and then answers something else entirely. Like he did the first time we met. He didn't care about what I told him then either. Now he only talks to my parents. The problem is: I don't want him!!! Oh, everyone is pressuring me. Mum and Dad are dark on the inside, they just pretend to be kind. They're not!

After a while Mahmoud began calling again. Usually, she didn't answer the phone. One day she tapped accept, and he just said a single sentence.

'Come and choose a bed!'

Ariana hung up.

She had never cried as much as she did after that call.

She stopped answering completely, but he continued to send texts.

Life felt increasingly constricted. Mahmoud was coiling himself around her. His texts felt like threats. She shared what he wrote in her diary.

He says:
  Though it may not be what you want
  You can't decide
  Your father agrees and that's more important than what you say
  Oh, how could I believe he was kind?

He says:
   Don't even think about calling it off
   You have only one choice
   And that's to marry me
   He threatens me
   I can't do this
   Now I understand
   This will be horrible
   Now I understand
   I can't do anything

Ariana decided to read out his messages to her parents. They were overwhelmingly on his side.

'You wrote lots of horrible things to him,' her mother said. 'He's hurt. He deserves an apology.'

She went to her room. She watched the fourth episode of *Stranger Things*. Soon it would be over. Soon everything would be over.

Everything else was decided above her head; this was the only thing she had control over, when to watch the last three episodes.

She looked around, taking in her room. All the notebooks from lectures. The diploma from the Jessup competition, when they made it to the semi-final. All the courses she had completed. Her books, clothes. She shut the world out and was in her own universe. Her headphones were her escape. She found out Beyoncé had released a new album. The star was suddenly talking to her.

   I'm 'bout to explode, take off this load
   Spin it, bust it open, won't ya make it go

Ariana slipped right into the song. She was inside it.

   You won't break my soul
   You won't break my soul
   You won't break my soul
   You won't break my soul

She got up and took out the nicest outfit she had ever bought, with the money she earned from student radio. Her mother had been angry when she heard how much it had cost. 'How could you use so much money on something like that?'

She ran her hands over it, smelled it, rubbed the smooth fabric against her cheek. The grey Adidas tracksuit with the green stripes on the sides belonged to another time. Every morning she used to wear it on a run round the campus. Half an hour, sometimes an hour, to wake up. She had loved that time. Afterwards she hurried into the shower before her roommates, still asleep in their bunk beds, woke up. Then she fried eggs and made tea for everyone. Those breakfast parties that lasted until one of them shouted 'Oh no! We're going to be late!' had once been part of her everyday life. Up until then life had consisted of her friends, her family, Justin Bieber and Netflix. She had never had a boyfriend, had never held someone's hand. Now she was going from here straight to living with a stranger who felt like an ever-increasing threat. She didn't share her misery with her friends; even now she couldn't bring herself to appear weak. The fall was too great, she was the one who could do anything, saw opportunities everywhere, was outstanding. She confided in her diary instead.

I like when night
Comes to my room
Darkness
No one bothering me
Don't want people around me
So much in my head
And I ask myself all the time:
How can I sleep with him?!!!
It's horrible
I'm scared

Just before falling asleep, she heard the tick of a text message arriving. It was a photo. Should she open it or not? She opened it.

It was a bed. The headboard was covered in a shiny copper-coloured material. Several golden cushions were propped against it on the bedspread. At the foot, a padded bench, also copper-coloured, was attached to the frame.

He had written one sentence.

'My choice of bed.'

A New Life

Hala was standing ready when Bashir arrived. Dressed in white. Everyone was to appear equal before God.

She only had a small bag. A pilgrim had to travel light.

Bashir's mother stood swathed in a sheet-like garment. On her head she wore a white shawl fastened to a headband, preventing it from slipping off.

She was going to be washed clean of her sins.

She was going to be born anew.

She was going to Mecca!

Whoever performs Hajj for Allah's pleasure . . . will return without sins, like on the day they were born, the Prophet had said.

Bashir had just got word.

'The plane is ready. It leaves tonight!'

He had called his mother at once.

For twenty years the Taliban had lived in the shadows, in the mountains and deep valleys, in ravines and dense forests, not able to travel. Their names were on no-fly lists, they were wanted by the authorities. To them, airports had been nothing more than terror targets.

Now they controlled Afghanistan and this year hordes of Taliban wanted to go to Mecca to give thanks to God and be washed clean.

Then there weren't enough places. Of course there weren't. The number wanting to go had piled up, and the Ministry of Hajj and

Religious Affairs had decided applicants would be selected by lottery. Saudi Arabia had announced that thirteen thousand Afghans would be granted visas during the period of pilgrimage, the first half of July, in this first year of their victory.

When Bashir's number came up and the opportunity to travel to Mecca became a reality, he had second thoughts. The plane tickets and accommodation were expensive. He did the maths. The price came to over one hundred thousand afghani.

Was that feasible?

It was the duty of every Muslim to go to Mecca, the Prophet had said. It was one of the five pillars of Islam alongside creed, prayer, fasting and charity.

But he needed one million afghani for wife number three. And money for a second house.

He had much to be grateful to God for. But there were others he had to thank too.

Who had taught him the creed? Who had shown him how to pray? When he fasted, who had made sure he ate some yoghurt before the sun rose, and a good meal when it went down? Who had taught him to be generous to those who had little? Who had supported him more than anyone in jihad?

Exactly. Her turn had come. She deserved to experience the fifth pillar of Islam after a life fulfilling the four others.

'Mum, do you want to go to Mecca?' he had asked.

Hala had just swatted at him with the end of her shawl.

'You're going,' he said. 'We have a place in the queue. It's yours.'

Hala had laughed through her tears. She straightened up, stretched her arms skyward and thanked God for life, for happiness, and for Bashir.

But then she backed out.

'You want to send me to Mecca, and we don't have money for flour!'

The family were often short of money. The entire country was short of cash. But Bashir had people to borrow from.

Then it was just a matter of standing ready. You didn't know which flight you would get a seat on.

Hala promised everyone in the house she would bring back *zamzam*. The spring water that came from the well by the Kaaba cured and gave strength for free. She was going to take home as many bottles as she could carry, she told the family as they went outside to wave her goodbye.

Then she was driven off in the white Land Cruiser.

Hala. The fatherless. The motherless. She had carried four sons, two still among the living. And one of them had given her a ticket to Mecca. As he always said, quoting the Prophet: paradise is at the feet of the mother.

Bashir had yet to raise the funds he needed to pay for Mariam.

In spring!

Then, after Ramadan.

Now, when his mother was back from Mecca.

Soon the heat of summer was upon them, and his best friend whispered in his ear: what's the hurry?

'Shouldn't you just enjoy her a bit?' Farid asked. After all, it was the sweetest time.

The engagement period, before the household with three wives, new babies, new nappies.

He had just about managed to afford the construction of the guest house. It comprised two rectangular rooms at an angle, with carpeted floors and mattresses along the walls. He had been captivated by a new trend – a simple, subdued style. The carpet was beige, without any pattern. The mattresses were creamy white with narrow brown stripes. The pillows were in natural colours, the curtains in the same tones, with some of the interior in mahogany brown.

The only departure was on the ceiling, where lights swung like glitterballs in intense fluorescent pink and purple, making a flickering impression on the wall.

Yes, he was going to just enjoy himself. On getting engaged he had entered into nikah, so he could visit the sixteen-year-old whenever he wished. Spending the night with her was now *halal*. While at the same time he was spared the household.

The war he had been looking forward to, the jihad in Pakistan, had been cancelled, or postponed at least. Pakistan and the TTP had agreed a ceasefire in mid-June. The negotiations had taken place in Kabul, with the interior minister as a mediator.

Sirajuddin Haqqani had held the key to the agreement, well acquainted as he was with both parties after spending two decades in Waziristan. He had managed to overcome deadlocks and avoid dead ends, and eventually the TTP had called off their jihad. For now.

Consequently, Bashir was left feeling restless.

'It's a little like *naswar*,' he told Farid. Naswar was a green powder you placed behind your bottom lip or under your tongue. In the course of the war Bashir had developed an addiction, but Bagram cured him; there was none available in prison.

'That's what jihad is like,' he reasoned. 'The urge comes over me in waves and I feel I just need to have it!'

Farid laughed.

'The time will come,' his faithful friend simply responded. He had known it the whole time. Bashir would never go against the caliph. He was brave but he wasn't foolhardy. That was the reason he had survived when others had been killed. That and a decent portion of luck, of course.

No, you were better off just enjoying life.

A dose of good fortune was certainly needed. Right after the shadow governor's visit to Bashir, two of his men were killed in a drone strike on the outskirts of Jalalabad. The Pakistani government took responsibility for the attack. Two more lives to avenge in the full moon operation had been Bashir's initial thought, but then the whole thing was called off.

One evening, a few days later, having had the boys place some rugs on the roof since the weather was so mild, he turned his prayer mat to face Mecca, where his mother was. There, with only the sky above, a sensation of happiness welled up within him.

Bashir wanted to sit at the front and lead the prayer.

When they were finished, he heard it. A buzzing broke the silence of the quiet neighbourhood.

Jamal glanced up.

'A drone!'

For several days after the shadow governor's visit the drone continued to fly over the house. The eye in the sky keeping tabs.

Not long after, the leader of al-Qaeda, the man who had been Osama bin Laden's personal physician, Ayman al-Zawahiri, was killed on his balcony in Kabul by a Hellfire missile fired from a drone. The house belonged to Sirajuddin Haqqani's son-in-law, but the Taliban denied any knowledge of al-Zawahiri being in the country. The question was, who had tipped off the Americans? Had the minister of interior affairs sold him out for a solution to the problem of the billions in frozen funds?

In any case, it was time to keep a low profile.

To just enjoy life.

* * *

Jamila was at the airport in Alta, dressed in jeans and trainers. Kakar and the children were with her. The trip had been postponed several times, and always for the same reason: some documents were lacking.

She had chosen a new homeland.

The children were crying. The children's friends were crying. Neighbours had come along; employees from the town council had turned up. The sun was shining, as it would light up every day and every night all through the summer. And they were leaving.

Jamila had been feeling down over the last few days. Why am I sad now, I've got what I wanted after all, she asked herself.

Some months earlier she had received an email from the immigration authorities in Canada informing her that the offer of residence in the country would soon expire. She was puzzled. She had never applied to go to Canada. But then she remembered. In Kabul, during that terrible August last year, she had received offers of evacuation from several countries. She had chosen Norway, deciding it would be good for the children, the country had a good health service and she liked the Norwegians she had met. She had believed that accepting one offer meant the others were automatically declined. But they weren't, and so nine months after arriving in Norway she had received the email from Canada.

'No!' Fatima said.

'No!' Khadija cried.

'I'm perfectly happy here,' Salahuddin said.

The children loved Alta. They had made lots of friends and had become accustomed to *friluftsliv* – the Norwegian concept consisting of the words 'free', 'air' and 'life'. Skiing, skating, sledging and running around outdoors was heaven after a life within the high walls of Kabul. Kakar also liked life in Alta. He enjoyed the Norwegian language course and loved living so close to nature. He could thrive anywhere, Jamila complained. He was like water. He flowed into a place, no matter where he was.

Jamila had explained why she wanted to leave. Norway required that you live there for at least seven years before obtaining citizenship. Only then were you permitted to travel to your home country without losing the right to protection. The Canadian rules weren't as strict. It would provide a safe haven while allowing her to visit Kabul and continue with her work for her country. Canada was a shortcut home.

'All of you are happy here, but I'm not,' she said.

The caseworker at the Directorate of Immigration had looked at her in incomprehension when she arrived to take care of the paperwork.

'But don't you have peace and security here?' he wondered aloud.

'Protection isn't enough to live,' Jamila countered.

For the most part she was resigned and despondent. There were no bright spots to be seen in Afghanistan, where her head was. She hoped Canada would restore her strength.

All the same the very thought of leaving was exhausting. Starting over yet again. After a year of darkness. After a year of ice and cold.

She viewed it as a wasted year.

Jamila had harboured such strong hopes of things improving in her home country, so the disappointment was all the greater when it didn't happen.

Within days of the women's meeting with the caliph, a message appeared on Twitter announcing the reopening of schools for teenage girls. Jamila rejoiced in her living room in Alta. They had all been on such a high after the meeting with Haqqani, after all the compliments, his flattery — *to think he actually said that, that he had never met such knowledgeable women.* They had got the impression he was being honest, and they figured the school reopening had come about as a result of the meeting.

But the tweet turned out to be fake.

It was quickly refuted.

They remembered how he had said he would send word to the airports. But the ban on women travelling without a guardian was still in effect.

He had assured them that women would be invited to the loya jirga in July. When they rang to enquire about their invitations and spoke to Haqqani's secretary, whose number he had so freely given out after the meeting, he told them that there wouldn't be any space for women this year, unfortunately. There were so many important matters to be discussed, from the economy and security to reform of the legal system, there wasn't time for women's issues. Perhaps next year.

Be patient, woman.

Wait.

Cover up.

And remember: the best burka is to stay at home.

Three thousand men were invited to the meeting in Kabul. Even amir al-mumineen, the supreme leader, had left Kandahar for the occasion.

'We will never allow ourselves to be dictated to by the infidels!

Even if they let atom bombs fall on us,' said the man who had seen to it that teenage girls stayed at home. 'We are many. We're not afraid of death. We'll do as we please.'

It was so dark.

But maybe it would be better in Canada.

Maybe her voice would carry from there.

* * *

Ariana had gone to bed. The room was in complete darkness when she heard the shuffle of feet outside the door. The doorknob turned and someone entered.

It was her father.

He just stood there, a few metres from her bed. Without saying anything. She didn't say anything either.

He cleared his throat, as if about to speak. Then burst into tears.

'Ariana,' he managed to say. 'You know I love you. It's awful, it feels so awful when . . . '

She had never seen her father cry. A feeling of tenderness spread through her limbs.

'Don't do this to our family, Ariana! Don't blacken our name!'

She had softened, had had time to think: it's my fault that Daddy's crying!

But the tears weren't for her, he was weeping for himself!

'I don't understand, Dad, this isn't divorce. It's an engagement that hasn't worked out. What is the big deal? Nothing has happened. I've only met him with you or Mum. Please, Daddy, don't ruin my life, don't make me marry him!'

'You're too young to understand,' Karim replied. 'Later on, you will. He's a fine boy. He's a fine man. You'll be safe with him.'

Then he left.

Her thoughts turned to what her sister had told her the previous night.

Zohal had overheard a conversation between their parents just before bedtime, and came in to tell Ariana straight away.

They had been talking about contacting a shaman.

'Maybe find one who could soften her attitude,' her mother had suggested. 'Who could temper her will for a few weeks.'

Their father had muttered something Zohal hadn't caught. Their mother had said she'd reach out to someone she knew. Either the shaman would have to make a home visit or perhaps he had something they could give her, a potion, or a serum?

A remedy for recalcitrance.

Ariana was all out of tears.

'Mum has never really tried to understand me,' she said to Zohal the next day. 'At least Dad came in and cried.'

One day, when Ariana lay on her bed sobbing, her mother had said, 'Nobody *wants* to get married, you just have to get on with it. Your tears won't change a thing.'

And now she wanted to dope her into obedience. Or let a shaman lay his hands on her. She didn't recognise her family.

Nor was it true that nobody *wanted* to get married. Lots of people did. She hadn't had the nerve to be honest with her friends about how she felt, so they were constantly sending pictures. Of beautiful brides. Hairstyles. Veils. Decorations and bouquets. Dresses. A multi-tiered cake with pink cream.

They were just like Mahmoud!

You won't break my soul didn't help any longer. There was no hope to be found anywhere.

In early August her father said to her, 'His family have booked the hotel. The wedding will take place in a week.'

She wrote in her diary:

I can never forgive them. They will regret.

She had once written about how she viewed her life as a book. You had to stay sharp and follow what was going on, otherwise you risked being left behind while the plot kept moving.

Now she wrote:

This is THE END.

She didn't have the strength to fight any more. She decided to involve her mother in what she called *the dreadful part*.

'Mum, listen, about the wedding, can you tell me . . . ' She mustered her courage: 'What I'm supposed to do on the first night?'

Her mother's face clouded over.

'Don't you know?'

'How would I know?'

'I'll tell you the night before the wedding,' Nadia said.

Her mother couldn't even talk about it! Her own mother didn't want to deal with what was about to happen.

On her way out the door Ariana said:

'The night before, then?'

The following day, when she was at home, Mahmoud rang. She didn't pick up. When he tried for the tenth time she answered.

'I was just wondering what you thought about the decorations?' he said.

'What the hell are you asking me for? *Gap nako!* Shut up and fuck off!'

Then she lay down and cried.

He sent her a photo. It was of a man striding into a white, dreamlike hall. A stage had been erected where the bride and groom were to enter. The tables had beautiful glass decorations with lights in them and the chairs were upholstered in white material with shimmering silver patterns. It was a publicity picture from the function room at the hotel his family had booked.

It was like he was living out the romance on his own.

I'm the luckiest man in the world, he wrote.

And you will be my queen.

It's a very good hotel.

Ariana, you'll soon see how I will shower you with love and affection.

Life is happier with love.

You're my life, I want to call you my life.

I hope you like the hotel.

I'll send you a video. Look.

She opened the link he had sent. It was Russian, from a dance studio in Rostov. The video showed a couple dancing. The woman was dressed in a gauzy, low-cut bridal dress, the man was wearing a suit. They were moving close together, gazing into each other's eyes. It was so tacky. She couldn't breathe. The song they were dancing to was 'Love Me Like You Do' — from the film *Fifty Shades of Grey*. *You're the cure, you're the pain, you're the only thing I wanna touch . . .*

How could he keep on texting and texting when she didn't respond?

It was so annoying!

He was deaf and blind and happy.

'I'll be gentle,' he wrote. 'Everything will be the way you want it. I won't do anything you don't like.'

Seven days isn't long.

Ariana lay in bed, where she had spent most of the last week. The wedding was to take place the following day. She felt sick. Dizzy. She had taken some pills. The more she thought about the next day, the weaker she felt.

The sound of dancing and laughter was coming from the living room. It was henna night, when the mother of the bride gathered family and friends to eat good food, dance, reminisce about the life that was past and dream about the one to come. But, most important, the bride was to have her hands and feet decorated with henna.

She didn't want to.

'You can't leave your mother's house without henna,' her oldest aunt, the wife of Karim's brother, told her. She added water to the powder and stirred.

Ariana's room was empty. Mahmoud's family had come to collect her books and clothes, and taken them to the new apartment. They had also brought the three outfits she was to wear the next day. A colourful, traditional Afghan dress with sewn-on pearls. A pink dress, tight at the waist, with a huge skirt. And last — a dazzling white bridal gown in tulle and lace with a long veil.

The two oldest aunts came into her room.

'I don't want to!' she said.

'You have to.'

They pulled up the sleeves of her sweater.
They pulled up the legs of her baggy trousers.
She let them have her hands.
She let them have her feet.

With practised hands her aunts drew patterns on Ariana's body. Then they covered her skin with plastic wrap. By the time she was to be collected the following day, the green paste would have turned red.

The long floral stems coiled along her limbs. Like tentacles.

* * *

The first contraction came in the middle of the night. Galai had thought she had a month left. Bashir was sleeping peacefully next to her. The summer heat lay heavy in the room. She got up, walked through the hall and out onto the wide steps. Outside, she inhaled the night air and waddled across the yard to the vines, already laden with grapes, where she sat down on a bench.

She had a black eye, the bruise extending down over her cheek. It looked like someone had given her a powerful blow to the face, but she told people it had happened when she had tended the grapes and one of the canes holding up the vines had hit her. She had been standing below it, here where she now sat, when it had come loose.

She gasped a little for air, before staggering the few steps back across the yard.

'Almighty God, have mercy,' she whispered, taking another break on the steps, before going inside and getting back into bed.

Sleep was impossible. She was impatient.

Another contraction.

Bashir lay beside her snoring quietly.

Another one. She let out a muffled groan.

Her husband slept.

She began to moan. The contractions were getting closer together.

Bashir continued sleeping.

A cry of pain escaped her.

He grunted.

It wasn't until the call to prayer sounded from the minarets at dawn that he awoke with a start.

Upon realising she was in labour, he wanted to drive her to the clinic. Galai refused. The last time she gave birth in a hospital she was left with a dead child. Her son had died during delivery. There was no way in the world she was going to a hospital again; all the children she had given birth to at home were healthy and strong.

She remained lying there. Bashir said he was going to the guest house to pray with the men who had stayed the night there.

Galai felt alone. Hala was in Mecca. Yasamin was in Mussahi. She heard Raouf leaving the adjacent room to pray with his brother on the other side of the yard.

It was time. She made her way towards the little room in the corner of the entrance hall. A thin red blanket hung in front of the doorway. She drew it aside and went in. The room measured about three metres square. At one end was a rudimentary squat toilet made of brick. A bucket of water, serving as a sink, and a low stool stood by the wall. She sat down heavily.

'Oh, Almighty God, have mercy on me!' she whispered again.

She pushed a little, counted to three then pushed again.

From outside, she heard Sima call out to her.

'Do you need help?'

'No!'

Sitting on the stool she pushed again. Clenched her teeth.

'I'll be all right!'

With her hands cupped beneath her she sat ready to receive the head when it came. She took a deep breath, pushed hard – and there it was! She saw the top of a head. Her eyes were fixed on the black hair as she pushed again and then . . . the baby was out.

It was a girl.

Sima heard the cry of the baby. She had been standing in the hall, right outside the bathroom, in case Galai needed her. Now she hurried back to her room, went to her closet and picked up the large scissors on the second shelf down.

She cut the umbilical cord, lifted the child from her mother's arms and washed her. Sima wrapped the baby in a white cloth, so the infant lay like a little package before her. If children were wrapped tightly in swaddling bands, they slept better and grew straighter. A white shawl was tied around the girl's head, to give it a nice shape.

The birth was over before the end of morning prayer. The newborn girl lay at Galai's breast when Bashir returned.

His face broke into a wide smile when he saw her.

'She's uglier than the others!' Galai exclaimed. 'Look at her nose, it's so small, it doesn't fit with the rest of her face.'

Bashir just smiled.

'Fazila,' he said. 'She'll be called Fazila – the brilliant one.'

He laughed. He was so happy.

As he always did after morning prayer, he went to lie down. While he was sleeping, Fazila's soul restlessly sought a home.

When a child was born, it didn't know to which religion it belonged, Galai had learned. The baby knew nothing about God. Her soul wandered about, looking around and asking everyone: who am I? Where do I belong?

When the sun was at its highest, Bashir woke up. Fazila lay dressed in the clothes Galai had sewn for her. Her skin was pink, her eyes big and clear. Sima had outlined her eyes with kohl and defined her eyebrows with a thick black pen. On her head, over the white shawl, Galai had placed a medallion in fabric, with glass beads and glitter, and tied it with a ribbon.

Bashir approached and bent down.

'My brilliant baby,' he murmured.

With his mouth close to her ear, he began to whisper. He called to the baby in the way the muezzin called to prayer. He called on her soul, helping it on the right path, so it would find God. In her right ear he whispered *azan* – to call her to the faith.

God is great! I bear witness that there is no God but the One God. I bear witness that Muhammad is the messenger of God . . .

Then he put his face to her other ear. Into it he whispered *iqama* — and in so doing incorporated the child into the ranks of the faithful: *la ilaha illa allah wa muhammad rasul allah . . . Hasten to the prayer! Hasten to the salvation!*

He took her in his arms.

Now she knew who she was. Now she knew where she belonged.

Islam means submission, to surrender to the Almighty.

Her parents smiled. Her life lay in God's hands. May his will be done.

The Basis of the Book

This is a book about the Afghans – by way of three of them – and how their country shaped them, but also how they themselves have tried to pull their country in the direction they want it to go.

It is a portrait of three people, at a moment in time.

The Afghans is first and foremost the stories of Jamila, Bashir and Ariana.

They appear in the book in the order they were born, each into a specific period of the country's history. Jamila came into the world in 1976, a few years prior to the Soviet invasion. Bashir was born in 1987, when the war was nearing an end, while Ariana was born at the turn of the millennium, the year before the terror attacks in the USA on 11 September 2001.

My first meeting with Jamila Afghani took place via a computer screen. In early September 2021 the Norwegian Afghanistan Committee held an open meeting with Afghan women's rights activists. Jamila, with her sharp analyses and courageous assertions, cut an impressive figure. After several meetings over Zoom, that were frequently disconnected due to the poor coverage at the reception centre for asylum seekers where they were staying, I went to meet her in person.

I asked Jamila if she would consider appearing in a book about Afghanistan, which at the time I had scarcely begun, and explained what that would entail with regards to interviews and research. She readily agreed. As did her husband Kakar.

Several meetings took place with Jamila, Kakar and their children, both in Alta, where they were sent later that autumn, and in Oslo.

Jamila is the principal source for the chapters pertaining to her. She is also the one who related her parents' story. Her mother had passed away and her father was too ill to be interviewed. The accounts of their childhoods and early lives in Ghazni, and later in Kabul, are therefore based on what Jamila recounted. Thus the thoughts and actions of her parents are Jamila's words, and part of her family history as she sees it. I have also interviewed one of her brothers.

Jamila has previously given accounts of her family, in *Contested Terrain: Reflections with Afghan Women Leaders* by Sally L. Kitch, from 2014, and *Peacemakers in Action: Profiles in Religious Peacebuilding* edited by Joyce S. Dubensky and published in 2016. Some of the depictions of her childhood have therefore appeared before. Sometimes the stories are strikingly similar, at other times the details differ slightly. I asked Jamila for clarification when there were discrepancies.

Jamila also sent me drafts of speeches she has made, as well as other written material from her life. The speech she delivered in Doha was reported by Al Jazeera and can be found online.

I have also visited locations in Kabul related to Jamila. In the building she owns, the organisations NECDO and WILPF have a floor each, and the library she and Kakar built up is to be found there, along with their own apartment. I have also met several of the female Islamic scholars she worked with.

Between January and July 2022, I undertook three extended trips to Afghanistan. My goal was to try to understand more about the Taliban and their rule. What has changed and what has remained the same? What do they wish to achieve?

On my first day in the country, I was required to have my press accreditation approved by the new authorities. In regard to this I was granted an audience with the spokesperson for the Ministry of Foreign Affairs, Abdul Qahar Balkhi, who told me I could just forget about the personal stories of the Taliban: they wouldn't talk.

All the more reason to try.

I travelled from police districts to provincial centres, visited people at home and set my sights on those midway up the hierarchy; the foot soldiers didn't have enough experience, while those in the upper echelons were inaccessible.

I found several interesting individuals. To take part in a book, above all the person must want to tell their story. They also need to be stable enough to stay the course.

I immediately sensed I had discovered such a character upon meeting Bashir. He was the first person to ask me questions before saying anything himself.

Why did I want to write a book about Afghanistan? Why was I interested in the Taliban? What sort of stories was I after? Why were all the wars I had covered in Muslim countries?

Much had been written about the Taliban as a group but more seldom as individuals. I was looking for someone who would tell their own story, I explained. I wanted to understand what motivated them and what kind of people the movement consisted of.

'The reason these accounts are lacking is obvious,' I added. 'If I had come here last year then you probably would have kidnapped me, wouldn't you?'

He had a good laugh at that. Yes, of course he would have.

All the interviews with people in the book were recorded and transcribed afterwards. The interviews in English were transcribed by me, sometimes with the assistance of transcription programs. In order to arrive at the correct meaning in Pashto, which Bashir and his family spoke, the interviews were sent to professional translators, to render them as verbatim as possible.

Regarding Bashir's childhood, adolescence and how he rose through the ranks of the Taliban, this is based on his own accounts and what members of his family told me. Only on rare occasions did I speak with people on the other side; that is, Bashir's enemies. But I did find one person who had worked as an interpreter for the American forces during Qalam's attack on Forward Operating Base Tillman. He recalled the mood on the base when the commander was killed and how they took him to cold storage.

The battles I chose to include in the book contain many details. How could Bashir remember so much in such a chaotic and confusing situation?

I used the following method: when I had decided which battles or reminiscences I wished to use in the book, I went back to Bashir and asked him to go through these stories in more detail. Bashir and his men were often exasperated by my nitpicking over points they viewed as inconsequential, but in my experience it's often in what is seen as unimportant that you find what is central. Many of Bashir's men also thought I asked stupid and repetitive questions. Others believed I had to be an intelligence agent, working for the West.

The sports reporter's refrain of ' . . . and what was going through your mind then?' is the best question in the world. I must constantly remind an interviewee to not only recount an event, but also say what they were thinking at the time it was occurring.

In this manner it's possible to construct scenes with factual content and at the same time breathe life into them. I attempt to find out what people are thinking and feeling in different situations, and what motivates them, so we can get to know them.

When Bashir and his men thought I was unduly fixated on details, it might have been around questions concerning what something looked like, smelled like, felt like or simply how they were sitting — were they sitting on cushions, on rugs, on mattresses? Ah, right, directly on the concrete, then?

Another method is to ask the same thing many times, in different circumstances. It may be to elicit more nuance, but it can also serve to check if the answers are consistent. Being in possession of the recordings, I can have what someone said many months previously fresh in my mind and ask them exactly the same thing to see if their version has changed. Bashir had an excellent memory and was always quick to mention that he had told me about this or that before. Had I not been listening?

My impression of Bashir was that he was guarded in his frankness, it was restrained.

He knew what he wanted to talk about and what he did not. The Taliban are a collective movement, and the identity of those behind specific kidnappings, killings, massacres, torture or attacks on civilian targets like hospitals and educational institutions is not something they want to come out. The collective are responsible for what is achieved and what you can be punished for, under different regimes, not the individual commander.

Acts of war – unadulterated warfare, in its pure sense – were on the other hand something it was safe to talk about.

The luckiest you can be in today's Afghanistan is a visiting female reporter. Then you have access to both men and women. At the same time as you can – for the time being – travel around, you also know that you can leave, and thereby avoid the intimidation that local journalists are subject to.

Most people associate the Taliban with men. Little has been written about those in the movement who hardly leave the house. The stories of Taliban wives and close family members have, in more than one sense, been concealed. There are many reasons for that, of which the most important is the ideal of a secluded life. I told Bashir at an early stage that I wished to meet his family, his mother, his wives and children. To my surprise he replied, 'Of course – when would suit you?'

But first he had to ask them.

They met me with friendly scepticism. Why did I want to hear their stories? What was behind it? And eventually: how had I managed to make it to Afghanistan *all alone*?

On these visits I had a female interpreter. She was cautious but dauntless, and through her gentle manner established a rapport with all the members of the family. Much of what the women told was as unfamiliar to her as it was to me, such as, for example, that you are not supposed to mourn the death of a child.

The main characters among the Taliban women are Hala, Galai and Yasamin – Bashir's mother and his two wives. I quickly discovered that the best way to interview them was to focus on one at a time, although most of our conversations ended up part of the chaos of their pink house, as toddlers came in and out, food was served and eaten, babies were breastfed, tea was drunk, garments repaired. Expectant mothers lay down to sleep beside me, others decorated my hands with henna or wanted to teach me how to bake bread. Like Bashir, they attempted to convert me. I spent many hours with the children at the Quran school, where Hasibullah walked around correcting pronunciation.

Women as active participants and facilitators in the war is a story that has barely been told. Bashir's wives told me about the making of the Taliban's most lethal weapon – roadside bombs – in the same matter-of-fact manner they talked about preparing dough for bread.

I also met Bashir's fiancée, Mariam, and her parents. Then I needed two interpreters, one female to translate her story, before I went into the adjacent room, where a male interpreter translated for her father. Only I could go freely between the rooms.

The book is built upon what the people in it have told me. The dialogue is reproduced based on what they have said about their lives. Just as Jamila told me about her parents, so Hala related the story of her late husband, the events around his death and the life they shared prior to it.

At other scenes I was present. Bashir took the task of having a biographer in tow seriously, informing everyone we met that 'what you tell me now, you're also telling her'. That was the case with the runaway, the shadow governor and the families of the martyrs.

The controlled frankness I found with Bashir, I also encountered with the women. They were surprisingly open about family and everyday life, including reactions to Bashir's polygamy. What I found no hint of was the wish for a more independent life. I cannot know if that was a desire that burned deep within, or if the truth was as they said, that a life like that did not interest them.

After spending some time in the house my impression is that the will of the girls is bent so early and gradually that resistance softens step by step. Four-year-old Hoda, for example, was similar to any other child of that age, playful and inventive. The eight-year-olds in the house were already covered up; they spoke with heads lowered, afraid of saying anything wrong. All they wanted, they said, was to learn the Quran by heart. When I asked if there was anything else they might wish for, they just shook their heads.

It was important to Bashir's women that their names weren't disclosed. I asked if they wanted to choose their own names for the book, but they didn't care and asked me to come up with some myself.

It was important to me to strictly define my role as a journalist, to avoid any misunderstandings around what was on and what was off the record. My recording device was always placed in the middle of the room, or close to whoever was speaking. Furthermore, I took notes of what the interpreter translated and of what I observed. There was never any doubt that I was there to work.

Like Bashir, the women were also puzzled about my search for details, and at times it was hard to have to ask about the specifics needed to build up a scene, such as when Yasamin lost her first child, and I asked about details like:

Did you look at Bashir? Was he looking at you? Were you sitting down? Was he standing? Why were you looking down? How did that make you feel?

But that is how a book comes about.

For a long time, I thought this book would have two main characters.
Then I met Ariana.
My first impression was of a nervous, pale young woman. She seemed wound up, her eyes flickering about as she attended a stress management course at Jamila's office in Kabul. Most of the women

in the room were older than her. She talked about a life consisting of nothing.

I met her again, and realised she was what the main changes centred around – the young women who thought they could achieve anything, if only they were smart and worked hard enough, and then everything was taken from them. She is who the main struggle between people like Bashir and Jamila is all about. When I told Bashir about Ariana graduating at the top of her class in law, he replied, 'Sorry, but there's no place for educated women in Afghanistan. Her parents should find her a husband.'

The first thing Ariana asked me when I wondered if she would be willing to be in the book was: can I be anonymous?

I told her she could, and she is.

Like Jamila, Ariana speaks fluent English, making the interviews easy to conduct. We had several face-to-face meetings, both at her home, where I was put up, at cafés in Kabul, or at my place. For long periods we had daily contact online.

Ariana is herself a person who writes. She kept two diaries, one in Dari and one in English. Over the last few years, she kept her diary on her computer and sent sections of it to me. Towards the end of our time working together, it was important for her to convey her thoughts around the marriage her parents wanted her to enter.

Her parents were also interviewed on several occasions, but primarily in the period before the conflict with their daughter came to a head. As she acted as the interpreter in her parents' interviews, and they would never allow an outside interpreter to gain insight into recent events, I do not have their version of what happened after the engagement.

What they said to Ariana in different situations, and how they acted, is based solely on what she has told me. The same applies to her translations of text messages from her fiancé, whom I have named Mahmoud. I have never met nor interviewed him.

Except for Jamila Afghani and the politicians in the book, all the Afghan women have had their names changed.

Both Jamila and Ariana have read the chapters about themselves in English translation and been given the opportunity to provide input and make corrections. They have both approved the chapters as they are printed in this book.

Bashir declined the offer to read an English translation and communicated via the interpreter that he would like to read through his chapters prior to the book being published in Pashto.

The historical sections in the book are drawn mostly from *Afghanistan – A New History* by Martin Ewans, which I bought at Shah M Book in Kabul in 2001. I have used specific quotations and dialogue from the following books:

The conversations between Osama bin Laden and Suleiman Abu Ghaith on 11 September 2001 are taken from *The Exile: The Stunning Inside Story of Osama bin Laden and Al Qaeda in Flight* by Cathy Scott-Clark and Adrian Levy.

The quotation 'I asked forgiveness from God Almighty, feeling that I had sinned because I listened to those who advised me not to go' is taken from *The Looming Tower: Al-Qaeda's Road to 9/11* by Lawrence Wright. Facts concerning life in Peshawar during the Soviet occupation are from the same source. In addition, for that chapter, I also used Thomas Hegghammer's *The Caravan: Abdallah Azzam and the Rise of Global Jihad*.

Communication between George W. Bush and God is taken from a 2005 article in the *Guardian*, where he referred to God telling him, 'George, go and fight these terrorists.'

Quotations from Lyse Doucet's phone call with Hamid Karzai are taken from 'The Karzai Years: From Hope to Recrimination', which she wrote for BBC News in July 2014.

The quotations from the Doha negotiations are taken from the *New Yorker* article 'The Secret History of the U.S. Diplomatic Failure in Afghanistan' by Steve Coll and Adam Entous. Details around Ashraf Ghani's security advisor Hamdullah Mohib are taken from 'Inside the Fall of Kabul' in the *New York Times Magazine*, written by Matthieu Aikins. The same journalist also wrote 'The Taliban's

Dangerous Collision Course with the West', where some of the background for the school closures was uncovered. The main source for the meeting in Kandahar, where it was decided that the schools would not be opened to teenage girls, is the report by Ashley Jackson in 'The Ban on Older Girls' Education: Taleban conservatives ascendant and a leadership in disarray', a report for Afghanistan Analysts Network.

With regard to the Haqqani Network, the book *Fountainhead of Jihad: The Haqqani Nexus 1973–2012* by Vahid Brown and Don Rassler is central. The description of the relationship between the Taliban and al-Qaeda, and a quote delivered to Osama bin Laden, is taken from *An Enemy We Created: The Myth of the Taliban–Al Qaeda Merger in Afghanistan, 1970–2010* by Alex Strick van Linschoten and Felix Kuehn.

The depiction of the use of drones in Afghanistan is taken primarily from the article 'Drone Warfare in Waziristan and the New Military Humanism' by Hugh Guterson, published in *Current Anthropology*. How the grieving parents of soldiers in the Soviet Union were disciplined is taken from '*Dedovshchina*: From Military to Society', issue 1 of the *Journal of Power Institutions in Post-Soviet Societies*.

Other books I have based my work on are *The Afghanistan Papers: A Secret History of the War* by Craig Whitlock, *The Taliban at War: 2001–2021* by Antonio Giustozzi, *No Good Men Among the Living* by Anand Gopal and *The Performance of Emotion Among Paxtun Women* by Benedicte Grima. A book that inspired me, and which I gave to Ariana when I left, is a collection of short poems, orally passed down by Afghan women: *I am the Beggar of the World: Landays from Contemporary Afghanistan*, collected and translated by Eliza Griswold.

In working on this book, I have received help from several experts.

Arne Strand, senior researcher at the Christian Michelsen Institute, with Afghanistan as his specialist field, has read through the manuscript along the way and offered useful feedback and comments. He also read through the finished manuscript and imparted his knowledge when we discussed the different themes in the book.

Amund Bjorsnes, a specialist in classical and oriental philology, helped me to understand the principles behind the recital of the Quran and has reviewed religious references. Bjorsnes went through the words in Dari, Pashto and Arabic, to render the spelling as consistent as possible. We prioritised readability rather than scientific methods of transcription. Extracts from the Quran are from *Al-Qur'an: A Contemporary Translation* by Ahmed Ali.

Arabist and lecturer in Arabic at the University of Bergen Pernille Myrvold looked through the transcription of Arabic words, and was one of several valued early readers. She requested a map, which was beautifully drawn by Audun Skjervøy for the Norwegian edition.

Abdul Sayed at the Carnegie Endowment for International Peace went through Bashir's stories from Waziristan. He listened to recordings in Pashto and helped me better understand Bashir's role in the Haqqani Network and in particular his relationship with Tehrik-e-Taliban Pakistan. I also discussed Bashir with the author Anand Gopal, who has written extensively on the Haqqani Network and the Taliban.

Humanitarian consultant in Afghanistan Ayesha Wolasmal helped me understand aspects of both traditional and modern Afghan life. She explained several of the terms the main characters used and commented extensively during the writing process.

In Kabul I took pleasure in and benefited greatly from conversations with Terje Watterdal, Country Director at the Norwegian Afghanistan Committee, and I would also like to thank General Secretary Liv Kjølseth from the same organisation for the first introduction to Jamila.

Former commanding officer of Norway's Special Operations Command, with experience in Afghanistan, Frode Kristoffersen tidied up some military terms, while diplomat Andreas Løvold, who has served for both Norway and the UN in Afghanistan, helped me understand the period under Ashraf Ghani. Historian Tore Marius

Løiten provided great help in researching the various themes of the book. Two readers who made invaluable suggestions regarding form and content are poet Ingrid Olava Brænd Eriksen and historian Marte Heian-Engdal.

My parents Frøydis Guldahl and Dag Seierstad have as always been my most loyal readers, and commented upon several different versions during the writing process. The youngest person to read the manuscript, Katja Sira Myhre, offered important correctives about what young people know about the history and the politics of Afghanistan. Thus the manuscript has had test readers ranging from seventeen-year-old Katja to eighty-six-year-old Dag.

Publishers have provided a fine bunch of readers, like author, traveller and publisher Erling Kagge, and editors Tuva Ørbeck Sørheim and Ivar Iversen, who all offered important observations and comments, while Charlotte Sabella provided technical assistance.

My editor Cathrine Sandnes has been a phenomenal sparring partner from the start to the finish line. I have been in the best of hands.

This book would not have been possible without my translators and fixers, all of whom have preferred to remain unnamed. I am forever grateful for helping me to find, to connect and to understand the complexity of the Afghan society and to guide me from place to place, and from person to person.

Finding an appropriate title was difficult, when the main characters were so clearly pulling in different directions and the only thing uniting them was a strong will – and a country.

Thus, the working title *The Afghans* has remained.

I am grateful that Jamila, Bashir, Ariana and the people around them agreed to share their stories with me – and with you.

Åsne Seierstad
Oslo, 25 January 2024

Credits

177   Lyrics from 'Boyfriend' by Justin Bieber, Mike Posner, Mason Levy and Matthew Musto. Copyright © Sony/ATV Tunes LLC, Universal Music Corp., Bug Music, Bieber Time Publishing, Artist Publishing Group West, North Greenway Productions, Bear Trap Publishing, Songs of Universal Inc.

228   Lyrics from 'My Heart Will Go On' by James Horner and Will Jennings. Copyright © Universal Music Publishing Group

242   Lyrics from 'Stay' by Justin Bieber, Michael Mule, Magnus Hoiberg, Isaac Deboni, Charles Puth, Omer Fedi, Blake Slatkin, Charlton Howard and Subhaan Rahman. Copyright © Universal Music Corp., Sony/ATV Songs LLC, Bieber Time Publishing, Artist 101 Publishing Group, Electric Feel Music, Charlie Puth Music Publishing, Back Hair Music Publishing, Songs of Universal Inc., Two Hands And A Bit Publishing, Omer Fedi Music

398 and 409	Lyrics from 'Break My Soul' by Adam Pigott, Allen George, Beyoncé Knowles, Christopher Stewart, Fred McFarlane, Freddie Ross, Shawn Carter and Terius Nash. Copyright © Kobalt Music Publishing Ltd, Sony/ATV Music Publishing LLC, Spirit Music Group, Warner Chappell Music, Inc.
411	Lyrics from 'Love Me Like You Do' by Max Martin, Savan Kotecha, Ilya Salmanzadeh and Tove Lo. Copyright © BMG Gold Songs, Universal Pictures Music, Warner/Chappell Music, Scandinavia AB, MXM Music AB, Wolf Cousins

Åsne Seierstad was born in 1970 and studied Russian, Spanish and the history of philosophy at Oslo University. An internationally bestselling author, she has also received numerous awards for her journalism. She has worked as a correspondent across the world, including in Russia, China, Iraq and Afghanistan. Her second book, *The Bookseller of Kabul*, has sold over three million copies and the paperback was in the *Sunday Times* top ten for over a year. Her other critically acclaimed works include *A Hundred and One Days: A Baghdad Journal* and *The Angel of Grozny*. Following the acts of terror in Oslo and Utøya in July 2011, she attended the trial of Anders Breivik and then began work on *One of Us*, which became a European bestseller. *Two Sisters*, her account of a family torn apart after two Norwegian girls join the war in Syria in 2013, was a number-one international bestseller and won the non-fiction category of the 2016 Brage Prize.